SHIELDED FROM JUSTICE:
Police Brutality and Accountability in the United States

Human Rights Watch
New York · Washington · London · Brussels

Cover photograph © Kathleen Foster/Impact Visuals

ISBN 1-56432-183-5
Library of Congress Catalog Card Number: 98-86155

Human Rights Watch is dedicated to
protecting the human rights of people around the world.

We stand with victims and activists to prevent
discrimination, to uphold political freedom, to protect people from inhumane
conduct in wartime, and to bring offenders to justice.

We investigate and expose
human rights violations and hold abusers accountable.

We challenge governments and those who hold power to end abusive practices
and respect international human rights law.

We enlist the public and the international
community to support the cause of human rights for all.

HUMAN RIGHTS WATCH

Human Rights Watch conducts regular, systematic investigations of human rights abuses in some seventy countries around the world. Our reputation for timely, reliable disclosures has made us an essential source of information for those concerned with human rights. We address the human rights practices of governments of all political stripes, of all geopolitical alignments, and of all ethnic and religious persuasions. Human Rights Watch defends freedom of thought and expression, due process and equal protection of the law, and a vigorous civil society; we document and denounce murders, disappearances, torture, arbitrary imprisonment, discrimination, and other abuses of internationally recognized human rights. Our goal is to hold governments accountable if they transgress the rights of their people.

Human Rights Watch began in 1978 with the founding of its Europe and Central Asia division (then known as Helsinki Watch). Today, it also includes divisions covering Africa, the Americas, Asia, and the Middle East. In addition, it includes three thematic divisions on arms, children's rights, and women's rights. It maintains offices in New York, Washington, Los Angeles, London, Brussels, Moscow, Dushanbe, Rio de Janeiro, and Hong Kong. Human Rights Watch is an independent, nongovernmental organization, supported by contributions from private individuals and foundations worldwide. It accepts no government funds, directly or indirectly.

The staff includes Kenneth Roth, executive director; Michele Alexander, development director; Reed Brody, advocacy director; Carroll Bogert, communications director; Cynthia Brown, program director; Barbara Guglielmo, finance and administration director; Jeri Laber special advisor; Lotte Leicht, Brussels office director; Patrick Minges, publications director; Susan Osnos, associate director; Jemera Rone, counsel; Wilder Tayler, general counsel; and Joanna Weschler, United Nations representative. Jonathan Fanton is the chair of the board. Robert L. Bernstein is the founding chair.

The regional directors of Human Rights Watch are Peter Takirambudde, Africa; José Miguel Vivanco, Americas; Sidney Jones, Asia; Holly Cartner, Europe and Central Asia; and Hanny Megally, Middle East and North Africa. The thematic division directors are Joost R. Hiltermann, arms; Lois Whitman, children's; and Regan Ralph, women's.

The members of the board of directors are Jonathan Fanton, chair; Lisa Anderson, Robert L. Bernstein, William Carmichael, Dorothy Cullman, Gina Despres, Irene Diamond, Adrian W. DeWind, Fiona Druckenmiller, Edith Everett, James C. Goodale, Jack Greenberg, Vartan Gregorian, Alice H. Henkin, Stephen L. Kass, Marina Pinto Kaufman, Bruce Klatsky, Harold Hongju Koh, Alexander MacGregor, Josh Mailman, Samuel K. Murumba, Andrew Nathan, Jane Olson, Peter Osnos, Kathleen Peratis, Bruce Rabb, Sigrid Rausing, Anita Roddick, Orville Schell, Sid Sheinberg, Gary G. Sick, Malcolm Smith, Domna Stanton, Maureen White, and Maya Wiley. Robert L. Bernstein is the founding chair of Human Rights Watch.

Addresses for Human Rights Watch
350 Fifth Avenue, 34th Floor, New York, NY 10118-3299
Tel: (212) 290-4700, Fax: (212) 736-1300, E-mail: hrwnyc@hrw.org

1522 K Street, N.W., #910, Washington, DC 20005-1202
Tel: (202) 371-6592, Fax: (202) 371-0124, E-mail: hrwdc@hrw.org

33 Islington High Street, N1 9LH London, UK
Tel: (171) 713-1995, Fax: (171) 713-1800, E-mail: hrwatchuk@gn.apc.org

15 Rue Van Campenhout, 1000 Brussels, Belgium
Tel: (2) 732-2009, Fax: (2) 732-0471, E-mail: hrwatcheu@gn.apc.org

Web Site Address: http://www.hrw.org

Listserv address: To subscribe to the list, send an e-mail message to majordomo@igc.apc.org with "subscribe hrw-news" in the body of the message (leave the subject line blank).

CONTENTS

ACKNOWLEDGMENTS

This report was written by Allyson Collins, senior researcher on the United States. It was edited by Cynthia Brown, program director, and legal review was provided by Dinah PoKempner, deputy general counsel. Kenneth Roth, Wilder Tayler, and Michael McClintock reviewed portions of the manuscript. Extensive research and production assistance were provided by Robby Peckerar; Sahr MuhammedAlly also provided research assistance. Production assistance was also provided by Patrick Minges.

Several experts on police abuse reviewed and commented on the text. We are particularly grateful to Prof. Paul Chevigny of New York University School of Law. Others who provided valuable comments include Prof. Samuel Walker, Department of Criminal Justice, University of Nebraska; Thomas R. Parker (retired F.B.I. special agent) of Human Rights Watch's California Committee; Paul Hoffman, attorney, Bostwick and Hoffman; Prof. James J. Fyfe, Department of Criminal Justice, Temple University; G. Flint Taylor, attorney, People's Law Office; Mary Howell, attorney, Howell and Snead; John Crew, director, Police Practices Project of the American Civil Liberties Union of Northern California; and Portland Copwatch. We also would like to thank David Burnham and Sue Long of the Transactional Records Access Clearinghouse of Syracuse, New York, for providing data and analysis regarding federal criminal civil rights prosecutions.

We wish to thank the scores of individuals we have interviewed in preparing this report, including community activists, police abuse experts, attorneys representing alleged victims of abuse, local politicians, journalists, civilian review agency personnel, police officers and officials at all levels, local and federal prosecutors, and Justice Department officials.

SUMMARY AND RECOMMENDATIONS

Police brutality is one of the most serious, enduring, and divisive human rights violations in the United States. The problem is nationwide, and its nature is institutionalized. For these reasons, the U.S. government – as well as state and city governments, which have an obligation to respect the international human rights standards by which the United States is bound – deserve to be held accountable by international human rights bodies and international public opinion.

Police officers engage in unjustified shootings, severe beatings, fatal chokings, and unnecessarily rough physical treatment in cities throughout the United States, while their police superiors, city officials, and the Justice Department fail to act decisively to restrain or penalize such acts or even to record the full magnitude of the problem. Habitually brutal officers – usually a small percentage of officers on a force – may be the subject of repeated complaints but are usually protected by their fellow officers and by the shoddiness of internal police investigations. A victim seeking redress faces obstacles at every point in the process, ranging from overt intimidation to the reluctance of local and federal prosecutors to take on brutality cases. Severe abuses persist because overwhelming barriers to accountability make it all too likely that officers who commit human rights violations escape due punishment to continue their abusive conduct.

This report is based on research conducted in fourteen U.S. cities over two and a half years. Rather than focusing on one city and its police department's problem with abuse, as most studies of police abuse have done, we examined large cities representing most regions of the nation to find common obstacles to accountability. The cities examined are: Atlanta, Boston, Chicago, Detroit, Indianapolis, Los Angeles, Minneapolis, New Orleans, New York, Philadelphia, Portland, Providence, San Francisco, and Washington, D.C. In researching this report, Human Rights Watch interviewed and corresponded with attorneys representing victims alleging ill-treatment by police, representatives of police department internal affairs units, police officers, citizen review agency staff, city officials, Justice Department officials, representatives of federal U.S. attorneys' offices, local prosecutors' office representatives, experts on police abuse, and victims of abuse.

Human Rights Watch recognizes that police officers, like all human beings, are fallible, and that the situations they confront are often dangerous and require quick decisions. But, as described in this report, the cost of pervasive police abuse is monumental – in the tens of millions of dollars in damages that cities pay every year in response to victims' civil lawsuits; in police criminality and the corruption of ideals of public service; in the ensuing public mistrust that – particularly in communities of racial minorities – creates a rift between the police and the public.

1

Race continues to play a central role in police brutality in the United States. Indeed, despite gains in many areas since the civil rights movement of the 1950s and 1960s, one area that has been stubbornly resistant to change has been the treatment afforded racial minorities by police. In the cities we have examined where such data are available, minorities have alleged human rights violations by police more frequently than white residents and far out of proportion to their representation in those cities. Police have subjected minorities to apparently discriminatory treatment and have physically abused minorities while using racial epithets. Each new incident involving police mistreatment of an African-American, Hispanic-American or other minority – and particularly those that receive media attention – reinforces a belief that some residents are subjected to particularly harsh treatment and racial bias.

If the barriers to accountability described in this report were removed, the number and severity of abuses that officers commit would no doubt be greatly reduced. Yet the administrative and legal procedures that should guarantee accountability are seriously flawed and have been extremely resistant to change. In fact, many of the problems we describe in this report have been highlighted in previous studies on police practices: the 1968 Kerner Commission report, the 1981 report of the U.S. Commission on Civil Rights, and several more recent studies on especially troubled city police departments. Nevertheless, most police departments examined by Human Rights Watch continue with "business as usual" until scandals emerge. Those who claim that each high-profile human rights abuse is an aberration, committed by a "rogue" officer, are missing the point: human rights violations persist in large part because the accountability systems are so defective.

Victims of police brutality have many options for reporting abusive treatment by officers but little chance of seeing those officers punished or prosecuted. Citizen review agencies are often overwhelmed and understaffed; reporting an abuse to such an agency may, eventually, lead to an investigation, but it is unlikely to result in the offending officer's being appropriately punished. Filing an abuse complaint with a police department's internal affairs unit can be intimidating, and police departments' excessive secrecy usually means that the complainant learns nothing about any disciplinary action that may have been taken against the accused officer. Filing a civil lawsuit is an option for some victims, but success rates vary widely from city to city, and typically it is the municipality rather than the officer that is held financially responsible. Also, most victims of abuse correctly perceive that criminal prosecution, either locally or federally, is rarely an option – except in highly publicized cases. As a result, resentment and frustration often exacerbate the original abusive treatment. Because it is an open secret that oversight procedures for police abuse do not function effectively, many abuse victims do not even bother to pursue a complaint at all. This series of factors results in violent officers remaining on the job.

In examining human rights violations committed by police officers and barriers to investigation, redress, and prosecution, we found common shortcomings in all of the cities we examined. These failings fall into three basic categories: lack of effective public accountability and transparency, persistent failure to investigate and punish officers who commit human rights violations, and obstacles to justice. We offer recommendations addressed to officials at all levels – departmental, municipal, and federal – and emphasize that reform at all levels and in all three areas is required to secure real change.

Public Accountability and Transparency

Reforms to curb abusive police conduct – or, at least, punishments of specific abusive officers – tend to occur only when the local news media or high-profile court cases focus public attention on the problem. That this happens relatively seldom, in comparison with the incidence of ill-treatment, is partly due to the lack of information supplied to the public regarding allegations of police brutality.

Citizen review agencies, tasked with monitoring and, in some cases, investigating cases of excessive force, are undermined from all sides: by police unions and others who attack them, by city officials who under-fund them, and by police officers who refuse to cooperate with them. Moreover, the limited mandates of many civilian review agencies discourage public involvement or support. Some citizen review agencies do not produce public reports, while others provide incomplete information to the public. None of the reports we examined indicates whether an officer was disciplined in a specific case or prosecuted in a criminal proceeding. Although these agencies are the point of greatest transparency in the system, their reports almost never include even the most basic facts on specific cases that are of interest to the public.

Police internal affairs units, the principal departmental investigators of physical abuse allegations, operate as a rule with excessive secrecy. The public, to whom police departments should be accountable, thus cannot ascertain whether, in fact, the police are policing themselves. Indeed, information about the operations and activities of internal affairs units is nearly impossible to obtain; in some cities, internal affairs representatives refused to answer, or ignored, Human Rights Watch's requests for basic information, with some refusing even to provide information about the number of investigators or other staff in their units. Essential information, such as the number of deaths in custody in a particular department, is generally withheld or is provided in a manner that is unhelpful in determining responsibility for the death. While police representatives claim privacy issues are the reason for protecting information about investigations or disciplinary hearings, police departments also resist providing information even when relevant names or other identifying information is excised.

Local prosecutors are no more transparent. When police officers are prosecuted for human rights violations, it is usually under state criminal charges of murder, manslaughter, assault, battery, or rape. Comprehensive statistics are generally not made available to the public regarding prosecution efforts against police officers, reasons for prosecutorial decisions, or prosecutorial success rates in these cases. Without information about the number of police officers prosecuted, which does not appear to be maintained by most district attorneys' offices, it is impossible to know with certainty whether local attorneys are appropriately handling cases (and, consequently, whether federal prosecutors need to initiate their own investigations).

Federal data are hardly more useful. Federal prosecutors do track the numbers of civil rights complaints filed with the Justice Department, as well as the number of ensuing indictments and prosecutions, but two different offices at the Justice Department maintain parallel and incompatible databases – and the Federal Bureau of Investigations maintains its own distinct data on civil rights investigations – so that no one office is able to provide the public with complete information regarding complaints against, and prosecutions of, police officers in a particular U.S. district or city. Nor does the Justice Department provide public analysis of the imperfect statistics it does have, such as to account for increases or decreases in alleged cases of brutality in any category or region.

Almost four years after Congress called on the Justice Department to produce a nationwide report on the use of excessive force by police officers, that report is still awaited. In November 1997, the Justice Department released a preliminary report describing a pilot household survey that focused on contact between police and the public; and in May 1998, the first status summary on a use-of-force data compilation project was made available. Yet, despite the congressional mandate, which requires the Justice Department to acquire data about the use of *excessive* force by law enforcement officers, the 1997 survey solicited information from households about all types of encounters with police, both favorable and unfavorable, and the use-of-force data project, headed by the International Association of Chief of Police, is collecting data submitted by a small percentage of police departments, which voluntarily provide information about incidents.

In sum, the preliminary reports have avoided the crucial question that Congress asked the Justice Department to answer. We call on the Justice Department to refocus its efforts, reallocate its research grants, and produce a report responsive to its mandate on this issue. Without the information requested by Congress, and more, it is extremely difficult, if not impossible, for governments and police departments to craft enlightened policies that balance the importance of public order with the absolute requirement that the state protect anyone in its jurisdiction from human rights abuses at the hands of police officers.

Investigation and Discipline

External pressures are essential to force police leaders to improve chain of command control of officers who commit human rights violations. But police brutality will subside only once superior officers judge their subordinates – and are judged themselves – on their efforts to provide sufficient and consistent oversight, appropriate administrative discipline and, when necessary, punishment of the perpetrators of abuse. There is no substitute for police leadership to make clear to new as well as veteran officers that human rights violations are not acceptable. The highest-ranking commanders must also hold to account superior officers who are found to have ignored or tolerated abuses committed by officers under their command. The current, longstanding and pervasive tolerance of abuse within police forces, which has been noted by specialized commissions, remains a crucial impediment to reducing police brutality.

Internal affairs divisions must be central to any examination of how police departments deal with abusive behavior by officers. Therefore, it is alarming that no outside review, including our own, has found the operations of internal affairs divisions satisfactory. In each city we examined, internal affairs units too often conducted substandard investigations, sustained few allegations of excessive force, and failed to identify and punish officers against whom repeated complaints had been filed. Rather, they, in practice, often shielded officers who committed human rights violations from exposure and guaranteed them immunity from disciplinary sanctions or criminal prosecution.

In many cases, sloppy procedures and an apparent bias in favor of fellow officers combine to guarantee that even the most brutal police avoid punishment for serious abuses until committing an assault so flagrant, so unavoidably embarrassing, that it cannot be ignored. Three major investigations and reports into police department misconduct in recent years (in Boston, Los Angeles, and New York) harshly criticized the operations of internal affairs units, blaming them for a climate of impunity that fostered human rights violations or corruption.

Even when police departments do try to hold officers who commit abuses accountable, many avoid dismissal or severe disciplinary sanctions because officers are provided with many opportunities to fight punishments; in many cases they prevail, thus sending a signal to fellow officers that they may not be held accountable no matter their actions.

Police officers accused of human rights violations or other misconduct are often protected by special law enforcement officers' "bills of rights," providing for specific protections for officers accused of misconduct. These special statutes have been initiated by police unions and their supporters in state legislatures, and in many states help to shield officers from appropriate punishment. Some of the "bills of rights" allow, for example, for the purging of officers' personnel files of all but sustained complaints; even the rare sustained complaint may be purged after a set number of years in some states; these files are required to appropriately discipline or dismiss officers in the future. The police unions, which provide legal counsel for accused officers, also negotiate contracts for police officers that make discipline or dismissal of officers difficult for police officials to accomplish – even in cases where sanctions are clearly appropriate. While officers are entitled to full due process safeguards, many of the protections they currently enjoy are exceptional and, in practice, undermine police leaders' efforts at accountability.

In some cities, police officers are afforded extensive protections as civil servants (government employees) so that strong disciplinary sanctions, including dismissals, are often weakened or reversed. In some cases, officers appeal directly to the courts when they are dismissed. In other cities, arbitration – a process relied upon to resolve disputes between officers and the city – typically serves to stack the deck further in the officers' favor. When a police department seeks to dismiss an officer, he or she may appeal the dismissal order and an arbitrator is appointed to decide whether the punishment should stand or not. The person chosen as the arbitrator is agreed upon between the police union and the city, but in practice the arbitration process usually favors the officer seeking reinstatement. Police unions provide experienced attorneys to represent the officer, while cities are often represented by far more junior and inexperienced attorneys who argue to uphold the dismissal. As described in this report, there have been many cases involving officers against whom repeated brutality complaints have been sustained, where the police department has sought to dismiss the officers, yet they have been reinstated, often due to minor technicalities, by arbitrators.

The apparent lack of collective official will to control officers who commit human rights violations– and to require all police forces to abide by the law and the police departments' own policies – is evident in the lack of linkage among various entities responsible for overseeing the police and for criminally prosecuting officers who break the law. Although prior to filing a civil lawsuit many plaintiffs will have already filed a complaint with the police department's internal affairs unit or citizen review agency, this is not always the case. When a complaint has not been filed, the filing of a civil lawsuit alleging violations of human rights by police should trigger an investigation by the relevant civilian review agency or internal affairs division; yet this occurs in only four of the cities we examined (including Los Angeles, which changed its policy in 1998). Some city attorneys "notify" the relevant internal affairs unit, but no investigation is automatically initiated, and in other cities, the city attorney's office fails to notify the department in a formal way at all.

Indeed, in most cities, even when the municipal government pays out large settlements or jury awards to the victim as a result of a civil lawsuit for brutality, there may not be an investigation into the incident by the police department. There may not even be an indication in the officer's personnel file that such a lawsuit was filed or settlement or jury award paid (or, if there is an indication, it may have no negative effect on his or her chances for promotions or positive performance reviews). Similarly, citizen review agencies do not track civil lawsuits in most cases. Thus, the wealth of information normally found in such lawsuits, and the enormous cost of abuse to city budgets (and thus the taxpayers), go unexamined.

Obstacles to Justice

From filing a complaint to pursuing legal recourse, the victim of police abuse is faced with unnecessary difficulties and, in some cases, concerted opposition from police officers and powerful police unions. The chances of local criminal prosecution are slim, and of federal civil rights prosecution, even for strong cases, remote.

One area where the federal role in checking police abuse recently has been the Justice Department's enhanced is its new powers to conduct investigations to determine whether there is a "pattern or practice" of abuse in particular police departments and to bring lawsuits ordering reforms to end abusive practices. (In two cases, cities agreed to implement reforms to end violative practices rather than risk the Justice Department taking a case to court for injunctive action.) And although privately filed civil lawsuits are sometimes successful, they do not provide real redress; frequently, the officer in question escapes not only administrative punishment for the offense but also, because of indemnity policies, any personal financial liability.

Police departments and citizen review units, as a rule, will not initiate an investigation into alleged police brutality without a formal complaint. Yet in all of the cities examined by Human Rights Watch, there are serious flaws in the way complaints from the public are initially received or forwarded for action. Filing a complaint is unnecessarily difficult and often intimidating, whether the person seeking to complain deals with a precinct sergeant, an internal affairs investigator or, to a lesser extent, a civilian review agency. Complainants may be met with hostile officers who do not wish to receive a complaint about a colleague. They may be dissuaded from filing a complaint by threats or other techniques. Officers receiving complaints may suggest that they do not believe the complainant, or ask intimidating questions about the complainant's criminal history or charges that may be pending as a result of the arrest that gave rise to the abusive incident. Most police departments prohibit attempts to impede or dissuade a complainant from filing a complaint, yet supervisors rarely confront or punish officers who do so. As noted above, even if a complaint is filed, often the complainant is not advised about whether it has been pursued and the results of any investigation or disciplinary sanction against the subject officer.

Criminal prosecutions are difficult and, in isolation, generally do not lead to improvement in police practices. Police abuse experts warn that when the criminal law is used as a substitute for departmental standards – that is, standards built into a police department's system of discipline and promotion – the results are almost invariably disappointing. As we argue above, stricter internal discipline is essential if a pattern of police abuse is to be interrupted. That said, however, it is clear that local prosecutors must do more to hold criminally abusive officers accountable in order to redress serious crimes, show that police are not above the law, and restore public confidence in the police.

There are many reasons why prosecutors choose not to pursue a case against an allegedly brutal police officer. The traditionally close relationship between district or county attorneys and police officers, who usually work together prosecuting criminals, militates against the vigorous pursuit of police abuse cases. Because it is hard to grand juries (bodies that review a prosecutor's evidence in a case and decide whether or not to indict) and trial juries that a police officer did not merely make an understandable mistake but actually committed a crime, local prosecutors tend to shy away from these cases. In some jurisdictions, special procedural protections for public officials (including police officers) accused of criminal behavior make criminal indictment even less likely.

When local prosecutors fail to pursue serious cases of human rights violations at the hands of the police, it is the responsibility of the federal government to prosecute. Specifically, the Criminal Section of the Civil Rights Division of the Justice Department is responsible for prosecuting these cases under federal criminal civil rights statutes (18 U.S. Code, sections 241 and 242). Yet federal prosecutors almost never pursue even strong cases, due in part to the high legal threshold required to win such cases (prosecutors need to prove the accused officer's "specific intent" to deprive an individual of his or her civil rights) and a shortage of resources (indicating that civil rights prosecutions of law enforcement officers are a low priority). Of the thousands of complaints the Civil Rights Division receives annually, it prosecutes only a handful. Although federal prosecutors claim they play a "backstop" role in prosecuting officers, it is notable that even when local prosecutors decline prosecution or do a poor job in presenting a case, federal prosecutors still fail to step in. And, despite the Clinton administration's rhetorical support for civil rights, its rate of prosecution for these cases changed little from the Bush administration's.

Absent administrative or criminal accountability, many police abuse victims or their families rely on privately filed civil lawsuits for redress. In practice, private civil lawsuits usually allow police departments to continue doing business as usual. Some victims have succeeded in obtaining compensation from municipalities, and a small percentage of civil lawsuits have forced police departments themselves to accept liability for ill-treatment, leading to reforms in training or flawed policies. But because most civil jury awards are paid by cities, most police departments acknowledge that they do not always track civil lawsuits, though an officer's behavior may have cost a city hundreds of thousands, or millions, of dollars in payments to victims. Moreover, even when a lawsuit demonstrates serious violations, there is usually no effort by police supervisors to consider civil lawsuits in an officer's performance evaluations. In the end, taxpayers are paying at least twice for officers who commit abuses, once for their salaries and again to pay victims of their abuse, while often getting little legitimate police work or protection from them.

When all of these systemic shortcomings in dealing with abuse by police officers are combined, it becomes understandable why officers who commit human rights violations have little reason to fear they will be caught, punished, or prosecuted.

International human rights treaties and guidelines set out standards for the conduct of law enforcement officers. The International Covenant on Civil and Political Rights (ICCPR) and the Convention against Torture and Other Cruel, Inhuman or Degrading Treatment or Punishment protect the right to life and prohibit torture, cruel, inhuman or degrading treatment; both treaties have been ratified by the United States. There are also internationally agreed-upon standards regarding the use of force and firearms by police officers. For example, the U.N. Basic Principles on the Use of Force and Firearms by Law Enforcement Officials, adopted in 1990, provides standards on recruitment, training, and the use of force. It calls for proportionality in the amount of force used when required, the adoption of reporting requirements when force or firearms are used, and for governments to ensure that "arbitrary or abusive use of force and firearms by law enforcement officials is punished as a criminal offence under their law."

International human rights monitoring entities have expressed concern over the problem of police abuse in the United States. For example, the Human Rights Committee, which is the international body charged with monitoring compliance with the provisions of the ICCPR by the U.S. and other States parties, concluded in 1995: "[T]he Committee is concerned at the reportedly large number of persons killed, wounded or subjected to ill-treatment by members of the police force in the purported discharge of their duties." Following a 1997 investigation into killings by police in the U.S., focusing on New York City and Los Angeles, the United Nations Special Rapporteur on Extrajudicial, Summary or Arbitrary Executions expressed his concern over reports of violations of the right to life as a result of excessive force by law enforcement officials and stated his intention to continue to monitor this issue closely.

Recommendations

Police, state, and federal authorities are responsible for holding police officers accountable for abusive acts: police officials must ensure that police officers are punished when they violate administrative rules, while state and federal prosecutors must prosecute criminal acts committed by officers. All of these officials are also responsible for requiring that the conduct of police officers meet international human rights standards and comply with human rights treaties by which the U.S. is bound, such as the International Covenant on Civil and Political Rights and the Convention against Torture. While only the federal government is responsible for reporting internationally on U.S. compliance with these treaties, local and state officials share responsibility for ensuring compliance within their jurisdictions.

Federal Aid Policy: It is common under federal law to condition a grant to state and municipal entities on compliance with provisions of federal law. It is also common for the U.S. government, pursuant to legislation on human rights, to condition foreign aid on other governments' compliance with international human rights practices. We believe that such conditionality is appropriate in the case of the rights to life, physical integrity, and humane treatment of persons in the United States – rights protected under international treaties, the U.S. Constitution, and under U.S. civil rights law. Directly and indirectly, local police departments receive billions of dollars annually in federal grants to support training, community relations, personnel hiring, and equipment purchases.

Congress should pass legislation that would withhold these funds from police departments or receiving cities unless they provide data regarding the use of excessive force – data that the Justice Department has failed to compile even though Congress instructed it to do so in 1994.

Congress should also pass legislation that would withhold grants if it can be shown that the police department requesting the funding fails to fully respect human rights. Specifically, when the Justice Department, as part of its new "pattern or practice" investigations, identifies widespread human rights violations in a police department, federal funding to that department should be ended if the police department fails, or demonstrates its unwillingness, to implement reforms.

Congress should also consider conditioning federal funds on all recipient police departments' demonstrable progress in adopting the reforms set out in agreements already made by the Justice Department with two police departments under the "pattern or practice" review, such as to create and utilize "early warning systems" to identify officers who are repeatedly the object of citizen complaints and including civil lawsuits against officers as part of the "early warning" tracking system; to develop and implement a use of force policy that is in compliance with applicable law and current professional standards; to require officers to file appropriate use of force and other reports; to conduct regular audits and reviews of potential racial bias, including the use of racial epithets by officers; to apply appropriate discipline following sustained complaints; and to appoint an independent auditor to ensure improvements. Since the Justice Department has endorsed these standards for some departments as essential for improved accountability, all police departments should be rewarded for taking demonstrable steps toward implementing similar procedures.

In the three areas we have highlighted – obstacles to justice, problems of investigation and discipline, and public accountability and transparency – we recommend the following changes.

Obstacles to Justice
(1) The U.S. federal government should remove obstacles to the fair and thorough investigation and, where appropriate, prosecution of human rights abuses committed by police officers.

- The Clinton administration should support the introduction of a bill in Congress to remove the "specific intent" requirement of the civil rights statutes which, in effect, undermines the spirit of the law. It should be sufficient for federal criminal prosecution that a police officer intentionally and unjustifiably beat or killed a victim without the additional burden of having to prove the officer specifically intended to violate the victim's civil rights by abusing the individual. Even without its removal, a finding of "specific intent" should be directed by the court in all cases of excessive force by on-duty officers because, by virtue of their profession, they should know that using excessive force deprives individuals of their rights and because jurors are often confused by the "specific intent" requirement.

- The Justice Department's Civil Rights Division, particularly its Criminal Section and Special Litigation Section, should be funded adequately so that it can fulfill its mandate. The funding should be in proportion with the growth of law enforcement agencies and their personnel who are subject to investigation or prosecution by the division.

- The U.S. Congress should pass implementing legislation for the International Covenant on Civil and Political Rights, the Convention against Torture and other Cruel, Inhuman or Degrading Treatment or Punishment, and the

International Convention on the Elimination of All Forms of Racial Discrimination (CERD), which include provisions on the prohibition of abusive, arbitrary, or discriminatory law enforcement activities, and President Clinton should request that the Senate consent to withdraw reservations that undermine the spirit and purpose of the treaties. Implementing legislation of the Convention against Torture would codify torture as a criminal offense in the U.S. If U.S. residents could invoke the race convention's provisions, the disproportionate impact of police abuse on minorities could be challenged in court because proving discrimination under the treaty requires proof of discriminatory intent or effect, while the U.S. Constitution has been interpreted by courts to require proof of both intent and effect. And if reservations attached to the treaties by the United States at the time of ratification that violate the spirit of the treaties were removed, U.S. residents would enjoy additional protections from police abuse. In particular, the reservations to Article 7 of both the ICCPR and the Convention against Torture, which prohibit "cruel, inhuman and degrading treatment or punishment" should be removed so that U.S. residents would be protected from "inhuman" and "degrading" treatment or punishment not currently prohibited by U.S. constitutional standards, which frame protections in the narrower terms of "cruel and unusual" punishment.

• The U.S. Congress should pass legislation that codifies torture as a federal crime whether or not implementing legislation for the Convention against Torture is approved.

• Due to the common reluctance of local district or county attorneys to prosecute police officers accused of human rights violations, each state should create a special prosecutor's office to handle criminal prosecutions of officers accused of criminal acts, including cases of brutality and corruption. The special prosecutor's office should also investigate district attorneys who, for extended periods, knowingly utilize evidence and testimony of notoriously abusive and corrupt officers and take no steps to prosecute them. Too often, scandal-ridden police departments, and usually low-level officers, bear the brunt of responsibility while higher-level officials escape scrutiny altogether. Until special prosecutor's offices are created, district attorneys suspected of misconduct in this regard should be referred to the state's bar association.

(2) State and city governments should create effective civilian review mechanisms, remove obstacles to the filing of complaints against police officers, fund citizen review agencies to allow them to fulfill their mandates, and should revise their laws

and practices to remove extraordinary protections for officers that shift the burden of abuse from the police onto the taxpayer.

- Cities should create an oversight system using an independent auditor office to: identify problematic practices and policies; review investigations by internal affairs divisions with the power to require additional investigations; and recommend reforms, monitor implementation of its recommendations, and participate in disciplinary hearings. Such an office should provide regular public reports on its activities. The oversight system should also include a fully empowered, independent fact-finding body (similar to some current civilian review boards) for receiving and investigating complaints that should work closely with the independent auditor. The oversight system should be supplemented by a city administrator who would track civil lawsuits relating to police abuse and identify trends in abuse allegations and officers named in the lawsuits.

- Barriers to the filing of complaints should be removed. For example, individuals wishing to file a complaint alleging police ill-treatment, whether with a citizen review agency or a police department official (or other office), should be provided with clear instructions, simple forms, and a telephone contact to check on the status of the investigation. Under no circumstances should any review agency or intake officer attempt to dissuade or intimidate a complainant. Anonymous complaints should be accepted for the purpose of triggering further investigation, but should not, on their own, be used for disciplinary purposes without verification by an appropriate senior official of the person's identity. Information about the complaints process and the complaint form itself should be made available in the languages of the community.

- Complainants should be provided with written, and regular, updates of the status of their complaints and the progress of the resulting investigation. At a minimum, the complainant should be advised that the citizen review agency or the police department's internal affairs unit has received the complaint, of any hearings or final determination regarding the complaint (including any disciplinary action taken), and complete explanations for the outcome.

- Any officer who attempts to dissuade a complainant from filing an abuse or other complaint should be punished appropriately. If necessary, training on receiving complaints should be provided.

- Citizen review agencies should be provided adequate resources to improve outreach efforts and demonstrate to skeptical residents that it is in their interest and worth their effort to file and pursue a complaint.

- When federal aid for police departments is considered, the U.S. Congress should reward municipalities that establish and adequately fund civilian or citizen review agencies and whose police departments cooperate with those bodies; this information should be provided to relevant congressional committees by the review agencies.

- Laws or policies that indemnify police officers from civil judgments should be modified in regard to serious human rights abuses. In the case of judgments against municipalities for the abusive conduct of a police officer, the municipality should seek some compensation from the officer to help pay the victim or his or her family.

- In those states where preferential grand jury rules apply for investigations of public officials, including police officers, those rules or laws should be revised so that justice is applied equally, regardless of occupation.

- Grand jurors have a unique role and unusual access to information about police practices in reviewing prosecutors' cases and deciding whether or not to indict police officers accused of criminal acts. Grand juries are permitted to make recommendations regarding police policies or practices in cases they consider whether or not they choose to indict the involved officers, and should do so.

Investigation and Discipline
(1) Federal, state, and city governments should coordinate to ensure that policies discouraging police abuse are reinforced at all levels.

- A tracking system should be established at the state or, ideally, federal level to prevent officers who have committed abuses and have been dismissed from one department from being hired as law enforcement officers elsewhere. Police departments and other law enforcement agencies should be required to submit relevant information to the tracking office when an officer is dismissed for serious misconduct (including human rights abuses) or when an officer resigns before a determination is made regarding the officer's alleged abuse. Police recruiters should be required to check with the tracking office prior to offering a position to any applicant. Further, uniform standards regarding the criminal background "acceptable" for police recruits should be created so that individuals with a record of violent criminal behavior are not hired due to low standards used by some police departments. That standard should exclude any officer convicted in any criminal court of any violent crime, whether prosecuted as a felony or misdemeanor.

- Police officer decertification procedures, which exist in thirty-nine states, should be reinvigorated and fully funded so that police officers who engage in serious misconduct (including human rights violations) will be "decertified" as officers and unable to serve on any police force in the state. The eleven states in which the Peace Officer's Standards and Training (POST) Commission, or its equivalent, does not have decertification powers should so empower the commission. All states should revise their statutes or regulations to require that police chiefs or commissioners report to the POST commission the dismissal or resignation of officers accused of serious misconduct (including human rights violations). Federal legislation should be introduced that would link the data currently collected by state POST commissions so that such officers are not allowed to obtain employment in a neighboring state or with federal law enforcement agencies.

(2) City and state governments and police department leaders should take measures to end impunity for all officers, but particularly for "problem" or "at-risk" officers – usually a small percentage of officers on each force that are repeatedly the subject of complaints and civil lawsuits – who persistently escape appropriate discipline and/or prosecution.

- Police leadership must send a strong and clear message to officers under their command, through words and actions, that human rights violations will not be tolerated and that departmental policies, and the law, will be strictly enforced.

- Whether conducted by civilian review agencies, internal affairs units, or other police personnel, all investigations should be prompt, thorough, and impartial.

- The findings of police investigators (by precincts/districts, internal affairs units, or homicide divisions) in cases involving the alleged use of excessive force or other serious human rights violations should always be reviewed by civilians at some level – whether civilian review agencies or auditors, civilian police commissions, or city councils.

- Whenever a police officer has been arrested or indicted, the officer should be removed from the field and assigned to desk duty or suspended with pay, depending upon the charges, until the case is resolved. Whenever a case against an officer is pending consideration by a grand jury or if authorities have reason to believe that the officer may have been involved in abusive conduct, the officer should – at a minimum – be placed on desk duty. Any officer convicted of any violent criminal offense, whether felony or misdemeanor, should be dismissed.

- Any officer involved in an on- or off-duty shooting should be assigned to desk duty or suspended with pay, depending upon the circumstances of the shooting, until the incident is investigated and resolved. Any officer against whom a complaint has been filed alleging the use of excessive force or other human rights violation resulting in the injury of the complainant or alleged victim should be assigned to desk duty or suspended with pay until the incident is investigated and resolved.

- When an officer who has been the subject of numerous complaints alleging human rights violations from citizens or fellow officers, or who has been repeatedly sued civilly for alleged abuse, yet is tolerated by his or her immediate superior who fails to discipline, retrain or otherwise address and curtail the officer's alleged ill-treatment of suspects or others, the superior officer should be investigated by the internal affairs unit or other appropriate investigators and held accountable for the subordinate officer's actions. If it is found the superior officer has failed to report the abuses or otherwise tolerated persistent abusive behavior on the part of any of the officers he or she supervises, the superior officer should be disciplined appropriately and the finding that he has failed to act to curtail abuses should become a permanent part of his personnel record and considered as a strong negative factor if promotion is considered. Those placed higher in the chain of command should routinely review those who directly supervise officers to ensure that they are appropriately handling their subordinates.

- Police officials must address seriously the code of silence that undermines efforts to hold police accountable for abuse. They must provide consistent positive reinforcement for those who report human rights violations and punishment for those who fail to do so. Supervisors should stigmatize abuse, not those who report it.

- Police officers who set a positive example by doing their job while dealing appropriately and respectfully with residents, intervening when fellow officers become abusive, and reporting violations when they do occur should be rewarded through preferred assignments and promotions to demonstrate that such officers will benefit professionally.

- Police departments must establish and utilize effective early warning systems to identify officers who repeatedly abuse the public they are sworn to serve, as well as programs for officers who are having emotional or other problems and need assistance to avoid committing a serious abuse. Early warning systems should take into account all complaints, use of force reports, civil lawsuits, and internal police management information concerning an officer. The threshold for triggering a review of an officer with repeated complaints or civil lawsuits should be low enough to ensure that officers receive attention and are handled appropriately before they repeatedly use excessive force against the public.

- Light-handed counseling should never replace strong disciplinary actions in serious cases of abuse in a misguided attempt to help officers who should, in fact, be punished or dismissed. Similarly, transfers should not be used as a tool to address an abuse problem; supervisors who choose to pass the problem to another precinct or district, thereby endangering residents and officers, should be punished appropriately.

- Sustained complaints against an officer should never be purged from an officer's file after a set period of time.

- The findings of civilian review agencies should be binding on the relevant police department unless the department can find – and describe fully and publicly – gross negligence or determinative factual errors on the review agency's part.

- When civilian review boards or internal affairs divisions have "sustained" a complaint against an officer, but the police department fails to discipline the officer at all, a detailed justification for the department's disregard of the "sustained" finding should be publicly provided as part of the review board's or the internal affairs unit's annual report, described below.

- When a complaint alleging possibly criminal behavior is sustained by either civilian review agencies or internal affairs units, it should be automatically forwarded to local and federal prosecutors for review. When a complaint is received by civilian review agencies or internal affairs unit alleging possibly criminal physical abuse involving injury, it should be forwarded at the time of its receipt to local and federal prosecutors for review.

- Each police department should create a disciplinary matrix or table, describing the range of penalties that officers should expect for various offenses, which should assist in removing the broad discretion currently exercised by some police officials in applying discipline.

- In some police departments, officers may not be disciplined if an investigation – by police personnel or a civilian review agency – take longer than a set period of time. In practice, abuse complaints have been sustained but officers have not been disciplined because of these statutes of limitations. These time limits should be removed or extended to reflect the amount of time investigations take; an arbitrary deadline should never be an excuse for allowing an officer who has committed a human rights violation to escape punishment.

- Civilian, non-police personnel should be involved in internal disciplinary hearings. The presence of "outsiders" can provide both the appearance and substance of public accountability.

- City governments must provide adequate legal resources to ensure that dismissals of officers by police departments are upheld. Arbitration and other procedures that, in practice, allow officers who have been found to engage in human rights violations or other misconduct to remain on the force should be revised to allow police chiefs, superintendents, or commissioners to fire officers who are deemed unsuitable for police work.

- State "bills of rights" for law enforcement officers should be examined and revised to ensure that the protections they grant officers in disciplinary proceedings do not inappropriately undermine accountability efforts.

- An internal investigation should be automatically triggered by the filing of a civil lawsuit alleging police abuse. If an internal investigation takes place and the complaint is not sustained, the investigation should be re-opened if a jury award or substantial settlement is made in favor of the complainant any evidence presented at the civil trial that was not considered by internal investigators. Once an internal affairs unit is notified about a lawsuit against an officer in its department, a notice should be sent to the plaintiff encouraging him or her to file a complaint with internal affairs if he or she has not already done so.

- The use of chokeholds is prohibited by most of the police departments examined in this report and should be banned by all law enforcement agencies. The degree of precision necessary in applying chokeholds without causing severe injury or death, combined with variables that contribute to the likelihood of injury or death that cannot be known immediately by the officer – including whether the arrestee is asthmatic, under the influence of particular drugs, or suffering from other pre-existing health problems – make chokeholds an unacceptable force option.

- Enhanced training should be provided on situations that often lead to abuse. For example, officers should be fully trained on how properly to use pepper spray, how to deal in a non-violent way with mentally ill individuals, and how to handle post-chase apprehensions.

- The effects of newer police weapon technology, such as pepper spray, should be fully studied before being made available for use by officers. In addition, officers should be trained to deal with the effects of these weapons, including providing prompt medical attention. Police administrators should create and enforce policies that fully protect the health and safety of individuals on whom these weapons are used.

- In choosing trainers, complaint histories and allegations of any kind of misconduct should be considered; police departments should never choose police officers who have been involved in abusive behavior to serve as trainers.

- Officers should be encouraged and trained to intercede when their partners or fellow officers threaten or begin to engage in abuse. When an arrest has been accompanied by any type of altercation – whether verbal or physical – between the arresting officer and arrestee, the arrestee should be processed at the station house by a different officer. Whether or not this type of "hand-off" takes place, it is essential that the identity of the arresting officer is included in the arrest report and other relevant documents.

- Officers who are witness to, or responsible for, shooting another individual should be required to provide statements immediately to investigators, in compliance with appropriate due process guarantees and whether or not they consult with legal counsel; special provisions for days-long delays that are now permitted in at least one of the cities examined can serve to obstruct justice and should be eliminated. Such delays impede investigators and undermine police-community relations because they give the appearance of impropriety.

- District attorneys' "roll-out teams," which respond to officer-involved shootings, should be created or, where they have been curtailed on budgetary grounds, reinstated. When district attorney's office personnel are on the scene of a shooting, they should be permitted to interview the officers involved in the shooting before police department investigators compel statements from officers that are inadmissible in criminal proceedings.

- Police departments should pay special attention to the "trilogy" of charges – resisting arrest, disorderly conduct, and assaulting an officer. Officers frequently use these charges against abuse complainants to cover up their own human rights violations. Police departments should determine whether certain officers are repeatedly using these allegations, particularly in the absence of underlying charges, in an effort to deter victims from pursuing complaints. If it is found that such charges are being applied to cover an officer's own abuses, the officer should be dismissed.

- City solicitors, attorneys, or corporation counsels should be required to report any lawsuit involving a police officer to the relevant police department without delay.

- Civil lawsuits should be paid from the police department's budget, not out of general city funds as is usually done. In this way, police departments would have a strong financial incentive to deal appropriately with officers who are frequently the subject of civil suits. Amounts, incidents, and trends in police misconduct lawsuits should be used in policy planning.

Public Accountability and Transparency
(1) The federal government should provide timely and thorough reports in compliance with its human rights treaty obligations, should disseminate information to state and local entities regarding U.S. obligations under international human rights law, and should cooperate with international human rights investigators in a manner consistent with its obligations.

- The United States is obliged to submit periodic reports to the U.N. Human Rights Committee, the Committee against Torture, and the Committee on the Elimination of Racial Discrimination, due to its ratification of these international instruments. To date, its reporting has been incomplete (in the case of the Human Rights Committee) or more than two years overdue (in the case of the other two committees). In the future, reporting could be made more responsive through better data collection, more candid descriptions of continuing shortcomings, and, perhaps most importantly, political will to compile timely and thorough reports.

- The federal government has a duty to disseminate information to state and local entities regarding U.S. obligations under international human rights treaties to which it is party. So far, no such efforts have been undertaken in a serious or consistent manner. The federal government must disseminate this information without delay.

- When Special Rapporteurs or other U.N. investigators conduct missions in the United States, relevant U.S. officials at all levels should assist them by providing information requested, arranging meetings with officials at all levels of government involved in police accountability issues, and studying the U.N. reports once released, including their recommendations. Specifically, local and federal officials should review the report released in April 1998 by the U.N. Special Rapporteur on extrajudicial, summary or arbitrary executions. He investigated killings by police and raised concerns regarding the absence of national data on this issue, the poor quality of some investigations of killings by police, and the low rate of criminal prosecution in cases of police abuse resulting in death. The Special Rapporteur recommended: enhanced training on international standards on law enforcement and human rights; independent investigations of deaths in custody; and the use of special prosecutors.

(2) The federal government should compile and publish relevant, nationwide statistical data on police abuse, to inform its own policymaking, to maintain oversight of local data-collection, and to facilitate monitoring by both governmental and nongovernmental entities.

- The Justice Department should provide an annual report on the number of complaints alleging human rights violations against police officers received and investigated, and the number of officers indicted or convicted under the federal criminal civil rights statutes. The report should contain an analysis of such issues as official acts of racial discrimination, trends in types of abuse, difficulties in prosecuting cases, and sources of information.

- The Justice Department should compile data on the excessive-use-of-force and produce an annual report on this topic, as instructed by Congress in 1994. Pilot surveys and preliminary reports released by the Justice Department so far have not yielded useful information on this topic. The data compilation should include information provided by citizen review agencies or mechanisms, and civil rights groups, rather than the current project's reliance on police departments to report voluntarily. As conducted so far, this project is unresponsive to Congress's instructions. The Civil Rights Division should provide additional oversight and guidance, and reallocate the Justice Department's grants to ensure that this congressional mandate is fulfilled.

- Congress should withhold federal grants intended for police departments that have failed to provide data on the use of excessive force. Congress, which has reportedly failed to provide adequate funding for data compilation on police use of excessive force should do so without delay, provided that the research projects are refocused to fulfill the congressional mandate. Members of Congress should also monitor the Justice Department's efforts to compile these data and insist that use of excessive force data be produced immediately.

- Under new authority, the Civil Rights Division's Special Litigation Section may bring "pattern or practice" lawsuits against abusive police forces. To date there has been no comprehensive public report on the investigations or lawsuits undertaken. The Justice Department's report on use of excessive force, or a separate report released by the Civil Rights Division, should include: information on the police departments examined by the Civil Rights Division; the findings of these investigations; cooperation with local attorneys or civil rights groups supplying information to Justice Department about the police force; the status of the police departments' compliance with reforms requested by the Justice Department to avoid a lawsuit; and consent decrees reached or injunctions filed prohibiting abusive treatment. Any progress in police department compliance with consent decrees or other agreements should be noted, as should the methodology employed to monitor compliance. Further, the report should identify the reasons for the examination of a particular city's police department. Without widespread dissemination of information about consent decrees reached, the positive aspects of the agreements are undermined and, absent information to the contrary, the public presumes the Justice Department is not living up to its obligations. Moreover, the public has a right to know how the Justice Department is using its new civil powers.

- The Justice Department should monitor and encourage local data collection efforts, to ensure that public access to useful, relevant data is maximized and to guarantee that federal policy can be made on the basis of sound assessments of the incidence and characteristics of police brutality.

• The U.S. Commission on Civil Rights publishes periodic reports on police brutality in particular cities and regions. We urge additional funding for the commission to enhance its ability to hold public hearings, produce useful and timely reports, and make and monitor reform recommendations.

(3) Civilian review agencies, police departments' internal affairs units, city governments, and local prosecutors should regularly publish reports on their activities in relation to human rights violations committed by law enforcement officers. Where this requires additional funding, that funding should be provided; under-funding is no excuse for ignoring this responsibility to provide information to the public.

• Citizen review agencies should publish reports, at least annually, presenting detailed statistics and information relating to complaints, trends, sustained rates for each type of complaint, disciplinary actions stemming from sustained allegations, policy recommendations (as well as the departmental responses to those recommendations), and community outreach efforts. The statistics should include breakdowns on the race and gender of the complainants and officers in question. The reports should also include examples of the types of abuse about which the agency has received complaints during the reporting period.

• In those cities where the citizen review agency has been provided with a mandate that clearly precludes its intended, effective review of police practices, these mandates should be revised.

• Review agencies should not limit themselves to handling individual complaints they have received, but should be empowered and financed to conduct investigations on their own initiative.

• Review agencies are in a unique position to observe types of complaints of abuse and shortcomings of the police departments they monitor. For this reason, they should provide policy recommendations to the relevant police department.

• Citizen review agencies should be automatically notified of the filing of civil lawsuits alleging police abuse, and should send the plaintiff information regarding his or her right to file a complaint with the review agency.

- Police departments should eliminate the secrecy surrounding their handling of abuse allegations that is not directly and narrowly necessary to provide due-process protection for allegedly abusive police officers. Police are accountable to the public and must demonstrate that their practices and policies are adequate and conform to human rights standards. Police departments that claim to handle officers suspected of committing human rights violations appropriately should provide evidence in this regard to the public, either through regular public reporting or improved responsiveness to requests for information. Police departments should provide a report, respecting privacy concerns, describing at least the number of officers disciplined, the offenses leading to punishment, and the types of punishment, over a set time period. Such a report should also include the names and number of officers indicted or convicted during the reporting period, and the charges brought against them; this information should never be withheld. District attorneys and federal prosecutors should provide information to the police department regarding the status of criminal charges against officers on the relevant police force.

- Local prosecutors should maintain a list, available to the public upon request, of law enforcement officers who have been arrested, indicted, or convicted. The vast majority of the district and county attorneys queried by Human Rights Watch did not acknowledge maintaining such a list. Without such tracking, there is no way for federal prosecutors to know whether local prosecutors are handling sensitive police brutality cases appropriately and whether they should initiate federal investigations. It also leaves the public without basic information about the nature of the police force sworn to protect and serve it.

- Nationwide, systematic data should be kept on the number and nature of civil lawsuits alleging police abuse, and how much is paid in each jurisdiction. As a start, cities should begin to publish reports on civil lawsuits, with descriptions of allegations, amounts paid through settlements or after a jury trial, and how the police department dealt with the officer named in each suit leading to significant settlements or jury awards, whether through retraining, counseling, or disciplinary sanctions.

OVERVIEW

Police abuse remains one of the most serious and divisive human rights violations in the United States. The excessive use of force by police officers, including unjustified shootings, severe beatings, fatal chokings, and rough treatment, persists because overwhelming barriers to accountability make it possible for officers who commit human rights violations to escape due punishment and often to repeat their offenses.[1] Police or public officials greet each new report of brutality with denials or explain that the act was an aberration, while the administrative and criminal systems that should deter these abuses by holding officers accountable instead virtually guarantee them impunity.

This report examines common obstacles to accountability for police abuse in fourteen large cities representing most regions of the nation. The cities examined are: Atlanta, Boston, Chicago, Detroit, Indianapolis, Los Angeles, Minneapolis, New Orleans, New York, Philadelphia, Portland, Providence, San Francisco, and Washington, D.C. Research for this report was conducted over two and a half years, from late 1995 through early 1998.

The brutality cases examined, which are set out in detail in chapters on each city, are similar to cases that continue to emerge in headlines and in survivors' complaints. It is important to note, however, that because it is difficult to obtain case information except where there is public scandal and/or prosecution, this report relies heavily on cases that have reached public attention; disciplinary action and

---

[1] "Excessive force" is used throughout this report to refer to force that exceeds what is objectively reasonable and necessary in the circumstances confronting the officer to subdue a person, as in Article 3 of the U.N. Code of Conduct for Law Enforcement Officials (*see* appendix H), which provides that: "Law enforcement officials should use force only when strictly necessary and to the extent required for the performance of their duty." GA resolution 34/169 passed on December 17, 1979, and in the U.N. Basic Principles on the Use of Force and Firearms by Law Enforcement Officials, which stipulates that, "Whenever the use of force and firearms is unavoidable, law enforcement officials shall exercise restraint in such use and act in proportion to the seriousness of the offence and the legitimate objective to be achieved." UN Doc. A/CONF.144/28/Rev.1 (1990). In *Graham v. Connor* 490 U.S. 386 (1989), the United States Supreme Court held that that the United States Constitution's Fourth Amendment requirement of "reasonableness" on the part of the police applies to "all claims that law enforcement officials have used excessive force – deadly or not – in the course of an arrest, investigatory stop, or other seizure of a free person." Throughout this report, the term "excessive force" refers to abuse occurring both during apprehension and while in custody. This report also describes sexual assaults and torture by police officers which are not, strictly speaking "excessive" use of force, but are unjustified and criminal assaults.

25

criminal prosecution are even less common than the cases set out below would suggest.

Our investigation found that police brutality is persistent in all of these cities; that systems to deal with abuse have had similar failings in all the cities; and that, in each city examined, complainants face enormous barriers in seeking administrative punishment or criminal prosecution of officers who have committed human rights violations. Despite claims to the contrary from city officials where abuses have become scandals in the media, efforts to make meaningful reforms have fallen short.

The barriers to accountability are remarkably similar from city to city. Shortcomings in recruitment, training, and management are common to all. So is the fact that officers who repeatedly commit human rights violations tend to be a small minority who taint entire police departments but are protected, routinely, by the silence of their fellow officers and by flawed systems of reporting, oversight, and accountability. Another pervasive shortcoming is the scarcity of meaningful information about trends in abuse; data are also lacking regarding the police departments' response to those incidents and their plans or actions to prevent brutality. Where data do exist, there is no evidence that police administrators or, where relevant, prosecutors, utilize available information in a way to deter abuse.[2] Another commonality in recent years is a recognition, in most cities, about what needs to be done to fix troubled departments. However, this encouraging development is coupled with an official unwillingness to deal seriously with officers who commit abuses until high-profile cases expose long-standing negligence or tolerance of brutality.

One recent, positive development has been the federal "pattern or practice" civil investigations, and subsequent agreements, initiated by the U.S. Justice Department.[3] In Pittsburgh, Pennsylvania and Steubenville, Ohio, the Justice

---

[2] In the Violent Crime Control and Law Enforcement Act of 1994, the U.S. Justice Department was tasked with collecting data on the frequency and types of abuse complaints filed nationwide. At the time of this writing, nearly four years later, no such report has been issued. (*See* below.)

[3] The Violent Crime Control and Law Enforcement Act of 1994 included a new statute under which the Justice Department may sue for declaratory relief (a statement of the governing law) and equitable relief (an order to abide by the law with specific instructions describing actions that must be taken) if any governmental authority or person acting on behalf of any governmental authority engages in: "a pattern or practice of conduct by law enforcement officers...that deprives persons of rights, privileges, or immunities secured or protected by the Constitution or laws of the United States." "Police Pattern or Practice" 42

Department's Civil Rights Division has examined shortcomings in accountability for misconduct in those cities' police departments; the cities agreed to implement reforms to end violative practices rather than risk the Justice Department taking a case to court for injunctive action. The reforms proposed by the Justice Department were similar to those long advocated by community activists and civil rights groups, and included better use-of-force training and policies, stronger reporting mechanisms, creation of early warning systems to identify current, and potential, officers at risk of engaging in abuse, and improved disciplinary procedures. The Justice Department does not usually make its investigative choices public, but several other police departments, including those in Los Angeles, New Orleans, New York, and Philadelphia, are reportedly under investigation by the Civil Rights Division.

Police abuse experts, and some police officials, refer to "problem" officers, by which they mean officers who either have significant records of abuse or significant records of complaints from the public, and who thus should receive special monitoring, training and counseling to counter the heightened risk that they will be involved in some future incident of misconduct or brutality. In this report, we will use this terminology where police officials and experts use it, to denote officers who, on account of their record of either sustained or unsustained complaints, appear to present a higher than normal risk of committing human rights violations.

Allegations of police abuse are rife in cities throughout the country and take many forms. This report uses specific incidents as illustrations of the obstacles to deterring, investigating and acting upon perceived abuses. Human Rights Watch is presenting these cases *not* to accuse any particular officer of an abuse, but rather to describe the barriers that exist to addressing such allegations meaningfully. Any alleged abuse has a corrosive effect on public trust of the police force, and it is imperative that the system be reformed to prevent human rights violations such as those described below.

- A seriously flawed background check of a new recruit who had a history of abusive behavior while working for another police department, apparent misuse of pepper spray, and poor investigation procedures were evident in the Aaron Williams case. (*See* San Francisco chapter for additional details.) Williams died while in the custody of San Francisco police officers after officers subdued him and sprayed him with pepper spray in the Western Edition neighborhood in June 1995. Williams, a burglary suspect, was bound with wrist and ankle cuffs, and according to witnesses was hit and kicked after he

---

U.S.C. §14141.

was restrained.[4] Departmental rules apparently were broken when the officers used pepper spray repeatedly on Williams, who appeared to be high on drugs, and officers did not monitor his breathing as required.[5] One of the officers involved in the incident, Marc Andaya, had reportedly been the subject of as many as thirty-five complaints while working with the Oakland police force before being hired by the San Francisco Police Department.[6] In Oakland, his supervisor reportedly had urged desk duty for Andaya because of his "cowboy" behavior.[7] It is not clear why the San Francisco Police Department hired Andaya in light of his background, but the press reported that Andaya may have given only a partial account of his complaint history and no thorough check was conducted.[8] Andaya was accused of neglect of duty and using excessive force, but the city's Police Commission initially deadlocked on the charges (two for, two against, with one police commissioner absent), which was in effect an exoneration. In large part due to community outrage over the Williams case, Andaya was eventually fired for lying about his disciplinary background in his application.[9]

•   A record of brutality complaints, inadequate supervision, and the code of silence were illustrated in the Anthony Baez case in New York City. (*See* New

---

[4] Mary Curtius, "Despite Progressive Policies, S.F. Police, Public at Odds," *Los Angeles Times*, July 21, 1997. Officer Marc Andaya was reportedly injured during the incident.

[5] Officers also reportedly placed a surgical mask on Williams during the encounter and the mask was discarded at the scene; examination of the mask may have made clear whether pepper spray was used after Williams was subdued or if its use contributed to his death by restricting breathing. Rachel Gordon and Katherine Seligman, "Did cops skirt rules in death of suspect?" *San Francisco Examiner*, June 8, 1995.

[6] Susan Sward, "S.F. panel fires officer in Aaron Williams case," *San Francisco Chronicle*, June 28, 1997.

[7] Jim Herron Zamora, "S.F. cop cleared of using excess force," *San Francisco Examiner*, November 21, 1996.

[8] Jim Herron Zamora, "Cop kicked suspect's head, say 3 witnesses," *San Francisco Examiner*, October 8, 1996; Zamora, "S.F. cop cleared of using excess force," *San Francisco Examiner*, November 21, 1996.

[9] Susan Sward, "S.F. panel fires officers," *San Francisco Chronicle*, June 28, 1997.

York City chapter for additional details.) Baez, age twenty-nine, was choked to death during an encounter with police Officer Francis X. Livoti on December 22, 1994. Livoti had been the subject of at least eleven brutality complaints over an eleven-year period, including one that was substantiated by the city's civilian review board involving the choking of a sixteen-year-old who was allegedly riding a go-cart recklessly.[10] In the Baez case, Livoti was acquitted of criminally negligent homicide in a judge-only trial ending in October 1996. But in finding the prosecution's case unproven, the judge nevertheless criticized conflicting and inconsistent officer testimony, citing a "nest of perjury" within the department.[11] Livoti was then prosecuted administratively to ascertain, in part, whether he had broken departmental rules that prohibit applying a chokehold.[12] Partially in response to substantial publicity and community outrage over Livoti's behavior, he was fired in February 1997 for breaking departmental rules.

- The case of Frank Schmidt in Philadelphia illustrated flawed investigative procedures and lax discipline. (*See* Philadelphia chapter for additional details.) Officer Christopher Rudy was on duty but reportedly visiting friends and drinking alcohol at a warehouse in November 1993.[13] A dispute arose between the warehouse owner and Frank Schmidt, with Schmidt accused of stealing items from the warehouse. Schmidt reportedly told investigators that the warehouse gates were locked behind him, a gun was put to his head, and he was beaten as Officer Rudy watched and poured beer over Schmidt's head.

---

[10] Clifford Krauss, "Case casts wide light on abuse by police," *New York Times*, April 15, 1995.

[11] In September 1997, the Bronx District Attorney's office announced it would reopen its perjury inquiry involving fifteen officers of the 46th Precinct, where Livoti worked.

[12] Of the fourteen city police departments examined by Human Rights Watch, only four – San Francisco, Washington, D.C., Los Angeles, and Minneapolis – still allow chokeholds. *1993 Law Enforcement Management and Administrative Statistics*, 1993, Bureau of Justice Statistics, Washington, D.C., pp. 169-180.

[13] Mark Bowden, "Major offenses by Philadelphia cops often bring minor punishments," *Philadelphia Inquirer,* November 19, 1995; and case files of off-duty actions provided to Temple University Prof. James Fyfe by the police department's Internal Affairs Division. He compiled case studies titled "Philadelphia police off-duty actions: Complaints and Shootings," May 23, 1994.

Throughout the ordeal, the warehouse owner reportedly threatened to cut off Schmidt's hands with a knife and to have warehouse workers rape him. Schmidt reported the incident to the police, but Rudy was not questioned for seven months and then denied everything. Rudy reportedly received a twelve-day suspension for failing to take police action and for conduct unbecoming a police officer; he was returned to active duty .[14]

- Lax oversight and the failure to act quickly to dismiss an abusive officer while he was still on probation were evident in Minneapolis. (*See* Minneapolis chapter for additional details.) Officer Michael Ray Parent was convicted in state court of kidnaping and raping a woman in his squad car and was sentenced to four years in prison in April 1995. In the early morning hours of August 5, 1994, Officer Parent stopped and questioned the woman. She acknowledged she had been drinking, and he put her in the back seat of his squad car and told her she was under arrest for driving under the influence of alcohol. He then forced her to have oral sex with him. After the incident was reported, investigators found several prior complaints about Parent involving inappropriate sexual conduct while on duty, even though he had been on the force for only a year and a half before the August 1994 incident; he had been accused of a sexual incident during his probationary period on the force, when dismissals are much easier.[15]

- Despite a civil jury trial leading to one of Indianapolis's largest awards following a judgment against an officer who fatally shot a burglary suspect, the officer remains on the force. (*See* Indianapolis chapter for additional details.) Officer Wayne Sharp, who is white, shot and killed Edmund Powell, who was black, in June 1991.[16] Sharp, a veteran officer, claimed the shooting was accidental and that Powell had swung a nail-studded board at him, yet according to at least one witness, Powell was on the ground and had apparently

---

[14] Telephone confirmation of Rudy assignment with Philadelphia Police Department, August 11, 1997.

[15] Pat Pheifer, "Minneapolis officer held on charges of assault," *Minneapolis Star Tribune*, September 2, 1994.

[16] Erica Franklin, "Witness saw suspect prone before officer shot him," *Indianapolis Star,* April 18, 1995.

surrendered when he was shot.[17] According to witnesses, Powell allegedly stole something from a department store, and Sharp chased him into an alley with his gun drawn. The Marion County prosecutor brought the case before a grand jury, and it declined to indict Sharp on any criminal charges. Community activists claimed that the shooting was racially motivated; Sharp had killed a black burglary suspect ten years earlier and a grand jury had declined to indict him. At that time, Sharp reportedly was removed from street duty because of his "flirtation" with the National Socialist White People's Party, a neo-Nazi group.[18] Powell's grandmother, Gertrude Jackson, alleging Sharp intentionally shot Powell, filed a civil lawsuit in 1992; the jury found in favor of Jackson and awarded $465,000 to Powell's family.[19] The city had not paid Jackson as of September 1997, and the status of any appeal was unclear.[20] Despite his history, Sharp was still on duty as of mid-1997 and according to the police chief there has received "high accolades and several awards for superior work."[21]

• A ranking New Orleans officer who himself was responsible for enforcing internal rules had a long history of abuse complaints, some sustained, but was only dismissed after he was convicted of a crime. (*See* New Orleans chapter for additional details.) Lieutenant Christopher Maurice was the subject of more than a dozen discourtesy and brutality complaints before being charged and convicted on two counts of simple battery in November 1995 (and fired two weeks later). The charges stemmed from a June 1994 incident in which Lt. Maurice allegedly slammed the head of radio personality Richard Blake

---

[17] Ibid.

[18] Sherri Edwards and Erica Franklin, "Jury finds police officer guilty of intentionally killing suspect," *The Indianapolis Star,* April 22, 1995; U.P.I., "FBI probes police shooting," June 20, 1991; "Police confrontations," *Indianapolis News*, July 27, 1995.

[19] Howard M. Smulevitz, "Jury award could bust IPD's bank," *Indianapolis Star*, April 25, 1995.

[20] Welton W. Harris II, "Officer loses fatal shooting suit," *Indianapolis News,* April 22, 1995; Sherri Edwards and Erica Franklin, "City may appeal verdict giving slain man's family $465,000," *Indianapolis Star*, April 23, 1995; telephone interview with Greg Ray of the Office of Corporation Counsel, July 28, 1997.

[21] Letter to Human Rights Watch from Chief Michael H. Zunk, dated January 26, 1998.

(known as Robert Sandifer) against the police car's hood.[22] Just after this encounter, Maurice was found in violation of department rules for getting into an argument and nearly a fistfight with a fellow officer during ethics training in early 1994. Also in June 1994, Maurice was served a warrant for another battery charge in St. Tammany Parish. Prior to the 1994 incidents, he had been suspended once (allegedly for brandishing his gun at a neighbor) and reprimanded twice since 1985, according to his civil service records. In a 1991 civil suit, the city paid a $25,000 settlement to a man who claimed that Maurice had hit him in the head with his police radio. Despite this record, Maurice was the commander in charge of enforcing the internal rules of the department. The city's citizen review agency (an external monitoring office) reportedly investigated several of the complaints against Maurice but did not uphold any of them as valid.

Human Rights Watch recognizes that police officers, like other people, will make mistakes when they are under pressure to make split-second decisions regarding the use of force. Even the best recruiting, training, and command oversight will not result in flawless behavior on the part of all officers. Furthermore, we recognize that policing in the United States is a dangerous job. During 1996, 116 officers died while on duty nationwide (from all causes – shootings, assaults, accidents, and natural causes).[23] Yet, precisely because police officers can make mistakes, or allow personal bias or emotion to enter into policing – and because they are allowed, as a last resort, to use potentially lethal force to subdue individuals they apprehend – police must be subjected to intense scrutiny.[24]

---

[22] Maurice's appeal of his battery conviction was pending at the time of this writing.

[23] National Law Enforcement Officers Memorial Fund, online at http://www.1nleomf.com/ and the Associated Press, December 31, 1996. The 1996 death total was the lowest since 1959. Of the 116, more officers died from traffic accidents, falls, plane crashes and heart attacks than by acts of criminal suspects or others (shootings, stabbings, or assaults). During 1997, 159 law enforcement officers were killed in the line of duty, including seventy who were shot to death. During the 1990s, 151 officers have been killed annually, on average.

[24] Principle 4 of the U.N. Basic Principles on the Use of Force and Firearms by Law Enforcement Officials states, "[L]aw enforcement officials, in carrying out their duty, shall, as far as possible, apply non-violent means before resorting to the use of force and firearms. They may use force and firearms only if other means remain ineffective or without any promise of achieving the intended result." UN Doc. A/CONF.144/28/Rev.1 (1990).

The abuses described in this report are preventable. Officers with long records of abuse, policies that are overly vague, training that is substandard, and screening that is inadequate all create opportunities for abuse. Perhaps most important, and consistently lacking, is a system of oversight in which supervisors hold their charges accountable for mistreatment and are themselves reviewed and evaluated, in part, by how they deal with subordinate officers who commit human rights violations. Those who claim that each high-profile case of abuse by a "rogue" officer is an aberration are missing the point: problem officers frequently persist because the accountability systems are so seriously flawed.

Police, state, and federal authorities are responsible for holding police officers accountable for abusive or arbitrary acts.[25] Police officials must ensure that police officers are punished when they violate administrative rules, while state and federal prosecutors must prosecute criminal acts committed by officers, and where appropriate, complicity by their superior officers.[26] Each of these entities apply different standards when reviewing officer responsibility for an alleged abuse.[27] All of these authorities have an obligation to ensure that the conduct of police officers

---

[25] Principle 7 of the U.N. Basic Principles on the Use of Force and Firearms by Law Enforcement Officials state, "Governments shall ensure that arbitrary or abusive use of force and firearms by law enforcement officials is punished as a criminal offence under their law." UN Doc. A/CONF.144/28/Rev.1 (1990).

[26] U.N. Basic Principles on the Use of Force and Firearms by Law Enforcement Officials, calls for accountability for superior officers: "Governments and law enforcement agencies shall ensure that superior officers are held responsible if they know, or should have known, that law enforcement officials under their command are resorting, or have resorted, to the unlawful use of force and firearms, and they did not take all measures in their power to prevent, suppress or report such use. Principle 24. UN Doc. A/CONF.144/28/Rev.1 (1990).

[27] There are several standards used by different entities when reviewing officer responsibility for an alleged abuse. In civil cases, a "preponderance of the evidence" standard is used. A more rigorous standard is used in state criminal cases (for charges such as assault, manslaughter, murder, etc.), "beyond a reasonable doubt," and in federal criminal civil rights cases, a prosecutor must also prove that the officer in question specifically intended to deprive an individual of his or her civil rights. Whether in state or federal court, an officer must be indicted by a grand jury before standing trial. And, when an officer is administratively charged by his police department for breaking the department's rules, the standard should be the same as in civil cases – preponderance of the evidence – but in practice is often similar to a criminal standard of "beyond a reasonable doubt."

meets international standards that prohibit human rights violations and that, in general, the U.S. complies with the obligations imposed by those treaties to which it is a party. While only the federal government is responsible for reporting internationally on U.S. compliance with the relevant treaties, local and state officials share responsibility for ensuring compliance within their jurisdictions.[28]

Contributing Factors

In looking at human rights violations common to most of the cities examined, we found:

- *Weak Civilian Review:* Citizen review agencies, tasked with monitoring and, in some cases, investigating cases of excessive force, are under-funded by city officials, undermined by police officers who refuse to cooperate with them, under attack by police unions and others, and under-utilized by the public. External citizen review should be an integral part of police oversight and policy formulation, but instead has been sidelined in most cities examined.

- *Leadership Failure:* Police administrators, the officials most responsible for addressing the problem of police abuse, are not yet taking this issue seriously enough. Notably, in Los Angeles, Philadelphia, and New Orleans, among other cities, high-profile cases and unflattering media attention have been required

---

[28] According to the Understanding filed by the U.S. upon its ratification of the International Covenant on Civil and Political Rights: "That the United States understands that this Covenant shall be implemented by the Federal Government to the extent that it exercises legislative and judicial jurisdiction over the matters covered therein and otherwise by the state and local governments; to the extent that state and local governments exercise jurisdiction over such matters, the Federal Government shall take measures appropriate to the Federal system to the end that the competent authorities of the state or local governments may take appropriate measures for the fulfilment of the Covenant." (As submitted by the U.S. Senate on April 2, 1992.) This provision is not a reservation and does not modify or limit the international obligations of the United States under the Covenant. Rather, it addresses the essentially domestic issue of how the Covenant will be implemented within the U.S. federal system. It serves to emphasize domestically that there was no intent to alter the constitutional balance of authority between federal government on the one hand and the state and local governments on the other, or to use the provisions of the Covenant to federalize matters now within the competence of the states. It also serves to notify other States Parties that the United States will implement its obligations under the Covenant by appropriate legislative, executive and judicial means, federal or state, and that the federal government will remove any federal inhibition to the abilities of the constituent states to meet their obligations in this regard.

to produce overdue and necessary reforms. The leadership gap is evident in the poor performance of police departments' internal affairs divisions around the country, which too often conduct sloppy and incomplete investigations that tend to be biased in favor of fellow officers. Early warning systems to identify and manage "problem officers" are not fully operational in most cities we examined – despite findings by oversight commissions and journalistic investigations that a small percentage of officers are responsible for a large percentage of abuses. Disciplinary actions against officers responsible for abusive treatment are lax, while internal review activities remain shrouded in secrecy.

- **Ineffectual Civil Remedies:** In part because police often are not held responsible for their actions through administrative or criminal procedures, many police abuse victims or their families rely solely on civil remedies for redress. In practice, civil lawsuits usually allow police departments to continue to ignore abuses committed by officers. Some victims have succeeded in obtaining compensation, and a small percentage of civil lawsuits have forced police departments to accept liability for abuses, leading to reforms in training or flawed policies. Still, most police departments we examined do not have to pay plaintiffs; the payments come instead from the city's general budget. And, though an officer's behavior has cost a city hundreds of thousands, or millions, of dollars in payments to victims, there is often no linkage to that officer's performance evaluations – even when the lawsuit alleges serious violations. In the end, taxpayers are paying at least twice for bad officers – once for their salaries and again to pay victims of their abuse.

- *Passivity on Criminal Prosecutions:* Local criminal prosecution of officers who commit human rights violations is far too rare, with many local prosecutors unwilling to prosecute vigorously officers who normally help them in criminal cases. Federal prosecutors, who can prosecute officers under criminal civil rights statutes, almost never pursue even strong cases, due in part to the high legal threshold required to win such cases and a shortage of resources. Of the thousands of complaints the Justice Department receives annually, it prosecutes only a handful. And, though federal prosecutors claim they should play a "backstop" role in prosecuting officers who commit human rights violations, they rarely do so even when local prosecutors decline prosecution or do a poor job in presenting a case.

When all of these systemic shortcomings in dealing with officers who commit human rights violations are combined, it becomes understandable why they have little reason to fear that they will be caught, punished, or prosecuted.

Recent police abuse scandals clarify that lack of will at the top of police departments is permitting abuses to recur. For example:

- In Philadelphia, a recent scandal uncovered widespread police corruption, often accompanied by brutality – which was tolerated by both police officials and prosecutors – and, as a result, scores of criminal cases that relied on corrupt officers' accounts have been overturned, while public distrust of the police is pervasive. Taxpayers have shouldered the burden of tens of millions of dollars paid out in police misconduct civil lawsuits against the city over the past four years. Some of the lawsuits' settlements or jury awards following trial are directly related to the recent scandal; others stem from the general damage done to the department's reputation, making jurors more likely to find in favor of plaintiffs alleging abuse and the city more eager to settle such cases.

- In New Orleans, public awareness of police corruption and abuse reached a new high in the mid-1990s, as dozens of officers were tried for felonies, including murder, armed robbery, and drug trafficking. These recent scandals followed decades of outrageous behavior. In recent years, one officer was convicted of hiring a professional killer to murder a woman for bringing a brutality complaint against him, and another was convicted for killing a brother and sister who worked at a family-run restaurant where the officer had been a security guard; this officer also killed an off-duty policeman working at the restaurant.

- In New York, abuse complaints climbed after the police began aggressively pursuing petty criminals in 1994, with serious on- and off-duty abuses reported regularly. Major police corruption scandals, recurring every twenty years, led most recently to the independent Mollen Commission's investigation of corruption, highlighting its link to brutality. But many of the commission's recommendations, issued in July 1994, have not been implemented as of this writing. Several recent abuse cases, including the alleged torture of Haitian immigrant Abner Louima in August 1997, have led to heightened tensions.[29]

---

[29] In response to the public outrage surrounding the Louima case, New York City Mayor Rudolph Giuliani created a task force to examine police-community relations in the city and to make recommendations for improvements. Yet once the task force reports were released, the mayor immediately criticized the findings and recommendations. His reaction

And it is an open question whether an officer who unlawfully kills a suspect will be convicted; only three New York City police officers have been convicted for an on-duty killing in the last twenty years.[30]

- In Los Angeles, following the March 1991 beating of Rodney King and the April 1992 acquittals of the four accused officers on all but one of the state charges, rioting erupted, sparked in part by frustration over the lack of accountability for officers. The Christopher Commission's ground-breaking 1991 report, which called for a "new standard of accountability," has led, very slowly, to reforms. But the force still falls short in many areas, as noted in the first reports released during 1997 by the Police Commission's inspector general. (In an indication of the sluggish pace of reform, it took five years to fill the inspector general's position.)

- In Indianapolis, a small riot erupted in July 1995 after the alleged beating of a drug suspect, and in an August 1996 incident, officers allegedly yelled racial epithets and beat and sexually harassed citizens, making front-page news. These incidents led to resignations of two successive chiefs of police in a city where police leadership is desperately needed.

Political Considerations and Aggressive Policing

Efforts to improve police accountability are undermined by the actions of some police unions and organizations that legally challenge citizen review agencies. These groups publicly deny all allegations against police officers, even those they know are brutal; encourage noncooperation with investigators and the "code of silence" when allegations arise; and in approximately half of the fifty U.S. states

---

appeared to be extremely counterproductive and may have lost him support from the task force, made up of activists, clergy members, community leaders and attorneys. Dan Barry, "Giuliani dismisses police proposals by his task force," *New York Times*, March 27, 1998.

[30] Former Transit Officer Paolo Colecchia, who had been convicted for second-degree manslaughter for fatally shooting Nathaniel Levi Gaines, Jr. in July 1996, was sentenced to one and one-half to four and one-half years in prison in July 1997. A New York Housing Authority officer was convicted of criminally negligent homicide in August 1995, for a fatal shooting that occurred in March 1992, before the housing authority merged with the NYPD. In 1977, Thomas Ryan was convicted of criminally negligent homicide for beating to death Israel Rodriguez in July 1975; the Ryan homicide conviction was the first ever recorded in the city of an on-duty policeman.

have obtained special bills of rights for law enforcement officers that make it more difficult to discipline or dismiss officers who commit human rights violations.[31]

Public officials, whether mayors, city council members or local prosecutors, are elected officials and subject to public scrutiny.[32] These officials often rely on the support and endorsement of politically powerful police unions for re-election and are loath to offend the unions' members. Their hesitancy to condemn police abuse or prosecute violators of human rights is reinforced when crime rates go down, as has happened in several major cities where "aggressive" policing has been implemented, even when brutality complaints rise at the same time.

After an apparently successful experiment in New York City beginning in 1994, aggressive "quality of life" policing (with reduced tolerance of non-violent or petty crimes) is being copied in many cities around the United States. Police officials and their supporters contend that this approach naturally leads to an increase in complaints of abuse, as officers question and apprehend more individuals. Or, as a caller to *New York Times* columnist Bob Herbert put it, "Crime is down. If the police have to kick a little butt to make the city safer, so be it."[33] Among those who dispute this assumption is a former Washington, D.C. police chief who testified in 1992 that, as an officer, he had made the highest number of arrests on the force and was never the subject of an abuse complaint, demonstrating that you can be aggressive without attracting complaints of brutality.[34]

There is no denying that police-community relations have suffered in minority neighborhoods, where some residents initially welcomed the enhanced police

---

[31] According to the National Association of Police Organizations, "Position Paper on a federal law enforcement officers' bill of rights," January 1997. NAPO is the leading police lobbying group in Washington. The paper states that the passage of a federal Law Enforcement Officers Bill of Rights is its number one legislative priority.

[32] District attorneys are elected in all of the cities examined by Human Rights Watch except Washington, D.C., where there is no such office. Providence, Rhode Island does not have a local prosecutor, but the state's attorney general is elected.

[33] Bob Herbert, "Good Cop, Bad Cop," *New York Times,* March 23, 1997.

[34] U.S. Commission on Civil Rights, *Racial and Ethnic Tensions in American Cities: Poverty, Inequality, and Discrimination, The Mt. Pleasant Report,* (Washington D.C.: U.S. Commission on Civil Rights, January 1993), p. 34. As described in the Washington, D.C. chapter, former Chief Soulsby resigned amid allegations of misconduct unrelated to brutality.

presence but eventually complained that aggressive policing often translates into harassment. In New York, complaints citywide rose more than 37 percent from 1993 to 1994, after the new police "quality of life" initiatives took hold. Said one New Yorker, "They [the police] will bother you just for looking at them....[They] throw you against the car and start searching you like you're a criminal."[35] By the end of 1996, complaints had reportedly increased by 56 percent from the 1993 level.[36] To his credit, Police Commissioner Howard Safir initiated a program teaching courtesy, professionalism and respect ("CPR") in response to the rise in complaints. The program attempts to hold police commanders responsible for citizen complaints. Following the August 1997 Abner Louima incident (during which Louima claims officers tortured him by beating him and sodomizing him with a wooden stick in the bathroom of a Brooklyn police station), there was a sharp increase in the number of citizen complaints filed, but the 1997 total was lower than in previous years.[37] In any event, complaints are still being filed at a higher rate than prior to the initiation of "quality of life" policing.[38]

Race as a Factor

Race continues to play a central role in police brutality in the United States. In the cities we have examined where such data are available, minorities have alleged human rights violations by police more frequently than white residents and far out of proportion to their representation in those cities. Police have subjected minorities to apparently discriminatory treatment and have physically abused minorities while using racial epithets. Mistreatment may be non-violent harassment and humiliation, such as allegations of racial profiling in which drivers are temporarily detained often for driving in certain areas or for driving certain types of cars. At worst, it includes the kinds of extreme violence we feature in this report. Each new incident involving police mistreatment of an African-American, Hispanic-American or other minority – and particularly those that receive media attention –

---

[35] Garry Pierre-Pierre, "Examining a jump in police brutality complaints," *New York Times,* February 22, 1995.

[36] Jane H. Lii, "When the saviors are seen as sinners," *New York Times*, May 18, 1997.

[37] "Complaints against police found to be undercounted," *New York Times*, December 11, 1997.

[38] Similarly, police abuse experts in New Orleans have noted a jump in complaints alleging police misconduct following the initiation of "quality of life" policing in that city.

reinforces a general belief that some residents are subjected to particularly harsh treatment and racial bias.

Since the mid-1960s, incidents of real or perceived police abuse have sparked civil unrest, including costly and violent uprisings, and a lingering distrust between racial minority communities and the police. The thirty-year-old findings of the National Advisory Commission on Civil Disorders (also known as the Kerner Commission), published in 1968, are still relevant:

> Almost invariably the incident that ignites disorder arises from police action. Harlem, Watts, Newark and Detroit – all the major outbursts of recent years – were precipitated by routine arrests of Negroes by white officers for minor offenses....[T]o many Negroes police have come to symbolize white power, white racism and white repression. And the fact is that many police do reflect and express these white attitudes. The atmosphere of hostility and cynicism is reinforced by a widespread perception among Negroes of the existence of police brutality and corruption, and of a "double standard" of justice and protection – one for Negroes and one for whites.[39]

Virtually the same conclusions relating to police-community tensions are found in the 1991 Christopher Commission report on Los Angeles, published in the aftermath of the notorious beating of Rodney King.[40] The report stated: "Within minority communities of Los Angeles, there is a widely-held view that police misconduct is commonplace. The King beating refocused public attention to long-standing complaints by African-Americans, Latinos and Asians that Los Angeles Police Department (LAPD) officers frequently treat minorities differently from whites, more often using disrespectful and abusive language, employing unnecessarily intrusive practices such as the 'prone-out,' and engaging in use of excessive force when dealing with minorities." [41]

These tensions helped spark Los Angeles's deadly and costly April 1992 disturbances in response to the acquittals of police in the Rodney King case. Fifty-

---

[39] *The 1968 Report of the National Advisory Commission on Civil Disorders (The Kerner Report)*, (New York: Bantam Books, 1968) p. 206.

[40] *Report of the Independent Commission on the Los Angeles Police Department*, July 9, 1991, (hereinafter Christopher Commission report).

[41] Ibid., p. 70. "Proning-out" refers to the police practice of placing individuals who are being questioned on the street face down on the pavement.

four people were killed, 2,383 injured (221 critically), and 13,212 arrested; property damage was estimated at more than $700 million for the county.[42] In less spectacular ways around the country, tensions mount with each new incident of publicized police brutality or corruption. Yet, in predictable cycles, as new abuses come to light, police administrative or court decisions remind the public that officers often avoid penalties for human rights violations they commit.

The 1991 Christopher Commission report and the 1992 St. Clair Commission report (examining Boston's police department) show that race still plays a central role in the use of excessive force.[43] The St. Clair Commission report found that during the period studied, 50 percent of complainants in the sample group were African-American, while 26 percent of Boston's population was African-American.[44] The impetus for the St. Clair report was the Stuart case, in which a white man reportedly murdered his pregnant wife and diverted suspicion by claiming the assailant had been a black man. His allegation led to round-ups and harassment of African-American men and to outrage once the truth was discovered, with many claiming a double standard.

The Christopher Commission in Los Angeles "also found that the problem of excessive force is aggravated by racism and bias...."[45] The report described a survey finding that 25 percent of 650 officers responding agreed: "racial bias (prejudice) on the part of officers toward minority citizens currently exists and

---

[42] James D. Delk, "Fires and Furies: The L.A. Riots," ETC Publications, Palm Springs, CA. 1995. Property damage was estimated to have exceeded $900 million in Lou Cannon, *Official Negligence* (New York: Random House, 1997), p. 347. In reaction to the verdict, protests that were sometimes violent also reportedly took place in Atlanta, Dallas, San Francisco, and Madison, Wisconsin.

[43] Comprehensive studies examining police brutality generally, or the racial component specifically, are lacking. In addition to the studies of the police forces in Boston, Los Angeles, and New York, the Los Angeles Sheriff's Department cooperated with a brutality study and undergoes six-month audits funded by the county. See Kolts Commission, James G. Kolts, et al., *Report of the Special Counsel on the Los Angeles County Sheriff's Department* (Los Angeles, 1992). There was also an independent study of Milwaukee's police department published in October 1991.

[44] St. Clair Commission, *Report of the Boston Police Department Management Review Committee*, January 14, 1992, (hereinafter St. Clair Commission report). The study does not provide a breakdown comparing the percentage of those arrested who are African-American as distinct from other ethnic groups.

[45] Christopher Commission report, foreword.

contributes to a negative interaction between police and the community....[and more than 25 percent agreed that] an officer's prejudice towards the suspect's race may lead to the use of excessive force."[46] The report stated that the Los Angeles Police Department had practices and procedures conducive to discriminatory treatment and officer misconduct directed to members of minority groups. Witnesses repeatedly reported that officers verbally harassed minorities, detained African-American and Latino men who fit certain generalized descriptions of suspects, employed unnecessarily invasive or humiliating tactics in minority neighborhoods, and used excessive force.[47]

Each of the cities examined in this study has had serious abuse problems that have exacerbated racial tensions, including the May 1991 Mt. Pleasant (Washington, D.C.) uprising after an African-American officer, Angela Jewell, shot Salvadoran Daniel Enrique Gómez; the September 1997 alleged beating of African-American Jeremiah Mearday by white Chicago police officers; the January 1995 videotaped beating of African-American Corey West in Providence, R.I. by a white officer; or the July 1996 fatal shooting of African-American Nathaniel Gaines, Jr., who was unarmed, by white New York City Transit Officer Paolo Colecchia on a subway platform.

Recent, widely publicized cases highlight the way perceived instances of abuse can ignite a racially-charged atmosphere. In St. Petersburg, Florida, a white police officer, Jim Knight, shot and killed a black motorist, eighteen-year-old TyRon Lewis, on October 24, 1996. The officer claimed that Lewis's vehicle had lunged toward him.[48] The shooting sparked rioting in a portion of the city, with twenty people arrested and eleven injured; two dozen buildings were destroyed or heavily damaged, at a cost estimated at $5 million. Three weeks later, rioting erupted again just hours after a grand jury declined to indict Officer Knight. Several citizens were injured, and an officer was shot in the leg; some one hundred more arson fires were set in houses and stores, causing an estimated $1 million in damages.[49] City

---

[46] Ibid., p. 69.

[47] Ibid., p. xii, *see* Los Angeles chapter.

[48] Michael A. Fletcher, "State of emergency declared in St. Petersburg following riots," *Washington Post,* October 26, 1996. According to press reports, this was the sixth incident involving a St. Petersburg police officer shooting at a car during 1996.

[49] "Authorities appeal for calm in St. Petersburg," *Reuters,* November 15, 1996, [Wire Service]; and telephone interview with St. Petersburg police department public affairs officer, April 15, 1997.

officials claimed that the second round of rioting was "calculated" and led by a militant black group. But a subsequent investigation by the U.S. Commission on Civil Rights pointed to a "clique within the Police Department with a significant pattern of misconduct" as the primary problem between the police and community.[50]

On November 13, the day of the second round of violence in St. Petersburg, a similar scenario played itself out in Pittsburgh, Pennsylvania. White police Officer Jon Vojtas was acquitted by an all-white jury in the killing of black motorist Jonny Gammage in Brentwood, a predominantly white Pittsburgh suburb. Following the acquittal, there was a protest outside the courtroom, with chants reminiscent of the King case, "No justice, no peace."[51] Vojtas later returned to the Brentwood police force.

Gammage had been driving in Brentwood in October 1995 when police officers pulled him over, claiming that he had been driving erratically. In a struggle with five officers after he emerged from his car, Gammage was subdued as officers pressed on his back and neck, suffocating him. He died at the scene. The case drew unusual attention because the victim was the cousin of a Pittsburgh Steelers football player, Ray Seals, a local celebrity, and he had been driving Seals's car at the time of the encounter. The trials of two other officers involved in the incident ended in mistrials in 1996 and 1997. [52]

Similarly, the October 1996 acquittal of New York City police Officer Francis X. Livoti on charges of negligent homicide in the death of Anthony Baez, of Puerto Rican descent, sparked protests and led to heightened tensions and police alerts around the 46th Precinct in the Bronx, where Livoti was stationed. After the verdict, Baez's parents stated, "We learned that for Latinos and blacks, justice is not equal."[53]

---

[50] "Rights official sees danger from police," *New York Times*, February 28, 1997. Officer Knight was reportedly cleared of wrongdoing by the department, and in November 1997, the federal Justice Department announced that it would not prosecute. "No rights prosecution in killing by Fla. officer," *Washington Post*, November 4, 1997.

[51] "White officer acquitted in death of black motorist in Pittsburgh," *New York Times*, November 14, 1996.

[52] "2 officers face new trial in death of a black motorist," *New York Times*, October 12, 1997; Associated Press, "2d mistrial for officers charged in motorist's death," *New York Times*, December 14, 1997.

[53] David Gonzalez, "Commentary: In Livoti case, 'not innocent' is no comfort," *New York Times*, October 9, 1996.

Special Commissions and their Aftermath

Just as predictable as new, outrageous cases of abuse or the failure to punish or prosecute officers who commit human rights violations are the commissions created to investigate problems of abuse. In 1981, for example, the U.S. Commission on Civil Rights published an important report on police abuse, titled *Who is Guarding the Guardians?*[54] The commission held hearings, subpoenaed documents, and worked with experts in preparing its study. The report contains dozens of recommendations dealing with recruitment of new police officers, internal review of misconduct allegations, external review of abuse complaints, and compilation and dissemination of nationwide data regarding police abuse.

Seventeen years later, most of the recommendations made by the commission remain unrealized. All of the police departments examined by Human Rights Watch had flawed complaint systems and provided inadequate information to the public about how to file a complaint. Multilingual complaint forms, status notification to complainants, and proper maintenance and use of data relating to those complaints are still lacking. The Civil Rights Commission had recommended adequate internal affairs systems, meaningful external review mechanisms, and effective early warning systems for officers with repeated abuse complaints. None of the cities we examined has all of these mechanisms in place. The commission had noted, as well, that one major barrier to federal prosecution of police officers who commit human rights violations is the "specific intent" standard: prosecutors must prove that an officer specifically intended to deprive an individual of a constitutional right in order to win brutality cases. Yet in the seventeen years since the commission's report, neither Congress nor the Executive Branch of the federal government has actively pursued a revision of the statute.

Since the Civil Rights Commission report in 1981, a handful of comprehensive studies on police misconduct in particular cities have been published: in Los Angeles (Christopher Commission), Boston (St. Clair Commission), and New York (Mollen Commission).[55] Investigators have held hearings, reviewed relevant police files, and produced piercing critiques of the police departments' shortcomings. In Boston, the scope of the report was limited, and many of the recommended reforms

---

[54] U.S. Commission on Civil Rights, "Who is Guarding the Guardians?" (Washington D.C.: U.S. Commission on Civil Rights, October 1981). In 1957, Congress established the U.S. Commission on Civil Rights as a bipartisan, independent agency to investigate civil rights complaints and to collect and disseminate information.

[55] *Commission to Investigate Allegations of Police Corruption and the Anti-Corruption Procedures of the Police Department*, July 7, 1994 (hereinafter Mollen Commission report).

were long overdue and have been implemented. In New York and Los Angeles, implementation is still underway, with mixed results. In general, reports from special commissions or human rights groups receive serious attention initially, but that attention fades until new incidents remind citizens that reforms were not implemented as promised.

All of the commissions' studies revealed disturbing common threads. In addition to racial components and seriously flawed internal affairs units, described more fully below, the commissions emphasized that police departments tolerate abuse. The Mollen Commission stated: "As important as the possible extent of brutality, is the extent of brutality tolerance we found throughout the Department....[O]fficers seem fairly tolerant – both outwardly and inwardly – of occasional police brutality."[56] The commission went on: "This tolerance, or willful blindness, extends to supervisors as well....[W]hen cops come to the stationhouse with a visibly beaten suspect...[supervisors] often do not question the story they hear."[57]

Serious failures on the part of high-ranking police officials were also noted. The Christopher Commission report found, for example: "[T]he failure to control these [repeatedly abusive] officers is a management issue that is at the heart of the problem. The documents and data that we have analyzed have all been available to the department; indeed, most of this information came from that source. The LAPD's failure to analyze and act upon these revealing data evidences a significant breakdown in the management and leadership of the Department."[58] Similarly, the St. Clair Commission found "substantial problems in the leadership and management of the [Boston] Department...."[59] Hubert Williams, the president of the Police Foundation, a Washington, D.C.-based research group, stated: "Most police chiefs are honest and have integrity, but they fail due to an ignorance of what

---

[56] Mollen Commission report, p. 49.

[57] Ibid.

[58] Christopher Commission report, p. iv.

[59] St. Clair Commission report, p. i.

is occurring in their own departments."[60] Williams noted a "disconnect between policies and practices" within police departments.[61]

The Mollen Commission also described the important link between corruption and brutality, with brutality against citizens serving as a sort of "rite of passage" toward corruption. Some officers told the commission that brutality was how they first "crossed the line toward abandoning their integrity," and when the line was crossed without consequences, it was easier to abuse their authority in other ways.[62] According to the commission, "....we found that cops did not simply become corrupt; they sometimes became corrupt and violent."[63] In some cities, newer officers – who are most likely to be "tested" by corrupt fellow officers – are assigned to poor and minority neighborhoods. The victims in these brutality "rites of passage" would most commonly be minorities.

Public Access to Information

Too often, the police and city officials respond to reports on police abuse by special commissions or nongovernmental organizations by criticizing the authors as misinformed or biased instead of considering the reports' findings. Generally, police departments will claim that they have fixed the problems identified, or that the authors have not provided a full story about the cases described, usually meaning that the police departments' views have not been accepted (or made available to the authors).[64]

In researching its 1996 report on New York City's police department, Amnesty International was denied statistics and case information it requested from the police department. Once the report was published, officials criticized it for not providing a complete picture of police abuse in the city, largely for the lack of information withheld by the department itself. The mayor and police commissioner called the report "one-sided," "inaccurate" and "anecdotal" for relying, in part, on information

---

[60] U.S. Department of Justice, *Police Integrity: Public Service With Honor, National Institute of Justice and Office of Community Oriented Policing Services*, (Washington, D.C.: National Institute of Justice), January 1997, p. 33.

[61] Ibid.

[62] Mollen Commission report, pp. 45-47.

[63] Ibid., p. 45.

[64] Few reports on the issue of police abuse are published by nongovernmental organizations, except in the largest cities.

from victims and their attorneys.[65] The accounts of victims, however, cannot be so easily disregarded; and if official data were lacking, this was because the department as a general rule refuses to release information about human rights violations committed by police and disciplinary responses.

The American Civil Liberties Union of Southern California has published several reports on Los Angeles-area police departments, and its reports have been criticized by officials as incomplete. For example, after the group published a report criticizing the LAPD's high-speed chase policies, one commander called it a "very hastily done report" and added: "[T]hey did not have all the facts."[66]

In researching this report, Human Rights Watch requested information from police departments and city attorneys' offices in all the cities covered. Few provided the requested information in a timely way. Indeed, a year or more after our initial requests, and despite repeated follow-up queries, several departments still had not provided information. Regarding disciplinary actions taken against officers, information is rarely provided: police departments will sometimes provide statistics regarding disciplinary actions taken, but the information is too general to link types of offenses with disciplinary sanctions, or police departments simply claim that a certain officer was dealt with "appropriately," leaving outside monitors and the public in the dark about what actually happened.

In each city we examined, activists, attorneys representing alleged victims of abuse, and members of the media reported enormous frustration in obtaining police department data that should, in fact, be public information. In New Orleans, an attorney who frequently represents police abuse victims has tried repeatedly to obtain information about civil-lawsuit settlements and civil jury awards paid by the city, but has been denied this information, though it is clearly covered under the state's public access law.[67] The *Atlanta Journal-Constitution* repeatedly requested information in 1995 and 1996 about police shooting cases in that city; although Georgia's Open Records Act requires disclosure, the department did not provide all of the information the newspaper requested.

---

[65] Graham Rayman, "Report sees brutality in NYPD," *New York Newsday*, June 27, 1996.

[66] Jim Newton, "LAPD calls its policy on chasing cars fundamentally sound," *Los Angeles Times,* October 2, 1996, quoting Commander Art Lopez.

[67] Louisiana Revised Statute Title 44:5. After a significant delay, Human Rights Watch was finally provided with this information in June 1997 after threatening to file a lawsuit to force the city to turn over the data.

Community police abuse monitors have been attempting to obtain files concerning citizen complaints, investigations, and disciplinary actions from the Providence, R.I. police department for the past seventeen years.[68] In June 1996, a Superior Court judge ruled in favor of the monitors, asserting:

> [T]ell me how it would be an unwarranted invasion of personal privacy to disclose the name of a police officer who performs his or her duties in public, who has one of the most visible and important jobs in this society, and now has been determined to have brutalized somebody. What is the privacy interest there, and why would the city want to protect the name of that individual?[69]

As stated succinctly by police abuse expert and attorney Lynne Wilson:

> Police misconduct is a matter of strong public interest. Even though many departments name their self-investigative units "internal affairs bureaus," police misconduct is the public's business, not simply an "internal" departmental matter....[C]itizens, not police department officials, are the ultimate arbiters of what police behavior is acceptable in a democratic society....Law enforcement officers wield extensive authority in the exercise of their duties....[W]hether those officers, trained and paid at taxpayers' expense, use excessive force in carrying out their responsibilities or otherwise misuse their authority is clearly the public's business.[70]

In Chicago, attorneys fought to have an internal police report about torture allegations by police detectives released to the public. The court found in favor of the public's right to know:

> No legitimate purpose is served by conducting [police internal] investigations under a veil of near total secrecy. Rather, knowledge that

---

[68] Bruce Landis, "Despite challenges, police-brutality complaints remain sealed," *Providence Journal-Bulletin,* May 18, 1997.

[69] Ibid. The State Supreme Court ordered a stay of the Superior Court order in July, after the city appealed the Superior Court decision; the case is now pending.

[70] Lynne Wilson, "The public's right of access to police misconduct files," *Police Misconduct and Civil Rights Law Report,* January - February 1994, vol. 4, no. 7.

a limited number of persons, as well as a state or federal court, may examine the file in the event of civil litigation may serve to insure that these investigations are carried out in an even handed fashion, that the statements are carefully and accurately taken, and that the true facts came to light, whether they reflect favorably or unfavorably on the individual police officers involved or on the department as a whole.[71]

Indeed, even complainants themselves are not allowed access to information relating to investigations into complaints they have filed. In an informal telephone survey conducted by Human Rights Watch, police departments examined in this report were asked whether a complainant would have access to internal investigation information.[72] In several cities – Atlanta, Boston, Chicago, New Orleans, New York, and Washington, D.C. – the internal affairs units responded that no investigative files could be obtained or viewed by the complainant. In Minneapolis, a complainant may access the investigative file if the complaint is sustained, while in Portland, if the complaint is sustained, the complainant does not have access to the file. In Philadelphia, we were informed that the file may be viewed after the investigation has been completed. Detroit's internal affairs unit stated that a formal freedom-of-information request would be necessary, but even then the file would probably not be made available. In Los Angeles, the complainant would need a subpoena to view the investigatory file. In San Francisco, some information is available to the complainant.[73]

Filing Complaints
In general, police departments and citizen review units will not initiate an investigation into alleged police brutality without a formal complaint. Yet, in all fourteen cities examined by Human Rights Watch, there are serious flaws in the way complaints from the public are initially received or forwarded.[74]

---

[71] *Wiggins v. Burge* (Slip Op. At 6,) quoting *Mercy v. County of Suffolk*, 93 F.R.D. 520, 522 (E.D.N.Y.)

[72] Telephone interviews during the weeks of December 15, 1997 and January 5, 1998.

[73] The Indianapolis and Providence police departments failed to respond.

[74] Officers may also file internal complaints against other officers, but little information is known about how those complaints are handled. It is clear that they are taken more seriously than complaints filed by members of the public, since statistics provided by some police departments show a much higher sustained rate for internally generated complaints.

Filing a complaint is unnecessarily difficult and often intimidating, whether the person seeking to complain deals with a precinct sergeant, an internal-affairs investigator or, to a lesser extent, with a civilian review agency. Former Minneapolis Police Chief Tony Bouza has stated, "The police world has a hundred different ways of deflecting complaints."[75] Complainants, whether they are victims or witnesses, may not know where to go to file a complaint. They may have difficulty communicating due to language barriers, or they may be met with hostility by officers who do not wish to receive a complaint about a colleague. They may be dissuaded from filing a complaint through threats or other techniques. Officers receiving complaints may ask questions that reveal they do not believe the complainant, or they may ask about the complainant's criminal history or charges that may be pending as a result of the arrest that gave rise to the alleged abuse incident.

One of the most notorious dissuasion efforts related to the Rodney King beating in Los Angeles. When King's brother Paul tried to complain following the beating, the sergeant on duty treated him skeptically, asked him whether he had ever been in trouble, and never filled out a complaint form.[76] Without the videotape that made it famous, the King case likely would have been just one more invisible, unrecorded incident.

Individuals who are arrested – among the most likely to become victims of abuse – can be reticent to file a complaint because they simply want to clear up the criminal matter they face. Many do not think their complaints will be believed. In a 1993 case in Washington, D.C., a man did not file a complaint with the police department after he was allegedly beaten by Officer Richard Fitzgerald. In an unusual move, Fitzgerald's fellow officers reported him to prosecutors, who eventually questioned the alleged victim. Fitzgerald was subsequently convicted on assault charges.[77] In explaining his reluctance to file a complaint, the man stated, "Who is going to believe a drug addict?"[78] While some criminals may believe, as police representatives have claimed, that filing a complaint will help their cases, many think filing a complaint would be futile and are afraid of angering the officers

---

[75] David Ashenfelter, "Police brutality a metro dispute," *Detroit Free Press*, April 17, 1991.

[76] Christopher Commission report, p. 10.

[77] Bill Miller, "D.C. officer convicted of assault on suspect," *Washington Post*, November 2, 1996.

[78] Ibid.

involved and making their criminal cases more difficult; criminal defense attorneys may also advise clients not to file complaints because they may reveal information that could be used as evidence against them in their own criminal trial.

Efforts to dissuade complainants have become extreme in some cities. In Seattle, the police officers' guild filed defamation lawsuits against six citizens who had filed complaints that were not sustained by the Internal Investigations Section of the police department in 1994 and 1995. In the six months following this retaliation, there was a drop of almost 75 percent in citizen complaints. The guild has stopped filing suits, but local rights advocates believe that its objective was met by sending a chilling message to prospective complainants.[79] More recently in California, attorneys representing plaintiffs alleging police abuse in civil lawsuits have reported that police officers have sued plaintiffs and attorneys after unsuccessful civil rights litigation.[80] The lawsuits filed by police officers allege defamation, malicious prosecution, or abuse of process. The civil rights attorneys believe that the lawsuits are intended to discourage such suits against the police by imposing costs on the civil rights attorneys to defend themselves.

Similarly, individuals who choose to file a complaint because of abusive treatment may face counter-charges by the police officer in question. If, for example, an officer uses excessive force while effecting an arrest, and the individual expresses interest in filing a complaint, the officer may attempt to explain his actions by charging the individual with what police abuse experts refer to as "the trilogy": disorderly conduct, resisting arrest, and assaulting an officer. Police abuse expert Prof. James J. Fyfe refers to these charges as "contempt of cop;" he has found that a small percentage of officers repeatedly file such charges and that they stem from an officer becoming offended by a citizen's demeanor rather than from any legitimate law enforcement purpose.[81] When an individual has been charged

---

[79] Lynne Wilson, "Cops vs. Citizen Review," *Covert Action Quarterly*, Winter 1995-96, p. 11.

[80] Paul L. Hoffman, "Defending Police Against SLAPP suits," (paper presented at the meeting of Police Watch, Los Angeles, Ca., May 1997). SLAPP refers to "Strategic Lawsuits Against Public Participation."

[81] Declaration of James J. Fyfe, Ph.D., *United States of America v. City of Steubenville, Steubenville Police Department, Steubenville City Manager, in his capacity as director of Public Safety, and Steubenville Civil Service Commission,* Civil No. C2 97-966, U.S. District Court for the Southern District of Ohio, Eastern Division, August 28, 1997, p. 7. For examples of "contempt of cop" incidents in New York City, see Dan Barry and Deborah Sontag, "Disrespect as catalyst for police brutality," *New York Times*, November 19, 1997.

with these types of offenses, he or she can then be persuaded to drop the complaint against the offending officers in exchange for the counter-charges being dropped.

Police departments have an obligation to train officers in how to accept a complaint and to deal appropriately with complainants.[82] Those who fail to accept a complaint according to departmental guidelines and with due respect for the individual filing a complaint should be disciplined appropriately. For a variety of reasons, some victims of abuse may choose not to file a formal complaint, but when they wish to do so, they must be treated with respect and provided with basic information about what to expect from the filing of a grievance.

In cases of alleged torture or cruel, inhuman, and degrading treatment or punishment, the Convention against Torture, to which the U.S. is a party, provides there need not be a complaint filed by the victim or others. Article 12 states: "Each State Party shall ensure that its competent authorities proceed to a prompt and impartial investigation, wherever there is reasonable grounds to believe that an act of torture has been committed in any territory under its jurisdiction." Article (16)1 of the Convention applies the same standards for the investigation of cruel, inhuman or degrading treatment or punishment.[83] According to Article 13, "[E]ach State party shall ensure that any individual who alleges he has been subjected to torture in any territory under its jurisdiction has the right complain to, and have his case promptly and impartially examined by, its competent authorities. Steps shall be taken to ensure that the complainant and witnesses are protected against all ill-treatment or intimidation as a consequence of his complaint or any evidence given."[84]

Superior officers often fail to encourage officers to report abuses by fellow officers. As described more fully below, officers within most police departments fear breaking the traditional "code of silence" and do not want to be considered disloyal or "rats." As a result, officers who are not abusive too often silently tolerate other officers' brutality rather than submit a complaint to the relevant internal affairs office or citizen review unit. Those officers and supervisors who

---

[82] Former San Jose Police Chief Joe McNamara was among those who told Human Rights Watch that officers should receive training on how to receive complaints from the public. Human Rights Watch interview with Joe McNamara, September 18, 1995.

[83] General Assembly Resolution 39/46, December 10, 1984, in Centre for Human Rights, *Human Rights: A Compilation*, p. 293. Article (16)1 of the Convention applies the same standards for the investigation of cruel, inhuman or degrading treatment or punishment.

[84] Ibid.

remain silent after observing abusive behavior usually avoid any punishment for their inaction.

External Review
Citizen Review Mechanisms

Following high-profile police brutality cases, or a series of such cases, communities often demand an external "check" on their police departments. Such calls may also follow investigations finding that the internal systems for holding officers accountable are inadequate. Citizen review agencies are often created – or reorganized – as a result.[85]

By 1997, thirty-eight of the fifty largest U.S. cities (76 percent) had some form of citizen review.[86] Of the fourteen cities examined by Human Rights Watch, all the police forces except those in Providence and Washington, D.C. had provisions for some form of external or citizen review.

The idea of citizen review is simple: history has shown that police are not able or willing to police themselves in a manner acceptable to the public. The public, in turn, believes that independent investigators will be more fair and objective.[87] An external review mechanism provides an independent forum where victims or witnesses of abuse may file complaints or testify at hearings to give their account of what took place. One of the first independent commissions to call for external review was the Kerner Commission, assembled by President Lyndon Johnson in 1967 following racial tensions and riots. More recently, the 1992 report of the St. Clair Commission, tasked with reviewing Boston's police force, agreed that the police should police themselves but that, "given the disturbing results of our case review and the profound lack of confidence and trust the community expressed in

---

[85] Also referred to throughout this report as citizen review mechanisms or civilian review agencies.

[86] Nearly all English-speaking countries have mechanisms for the external review of police complaints. Samuel Walker, *Citizen Review Resource Manual,* (Washington, D.C.: Police Executive Research Forum, 1995), p. 4, citing Andrew Goldsmith, *Complaints against the police: the trend toward external review,* (Oxford: Clarendon Press, 1991).

[87] Civilian review expert Prof. Samuel Walker defines citizen review as a procedure for handling citizen complaints about police officer misconduct that, at some point in the process, involves people who are not sworn officers.

the department's current methods of handling citizen complaints we believe that the public must be given access into the system for it to work properly."[88]

Effective external review requires the review of police files about specific incidents, the ability to compel police cooperation, and the obligation to provide comprehensive periodic reports to the public about the types of complaints received, trends, and recommendations made to the relevant police department.[89] Citizen review units must also have independence, civilian control, and some role in disciplinary proceedings.

When review agencies become involved in high-profile, divisive cases, public support is key. In Philadelphia, for example, the civilian review agency has been under attack from police organizations since its inception, yet with support from community activists and concerned city council members, it has successfully fought off legal challenges. With this in mind, the leadership of the oversight system must actively educate the community about the merits of civilian oversight. This education must demonstrate that citizen review is useful; only with public support will external review agencies be able to survive during political or funding disputes.

Furthermore, an essential component of the work of any modern review agency should be making concrete policy recommendations to police administrators about how to prevent abuses from occurring in the first place (through improvements in recruiting and training and clearly articulated policies) and how to respond to abuses once they do occur (through fair and consistent disciplinary actions, assistance in criminal prosecutions, where warranted, and repeated emphasis in word and deed that abuse will not be tolerated). In cities where review agencies have pushed for specific reforms and seen them implemented – as has happened occasionally in Portland, San Francisco, and Minneapolis – trust in both the review agency and the police department has been enhanced.

An increasingly popular method of citizen review is the appointment of an auditor who does not investigate individual complaints but reviews procedures for investigating charges of excessive force and other allegations and recommends policy changes. Portland, San Jose (California), Los Angeles County, and the city of Los Angeles, through its newly created Office of the Inspector General, are

---

[88] St. Clair Commission report, p. v.

[89] Walker, *Citizen Review Resource Manual*, pp. 12-13. Nationally, almost 40 percent of review bodies have subpoena power, and almost half conduct public hearings.

among the cities that use this form of review.[90] Following reports of the alleged torture of a Haitian immigrant in New York City in August 1997, and the subsequent public uproar, discussions regarding the creation of an auditor to review brutality investigations were renewed.

One positive aspect of auditor systems is that they avoid the backlog problem experienced by many review boards with broad mandates to examine each complaint and conduct hearings. But there are negative aspects as well: auditors can do little to assist an individual who wishes to file a complaint but is hesitant to approach police officers. Auditors usually do not conduct independent investigations or hold hearings. So, while they play an important oversight role, auditors need to be supplemented by review agencies carrying out other essential parts of police oversight.

Some experts support a more comprehensive tripartite oversight system. On the one hand, an auditor or inspector general's office would identify problematic practices and policies, recommend reforms, monitor implementation of its recommendations, participate in disciplinary hearings, and report to the public on the outcome of disciplinary proceedings. On the other hand, an independent fact-finding body would investigate individual complaints and participate in investigations of high-profile incidents. In addition, a city administrator would provide information and track civil lawsuits relating to police misconduct.

Few believe that citizen review mechanisms alone are the solution to the problem of police brutality. In the end, police administrators and their political superiors are responsible for the actions of officers. But, as former New York Police Commissioner Ray Kelly observed, external review "keeps the department's feet to the fire."[91] Review agencies can provide important information to police administrators about management problems that might otherwise go unnoticed, and they provide information to the public about police actions to prevent, or respond appropriately to, violations. Without public knowledge and scrutiny, reforms will not normally take place. It is rare, indeed, for a police department, on its own initiative and without public pressure, to take steps to improve police conduct and enhance accountability for officers who commit human rights violations. For this reason alone, citizen review is essential.

In most cases, police departments and officers, usually through their union representatives, strenuously oppose the creation of citizen review mechanisms,

---

[90] So do Seattle, Washington, and Albuquerque, New Mexico, with less impressive results. Portland's auditors are volunteer citizen monitors who report to the City Council and mayor.

[91] Mollen Commission report, p. 6.

claiming that the external reviewers will undermine police authority to handle officer misconduct, know nothing about how police departments or officers operate, and harbor political, anti-police motivations. Opposition to the creation of external review has taken the form of public demonstrations, legal challenges, and pledges of non-cooperation.

Police opposition to citizen review mechanisms is reflexive, even in cases where a police department has been plagued by scandal or when the proposed review mechanism is carefully designed to avoid infringing upon police administrators' ability to investigate or discipline officers. Police abuse expert John Crew has noted three stages in police union resistance to citizen review: "over my dead body"; advocating for the weakest possible external review if its creation becomes politically inevitable; and legally challenging any review unit once created and effective.[92] This response has often further undermined public trust or respect for police departments.

In recent years, New York and Philadelphia have witnessed orchestrated and strenuous opposition to citizen review. When former New York City Mayor David Dinkins supported an independent civilian complaint review board in September 1992, police protested and engaged in actions that, according to a police department report, were "unruly, mean-spirited and perhaps criminal."[93] The officers' protest, sponsored by the police union, involved thousands of officers demonstrating at City Hall, blocking traffic to the Brooklyn Bridge, with some reportedly shouting racial epithets about then-Mayor Dinkins, who is black, while Dinkins's political opponent, current Mayor Rudolph Giuliani, who is white, participated in the protest.[94]

In addition to opposing the independence of New York's Civilian Complaint Review Board (CCRB), the police department has often refused to accept its findings or has stalled action on the board's recommendations beyond the statute of limitations, ensuring impunity for officers that the CCRB has found responsible for misconduct. These tactics led one of the board's key backers to declare, "What did we create here? We created a monster. People have to remember, I drafted this

---

[92] Wilson, "Cops vs. Citizen Review," *Covert Action Quarterly*. Crew is the director of the American Civil Liberties Union's Police Practices Project.

[93] George James, "Police dept. report assails officers in New York rally," *New York Times*, September 29, 1992.

[94] Ibid. and Paul Chevigny, *Edge of the Knife* (New York: The New Press, 1995), pp. 64-65.

legislation [to create the new board]. But we failed."[95] Joel Berger, formerly of the city's Corporation Counsel office, asks, "What is the point of having a CCRB if the final product, discipline of officers, does not happen?"[96] Police Commissioner Howard Safir has acknowledged that CCRB findings are not given much weight; during the independent CCRB's first three-and-a-half years, only 1 percent of all cases disposed of led to the disciplining of a police officer, and out of 18,336 complaints, there has been just one dismissal of an officer stemming from a CCRB-substantiated case.[97]

In Philadelphia, the Police Advisory Commission, also created in 1993, has been vociferously opposed by the Fraternal Order of Police (police officers' union), which has filed several lawsuits challenging the legality of the PAC and its operations.[98] Defending its existence against these lawsuits has occupied a great deal of the commission's first few years. During the PAC's hearings on a high-profile police brutality case, Fraternal Order of Police members disrupted the hearing room with shouts of "Kangaroo, kangaroo!"[99]

One common tactic by opponents of citizen review is to decry shortcomings in the agency's performance while ignoring factors beyond the agency's' control, such as lack of financial and political support. In Washington, D.C., the Civilian Complaint Review Board was abolished in 1995 due to lack of funds and an enormous backlog of cases; the board's pending cases were transferred back to the police department, which was later unable to provide Human Rights Watch with the status of investigations in the majority of cases transferred to it. In Atlanta, the Civilian Review Board has a limited mandate, minimal staff, and remains one of the best-kept secrets in the city, since it lacks the means to promote community

---

[95] Joyce Purnick, "Policing police proves hard for civilians," *New York Times,* December 5, 1996, quoting Norman Siegel of the New York Civil Liberties Union.

[96] Ibid.

[97] New York Civil Liberties Union report: a fourth anniversary overview of the Civilian Complaint Review Board, July 5, 1993 - July 5, 1997.

[98] The Fraternal Order of Police functions as a union in some cities, and as a police professional organization generally.

[99] These hearings concerned the August 1994 death in custody of Moises DeJesus. "Kangaroo courts" are tribunals disregarding or parodying existing principles of law. Paul Maryniak, "Philadelphia's story," *Pittsburgh Post-Gazette,* April 21, 1996.

awareness of its work. In New Orleans, where police brutality and corruption have been undisputed, the city's review agency is under-utilized and ineffective.

Other police departments and their supporters have successfully avoided citizen review. Until the long-delayed appointment of an inspector general in 1996, the Los Angeles Police Department had no operational review agency at all. Providence, despite having one of the highest per capita rates of complaints according to a 1991 Justice Department report, has no external check.[100] Some of the cities we examined have weak review agencies, due to either poor leadership within the agency or weak mandates, while other cities have settled for "appeals boards" that respond to individuals who are not satisfied with the police department's own investigation but do not receive or investigate complaints.

Of the cities examined, Portland's Police Internal Investigations Auditing Committee (PIIAC) and Minneapolis's Civilian Police Review Authority (CRA) – though imperfect – seemed to be working productively with their respective police departments. The PIIAC's role is limited to reviewing the police department's internal investigations, rather than the broader duties assigned to many review agencies. (The PIIAC is actually the city council, and the PIIAC's paid staff auditor is part of the mayor's office. PIIAC staff work with designated "citizen advisors" in reviewing internal investigations conducted by the police department's Internal Affairs Division.) At the time of our investigation, PIIAC's citizen advisors seemed to have good relations with relevant police officials, and, in addition to conducting reviews as stipulated in its mandate, PIIAC had successfully identified and promoted necessary reforms and seen them carried out in some instances.

Minneapolis's CRA provides an external check by receiving and investigating complaints. After a shaky start, the CRA appears to function well under the leadership of a strong executive director. The CRA emphasizes mediation of some complaints to avoid a backlog of minor cases, publishes useful reports, and makes policy recommendations. The CRA proposed, for example, the creation of a disciplinary table that seeks to limit supervisors' arbitrary decisions by clarifying what punishment officers face for different disciplinary offenses. This reform was carried out. Even with its positive aspects, however, the CRA's procedures are cumbersome and result in only a small percentage of allegations making their way to a hearing for full consideration of their merits.

Although at the time of our on-site investigation, in 1995, Los Angeles had no external review entity, and San Francisco's Office of Civilian Complaints (OCC) was experiencing rapid turnover in its executive director position, during the

---

[100] Criminal Section, Civil Rights Division, Department of Justice, "Police Brutality Study: FY 1985 - FY 1990," April 1991. (*See* Providence chapter.)

intervening period there have been positive changes. The inspector general post in Los Angeles has been filled, and her reports have impressed many police abuse experts in the city by highlighting continuing shortcomings and challenging department leaders to make reforms. In San Francisco, the current OCC director has a long history in civil rights activism and has received high marks from observers there. It would appear that, as in police departments themselves, leadership counts when the effectiveness of review mechanisms are judged. Communities must have faith in their proper operation for them to be effective, and leadership is crucial to winning this confidence.

The other citizen review agencies examined either had strong mandates but weak practices (as in New Orleans, New York's CCRB, and the now-abolished CCRB in Washington, D.C.) or are weak both on paper and in practice (Atlanta, Boston, and Indianapolis). Chicago's Office of Professional Standards is an odd mix: it has a large civilian staff and investigators who are not part of the Chicago police force, but the OPS itself is part of the police department, so that the appearance is not one of independence. Community activists and attorneys complain that, even with independent investigators, the OPS often conducts substandard investigations and can be biased in favor of officers.

Measuring the success of these review mechanisms is difficult. Some observers point to a drop in complaints as a gauge of success, but many different factors may explain a drop in complaints; for example, a community may become discouraged by an external review body's delays or lack of power and cease using the mechanism because it is, or appears, ineffectual. A drop in complaints could result from poor communication with affected communities, or from complaint forms that are available only in English or only at an inconvenient or intimidating location. On the other hand, while an increase in complaints may mean a jump in abuses, it may also demonstrate a successful community outreach effort and a belief that the external check will make a difference in the way cases are handled.

Review mechanisms could also be judged by their "sustained" rate – the percentage of abuse complaints that are found substantiated.[101] For example, a citizen review expert found, in studying seventeen law enforcement agencies, that internal affairs divisions sustained about 12 percent of brutality complaints (filed by citizens and other police personnel, with the latter sustained at a higher rate typically) compared to a 19 percent sustained rate for citizen review oversight

---

[101] Nationally, municipal law enforcement agencies sustain an average of 10 percent of all citizen complaints reviewed internally. Walker, *Citizen Review Resource Manual,* p. 3.

agencies.[102] Unfortunately, many internal affairs units examined in this report did not know, or would not provide, sustained rates, and in other cases, sustained rates are made available but not broken down by type of complaint. For these reasons, identifying an average sustained rate for internal affairs units in this report is not possible.

At the same time, judging a review agency by its sustained rate can be misleading. As noted by citizen review expert Prof. Samuel Walker, some review agencies do such a poor job in communicating their mission to affected communities that they are able to have a high sustained rate because they receive a very small number of complaints. In Atlanta, the civilian review office has a very low profile and has reviewed only a handful of cases; if, for example, it examined four cases and it sustained two, it would have a 50 percent sustained rate, which is hardly an indicator of its success. Furthermore, if police departments do not accept the review agencies' findings or act on them through disciplinary sanctions against offending officers, the sustained rate means very little as an accountability tool.

Perhaps the best way to judge citizen review mechanisms is by the amount and quality of information they provide to the public and the quality and implementation of their disciplinary and policy recommendations. If successful, the review mechanisms serve as a check on police departments by applying consistent pressure for improvements in policies and practices. They also aid these departments by highlighting trends in abuse or areas needing attention that may otherwise go unnoticed for long periods. When police departments realize that review agencies can be important tools for better police administration – and when their resistance to the review agencies ends – significant improvements are possible.

Though seriously flawed in many respects (as described below in the New York chapter), New York's Civilian Complaint Review Board in its semi-annual reports does provide detailed statistics relating to the race, gender, and age of the complainant and the involved officer and precinct. It also provides tallies of disciplinary sanctions, although there is no way to ascertain from the information provided which offender was disciplined. By providing the public with a general idea of the number of officers being disciplined for misconduct, including human

[102] Eileen Luna, "Accountability to the community on the use of deadly force," *Policing by Consent,* (publication of the National Coalition on Police Accountability based in Chicago, IL), December 1994.

rights violations, during a given time period, it is doing more than many of the citizen review agencies examined.[103]

Media Scrutiny

The media can provide a degree of external monitoring. Extensive investigative articles and consistent reporting when abuses arise have played a central role in generating pressure for reforms. For example, the *Boston Globe* provided extensive coverage of the police abuses surrounding the Stuart case, leading to the appointment of the St. Clair Commission; the *Atlanta Journal-Constitution* published consistent reports on the police department's inadequate investigation following a 1995 fatal shooting, and has reported its own difficulty in obtaining information from the police department about brutality investigations; the *Philadelphia Inquirer* has published investigative reports on that city's police force and its recent corruption and brutality scandals; the *San Francisco Examiner* published a 1996 series of articles on serious shortcomings in the official response to police shootings; and free weeklies in Chicago, Portland, and Washington, D.C. have published in-depth investigative articles about police abuse.

Still, newspapers or television news programs are not required to cover this issue, and informed reporters move on to other beats, taking their expertise with them and leaving police abuse issues under-reported. Journalists also face some of the same barriers to information encountered by attorneys and human rights monitors. In some instances, reporters cover high-profile cases without providing follow-up or context. Only when reporters cover police abuse consistently do they increase the public interest in the issue and the pressure on city and police officials to address brutality.

Police Administration: The Key to Reform

External pressures are essential to force police administrators to improve accountability, but police brutality will only subside once higher-ranking police officials judge their subordinates – and are judged themselves – on their efforts to provide sufficient and consistent oversight.[104] As the Christopher Commission

---

[103] Portland's PIIAC, San Francisco's OCC, and Minneapolis's CRA also publish periodic reports containing useful information to the public regarding abuse allegations and investigations.

[104] For example, the U.N. Basic Principles on the Use of Force and Firearms by Law Enforcement Officials, calls for accountability for superior officers: "Governments and law enforcement agencies shall ensure that superior officers are held responsible if they know, or should have known, that law enforcement officials under their command are resorting, or

stated, "The problem of excessive force in the LAPD is fundamentally a problem of supervision, management and leadership."[105] Absent constant vigilance, clear departmental policies, consistent enforcement of those policies, and a "zero tolerance" approach to both abuse and the code of silence that surrounds it, police brutality will continue to undermine police-community relations.

Unfortunately, in every city we examined, police leadership on this issue is lacking. Most high-ranking police officials, whether at the level of commissioner, chief, superintendent, or direct superiors, seem uninterested in vigorously pursuing high standards for treatment of persons in custody. When reasonably high standards are set, superior officers are often unwilling to require that their subordinates consistently meet them.

The heads of police departments set a tone, whether openly hostile toward victims of abuse, such as during the eras of Frank Rizzo in Philadelphia (who served as police commissioner and then mayor and who reportedly vowed to "make Attila the Hun look like a faggot"[106]) and Police Chief Daryl Gates in Los Angeles, or a positive tone, such as that set by reformers Patrick Murphy, the New York City police commissioner during the 1970s, or Joseph McNamara, the former police chief in San Jose, California from 1976 to 1991. Tone-setting is particularly important following police corruption or brutality scandals. Willie Williams, for example, became Los Angeles police chief in the aftermath of the King beating, and most observers credited him with injecting a sense of professionalism in the department. Currently, Richard Pennington, the police superintendent in New Orleans since October 1994, is attempting to "clean house" and implement reforms in an exceptionally troubled department; Chief Robert Olson in Minneapolis appears dedicated to instilling a culture of accountability, and the new LAPD chief, Bernard Parks, has a reputation as a strict disciplinarian in misconduct cases. Unfortunately, even when good chiefs attempt to improve accountability for

---

have resorted, to the unlawful use of force and firearms, and they did not take all measures in their power to prevent, suppress or report such use. Principle 24. UN Doc. A/CONF.144/28/Rev.1 (1990).

[105] Christopher Commission report, p. 32.

[106] Indeed, during Rizzo's tenure as mayor, Philadelphia police officers made no more arrests than New York City officers, but were thirty-seven times more likely to shoot unarmed citizens nonviolent crimes. Michael Kramer, "How cops go bad," *Time Magazine*, December 15, 1997, citing James J. Fyfe, "Philadelphia police shootings, 1975-78: a system model analysis," a report for the Civil Rights Division, U.S. Department of Justice, March 1980.

misconduct, progress falters once the individual leader leaves the department. In other cases, police chiefs or commissioners have made good-faith efforts to reform, only to be faced with overwhelming resistance among deputies or others on the force.

Internal Affairs Units

Internal affairs divisions are at the center of any examination of how police departments deal with human rights abuses committed by officers. It is alarming, therefore, that no outside review, including our own, has found the operations of internal affairs divisions in any of the major U.S. cities satisfactory.[107] In each city we examined, internal affairs units conducted substandard investigations, sustained few allegations of excessive force, and failed to identify, or deal appropriately with, problem officers against whom repeated complaints had been filed. In many cases, sloppy procedures and an apparent bias in favor of fellow officers combine to guarantee that even the most brutal police avoid punishment for serious violations until committing an abuse that is so flagrant, so unavoidably embarrassing, that it cannot be ignored. Since oversight commissions and journalistic investigations have found that a small percentage of officers are responsible for large percentages of abuses, this failure to identify and punish repeat offenders is evidently at the hub of the problem.

The workings of internal affairs divisions are cloaked in excessive secrecy: information about their operations is only disclosed in incomplete and occasional fashion through investigative newspaper articles, books, and special commission studies on police departments, usually following major scandals. Otherwise, the public is prevented from participating in, or even knowing about, the way police officers patrolling their streets are dealt with when they commit abuses. While police representatives claim privacy issues are the reason for protecting information about investigations or disciplinary hearings, police departments also resist providing information even when relevant names and other identifying information are excised. Observers are left wondering why no information is disclosed to support the contention that the police are policing themselves.

The few occasions the public has been allowed a glimpse of the inner workings of police departments in the 1990s have given cause for alarm. All of the three

---

[107] An exception to entirely negative reviews of internal affairs units may be a November 1997 report by the new "Integrity and Accountability" officer in Philadelphia. While noting continuing deficiencies, the officer found the investigations thorough and unbiased. His positive assessment was not shared by community activists who also viewed internal affairs files, as part of an agreement between the city and civil rights groups. *See* Philadelphia chapter.

commissions reviewing police misconduct in major cities since 1991 (in Boston, Los Angeles, and New York) found serious shortcomings in the way internal affairs divisions handled complaints.   In other cities (including Philadelphia, San Francisco, Chicago, Atlanta, and New Orleans), investigative reporters and police abuse experts have also concluded that internal investigations were not being conducted properly.

After reviewing 250 internal-affairs division cases, the St. Clair Commission in Boston concluded that the division was sustaining an abnormally low number of complaints:

> Our investigation into the Department's handling of citizen complaints of police misconduct...was particularly troubling. Our study revealed an investigative and hearing process characterized by shoddy, halfhearted investigations, lengthy delays, and inadequate documentation and record-keeping. The present Internal Affairs process is unfairly skewed against those bringing a complaint. Given the Internal Affairs Division's ("IAD") failure to routinely provide thorough and timely investigations of alleged misconduct, and the fact that the department sustains less than 6% of complaints against officers, it is no surprise that the overwhelming majority of community residents we spoke to have little confidence in the department's ability or willingness to police itself....[108]

The Christopher Commission in Los Angeles found that the Internal Affairs Division (IAD) of the LAPD had sustained only 2 percent of the excessive force complaints and stated: "Our study indicates that there are significant problems with the initiation, investigation, and classification of complaints." It called the IAD investigations "unfairly skewed against the complainant."[109]

When Temple University police abuse expert Prof. James J. Fyfe reviewed Philadelphia's internal affairs unit's files, he found documents missing and the files generally in disarray. The *Philadelphia Inquirer* has published many in-depth investigative reports finding the Internal Affairs Division's work seriously flawed. In 1997, one monitor found Philadelphia's internal affairs files reflected thorough investigations, while attorneys who were allowed to view some internal affairs records as part of a court-monitored agreement with the city found "significant shortcomings in too many of the investigative files that we reviewed," and that IAD

---

[108] St. Clair Commission report, pp. iii-iv.

[109] Christopher Commission report, p. 153.

investigators were "justifying the officers' actions where an independent analysis would find misconduct."[110] When a *San Francisco Examiner* reporter reviewed the San Francisco Police Department's internal affairs unit's record on police shootings, he found that internal investigations were seriously botched, allowing officers to avoid disciplinary sanctions or prosecution.[111] The Internal Affairs Division of the Metropolitan Police Department in Washington, D.C., is unable to account for case files it received from the now-abolished review board. When the *Atlanta Journal-Constitution* was able to obtain Internal Affairs Division files of that city's police force, after a lengthy delay, and reviewed the "contents list" in those files, it found that key items listed were missing.

In New Orleans, an attorney who represents victims of police abuse obtained internal affairs files and found them disorganized; she also found that the department was using an incorrect standard of proof in deciding whether to sustain complaints – the criminal "beyond a reasonable doubt" standard, instead of "preponderance of the evidence," which is the generally accepted standard for internal inquiries.[112] The records showed a sustained rate of about 1 to 2 percent for excessive force complaints filed against officers by civilians, with the sustained rate for officer-reported complaints a bit higher.[113]

Although off-duty conduct is not the focus of this study, we note that in the cities examined, off-duty criminal or violent behavior, particularly abuses that take place while officers "moonlight" as security guards in their off-hours, are not sufficiently monitored by internal affairs units. Police officers who become involved in altercations, bar fights, or domestic violence escape appropriate scrutiny due to poor tracking by internal affairs units. This is particularly true when the

---

[110] Mark Fazlollah, "Police get a 'C' for reviews of citizen complaints," *Philadelphia Inquirer*, September 30, 1997.

[111] Seth Rosenfeld, "S.F. pays big when cops shoot civilians," *San Francisco Examiner,* December 29, 1996; "Cops fail to police selves in shootings," *San Francisco Examiner,* December 30, 1996.

[112] In practice, the standard of proof in disciplinary proceedings is somewhat higher than "preponderance of the evidence" because complainants usually will not prevail without a corroborating witness. Chevigny, *Edge of the Knife*, p. 94.

[113] Human Rights Watch interview with attorney Mary Howell, New Orleans, October 1995. More recently, when Howell requested information regarding the standard of proof currently used by the internal affairs unit in December 1997, no answer to this question could be found in a stack of documents provided in December 1997, in response.

incident takes place beyond the jurisdiction where the officer works. At the same time, off-duty police officers who commit abuses frequently enjoy the protection of colleagues from their own and other forces. As of this writing, police forces around the country are grappling with, and in some cases opposing, implementation of new federal legislation prohibiting anyone, including police officers, with misdemeanor or felony convictions relating to domestic violence from carrying a gun or ammunition, thus requiring desk duty, and, in practice, dismissal for those officers.[114]

"Problem" Officers

As Human Rights Watch reviewed police abuse cases, it became apparent that there is a difference between an officer with a clean record and non-violent reputation who makes a mistake and hurts a civilian and an officer who has a long history of complaints and a reputation as a "problem." While all officers committing abuses must be disciplined appropriately, whether their use of force was simply unnecessary or malicious brutality, differing severities of abuse may require different approaches. Some officers should remain on the force after receiving retraining on specific tactics or counseling to deal with job frustration or other issues. Other officers should probably never have been hired, and it is questionable whether any amount of training or punishment would make them good, or even acceptable, police officers.

"Rogue" or problem officers – often called an aberration by police leaders fending off scandal – in fact account for a large percentage of abuse complaints and civil lawsuits. Yet internal affairs divisions generally fail to track problem officers or utilize early warning systems to identify those officers who are the subject of repeated complaints or legal actions. Although a handful of officers with a record of repeated acts of brutality can undermine the reputation of an entire police force, most of the departments examined by Human Rights Watch have failed to identify and take sufficient action to manage officers who repeatedly break departmental rules or, in some cases, the law.

Where they exist, most early-warning-system (or "at risk") reviews are triggered only after many complaints are lodged against an officer in a short period. Due to barriers to filing complaints and the code of silence, among other impediments, many problem officers are not identified. Civil lawsuits, even when they are found in favor of plaintiffs alleging serious violations, are usually not counted in the tallying of complaints. Thus, the detailed information they offer

---

[114] The Lautenberg Gun Ban, a rider to the Omnibus Consolidated Appropriations Act of 1997, PL 104-208, passed in September 1996.

about abuses usually does not find its way into personnel files in most of the fourteen cities reviewed.[115] Further, as described below, it should be noted that in two consent decrees reached by the Justice Department with police departments exhibiting a "pattern or practice" of abuse, civil lawsuit data are required to be part of future, stronger oversight systems.

The St. Clair Commission summarized its concerns about the handling of "problem" officers in Boston:

> [O]ur review of IAD files revealed a disturbing pattern of allegations of violence toward citizens by a small number of officers. The failure to monitor and evaluate the performance of police officers – particularly those with established patterns of alleged misconduct – is a major deficiency in the management of the department and results in an unnecessarily dangerous situation....No police department and no community should tolerate a situation where officers with a long record of alleged misconduct, including some with histories of alleged physical abuse of citizens, remain on the street largely unidentified and unsupervised.[116]

According to the Christopher Commission: "[T]here is a significant number of officers in the LAPD who repetitively use excessive force against the public and persistently ignore the written guidelines of the Department regarding force."[117] The police department in Los Angeles not only failed to deal with these; it often rewarded them with positive evaluations and promotions.[118] Former LAPD Assistant Chief Jesse Brewer testified: "We know who the bad guys are. Reputations become well known, especially to the sergeants and then of course to lieutenants and captains in the areas....But I don't see anyone bring these people up...."[119]

---

[115] A police-community agreement reached in Philadelphia in September 1996 should result in the use of civil liability information as part of that city's early warning system.

[116] St. Clair Commission report, p. iv.

[117] Christopher Commission report, foreword.

[118] Ibid., p. iv.

[119] Ibid., p, ix.

Code of Silence

The Christopher Commission, writing on the LAPD, found that "perhaps the greatest single barrier to the effective investigation and adjudication of complaints is the officers' unwritten 'code of silence'....[the principle that] an officer does not provide adverse information against a fellow officer."[120]   The commission concluded:

> [P]olice officers are given special powers, unique in our society, to use force, even deadly force, in the furtherance of their duties. Along with that power, however, must come the responsibility of loyalty first to the public the officers serve. That requires that the code of silence not be used as a shield to hide misconduct.[121]

In its first report, the Los Angeles Board of Police Commissioners' Office of the Inspector General (IG) found a decrease in the number of code-of-silence administrative actions – brought against officers who failed to provide information on alleged violations. These had dropped from fourteen in 1993, to twelve in 1994, ten in 1995, and none, at the time of the report, in 1996. Only four of the cases related to excessive force allegations. The IG was unable to ascertain whether the decrease related to a decline in the use of the informal code of silence to protect themselves or other officers, or lax enforcement of prohibitions on the code.[122]

The New York police force is also notorious for its officers' silence when misconduct occurs. As the Mollen Commission noted: "The pervasiveness of the code of silence is itself alarming."[123] The commission found that the code of silence is strongest in the most crime-ridden and dangerous neighborhoods and is considered essential to prove loyalty to other officers in those areas of the city. One policeman who admits to corrupt and brutal practices, former NYPD officer Bernard Cawley, testified that he never feared another officer would turn him in because there was a "Blue Wall of Silence. Cops don't tell on cops....[I]f a cop

---

[120] Ibid., p. 168.

[121] Ibid., p. 170-1.

[122] Los Angeles Board of Police Commissioner's Office of the Inspector General report, January 1997, p. 41.

[123] Mollen Commission report, p. 53.

decided to tell on me, his career's ruined....[H]e's going to be labeled as a rat."[124] Other officers who testified concurred with Cawley, including one who kept his identity hidden during the Mollen Commission hearings precisely because of the code, and who stated that officers first learn of the code in the Police Academy, with instructors telling them never to be a "rat."[125] He explained, "[S]ee, we're all blue...we have to protect each other no matter what."[126]

There is even a name for the way officers cover for each other and cover their own misconduct in court. It is called "testilying," offering false testimony in court. In justifying his inability to find NYPD Officer Francis X. Livoti guilty beyond a reasonable doubt for the "negligent homicide" of Anthony Baez, Acting New York Supreme Court Justice Gerald Sheindlin asserted that officers had committed perjury during the trial.[127]

Repercussions for breaking the code of silence include ostracism, threats, and the fear that officers will not "back up" or protect an officer who breaks the code.[128] In Officer Livoti's trial, for example, one officer's account differed in important ways from those of fellow officers who supported Livoti's claim that Baez had resisted arrest.[129]   After her testimony at Livoti's trial, she asked for an administrative assignment because she reportedly feared she would not get back-up in dangerous situations from fellow officers.

In an unprecedented move in Philadelphia, eight officers were ordered suspended for ten days without pay in May 1996 for their silence in the citizen review board's hearings on a high-profile death in custody. Police Commissioner Richard Neal said that the suspensions were necessary because the officers had

---

[124] Ibid.

[125] Ibid., p. 55.

[126] Ibid. p. 58.

[127] Michael Cooper, "Revenge cited in shooting of a captain," *New York Times,* January 8, 1997. In September 1997, the Bronx District Attorney's office announced it would reopen its perjury inquiry involving fifteen officers of the 46th Precinct.

[128] Mollen Commission report, p. 53.

[129] The officer had also filed a sexual harassment suit about the treatment she and other policewomen received at the 46th Precinct. Joyce Purnick, "The Blue Line Between Rat and Right," *New York Times*, October 10, 1996.

shown a "lack of candor."[130] The officers' punishment was somewhat ironic because, during hearings on the case, Commissioner Neal did not require the officers to comply with the board's requests for information, and the department was known for its strong code of silence. Fraternal Order of Police lawyer Jeffrey Kolansky told a reporter that he rejected the notion that there is a code of silence, but then refused to answer a reporter's questions on the subject.[131] To its credit, and in response to growing corruption and abuse scandals in the Philadelphia force, the black officers' Guardian Civic League called on fellow officers to turn in corrupt colleagues and report misconduct.[132]

In a 1993 study of the New Orleans police force, the city's Advisory Committee on Human Relations found a relatively small percentage of bad officers. One of the report's authors stated: "[T]he police department itself helps to cover up such people through the code of silence, and anyone who rats on another guy will find himself never promoted. Those signals come from the top and work their way down."[133]

In Boston, the police force's claims of reform were brought into serious question after a black plainclothes officer, Michael Cox, was allegedly beaten severely by fellow officers, who apparently believed he was a suspect.[134] Following the January 1995 incident, the officers accused of the beating gave wildly inconsistent accounts of it, initially contending that Cox was either not at the scene at all or that he was not hurt. The two dozen other officers present at the end of the chase denied seeing Cox at all, or claimed they were not near him at the time of the beating. Because of the code of silence, the officers identified by Cox as the

---

[130] Jeff Gammage, Mark Fazlollah and Richard Jones, "8 City officers suspended in DeJesus case," *Philadelphia Inquirer*, April 30, 1996. The commissioner also stated he would "disregard" the findings of the Police Advisory Commission, which found that one of the officers had used excessive force, and was responsible for the death; the PAC also found that five officers had shown a "lack of candor." PAC report on DeJesus case, December 19, 1995, PAC. NO. 94-0015.

[131] Jeff Gammage, "Code of silence: a barrier to truth in investigations of police," *Philadelphia Inquirer*, May 5, 1996.

[132] Editorial, *Philadelphia Inquirer*, September 27, 1995.

[133] Susan Finch, "NOPD told to put stop to brutality," *Times-Picayune*, May 20, 1993.

[134] Dick Lehr, "Department unwilling to face brutal facts," *Boston Globe*, December 8, 1997.

assailants have not been disciplined by police officials or charged criminally more than three years after the incident. (Federal and local prosecutors intervened in 1997, and brought obstruction of justice and perjury charges against one of the officers present during the Cox beating who gave a particularly unbelievable account of the incident.)

In all the cities we examined, and particularly in those like Philadelphia or New Orleans where police abuse and corruption have been visibly rampant, the code of silence is not limited to the street officers who witness abuses and fail to report them, or who lie when asked about reported incidents. In these cases, responsibility for the "blue wall of silence" extends to supervisors and ultimately police commissioners and chiefs. Furthermore, local district attorneys, when they prosecute criminal suspects based on officers' patently fabricated justifications of searches or suspects' injuries, and who continue to cooperate with officers who commit human rights abuses rather than attempt to prosecute them on criminal charges, join in complicity.

In the end, the code of silence all but assures impunity for officers who commit human rights violations since, without information about brutal incidents from fellow officers, administrative and criminal penalties are much less likely. In such a climate, officers who commit abuses flourish.

Disciplinary actions

Following a finding by a police department's internal affairs unit (or by precinct/division investigators) or a citizen review agency that an officer violated departmental policy, the officer should be subjected to disciplinary action. Usually authorized at the level of deputy chief or commissioner, disciplinary actions may include verbal reprimands, reprimand letters, suspensions, or dismissals. In addition, and in some cases instead of "punishments," officers may receive retraining or counseling. In most cases, they are assisted throughout the disciplinary process by police union representatives who utilize civil service laws and special "law enforcement officers' bills of rights" (statutes delineating specific "rights" provided for officers who are investigated for misconduct) to shield officers from punishment.[135]

---

[135] The bills of rights may limit the ability of a police chief or commissioner to suspend an officer, and require that suspended officers continue to receive their salaries and benefits. In some states, there is no requirement of dismissal or loss of benefits even for an officer convicted of a felony. Many of the "bills of rights" also allow for the purging of officers' personnel files of all but sustained complaints; even the rare sustained complaints may be purged after a set number of years in some states. While officers are entitled to full due process safeguards, many of the protections they currently enjoy are exceptional and, in

When, in a small percentage of cases, complaints alleging excessive force are sustained (following citizen or internal review procedures), there is no guarantee that the offending officer will be punished appropriately. Ranking officers, who should themselves be judged by how they handle sustained complaints of misconduct by their subordinates, may choose to apply lenient sanctions or none at all. If they do choose to discipline an officer, arbitrary statutes of limitations in some cities prevent them from taking any action when investigations have been delayed. Furthermore, when higher-ranking police officials order disciplinary measures, subordinates often bring administrative appeals and win them. Even in cases where heads of police departments have ordered the dismissal of officers known to be brutal, the officers have won reinstatement, with back pay, through arbitration or court appeals.

In Los Angeles, the Christopher Commission found that, "even when excessive force complaints are sustained, the punishment is more lenient than it should be."[136] As Assistant Chief David Dotson testified, "[H]igher command officers when learning of [incidents of excessive force] having occurred took no action or very indecisive action, a very weak and slow approach to doing something....And so, that's an area that I believe we have failed miserably in, is holding people accountable for the actions of their people."[137] The commission concluded that "a major overhaul" of the disciplinary system was required.[138]

According to a series of investigative articles in the *Philadelphia Inquirer*, firing even the most violent officers on the city's force is nearly impossible. In studying cases between 1992 and 1995, the journalists found that punishment imposed by the department was lessened or reversed two-thirds of the time, or in fifty-two of seventy-eight cases that went to arbitration; in twenty of the fifty-two, the arbitrator completely reversed the department's punishment.[139] Police Commissioner Neal called it "frustrating to no end.... [T]hese people who are being

---

practice, undermine police management efforts at accountability.

[136] Christopher Commission report, p. xx.

[137] Ibid., p. 33.

[138] Ibid., p. xx. (*See* Los Angeles chapter.)

[139] Jeff Gammage and Mark Fazlollah, "Arbitration offers a route back to work," *Philadelphia Inquirer*, November 21, 1995.

fired are people who should not be part of the department."[140] Yet attorneys defending the officers claim that they succeed in arbitration hearings because the city gives low priority to defending punishment decisions against officers, virtually ensuring that the officers will prevail.

In Portland, an Internal Affairs Division staff person told Human Rights Watch that most supervisors do not want to deal with officers with complaint histories, and firing them is made difficult by civil service protections.[141] He asserted that these officers are instead ignored, transferred to another precinct, or sometimes promoted. The unwillingness to deal with officers with a history of misconduct complaints was also evident in New York. The Mollen Commission found that certain police precincts were used as "dumping grounds" for incompetent or undisciplined officers.[142] Officers assigned to dangerous, high-crime precincts, it found, took a "perverse pride" in their reputation for being thuggish and believed that supervisors and internal affairs investigators would not venture into their "territory." The commission recommended transferring officers with disciplinary problems equally among all precincts to avoid this concentration and reinforcement of corrupt or brutal behavior.

In the most severe cases, police departments should utilize decertification procedures for officers found to have committed serious abuses. Thirty-nine states have police officer decertification procedures, by which police officers who engage in serious misconduct are "decertified" and prevented from serving on any police force in the state. Professional boards conduct the decertification reviews, much as similar boards operate in other professions. Hearings are held by a state agency usually known as the Peace Officer's Standards and Training (POST) Commission. In states with decertification procedures, a police officer whose conduct has been found to be in violation of state statutes or regulations will have his or her police officer certificate (or license) removed; this prevents him or her from continuing to serve as a law enforcement officer in the state. It also helps to curtail the practice of some "problem" officers who outrun disciplinary efforts by resigning their positions in one jurisdiction to take up work in a neighboring jurisdiction in the

---

[140] Ibid.

[141] Human Rights Watch interview with Lt. Ron Webber, Portland, September 21, 1995.

[142] Mollen Commission report, pp. 123-5.

same state.[143] Of the states we examined, Illinois, Indiana, Massachusetts, Michigan, New York, and Rhode Island are among eleven states without decertification powers, largely due to opposition from police unions. Louisiana has limited powers to revoke certification. Of the states examined, Georgia has used its POST most actively in recent years, with hundreds of law enforcement officers receiving some manner of "discipline" from the POST.[144]

In the eleven states in which the POST Commission or its equivalent does not have decertification powers, they should be so empowered. All states should revise their statutes or regulations to require that police chiefs or commissioners report the dismissal or resignation of officers accused of serious misconduct. Federal legislation should be introduced that would link the data currently collected by state POSTs so that "problem" or abusive officers are not allowed to obtain law enforcement employment in a neighboring state. Where decertification procedures currently exist, they should be reinvigorated and fully funded.

Investigations into Shootings

Though less frequent than beatings, shootings by police officers occur in every city we examined and are often the source of police-community tensions. In the face of such serious abuses, community trust and accountability are undermined by investigative procedures that are biased in favor of the officers involved. Police investigators may be inclined to accept the officers' accounts uncritically, and responsibility for investigating shooting cases may be left solely to police investigators (from internal affairs and/or homicide divisions), with no external review. Even where citizen review agencies have investigative powers, shooting investigations are usually led by the department itself (which may or may not work with the district attorney's office).

Even though investigators agree that an essential part of any successful investigation is the collection of statements from involved parties and other witnesses as soon as possible so that memories do not fade or become influenced by others, police officers who are involved in shootings may be allowed to delay providing a statement to investigators. In New York, for example, officers involved in shootings are allowed to wait forty-eight hours before providing statements to

---

[143] See forthcoming article, Steven Puro, Roger Goldman, and William C. Smith, "Police Decertification: Changing Patterns Among the States, 1985-1995, " in *Policing: An International Journal of Police Strategies and Management.*

[144] "A Sourcebook of Information by the International Association of Directors of Law Enforcement Standards and Training, 1996," p. 69, as provided to Human Rights Watch by the Florida Department of Law Enforcement on June 15, 1997.

investigators; in practice, the officer is often allowed more than forty-eight hours because an investigator must request an interview before the forty-eight hour clock begins, and weekends are not counted.[145]

In Los Angeles, after an "officer-involved" shooting, internal investigators conducted group interviews of the police involved. As the Christopher Commission noted, this allowed officers under investigation to "get their stories straight."[146] In cases reviewed by the commission, officers' statements were not recorded until after a pre-interview, and the district attorney's office was not allowed to interview the officer or witnesses until the police department was finished. The commission concluded, "[O]ther law enforcement agencies have successfully conducted shooting and other investigations without resorting to these techniques. The commission perceives no legitimate reason why the LAPD continues to engage in these practices."[147] The department did discontinue this practice.

Police departments may compel officers involved in shootings (and other abuses) to provide statements as a condition to remaining on the force. Under U.S. law, such statements cannot be used in criminal proceedings.[148] Such a warning is required when a police officer is ordered to give a statement regarding actions taken by him or her while employed with a police department. Because the failure to answer such questions may form the basis of an officer's dismissal or result in disciplinary proceedings against that officer, the officer's right not to be forced to incriminate him or herself has been interpreted by the U.S. Supreme Court to mean that any such statement, or its fruits, cannot then be used in any subsequent criminal proceeding against the employee, except in cases of alleged perjury by the employee giving the statements in which the criminal charge is based upon the falsity of the given statement. As a result, criminal prosecution of officers is more

---

[145] For example, after the December 25, 1997, fatal shooting of William Whitfield by a Brooklyn police officer, investigators did not immediately request an interview and the officer was to be interviewed at least six days after the shooting. Robert D. McFadden, "Police officer has yet to give his account of fatal shooting," *New York Times*, December 28, 1997. Some experts believe that investigators delay taking the statements of involved officers to avoid compelling testimony that as a result would not be admissible in court if the officer engaged in a possibly criminal offense. *(See below.)*

[146] Christopher Commission report, p. 161.

[147] Ibid., pp. 161-162.

[148] In these circumstances, officers under investigation receive a "Garrity warning." *Garrity v. New Jersey*, 385 U.S. 493 (1967).

difficult. Once an officer's statement is compelled, the officer is effectively shielded from prosecution on the basis of that statement. If applied in good faith, this Supreme Court ruling would often require a trade-off between purging bad officers through administrative means versus criminal prosecution. In practice, compelled statements tend to protect officers from any sanctions, since criminal prosecution is unlikely and administrative disciplinary sanctions are applied inconsistently if at all.

Officers are usually allowed to have an attorney present before speaking with investigators following a shooting. In some of the cities we examined, however, procedures do not provide for any non-police personnel to respond to the scene as representatives of a person who may have been shot unjustifiably. Oversight of officer-involved shooting investigations in Los Angeles, for example, was dealt a setback in 1995 when the district attorney's (D.A.'s) office discontinued its "roll-out" program of sending assistant district attorneys or special D.A. investigators to all shooting scenes. And in September 1995, the D.A.'s office ended its review of officer-involved shootings unless the relevant police agency requests the office's involvement. Around the same time, the police union created a roll-out team for officers involved in shootings, meaning that D.A. investigators are not on the scene, but attorneys to assist the officers under investigation always are.

This unequal provision of oversight at the shooting scene may pose a serious risk to the integrity of an investigation. For example, the Atlanta police department's investigation into a December 1995 fatal shooting of a motorcycle shop customer during a botched police raid revealed serious problems of bias and incompetence among police investigators. Witness accounts disputed the officers' version of events and indicated that one of the police shot an unarmed man while he lay on the ground, but Homicide Division investigators ignored these accounts. (Witnesses went to the press with their story. In response to the publicity surrounding the shooting investigation, the head of the Homicide Division was transferred to the internal affairs unit – a response that did little to improve investigative tactics in sensitive cases involving the Atlanta police force.)

In many cities we examined, the officer involved in a shooting is allowed to remain on the scene as fellow officers investigate. The officer is thereby allowed to provide his version of events, if he so chooses, and to convince investigators that he acted in a justifiable manner. Even if the involved officer does nothing untoward, his presence on the scene gives the appearance of impropriety.

Civil Remedies

Civil lawsuits against police officers and departments have become a common way of seeking "accountability" of a sort, with larger municipalities paying victims and their families tens of millions of dollars, through either pre- or mid-trial settlements or civil jury awards following judgments against officers and/or the police department.[149] While victims certainly deserve compensation when officers violate their human rights, civil remedies are never a sufficient form of accountability because they almost never address flawed management, policies, or patterns of abuse, nor do they hold an individual officer financially responsible.[150] And settlements in particular are problematic, especially in high-profile cases, by leaving responsibility for an abuse incident unresolved in the minds of the both the community and police department.

Under Title 42 U.S. Code Section 1983, the federal civil rights civil statute, individuals may file lawsuits against an offending officer, police department, or jurisdiction.[151] The statute mandates that:

> Any person who, under color of any statute, ordinance, regulation, custom, or usage, of any State or Territory or the District of Columbia, subjects or causes to be subjected, any citizen of the United States or other person within the jurisdiction thereof to the deprivation of any rights, privileges, or immunities secured by the Constitution and laws, shall be liable to the party injured in an action at law, suit in equity, or other proper proceeding for redress....[152]

Success rates in bringing civil lawsuits against officers vary dramatically from city to city, with some cities settling early and quietly while others vigorously fight brutality suits. If a case goes to trial, some juries have shown a predisposition to believe police officers' accounts, particularly when the victim has a criminal record. The strongest cases presented by victims of serious abuse are often settled by a city to avoid embarrassing attention; in such settlements, the department rarely acknowledges that an officer was in the wrong. Often, parties are sworn to secrecy

---

[149] Even if administrative or criminal accountability systems worked better, civil lawsuits would still be filed, yet the absence of other avenues for redress makes lawsuits more likely.

[150] As described in the legal section below, cities may pay plaintiffs in settlements, yet not admit liability for the officers' misconduct, thereby not actually accepting legal responsibility for the harm.

[151] Although the federal law, Section 1983, is used most frequently, plaintiffs may also use state-level statutes in bringing abuse lawsuits.

[152] 42 U.S.C. §1983.

regarding the amount of the settlement or information about the officer that may have been disclosed during the process.[153]

The amounts paid in civil lawsuit settlements and following judgments in police brutality cases varied greatly in the cities examined by Human Rights Watch. In New York City, taxpayers paid plaintiffs about $70 million in settlement or civil jury awards in claims alleging improper police actions between 1994 and 1996.[154] In Los Angeles, the city paid approximately $79.2 million in civil lawsuit awards and pre-trial settlements against police officers (not including traffic accidents) between 1991 and 1996. In other cities, the amounts paid were quite small. In Atlanta, where the city "litigates aggressively" to defend itself against police abuse lawsuits, the city paid just over $1 million between 1994 and 1996, although in June 1997 the city paid out $750,000 in a single case – one of the largest single payouts in Atlanta's recent history. Between 1994 and 1996, Indianapolis paid approximately $750,000 total in police misconduct lawsuits, pre-trial and post-verdict.[155]

Of the cities examined, Philadelphia was among those paying the largest amounts to settle civil lawsuits alleging police misconduct. Between July 1993 and November 1996, the city agreed to pay $32.6 million in settlements and civil jury awards arising from lawsuits alleging police misconduct.[156] The former deputy city solicitor (and newly appointed anti-corruption director) stated, "This is not Monopoly money. This is real money. How do we save the taxpayers millions of

---

[153] Total amounts of settlements may be made available, however, through city solicitors or city attorneys. No nationwide, systematic data are kept regarding the numbers of Section 1983 lawsuits filed.

[154] Matthew Purdy, "What does it take to get arrested in New York City? Not much," *New York Times*, August 24, 1997. Figure includes lawsuits alleging brutality and other police misconduct.

[155] The city appealed a $3.55 million jury verdict award in favor of the family of Michael Taylor in 1996.

[156] Mark Fazlollah, "Bill soars on police claims," *Philadelphia Inquirer*, November 21, 1996.

dollars?"[157] The *Philadelphia Inquirer* estimated in 1996 that the year's payouts would fund 250 police officers for a year.[158]

Washington, D.C. paid $4 million in settlement or post-verdict payments in police misconduct suits by individuals claiming false arrest/assault during a three-year period between 1993 and 1995. This amounted to four times the budget of the city's Civilian Complaint Review Board; the board was abolished in 1995, in part due to budgetary constraints.[159] In Detroit, the police department announced new training programs for recruits in April 1997 in an attempt to stem the enormous amounts paid by the city's taxpayers in civil lawsuits alleging police misconduct. Between 1987 and 1994, the city reportedly paid $72 million in settlements or jury awards stemming from police misconduct lawsuits (excluding claims based on vehicle accidents and chases), and in the twenty-two-month period between July 1, 1995 and April 1997, the city paid just under $20 million in cases involving alleged police brutality, police chases and minor accidents.[160]

The New Orleans Law Department resisted providing any information regarding payouts in civil cases to individuals alleging police abuse.[161] Between 1994 and 1996, the city reported paying approximately $1 million for excessive force and wrongful death suits. According to local attorneys who represent plaintiffs in these cases, the state has not actually paid on a police misconduct claim since mid-1995.

Taxpayers in some cities, such as New York and Philadelphia, are paying three times for officers who repeatedly commit abuses: once to cover their salaries while

---

[157] Ibid.

[158] Human Rights Watch attempted to obtain these figures directly, in writing, from the city solicitor's office. A request was sent on September 18, 1996, and the same request was sent repeatedly thereafter. As of this writing, and despite repeated telephone calls, we have not received a response.

[159] ACLU National Capital Area, testimony before the Committee of the Judiciary, City Council, October 11, 1995.

[160] Roger Chesley, "Police training program could cut lawsuits,"*Detroit Journal,* April 20, 1997; information provided by the city's legal department; and $72 million figure compiled by Detroit City Councilman Mel Ravitz's office.

[161] Other cities required many reminders, and several city solicitor or city attorney office representatives provided information by telephone but never sent the documentary material they promised.

they commit abuses; next to pay settlements or civil jury awards against officers; and a third time through payments into police "defense" funds provided by the cities. For all of the coverage, city residents get in return an erosion of standards and heightened tension in poor and minority neighborhoods.

The positive aspects of civil lawsuits, which provide some plaintiffs or their families with compensation, are undermined by several factors. In many instances, an attorney representing a police abuse victim will instruct him or her not to file a complaint with citizen review agencies or internal affairs units for fear of making a statement that may be unhelpful in pursuing the civil case or in defending the client if criminal charges are pending against him or her.[162] Therefore, because attorneys choose the strongest cases to pursue, some of the most important abuse complaints may not be filed with external or internal review units. Since these units are complaint-driven, no investigation will ensue.

Another problem in most cities is that civil settlements paid by the city on behalf of an officer usually are not taken from the police budget but are paid from general city funds. In larger cities, even significant payouts in these cases do not have much of an effect on the city's operations, and only lead to change when they become an embarrassment. In Philadelphia, for example, civil lawsuits on behalf of victims of police misconduct made headlines after they reached record highs in 1995 and 1996. Eventually, the threat of more lawsuits that could significantly affect the city's budget forced city officials to accede to a reform plan backed by community leaders. But that was an exceptional case; other cities continue to pay large amounts without examining, acknowledging, or correcting the police activities that led to the lawsuits.

The individual officer who is the subject of a police misconduct lawsuit found in favor of the plaintiff is rarely forced to pay the victim. In fact, an officer who is the subject of a successful lawsuit alleging abuse may escape any sanction. Most of the departments examined by Human Rights Watch did not initiate an internal affairs or review agency investigation when a civil claim or suit alleging serious abuse is filed or a settlement or award is made favoring the plaintiff. There are notification systems in some cities whereby the city attorney's office informs the relevant internal affairs unit that a suit has been filed or resolved, but that information is not necessarily used in evaluating the officer; indeed, some internal affairs units investigate complaints made in civil lawsuits only in order to assist the city in defending itself against plaintiffs' claims.

---

[162] Attorneys who frequently represent victims in police brutality civil cases have told Human Rights Watch that their clients are often badgered and intimidated by internal affairs investigators, thus reinforcing their lack of interest in filing a complaint with the relevant police department.

Some internal affairs investigators – in defending their inaction when civil suits alleging misconduct are filed or decided in favor of the plaintiff – state that plaintiffs' attorneys will not allow them to interview the alleged victim. Yet there is no reason why they could not use the information developed through a lawsuit, including names of witnesses and officers present, to begin an investigation even without a formal complaint or direct statement from the alleged victim. As it is, a city may pay hundreds of thousands, or millions, of dollars on behalf of a brutal officer, yet the officer pays no price whatsoever.

Even in cities where some type of early warning system is utilized to identify potential problem officers – as in Boston, Los Angeles, New Orleans, New York, and Portland – civil lawsuits filed against officers are not monitored the way complaints filed with citizen review agencies or internal affairs units are. This is so even though civil suit complaints include detailed information about serious violations that should be investigated. While clearly frivolous cases should not be used in assessing an officer's performance, this disconnect between lawsuits and internal investigations is baffling, because the suits could be used as a management tool; they should also be monitored by prosecutors in case criminal acts are credibly alleged.[163]

Yet, most internal affairs staff interviewed by Human Rights Watch made statements such as "civil cases are not our problem," or asserted that the settled suits do not indicate the "guilt" of an officer, disregarding the important information that citizen-initiated lawsuits could provide. City attorney offices seemed to share this perspective; for example, the New York City Law Department wrote to Human Rights Watch, "concerning notification procedures where a lawsuit alleges police misconduct, the Law Department does not have a formal procedure for notifying IAB or the CCRB of such lawsuits."[164]

In Portland, the police chief explained why "risk management data" (civil lawsuit information) are not used as a tool in reviewing officers, as suggested by

---

[163] Under Rule 11 of the Federal Rules of Civil Procedures (1996), attorneys who present federal civil lawsuits, such as suits under Section 1983, affirm their contention that the suit is not frivolous, baseless, or filed for improper purposes. If a court determines that an attorney violated this rule, it can impose fines or other "non-monetary directives." This is a stronger deterrent to filing unwarranted lawsuits than those faced by complainants using internal or external review procedures; therefore, lawsuits detailing incidents of police abuse should be taken at least as seriously as citizen complaints in initiating investigations by internal and external units.

[164] Letter from Assistant Corporation Counsel Michael Sarner, New York City Law Department to Human Rights Watch, November 8, 1996.

Portland's citizen review agency: "I have not been able to determine a way to utilize Risk Management Information to label employees as problem officers. Tort claim notices do not contain all of the facts and I do not think it is fair to attempt to determine the involvement of an individual without examining all of the facts."[165] Like many other high-ranking police officials, the chief fails to recognize that the information in such lawsuits could be valuable, at a minimum, in determining whether to launch an investigation.

Gannett News Service published a series of investigative articles in March 1992 examining the fate of police officers named in one hundred civil lawsuits in twenty-two states in which juries ordered $100,000 or more to be paid to plaintiffs between 1986 and 1991.[166] The awards from the lawsuits totaled nearly $92 million dollars. Of 185 officers involved in these cases, only eight were disciplined. No action was taken against 160, and seventeen were promoted. The reporter concluded, "[T]axpayers are penalized more for brutality than the officers responsible for the beatings."[167]

The Christopher Commission examined eighty-three civil cases with settlements, judgments or jury verdicts of more than $15,000 between 1986 and 1990 against officers with the Los Angeles Police Department. During this period, Los Angeles paid more than $20 million in over 300 lawsuits alleging excessive force through judgments, settlements and jury verdicts. A majority of cases involved clear and often egregious human rights violations committed by officers, resulting in the victim's serious injury or death. The commission found the department's investigation of these cases deficient in many respects and noted that discipline against the officers involved was frequently light or nonexistent. Eighty-four percent of the officers investigated received positive ratings in their personnel evaluations, and 42 percent were promoted following the incident.[168] The commission recommended establishing procedures to monitor results of civil litigation and to make use of the information obtained. It called on the city attorney to notify promptly the Police Commission and the department when lawsuits are filed alleging police misconduct, and called on the Internal Affairs Division to

---

[165] December 20, 1995 Memorandum from Portland Police Chief Moose to Portland Mayor Vera Katz.

[166] Rochelle Sharpe. (March 1992). "How Cops Beat the Rap," [News Wire] *Gannett News Service.* [Online].

[167] Ibid.

[168] No data were available for the remainder. Christopher Commission report, p. 57.

investigate every "significant" claim. In its November 1997 report, the Office of the Inspector General (OIG) of the Los Angeles Police Commission reviewed 561 civil claims for damages involving department employees forwarded from the City Attorney's office to the department in 1995.[169] The department did not sustain a single allegation of misconduct against a sworn employee, of the 561 claims reviewed. While the City Attorney's office does notify the department when a claim is filed in state court, the OIG found that there has been no procedure in place for the City Attorney to notify the department of federal lawsuits.

As with most aspects of police abuse, data collection on lawsuits is inadequate. Some cities do not distinguish amounts paid in cases of misconduct, including excessive force, from damages arising because of mishaps such as traffic accidents. Others compile statistics that combine information on wholly different issues, such as false arrest and excessive force. In Atlanta, because it claimed no data had been collected in a systematic manner, the city attorney's office provided Human Rights Watch with some information by asking its staff the amounts they remembered the city having paid. Despite repeated letters and telephone calls from Human Rights Watch, no civil lawsuit data relating to police misconduct were provided by Chicago or Philadelphia.

The city of Boston is unique among the cities examined in that it apparently does not compile, or acknowledge compiling, amounts paid in police abuse lawsuit settlements or jury awards. Nine months after Human Rights Watch's initial inquiry, we received a letter from the staff attorney with the Office of the Legal Advisor of the police department, stating: "[N]either the Department, nor the City of Boston, maintain records in a form responsive to your request, i.e., a list or compilation of the amount of money paid to settle police brutality cases."[170]

Although they usually do not affect policies, civil lawsuits have led to reform occasionally. In *Tennessee v. Garner* (1985), the U.S. Supreme Court held that police shootings under the authority of laws and policies that allowed officers to use deadly force to apprehend nonviolent fleeing suspects violated the Fourth Amendment of the U.S. Constitution, which protects against unwarranted search or

---

[169] Office of the Inspector General, "Status update: management of LAPD high-risk officers," November 1997, pp. 6-7.

[170] Letter from Robert E. Whalen, Staff Attorney, Office of the Legal Advisor, to Human Rights Watch, September 16, 1997.

seizure.[171] As a result, police departments were compelled to formulate more restrictive policies on the use of deadly force or face future liability for officers' exercise of the broad – and unconstitutional – discretion allowed them by state legislation.[172] Decisions in other cases under Section 1983 (the federal civil statute commonly used by individuals alleging police abuse) have held police agencies liable for inadequate policy and training regarding nonlethal force, strip searches, and vehicle pursuits. As described below in the chapter on Philadelphia, the threat of overwhelming civil lawsuits filed on behalf of victims of police abuse and court-ordered reforms in that scandal-ridden department forced police officials to agree to wide-ranging reforms.

Civil lawsuits also can lead to the disclosure of information – particularly when a case goes to trial – that otherwise would not have been available. Even initial complaints filed by alleged victims or their families provide information of interest to police abuse monitors.

Citizen review agencies generally do not utilize civil lawsuits, instead relying on individuals to come to the agency to file a complaint. Some agencies are overburdened and hardly interested in seeking out additional complaints. Others have respected concerns voiced by attorneys representing plaintiffs who prefer that their clients not speak to any investigator. A more proactive approach, however, is that of San Francisco's Office of Citizen Complaints, which has established a new procedure: once it is notified of police abuse lawsuits by the city attorney's office, it sends the plaintiff an OCC complaint form, explaining how the OCC works, and suggesting that the victim file a complaint.

Civil suits should be used in addition to, not instead of, other accountability avenues. When police departments or criminal prosecutors deflect criticisms by stating that victims of abuse can always sue, they forsake their responsibilities.

---

[171] Prior to *Tennessee v. Garner*, officers were not prohibited from shooting at any fleeing felon. According to international human rights standards, "[L]aw enforcement officials shall not use firearms against persons except in self-defence or defence of others against the imminent threat of death or serious injury, to prevent the perpetration of a particularly serious crime involving grave threat to life, to arrest a person presenting such a danger and resisting their authority, or to prevent his or her escape, and only when less extreme means are insufficient to achieve those objectives. In any event, intentional lethal use of firearms may only be made when strictly unavoidable in order to protect life." Principle 9, Basic Principles on the Use of Force and Firearms by Law Enforcement Officials, UN Doc. A/CONF.144/28/Rev.1 (1990).

[172] James J. Fyfe, *Police Administration* (New York: McGraw-Hill, 1997), p. 204.

Civil remedies must always be available, but they cannot be a substitute for police department mechanisms of accountability or prosecutorial action.

Local Criminal Prosecution

Local prosecutors (district, county or state's attorneys) may prosecute police officers who engage in behavior, on- or off-duty, that violates the law. When officers are prosecuted, it is usually under state law for crimes such as murder, manslaughter, assault, battery, or rape. Comprehensive statistics on prosecution efforts, reasons for prosecutorial decisions, or prosecutorial success rates are generally not available to the public. But our investigation leads us to conclude that local prosecutions of police officers on charges relating to the excessive use of force are rare.[173] Without information about the number of cases prosecuted against police officers, which does not appear to be maintained routinely by district attorney's offices or their clerks, it is impossible to know with certainty whether cases are being appropriately handled by local attorneys (and, consequently, whether federal prosecutors need to initiate their own investigation).

Experts have noted that because criminal prosecutions of officers are difficult, they frequently do not succeed in improving human rights practices. Police abuse experts warn, "When we try to use criminal law as a substitute for standards that should be applied within a profession or occupation, we almost invariably are disappointed with the results."[174] Even in cases where federal officials do actively investigate, "police brutality cases are incredibly difficult to prove in court," according to Steven D. Clymer, law professor at Cornell University. "Historically, most jurors have had a presumption in favor of the police officers. In most cases, jurors go into a case looking for reasons to convict. In police misconduct cases, they are searching for reasons to acquit."[175] Prosecutors, therefore, are hesitant to bring cases against police officers that are difficult to win, while one reason for the difficulty in successfully prosecuting officers may be the rarity of such efforts,

---

[173] Human Rights Watch attempted to compile statistics from relevant prosecuting agencies in the cities examined. Telephone inquiries, May 13 and 14, 1997 and June 3, 1997. We were repeatedly referred to police departments to obtain these statistics and told that prosecutors "don't track cases that way."

[174] Jerome H. Skolnick and James J. Fyfe, *Above the Law,* (New York: The Free Press, 1993), p. 198. Please note that there are two books with the title of *Above the Law* cited in this report. David Burnham is the author of the other *Above the Law,* cited below.

[175] Mark Curriden, "When good cops go bad," *ABA Journal,* May 1996.

causing jurors to disbelieve allegations of criminal activity that differ from their typical image of police officers.

Among the reasons prosecutors may choose not to pursue a case against a police officer accused of abusive behavior are:

- the traditionally close relationship between district or county attorneys and police officers who usually work together to prosecute other alleged criminals;

- difficulties in convincing grand juries and trial juries that a police officer did not merely make an understandable mistake, but committed a crime;

- special proceedings that, in some jurisdictions, provide additional protections for police officers accused of criminal behavior; and

- lack of information about cases that could be prosecuted or systems for reviewing possibly prosecutable cases.

There is a natural conflict of interest when district attorneys – who typically work closely with the police to bring cases against suspected criminals – are faced with prosecuting those same officers. District attorneys count on officers' testimony to support their cases during trials of alleged criminals. There is a particular reticence in bringing charges against officers who have been "productive" and who have worked closely with the district attorney's office. In some jurisdictions, district attorneys are elected and are aware that the powerful police unions and their supporters may withdraw their support if a police officer is prosecuted.

Prosecutors are also aware of juries' tendency to support the police. Even with apparently foolproof cases against police officers, juries have often been reluctant to find officers guilty of criminal conduct, particularly when the incident occurred while they were on duty. Because cases against police officers are usually difficult to win, prosecutors contend that it is best to pursue only the cases with the greatest chances of conviction. Of course, by only pursuing rare, overwhelmingly strong cases, the deterrent effect of criminal prosecution of officers is undermined significantly. Prosecutors contend that trying, and losing, a case against an officer is a worse signal to send to officers, and the affected communities, than not trying the case at all.

In explaining her office's low rate of prosecution of officers, the Philadelphia district attorney argued that the problem with criminal prosecution of officers is that if they are acquitted (after being suspended or dismissed), they almost always avoid additional discipline or win back their jobs through arbitration. For this reason, her office will pursue only exceptionally strong cases.[176] In New York, despite scores of fatal shootings during the past twenty years, no officer was convicted on homicide charges for an on-duty shooting between 1977 and 1995.[177]

In Atlanta, the spokesperson for the Fulton County district attorney's office told Human Rights Watch that he could recall only three cases that his office had prosecuted against police officers during the previous five years.[178] He stated that few excessive force cases reach the stage of charges being filed because they seem to "wash out" with the Atlanta police department's internal affairs unit. He attributed this tendency to "the police looking out for themselves."[179] New Orleans, despite a police force renowned for abusive behavior, has seen few criminal prosecutions of officers who have committed human rights abuses. When cases go before the grand jury, officers are frequently cleared. When the district attorney has been questioned about the lack of prosecutions, he has blamed the police department for the troubled force.

In some jurisdictions, the special procedures used in indicting or prosecuting an officer may help him or her avoid indictment or conviction. In Georgia, state officials (including police officers) are allowed to be present with legal counsel during grand jury proceedings, and the defendant officer may make a statement to the jurors after the state presents its evidence.[180] Normally, defendants are not present during grand jury proceedings (except during their own testimony), are not allowed to have a lawyer in the courtroom, and are not allowed to make concluding statements.

---

[176] Gammage and Fazlollah, "Arbitration offers a route ..," *Philadelphia Inquirer.*

[177] In 1992, prior to the 1995 merging of the New York City Housing Authority with the NYPD, Housing Authority police officer Jonas Bright shot and killed Douglas Orfaly, and in 1995 was convicted of criminally negligent homicide. More recently, in May 1997, New York City transit officer Paolo Colecchia was found guilty of second-degree manslaughter in the fatal July 1996 shooting of Nathaniel Levi Gaines, Jr.

[178] Telephone interview with Melvin Jones, Fulton County District Attorney's office, April 1, 1996.

[179] Ibid. It is worth noting that the *Atlanta Journal-Constitution* and the internal affairs unit of the Atlanta police force have reported that files regarding police shootings sent to the district attorney's office in recent years have been "lost," which may help explain the lack of action in such cases.

[180] Official Code of Georgia Annotated (O.C.G.A.) Title 17-7-52, which refers to Title 45-11-4, describing special grand jury procedures for public officials.

There is a lack of communication between prosecutors and agencies with information regarding possibly criminal police abuse. Internal affairs units submit cases to prosecutors in an ad hoc, arbitrary manner. When questioned by Human Rights Watch, most internal affairs units' representatives were unable (or unwilling) to provide even an estimate of how many cases they had submitted to local prosecutors involving excessive force by the police department's officers. Some internal affairs staff mistakenly believe that they must decide whether a case could be prosecuted successfully before providing it to local prosecutors instead of submitting any evidence regarding a possibly criminal act, while others simply lack a system for routinely submitting cases that may require criminal prosecution.[181] Internal affairs divisions are often reluctant to push for criminal prosecution of fellow police personnel, while prosecutors rarely insist on learning of all possibly criminal behavior on the part of officers. As a result, prosecutions are often fueled by press attention to particular cases rather than a regular review of cases that may require further action.

Furthermore, district attorneys' offices themselves do not appear to compile information relating to the prosecution of police officers. Human Rights Watch contacted district attorneys' offices for the cities examined in this study, and only Portland and Minneapolis kept a log of criminal cases in which police officers were defendants. None of the others knew, or would disclose, how many police officers had been prosecuted by their offices during the past several years. Each claimed that that information must come from the relevant internal affairs unit. Yet internal affairs units contacted are typically unwilling, to provide this information.

Citizen review agencies, despite receiving hundreds or thousands of complaints about police officers annually – some alleging clearly criminal behavior – have little or no contact with local prosecutors. When interviewed by Human Rights Watch, most representatives of citizen review units claimed their mandates did not include dealing with prosecutors, yet acknowledged nothing precluded them from passing particularly serious allegations to relevant prosecuting agencies. Most assumed that internal affairs units worked closely with prosecutors and would raise any cases of concern. As a rule, citizen review agencies that publish reports do not include any information about the agencies' dealings with prosecutors.

---

[181] The January 1997 report by the Los Angeles Police Commission's Office of the Inspector General report, for example, found that the LAPD's Internal Affairs Division (IAD) was not sending all possibly criminal cases involving police officers to prosecuting agencies, because they claimed prosecutors objected to reviewing anything but "good cases"; the IAD therefore submitted only what it believed to be "good cases" rather than forwarding those with prima facie evidence of criminal wrongdoing. Inspector General's report, p. 45.

It is clear that local prosecutors should prosecute far more cases against criminally abusive police officers. When members of the force are successfully prosecuted, it sends an important signal to fellow officers that there will be serious repercussions for abusing their authority. It also sends a message to internal affairs units that may be lax in dealing with officers who commit abuses to do more to hold officers accountable. Finally, successful prosecution of officers who commit human rights violations, and even clearly vigorous prosecutorial attempts that fail, send a signal to the community that prosecutors are attempting to uphold the law.

Federal Criminal Civil Rights Prosecution
Federal Passivity

When local prosecutors fail to pursue police brutality cases, it is the responsibility of the federal government to prosecute if an individual's civil rights may have been violated. Specifically, the Criminal Section of the Civil Rights Division of the U.S. Justice Department is responsible for prosecuting these cases, using Reconstruction-era (1871) civil rights statutes. The federal criminal civil rights statute, which may be used to prosecute officers accused of excessive force, states:

> Whoever, under color of any law, statute, ordinance, regulation, or custom, willfully subjects any person in any State, Territory, Commonwealth, Possession, or District to the deprivation of any rights, privileges, or immunities secured or protected by the Constitution or laws of the United States...shall be fined under this title or imprisoned not more than one year, or both; and if bodily injury results from the acts committed in violation of this section or if such acts include the use, attempted use, or threatened use of a dangerous weapon, explosives, or fire, shall be fined under this title or imprisoned not more than ten years, or both; and if death results from the acts committed in violation of this section or if such acts include kidnaping or an attempt to kidnap, aggravated sexual abuse, or an attempt to commit aggravated sexual abuse, or an attempt to kill, shall be fined under this title, or imprisoned for any term of years or for life, or both, or may be sentenced to death.[182]

---

[182] 18 U.S.C. §242. Until 1988, an abuse by a federal official acting alone, absent a conspiracy, was only a misdemeanor, no matter how serious the injury to the victim. In 1994's omnibus crime bill, civil rights violations became capital crimes. Human Rights Watch opposes capital punishment in all cases due to its inherent cruelty, its arbitrary and discriminatory application, and its irreversible nature.

A conspiracy charge may also be filed:

> If two or more persons conspire to injure, oppress, threaten, or intimidate
> any person in any State, Territory, Commonwealth, Possession, or District
> in the free exercise or enjoyment of any right or privilege secured to him
> by the Constitution or laws of the United States, or because of his having
> so exercised the same....[T]hey shall be fined under this title or imprisoned
> not more than ten years, or both; and if death results from the acts
> committed in violation of this section or if such acts include kidnaping or
> an attempt to kidnap, aggravated sexual abuse or an attempted to commit
> aggravated sexual abuse, or an attempt to kill, they shall be fined under
> this title or imprisoned for any term of years or for life, or both, or may be
> sentenced to death.[183]

There are many obstacles to successfully prosecuting police officers under the
federal civil rights statutes. Due to inadequate resources and, in some cases, an
apparent lack of will or interest by investigators or prosecutors (in the Civil Rights
Division, or among the ninety-three U.S. Attorney's offices around the country that
work with the Civil Rights Division to prosecute these cases), federal authorities do
not routinely collect and review cases that may be viable for prosecution under
federal civil rights statutes. When they do learn of cases, before or after preliminary
investigation by the Federal Bureau of Investigation (FBI), they choose to pursue
and prosecute less than 1 percent.

The poor performance of federal prosecutors is due, in part, to the difficulties
in prosecuting police officers generally (such as typically unsympathetic victims,
witnesses who are not credible, the public's predisposition to believe police
officers) and by the added requirement, as interpreted by the courts, that prosecutors
prove the accused officer's "specific intent" to deprive an individual of his or her
civil rights.[184] As a result of the "specific intent" requirement and other stringent
standards, federal prosecutors – who like their local counterparts are interested in
winning cases, not merely trying them – may be less than eager to pursue cases

---

[183] 18 U.S.C. §241. The 1994 omnibus crime bill made conspiracy charges a capital
offense.

[184] In *Screws v. United States,* the Supreme Court held that a conviction under 18
U.S.C. §242 required proof of the defendant's specific intent to deprive the victim of a
constitutional right. *Screws v. United States*, 325 U.S. 91 (1945). In *United States v. Guest*,
the Supreme Court read this same requirement into §241, the conspiracy statute. *United
States v. Guest*, 383 U.S. 745 (1966).

against police officers. Human Rights Watch believes that it should be sufficient for federal criminal prosecution that a police officer intentionally and unjustifiably beat or killed a victim without the additional burden of having a specific intent to violate the victim's civil rights.

During 1991 Congressional hearings, John R. Dunne, assistant attorney general for the Civil Rights Division, described his office's view of its responsibilities in prosecuting officers: "We are not the front line troops in combating instances of police abuse. That role properly lies with the internal affairs bureaus of law enforcement agencies and with state and local prosecutors. The federal government program is more of a backstop, if you will, to these other resources."[185] In response to this description of the federal role, police abuse expert Paul Hoffman noted, "This philosophy might be sensible if the Justice Department took its backstop role seriously and devoted the resources and attention necessary to make the federal government the guarantor of constitutional rights in situations where local institutions are incapable of playing this role. Instead, this philosophy is too often a convenient excuse for federal inaction."[186]

In large part due to lack of funding and staffing at the Criminal Section of the Civil Rights Division, which reflects the government's overall lack of commitment to prosecuting these types of cases, little has changed since Assistant Attorney General Dunne testified in 1991 about the Civil Rights Division's understanding of its "backstop" role. The current chief of the Criminal Section of the Civil Rights Division told Human Rights Watch, "The federal government is not here to stand in the way of good faith and vigorous [local] efforts" but left unanswered how the division proceeds when local efforts, and its own resources, are lacking.[187]

In the cities examined by Human Rights Watch, most community activists, citizen review agency staff, and internal affairs representatives had no idea how many cases federal prosecutors had prosecuted in their cities, if any. There was little outreach by the Justice Department to educate citizens and officials about its mandate and interest in prosecuting abuse cases, and there was little contact between internal affairs units and local U.S. Attorney's offices or the Justice

---

[185] Statement of John R. Dunne, Subcommittee on Civil and Constitutional Rights, House of Representatives, Washington, D.C., March 20, 1991.

[186] Paul Hoffman, "The Feds, Lies, and Videotape: The Need for an Effective Federal Role in Controlling Police Abuse in Urban America," *Southern California Law Review*, vol. 66, number 4, May 1993.

[187] Telephone interview, Richard Roberts, Criminal Section, Civil Rights Division, Department of Justice, November 17, 1997.

Department; internal affairs unit representatives generally did not believe it to be their responsibility to pass on cases for possible prosecution to federal authorities.[188] Citizen review agencies, likewise, had little knowledge of federal prosecutors' actions and rarely passed them appropriate cases.

Informally, some representatives of U.S. Attorney's offices did speak with Human Rights Watch and acknowledged that many of the decisions regarding which cases to pursue were fueled by media attention and that the receipt of cases for possible prosecution was ad hoc. Community activists and local attorneys who represent individuals in police abuse cases have often submitted cases to local U.S. Attorney's offices or the Justice Department. Of those we interviewed, most who attempted to bring such cases to the Justice Department's attention received no response, and none was certain if an investigation had been initiated as a result of information they provided, even in cases where the information was specifically requested by the Justice Department.

Low Rate of Federal Prosecutions

As the charts below show, even when a complaint does make its way to the Civil Rights Division, it is unlikely to lead to a conviction. While many of the complaints received by the Justice Department may be unfounded or weak, and do not merit prosecution, the fact that so few cases make their way through the review process is cause for concern.

Table 1.

CIVIL RIGHTS DIVISION PERFORMANCE MEASUREMENT – COMPLAINTS RECEIVED			
Number of Complaints	**1994**	**1995**	**1996**
From Citizens	5,312	6,083	8,538
From the FBI	3,030	2,781	3,183
Total	8,342	8,864	11,721

---

[188] As described above, some statements given by officers to internal affairs investigators may not be shared with prosecutors.

According to the Civil Rights Division[189]

Table 2.

FY 1996 CIVIL RIGHTS DIVISION PERFORMANCE MEASUREMENT	
Complaints Received	11,721 (up from 8,864 in FY95)
Complaints Reviewed (includes cases reviewed during FY96, but not necessarily received in FY96)	10,129
Number of Matters Investigated (FBI-initiated or sent to FBI by Civil Rights Division for investigation)	2,619
Number of New Matters Sent to Grand Jury (Grand Jury investigations initiated during FY96, not necessarily from FY96 complaints received)	70
Number of all Civil Rights Cases Filed (may include non-felonies not requiring Grand Jury approval)	79
Number of Cases Filed as Official Misconduct (including police abuse)	22 (down from 34 in FY94)

Of the 10,129 civil rights cases reviewed in FY1996(which included official misconduct complaints), just over .2 percent resulted in official misconduct cases filed for prosecution. If compared to the number of all civil rights matters fully

---

[189] Justice Department, "Performance Measurement Table: Presented by Decision Unit," undated but provided to Human Rights Watch on April 25, 1997. FBI totals include less serious complaints, but the majority are brutality complaints that become "matters investigated," meaning that they are assigned to an attorney.

investigated – by the FBI initially or after being referred to the FBI by the Civil Rights Division – the prosecution rate for official misconduct cases (including police abuse) is still less than 1 percent of cases investigated.

In explaining the low rate of prosecution, Richard Roberts, chief of the Criminal Section of the Civil Rights Division, told Human Rights Watch that federal civil rights prosecutions are difficult due to the requirement of proof of the accused officer's "specific intent" to deprive an individual of his or her civil rights as distinguished, for example, from an intent simply to assault an individual. When asked whether the intent provision of the statute creates too rigorous a standard to provide the civil rights protections intended or needed, Roberts contended that while the cases are difficult, his office is able to pursue them and does not advocate revising the civil rights statutes.

There is nearly a 100 percent success rate for cases other than those involving official misconduct that are fully prosecuted by the Civil Rights Division: hate crimes, cases brought under the Freedom of Access to [Abortion] Clinic Entrances laws, involuntary servitude, and beginning in 1996, church arson/desecration. By contrast, in official misconduct cases, including cases involving police officers, the conviction rate was much lower, only 78 percent in Fiscal Year (FY) 1994 and FY 1995 and declining to 64 percent in FY 1996.[190] Official misconduct prosecutions, including of police officers, went down as hate crime prosecutions went up, which may indicate a staffing shortage within the division as priorities changed.[191]

Not only are police misconduct cases prosecuted at the lowest rate among civil rights prosecutions, but civil rights offenses themselves are prosecuted less than any other category of offense handled by the U.S. Justice Department. For example, official corruption cases, which involve similar obstacles for investigators and prosecutors, were prosecuted at ten times the rate of civil rights cases in 1996.[192] Justice Department officials have explained the low rate of prosecution for civil rights cases by stating that they are interested in encouraging local authorities to

---

[190] Percentages determined by comparing matters presented to grand juries to convictions.

[191] In November 1997, President Clinton announced that the Civil Rights Division would bolster its efforts to address an increase in hate crimes, and that fifty FBI agents would be assigned to investigating such crimes.

[192] Update provided by David Burnham based on data provided by the Justice Department. In 1992, official corruption was prosecuted at nine times the rate of civil rights cases, David Burnham, *Above the Law*, (New York: Scribner Books, 1996), p. 264.

deal with civil rights violations in their communities, without explaining why the same could not be said regarding corruption.

In its explanation of resource distribution, the Civil Rights Division notes the inexperience of its staff, stating: "In addition, the current level of lawyers with little criminal experience has limited our ability to assign these attorneys to work independently on grand jury investigations."[193] It is unclear why attorneys without appropriate experience are being assigned to the Civil Rights Division. The division also explains that high-profile, complex cases overwhelm the resources of the division, with a few cases consuming the time of many of the experienced attorneys.

There is good reason to question whether staffing levels are sufficient at the Civil Rights Division. The Department of Justice had 108,700 employees as of March 1997; of these, 9,168 were attorneys.[194] According to the Civil Rights Division, as of April 1998, there were only thirty-two full-time attorneys in the Criminal Section of the Civil Rights Division, the office responsible for prosecuting police abuse and other official misconduct cases.[195] Moreover, as local (and all) law enforcement agencies grow dramatically, the number of Civil Rights Division attorneys available to prosecute cases of civil rights violations has remained steady or dropped.[196] In 1993, there were 665,803 sworn officers serving full- and part-time in 17,120 city, county, and state law enforcement agencies, and an additional 68,825 sworn federal law enforcement agents, for a total of 734,628.[197] Those numbers have certainly increased in the meantime, but even at that level, there would be one federal civil rights prosecutor for every 22,950 law enforcement

---

[193] Justice Department, "Performance Measurement Table...," received April 25, 1997.

[194] According to the most recent Legal Activities Book, released in March 1997 and available at http://www.usdoj.gov/careers/oapm/lab.

[195] Information provided by the Justice Department's personnel office, April 27, 1998.

[196] According to Skolnick and Fyfe, *Above the Law*, there were forty-four Criminal Section attorneys in 1993, and in November 1997, Human Rights Watch was told that there were thirty-three attorneys in the section. The discrepancy may stem from including as attorneys those who serve as managers.

[197] Bureau of Justice Statistics, *Sourcebook of Criminal Justice Statistics 1995*, citing the last census figures available for law enforcement agencies.

officers.[198]   Although the Civil Rights Division should insist on attaining a reasonable ratio between the number of prosecutors and law enforcement officers, the White House and Congress are equally responsible for allowing civil rights concerns to be pushed aside while supporting massive expansion of law enforcement personnel.   Clearly, civil rights crimes are a part of the law enforcement challenge that has been neglected.

Prosecutors rely on the Federal Bureau of Investigation (FBI) to conduct inquiries into allegations of criminal civil rights violations. Unfortunately, the typical FBI investigation of police abuse complaints may be limited to information provided by the local law enforcement agency itself – information that is routinely inadequate or biased, as described above. Furthermore, Justice Department rules require that a preliminary FBI report be made within twenty-one days, a requirement that virtually eliminates the possibility of a thorough investigation. The preliminary FBI report can be supplemented, but an investigative policy that does not involve monitoring subsequent civil proceedings or disciplinary actions will tend to place undue weight on initial, official explanations of the incidents involved.[199]   The FBI reportedly has no decision-making authority regarding whether to initiate a full investigation; that decision is left entirely to the Civil Rights Division.[200]

New Data on Federal Prosecutions and Sentencing

To obtain more detailed information regarding prosecution under federal criminal civil rights statutes, Human Rights Watch worked with the Transactional Records Access Clearinghouse (TRAC), a private data collection and analysis agency that has collected Justice Department records through the Freedom of Information Act. To our knowledge, these data have not been made public prior to

---

[198] In addition, assistant U.S. Attorneys around the country also play a role in federal civil rights prosecutions.

[199] Hoffman, "The Feds, Lies, and Videotape," *Southern California Law Review*.

[200] Telephone interview with Tron Brekke, chief of the Civil Rights Section, F.B.I., August 26, 1997.

this report's publication.[201] Tables of the TRAC analysis are in Appendices A through C, and some material appears below and in individual city chapters.

The TRAC data show exactly how rare it is for police officers to be federally prosecuted for civil rights violations, district-by-district. They also show that, despite applying the same law for the same type of offense, each district varies dramatically in the number of complaints referred for prosecution and the number pursued. Finally, the TRAC data show that the officers who are occasionally prosecuted successfully – presumably for the most serious crimes and with the strongest evidence – do not generally receive long sentences.

The Civil Rights Division does not compile information broken down by federal district, but the Justice Department's Executive Office of United States Attorneys (EOUSA) does.[202] Unfortunately, the EOUSA said its data are not broken down so that cases involving law enforcement agents can be examined separately.[203] The office, therefore, said it could not provide the information requested by Human Rights Watch regarding the number of referrals for federal criminal civil rights prosecutions of law enforcement agents acting under color of law for the fourteen U.S. districts examined in this study.[204] The EOUSA wrote: "In response to your Freedom of Information Act and/or Privacy Act request, a search for records located in this office has revealed no record for the information you seek. We have been advised by our Case Management staff that our computer system cannot identify defendants who are law enforcement agents."[205] In other words, both offices are maintaining somewhat similar, yet incomplete, data: by

---

[201] None of the information compiled by TRAC and cited below and in the appendices was easily available to the public. TRAC tirelessly pursues Freedom of Information Act requests and received these data in a form that required special data entry and analytical skills to be understood by the lay reader. A summary of these data is provided below, with fuller charts describing the data can be found in Appendices A through C.

[202] The Civil Rights Division does compile summaries of cases it has prosecuted in a given fiscal year, and that information contains federal district information, but no tally is kept and made public, and its summaries do not include the number of referrals by district.

[203] When Human Rights Watch submitted basic questions to the fourteen U.S. Attorney's offices relevant to this study, the two offices that responded directed us to the Executive Office for U.S. Attorneys at the Justice Department.

[204] 18 U.S.C. §§241 and 242

[205] Letter from Bonnie L. Gay, Acting Assistant Director, Executive Office for U.S. Attorneys to Human Rights Watch, May 16, 1997.

failing to monitor criminal prosecutions of law enforcement personnel in their respective federal districts, these offices cloud assessment of the adequacies of their own law enforcement efforts.

To add to the difficulty in analyzing the data compiled by the Justice Department, a third agency – the FBI's civil rights section, which is responsible for investigating possible federal criminal civil rights violations – compiles its own statistics that do not match those compiled by either the Civil Rights Division or the EOUSA at the Justice Department. For example, in Fiscal Year 1996, the FBI reports initiating 3,700 civil rights investigations (with approximately 70 percent, or 2,590, related to law enforcement officers).[206] Yet the chart provided by the Civil Rights Division of the Justice Department states that the FBI initiated 2,619 civil rights investigations, without a breakdown provided for law enforcement. Neither the FBI nor the Civil Rights Division could provide a reason for this discrepancy. Said the FBI representative, "[Y]ou'd think we'd all be counting from the same page."[207] The FBI notes that it initiates its own preliminary investigations in the vast majority of cases, meaning that cases passed from Justice Department headquarters are not necessarily acted upon because the FBI typically will have already started investigating the complaint. The FBI's local field offices receive complaints from the public, and learn about high-profile cases from local newspapers.

According to the data provided by the EOUSA and analyzed by TRAC, prosecution rates differ greatly among the ninety-four different federal districts in the nation. TRAC collected and analyzed data on prosecution rates for federal criminal civil rights violations under 18 U.S. Code, sections 241 and 242 between 1992 and 1995.[208] Of the districts including the cities examined in this report, the federal district of Georgia North (including Atlanta) decided on how to proceed with 133 cases during this four-year period, and prosecuted none. Rhode Island (including Providence) decided on 164 and prosecuted three. California North (including San Francisco) decided on 342 and prosecuted two. And Louisiana East (including New Orleans) decided on 819 cases and prosecuted just nine.

---

[206] Telephone interview with Tron Brekke, chief of the Civil Rights Section, F.B.I., August 26, 1997.

[207] Telephone interview with Tron Brekke, chief of the Civil Rights Section, F.B.I., September 3, 1997.

[208] Those prosecuted under this statute include all types of law enforcement officers (city, state or federal law enforcement officers, sheriffs' deputies, correctional officers), magistrates and judges.

Prosecution efforts were much more likely in California Central (including Los Angeles), where of thirty-nine cases considered, twelve were prosecuted, and in Pennsylvania East (including Philadelphia), where of fifty cases considered, thirty were prosecuted.[209] Although these numbers represent just a piece of the picture, they show wide variation district by district regarding the percentage of cases prosecuted by the relevant U.S. attorney (in consultation with the Civil Rights Division).

Except in rare instances, such as the Rodney King beating in Los Angeles, federal prosecutors do not pursue cases in which local prosecutors attempt but fail to indict or convict. In deciding whether to proceed with a case in which local prosecutors have failed to obtain a conviction, federal prosecutors consider whether the original trial was affected by prosecutorial incompetence, corruption, or jury tampering, whether they can introduce crucial evidence not allowed in state proceedings, or whether there is a compelling federal interest to prosecute. In practice, following a high-profile failure to indict or convict, federal prosecutors generally report that they are "reviewing" the case, but that is often the last the public hears about federal action.

In the vast majority of cases, the Civil Rights Division "declines" prosecution for a variety of reasons. According to TRAC analysis of fiscal years 1994 and 1995, the most common reasons for declining prosecution were: weak or insufficient admissible evidence (this was the most common reason for both years); lack of evidence of criminal intent; declined per instructions from the Justice Department; staleness; prosecution by other authorities anticipated; statute of limitations; and lack of investigative or prosecutorial resources.[210]

Even in the rare cases in which police officers and others are convicted on federal criminal civil rights charges, they spend little or no time incarcerated.[211] In 1994 and 1995, twenty-five defendants, out of ninety-six convicted, were sentenced to three months or less in prison (including serving no time at all). Forty-eight, or half, were sentenced to twelve months or less. These data are not linked to specific cases, making it difficult to assess whether the sentences were adequate, yet given

---

[209] *See* Appendix A.

[210] *See* Appendix B for complete listing of justifications provided for declinations.

[211] *See* Appendix C.

the serious nature of the civil rights crimes prosecuted by the Justice Department, the sentences do appear to be lenient.[212]

The Civil Rights Division of the Justice Department provides these statistics on its activities.

---

[212] Under 18 U.S.C. §§241 and 242, ten years in prison and a fine are the maximum penalties when bodily injury is inflicted. When death results, the convicted officer (or other individual who commits an offense "under color of any law") shall be subject to imprisonment for any term of years or for life. It appears no life sentences were given during 1994 and 1995.

Table 3a.[213]

SUMMARY OF CRIMINAL SECTION ACTIVITIES UNDER THE BUSH ADMINISTRATION – FISCAL YEARS 1989 - 1992								
Fiscal Year	1989		1990		1991		1992	
Numbers of:	Total	LE	Total	LE	Total	LE	Total	LE
Complaints	8053		7960		9835		8599	
FBI Investigations	3177		3050		3583		3212	
New Grand Juries	40	25	47	25	63	41	74	46
Indictments	26		30		44	26	38	21
Informations	34		36		25	10	26	6
TOTAL Cases Filed	**60**	**18**	**66**	**23**	**69**	**36**	**64**	**27**
Defendants	**85**	**22**	**101**	**37**	**137**	**67**	**112**	**59**
Convictions	23	20	17	5	36	26	16	6
Pleas	68	13	51	9	73	24	80	22
Acquittals	10	10	3	3	13	12	17	17

---

[213] LE refers to Law enforcement officers. Without LE information for the number of complaints or investigations, LE breakdown on grand jury presentations is useless. Indictments are brought by grand juries, while "informations" come from magistrates.

Table 3b.

SUMMARY OF CRIMINAL SECTION ACTIVITIES UNDER THE FIRST CLINTON ADMINISTRATION – FISCAL YEARS 1993 - 1996								
Fiscal Year	1993		1994		1995		1996	
Numbers of:	Total	LE	Total	LE	Total	LE	Total	LE
Complaints	9620		8342		8864		11721	
FBI Investigations	3026		2633		2310		2619	
New Grand Juries	51	30	64	34	68	38	70	37
Indictments	34	18	40	18	46	17	50	13
Informations	25	10	36	16	37	10	29	4
TOTAL Cases Filed	**59**	**28**	**76**	**34**	**83**	**27**	**79**	**22**
Defendants	**97**	**50**	**139**	**46**	**138**	**50**	**128**	**33**
Convictions	36	16	22	12	32	6	22	10
Pleas	45	21	81	25	75	23	85	19
Acquittals	29	26	11	10	13	8	14	14

In fiscal year 1997, the Civil Rights Division received a total of 10,891 complaints, with thirty-one grand juries and magistrates to consider law enforcement officers leading to twenty-five indictments and informations, involving sixty-seven law enforcement agents; nine were convicted, nineteen entered guilty pleas, and four were acquitted. It appeared that more law enforcement defendants were prosecuted per case in the same number of total cases, on average, than in previous years.

These data are of interest for several reasons. First, they show that, despite rhetoric to the contrary, the Clinton administration has neither dedicated significantly greater resources nor had much more success than previous administrations in, prosecuting law enforcement officers for civil rights violations. Between fiscal years 1993 and 1996 (four years), there were forty-four law enforcement officers convicted after trial on civil rights charges, and eighty-eight plea bargains, for a total of 132 convictions.[214] Between fiscal years 1989 and 1992 (four years primarily under President Bush's administration), there were fifty-seven convictions after trial of law enforcement officers, and sixty-eight plea bargains, for a total of 125 convictions. There does not appear to be a great difference in the outcome in these cases from one administration to the next.

Second, these data show a dramatic rise in the number of citizen complaints received by the Justice Department between fiscal years 1995 and 1996, from 8,864 to 11,721. The 1996 figure is the highest number at least since 1981 (the first year for which data were made publicly available). Unfortunately, the Civil Rights Division's data do not distinguish between types of civil rights complaints, meaning that no explanation or analysis of the 25 percent increase in complaints is possible. If police abuse complaints make up a large percentage of this jump, it may indicate an increase in abusiveness, an increase in community awareness about the Justice Department's role in handling these complaints leading to more complaints being filed, or an increase due to the large influx of new officers on the streets.

Third, the data show law enforcement officers make up almost all of the acquittals in cases prosecuted by the Civil Rights Division, yet constitute only half of the indictments in civil rights cases. These data demonstrate juries' general unwillingness to hold police officers responsible for criminal acts.

Federal Civil Actions

The Violent Crime Control and Law Enforcement Act of 1994 included a new statute under which the Justice Department may sue for declaratory relief (a statement of the governing law) and equitable relief (an order to abide by the law with specific instructions describing actions that must be taken) if any governmental authority or person acting on behalf of any governmental authority engages in: "a pattern or practice of conduct by law enforcement officers...that deprives persons of rights, privileges, or immunities secured or protected by the Constitution or laws of the United States."[215] Police abuse experts had long recommended giving federal authorities the power to bring a civil action against any police department engaging in a pattern or practice of misconduct to enjoin, or direct the police department to end, abusive practices.

In April 1997, the Special Litigation Section of the Civil Rights Division, which is responsible for actions under the new law, reached its first consent decree

---

[214] A plea bargain usually involves the accused and prosecutor agreeing, with court approval, to a guilty plea by the defendant on a lesser offense.

[215] "Police Pattern or Practice" 42 U.S.C. §14141

with a police department, that of Pittsburgh, Pennsylvania.[216] In the consent decree, the city denies "any and all allegations" regarding inadequate training, misconduct investigation, supervision, and discipline, yet agrees to: establish a comprehensive early warning system; develop and implement a use-of-force policy that is in compliance with applicable law and current professional standards; require officers to file appropriate use of force and other reports; conduct regular audits and reviews of potential racial bias, including the use of racial epithets by officers; improve investigative practices when an officer has allegedly engaged in misconduct; apply appropriate discipline following sustained complaints; and appoint an independent auditor to ensure compliance with the consent decree. At the time of this writing, a dispute over the scope of the early warning system was ongoing between the department's police union and the city.[217]

In August 1997, a second consent degree was reached with a police department under the "pattern or practice" provision, with the city of Steubenville, Ohio and its police force.[218] In its complaint, the Justice Department alleges the city and the police department have engaged in a pattern or practice of subjecting individuals to excessive force, false arrests, charges, and reports, improper stops, searches, and seizures.[219] The complaint states that Steubenville officials have caused and condoned this conduct through their inadequate use-of-force policies; inappropriate off-duty-conduct policies; and failure to supervise, train, discipline, monitor and investigate police officers and alleged misconduct. Among the offenses, Steubenville police officers allegedly used excessive force against individuals who witnessed incidents of police misconduct, who were known critics of the department or were disliked by individual officers, and who were falsely arrested or charged

---

[216] A judgment entered by consent of the parties whereby the defendant agrees to stop alleged illegal activity without admitting guilt or wrongdoing to force reforms in Pittsburgh's police force. *United States of America v. City of Pittsburgh, Pittsburgh Bureau of Police, and Department of Public Safety*, U.S. District Court for the Western District of Pennsylvania, Civil No. 97-0354, April 16, 1997.

[217] Kris B. Mamula, "City files civil action over police records system dispute," *Tribune Review*, Greensburg, PA, February 20, 1998.

[218] The court approved the consent decree on September 3, 1997.

[219] *United States of America v. City of Steubenville, Steubenville Police Department, Steubenville City Manager, in his capacity as director of Public Safety, and Steubenville Civil Service Commission*, Civil No. C2 97-966, U.S. District Court for the Southern District of Ohio, Eastern Division, August 28, 1997.

persons believed likely to complain of abuse. Further, officers allegedly falsified reports and tampered with official police recorders so that misconduct would not be recorded.

The city agreed to improve training, implement use-of-force guidelines and reporting procedures, create an internal affairs unit, and establish an early warning system to track use-of-force reports, civilian complaints and civil lawsuits to identify officers requiring increased training or supervision.

The Justice Department is reportedly investigating or monitoring at least three other police departments – Los Angeles, New Orleans, and Philadelphia – to decide whether to seek judicial orders on respect for governing law. And in August 1997, Zachary Carter, U.S. attorney for the Eastern District of New York, announced that a preliminary "pattern or practice" investigation of the NYPD would be initiated.[220] According to the Justice Department's Special Litigation Section, there are other police forces under scrutiny, but neither the Justice Department nor any monitored force has chosen to disclose information.[221] Under the statute, there is no public reporting requirement, leaving the public with little knowledge of an inquiry. And even when a consent decree is reached, there is little effort by the Justice Department to publicize its actions.

Under the new law, the Justice Department is also able to investigate and enjoin abusive behavior in particular precincts or districts within a given police department. In many of the largest cities' citizen review agency and internal affairs reports, detailed statistical analysis is provided, broken down by district or precinct. Federal investigators should fully utilize the information of this kind that is available in many cities, but it appears they do not.[222]

---

[220] Blaine Harden, "Civil rights investigation targets N.Y. Police," *Washington Post*, August 19, 1997.

[221] Telephone interview with Steven Rosenbaum, Chief, Special Litigation Section, Civil Rights Division, June 9, 1997. When the NYPD investigation was announced, Philadelphia was listed as a city that had been investigated under the new "pattern or practice" statute, yet that investigation was not mentioned by Justice Department officials interviewed by Human Rights Watch.

[222] Ibid. According to Rosenbaum, these reports were not reviewed to ascertain whether certain precincts or districts deserved special attention. Rosenbaum did note that information gathered by the FBI when it investigates a possibly criminal act under Sections 241 and 242 can be used by the Special Litigation Section, with special rules to protect secrecy provisions of grand jury proceedings, where relevant. When asked whether there are any set guidelines for pattern-or-practice investigations, Human Rights Watch was told that each investigation, and subject of investigation, is different, so guidelines are not used.

Federal Data Collection

It is self-evident that the Justice Department needs a more coherent and accessible approach to the collection and analysis of police abuse data. Without essential information about the problem of police brutality, the department cannot act effectively to combat it. Data collection on police abuse is particularly important because the lack of national data has served to perpetuate a situation in which local and national officials can claim that there is neither a continuing nor a nationwide problem; it also makes it more difficult to identify which police departments are most abusive. Moreover, the lack of information supports the federal position that the problem is "local," because the national government has no useful knowledge about it. And knowledge about the problem on a national scale is, of course, essential to the formulation of policy.[223]

In 1991, in response to the uproar over the King beating in Los Angeles, the Justice Department compiled a report on "official misconduct" complaints between 1985 and 1990, with the purpose of determining "to what extent, if any, a pattern of police brutality by employees of law enforcement agencies is shown from the data maintained by the Civil Rights Division."[224] The report acknowledged that, because there is no agency that collects data on police brutality nationwide, the computer data on official misconduct complaints received by the Civil Rights Division were used, and these were severely limited because:

- the number of complaints reflected only complaints reported directly to the Justice Department and did not purport to capture all, or even most, instances where official misconduct had occurred;

- the data base from which numbers were derived did not indicate the nature and/or severity of the alleged official misconduct;

- the information entered was not always sufficiently exact for purposes of the study; one reported complaint may in fact involve multiple incidents, multiple victims and/or multiple law enforcement officers and agencies; and,

---

[223] *See* Human Rights Watch position paper, "Police brutality in the United States," July 1991, p. 8.

[224] Criminal Section, Civil Rights Division, Department of Justice, "Police Brutality Study: FY 1985 - FY 1990," April 1991, p. 1.

- complaints were dated by their time of receipt by the Civil Rights Division only, and complaints were allegations, while no record was kept on the relative merits of complaints.[225]

The Justice Department report summarily concluded, "We respectfully submit that no pattern emerges from these figures."[226]

At the time the 1991 report was announced, police abuse experts scoffed at plans for producing it because, they contended, it required a sophisticated complainant to seek redress from the federal government. The number of complaints received at the federal level was, and remains, so insignificant that there was little reason to suppose that the number and type of complaints would reflect the severity of problems in communities around the country. At the time the study was announced, a newspaper reported, "[T]he justice department move was a finely calculated attempt to deal with the anger of lawmakers, civil rights groups and others over the L.A. [King] case while not offending police officers and their advocates."[227] Others asserted that if the Justice Department really wanted to know which cities had serious abuse problems, it could simply have asked attorneys and activists working on the issue.

In addition to the acknowledged shortcomings of the data maintained by the Civil Rights Division – and of the Executive Office of U.S. Attorneys' own, incompatible but somewhat parallel database, described above – critics of the report found its analysis to be flawed. In their study of police abuse, *Above the Law*, the authors pointed out, for example, that the Justice Department found no nexus between the number of complaints received by a police department and three key variables: the number of arrests, the number of sworn officers, and the size of service population. The Justice Department's conclusion that no pattern had emerged appeared to be misleading: As observed in *Above the Law*: "In the gentlest possible terms this is a *non sequitur* of such obvious dimensions that it can only reflect conscious avoidance of the facts."[228]

Finally, in 1994, Congress required that the Justice Department collect those data on police abuse that had clearly been lacking. The Violent Crime Control and

---

[225] Ibid., pp. 1 and 2.

[226] Department of Justice, "Police Brutality Study," p. 37.

[227] Human Rights Watch, "Police brutality in the United States," July 1991, p. 8, citing "National review of claims of police brutality," *San Francisco Chronicle*, March 15, 1991.

[228] Skolnick and Fyfe, *Above the Law,* p. 213.

Law Enforcement Act of 1994 requires the attorney general of the United States to collect data on excessive force by police and to publish an annual report from those data.[229] Nearly four years later, the Justice Department is still wrestling with this task, and no annual report has been produced. In April 1996, the Bureau of Justice Statistics (BJS) and the National Institute of Justice (NIJ), both of the Justice Department, published a status report on their efforts to fulfill the requirements of the law.[230] And in November 1997, the BJS released a second "preliminary" report about its efforts, titled, "Police Use of Force: Collection of National Data."[231]

The 1997 report described the findings of a 1996 pilot survey of 6,421 residents, which was intended to guide future development of a questionnaire on this topic. The survey attempted to ascertain from respondents the types of encounters with the police they had experienced during the previous year – both favorable and unfavorable. Its sample contained residents whose sole encounters with police had been at their own initiative, as in asking directions or complaining about a noisy neighbor along with those who had been the object of police action; and in the unfavorable category, its polling concerning individual perceptions of treatment by the police was not geared to distinguishing the legitimate use of force as an aspect of law enforcement from the excessive use of force. The findings were accordingly of little or no relevance to the congressionally mandated task at hand.[232]

The survey's limited pool makes analysis difficult, but it does appear to indicate that police officers generally do not use or threaten to use force against most residents – a point that was not contested by those concerned about the use of excessive force. What the survey fails to show is any type of trend regarding: situations commonly leading to the use of excessive force, police departments that appear to use force more frequently than others in similar situations, or what type of investigation or finding followed the reported abuse. Instead, a great deal of the report describes findings from the survey that are entirely unrelated to incidents

---

[229] Sec. 210402, "Violent Crime Control and Law Enforcement Act of 1994," PL 103-322, 42 U.S.C. §14142.

[230] Bureau of Justice Statistics and National Institute of Justice, "National Data Collection on Police Use of Force," (NCJ-160113) April 1996.

[231] BJS and National Institute of Justice, "Police Use of Force: Collection of National Data,"U.S. Department of Justice, NCJ-165040, November 1997.

[232] It should be noted that this type of household survey does not, by definition, include individuals who are homeless, institutionalized, or incarcerated – groups likely to have had negative encounters with police officers, including the use of excessive force.

involving the excessive use of force by police officers, and instead describe situations in which residents request assistance from the police.[233]

The November 1997 BJS report also included a summary regarding the second half of its efforts to collect information on use of force (there was no mention of use of *excessive* force, as mandated by Congress). To this end, the BJS and NIJ had funded a project by the International Association of Chiefs of Police (IACP), which in turn was working with the State Associations of Chiefs of Police, to develop a uniform set of data on use-of-force incidents, as reported by police officers themselves. Having left the reporting on themselves to the police, the federal government received predictably partial and inconclusive responses. The report stated that nearly 400, out of more than 13,000 city, county, and state police agencies, "indicated an interest" in the project, but it appeared far fewer than 400 agencies were actually providing any information.[234] Under the "procedures to protect agency identification," the report explained that these data, as provided to the Justice Department, did not include the name and location of each participating agency, making its stated goal of "comparable statistics on the use of force" impossible.[235]

As this report is completed, a preliminary summary of the IACP's use-of-force project has recently been made available. Time does not permit a thorough analysis of the summary, but the report notes that information was collected on a voluntary and anonymous basis from a small percentage of police agencies and that the

---

[233] The report contains appendices, but only one table out of six addresses the questions relating to the use of force; one appendix is dedicated to sample answers from respondents, all of which are unrelated to use-of-force incidents and answers to those questions. For example, a sample survey form shows that individuals who alleged use of force were also asked whether they attempted to file a complaint or lawsuit about the incident, but no information is provided regarding actions taken, or not taken, by individuals alleging threats, or use, of force by officers.

[234] The May 1998 preliminary summary of the IACP's use-of-force project states that, at most, 110 agencies reported in any given year since 1994.

[235] The report also stated that, among the Justice Department's goals, is "learning from police what kinds of information they maintain on their contacts with the public." So far, whatever the BJS has learned about police departments' record-keeping on incidents of excessive force has not been made public.

information was not nationally representative.[236] The summary states that one of "the most striking results" of the project has been the scarcity of force-related complaints against officers (as reported by the agencies) when force has been used. During 1996 and 1997, the summary found that there were 3,972 incidents of the use of force, with twenty complaints – one complaint was sustained.

In sum, the preliminary reports have avoided the crucial question that Congress asked the Justice Department to answer. We call on the Justice Department to refocus its efforts, reallocate its research grants, and produce a report responsive to its mandate on this issue. Without the information requested by Congress, and more, it is extremely difficult, if not impossible, for governments and police departments to craft enlightened policies that balance the importance of public order with the absolute requirement that the state protect anyone in its jurisdiction from human rights abuses at the hands of police officers.

According to the reports, inadequate funding had been provided for the data collection project (the police-public contact survey or use-of-force database). The BJS and NIJ fund the IACP's use-of-force database project, and the IACP had not requested funding for 1998. The November 1997 report stated, "[I]t is unclear whether the pilot efforts can be continued;" funding has been requested by the Justice Department for the pilot survey and use-of-force database, but none has been provided during the past three years. It is possible that, without funding, the last three years of pilot surveys and conferences about how to conduct this research will lead to no progress in gathering basic and essential information about the use of excessive force. And, if funding is made available, the continued reliance on random sampling that provides little information about excessive force incidents and counts on police officers voluntarily to report relevant incidents will lend little insight into this issue. A less superficial approach is required. Random surveys alone – such as the one initiated – tell the public very little about the extent of this problem, or the ways individuals who feel that they have been abused are able to seek accountability for violations by officers. Community activists, civilian and citizen review agencies, civil lawsuits filed against the police, and specialized reports on police abuse (such as past reports by special commissions) should be utilized. Furthermore, continued reliance on voluntary reporting should be replaced with a federal requirement that police departments receiving federal grants provide data on the use of excessive force. *(See* Recommendations.)

---

[236] The summary states that anonymity and volunteerism were necessary to "bridge the natural reluctance of the contributor and inspire the accuracy of the contribution." The summary also states that police agencies would have feared providing raw data that could be used to support a pattern or practice investigation by the Justice Department, even though that use of the data is prohibited.

The Law
International Human Rights Standards

In addition to violating state and federal law, the use of excessive force also violates international human rights law as set out in treaties to which the U.S. is a party.[237] International human rights law reinforces the U.S. civil rights standard but also goes beyond it. In recent years, the United States has ratified three major human rights treaties, which once ratified are binding on the government as laws of the land. While the executive and legislative branches of the federal government are responsible for the submission and ratification of the treaties, once ratified the treaties are binding on all levels of government, federal, state, or municipal. It is the duty of all relevant officials to uphold the treaties' obligations.

Police abuse, including the excessive use of force by police officers, is explicitly prohibited by two major international human rights treaties to which the U.S. is party.[238] In 1992, the United States ratified the International Covenant on Civil and Political Rights (ICCPR). The ICCPR states: "[E]ach State Party to the present Covenant undertakes to respect and to ensure to all individuals within its territory and subject to its jurisdiction the rights recognized in the present Covenant, without distinction of any kind, such as race, colour, sex, language, religion, political, or other opinion, national or social origin, property, birth or other status."[239] Article 6 of the ICCPR states: "Every human being has the inherent right to life. This right shall be protected by law. No one shall be arbitrarily deprived of his life."[240] Article 7 states: "No one shall be subjected to torture or to cruel, inhuman or degrading treatment or punishment...." Article 10 requires that all persons "deprived of their liberty should be treated with humanity and with respect

---

[237] "Excessive force" is force that exceeds what is objectively reasonable and necessary in the circumstances confronting the officer, as in Article 3 of the U.N. Code of Conduct for Law Enforcement Officials, which provides that: "Law enforcement officials should use force only when strictly necessary and to the extent required for the performance of their duty." GA resolution 34/169 passed on December 17, 1979, and *Graham v. Connor* 490 U.S. 386 (1989), and refers to abuse occurring during apprehension and while in custody.

[238] Furthermore, Article 5 of the Universal Declaration of Human Rights, the overarching international human rights norm, prohibits torture and other cruel, inhuman or degrading treatment or punishment.

[239] Article 2.1, ICCPR, A/RES/2200 A (1966). In Centre for Human Rights, *Human Rights: A Compilation of International Instruments*, vol. I, ST/HR/1/Rev. 5 (New York: United Nations, 1994), p. 20.

[240] Ibid.

for the inherent dignity of the human person," and Article 26 asserts that "all persons are equal before the law and are entitled without any discrimination to the equal protection of the law."

The Human Rights Committee, which is the international body charged with monitoring compliance to the provisions of the ICCPR by the U.S. and other States Parties, expressed concern regarding police abuse in its 1995 response to the initial report of the U.S. under this covenant:

> The Committee is concerned at the reportedly large number of persons killed, wounded or subjected to ill-treatment by members of the police force in the purported discharge of their duties.[241]

Furthermore, the Human Rights Committee urged the U.S. to:

> ...take all necessary measures to prevent any excessive use of force by the police; that rules and regulations governing the use of weapons by the police and security forces be in full conformity with the United Nations Basic Principles on the Use of Force and Firearms by Law Enforcement Officials; that any violations of these rules be systematically investigated in order to bring those found to have committed such acts before the courts; and that those found guilty be punished and the victims be compensated.[242]

Similar protections are included in the Convention against Torture and Other Cruel, Inhuman or Degrading Treatment or Punishment, which the U.S. ratified in 1994.[243] In addition to prohibiting torture, the States Parties have an obligation "to prevent in any territory under its jurisdiction other acts of cruel, inhuman or degrading treatment or punishment which do not amount to torture."[244] Article 10 of the treaty specifically requires that education and information regarding the prohibition against torture be included in the training of law enforcement personnel,

---

[241] Concluding observations of the Human Rights Committee: United States of America. 03/10/95, A/50/40, para. 282.

[242] Ibid., para. 297.

[243] General Assembly Resolution 39/46, December 10, 1984, in Centre for Human Rights, *Human Rights: A Compilation*, p. 293.

[244] Ibid., Article 16.

and Article 12 requires a prompt and impartial investigation when there is reason to believe an act of torture has been committed.

The International Convention on the Elimination of All Forms of Racial Discrimination (CERD), to which the United States became party in 1994, calls on states to eliminate racial discrimination and to seek to prohibit discrimination under law as well as to guard against discriminatory effects of the law. CERD provides broader protection against discrimination than that offered by the courts' interpretations of the U.S. Constitution. Under U.S. law, an individual must prove a discriminatory intent *and* effect, while CERD requires an intent *or* effect. CERD is relevant in considering police brutality because racial minorities are disproportionately represented among abuse complainants, showing a discriminatory impact that is prohibited by the convention. It is difficult to ascertain whether minorities make up a disproportionately high percentage of complainants because of more frequent arrests or encounters, or because they are singled out for rougher treatment. According to FBI data, African-Americans (adults and juveniles) made up nearly 34 percent of those arrested in cities, yet in cities where data are available regarding the race of complainants, minorities make up more than 60 percent of complainants alleging misconduct by police officers.[245] Even so, many abuse allegations stem from encounters that do not lead to the arrest of the complainant, making such comparisons imperfect.

As ratified treaties, these covenants are now U.S. domestic law and, in some cases, should provide enhanced human rights protections for those within the U.S. Unfortunately, the United States has ratified these treaties with reservations, declarations and understandings that carve away many of their expanded protections. Principal among these is the declaration that none of the treaties' provisions are self-executing, meaning that upon ratification they do not automatically become available as the basis for lawsuits, but must await the passage of implementing legislation. At the same time, the Executive Branch specifically declares that no implementing legislation is necessary – i.e., that U.S. law already adequately protects the rights embodied by the treaty – even when this is not so.

---

[245] U.S. Department of Justice, Federal Bureau of Investigation, *Crime in the United States, 1995,* (Washington, D.C.: U.S. Government Printing Office, 1996) p. 235. Individuals of Hispanic origin are divided among whites and blacks. Cities are defined as having a population of 10,000 or more. As described in civilian review agency reports in New York City, Philadelphia, and Minnesota. The exception, where data from the cities examined in this report are available, is in San Francisco, where in 1996 African-Americans made up 11 percent of the city's population and 25 percent of police abuse complaints.

The effect is that ratification is more or less meaningless for Americans who would invoke the treaties to see their rights protected.[246]

The Human Rights Committee noted:

> Under the federal system prevailing in the United States, the states of the union retain extensive jurisdiction over the application of criminal and family law in particular. This factor, coupled with the absence of formal mechanisms between the federal and state levels to ensure appropriate implementation of the Covenant rights by legislative or other measures may lead to a somewhat unsatisfactory application of the Covenant throughout the country.[247]

Indeed, in his report released in April 1998 regarding the application of the death penalty and killings by police in the U.S., the U.N. Special Rapporteur on Extrajudicial, Summary, or Arbitrary Executions, Bacre Waly Ndiaye, noted that:

> [T]here seems to be a serious gap in the relations between federal and state governments, particularly when it comes to international obligations undertaken by the United States Government. The fact that the rights proclaimed in international treaties are already said to be part of domestic legislation does not exempt the Federal Government from disseminating their provisions. Domestic law appears de facto to prevail over international law, even if they could contradict the international obligations of the United States."[248]

Still, none of these reservations, declarations or understandings affect the international obligations the United States has assumed to eradicate these forms of police abuse in order to "ensure" to all persons within U.S. territory enjoy the rights

---

[246] Human Rights Watch/American Civil Liberties Union, *Human Rights Violations in the United States* (New York: Human Rights Watch/American Civil Liberties Union, 1993 and Human Rights Watch, *Modern Capital of Human Rights? Abuses in the State of Georgia* (New York: Human Rights Watch, 1996).

[247] Concluding observations of the Human Rights Committee: United States of America. 03/10/95, A/50/40, para. 271.

[248] *Report of the Special Rapporteur on extrajudicial, summary or arbitrary executions*, submitted pursuant to Commission resolution 1997/61, Mission to the United States of America, E/CN.4/1998/68/Add.3, III (C).

provided for in the covenants. For the United States to comply with its international human rights obligations, it is not enough for officials to refrain from abusing those under their jurisdiction. The government must also take affirmative steps to ensure that individuals within its territory and subject to its jurisdiction are able to enjoy the rights embodied in the ICCPR and the conventions against torture and racial discrimination. In addition to the manner by which it has ratified these treaties, the U.S. federal authorities have failed to educate not only their own federal law enforcement agencies, but also state and local police officials, regarding the international human rights obligations by which they are bound.

After ratification, the U.S. is required to submit "compliance" reports to the United Nations to describe its progress in meeting a treaty's standards. In its first compliance report on the ICCPR, the U.S. barely mentioned the issue of police brutality. Instead, that July 1994 report merely cited federal criminal civil rights statutes that could be used, but rarely are used, to prosecute police officers who commit serious abuses. The report contained no statistical information or descriptions of incidents of police abuse. At this writing, the U.S. compliance reports on the torture and race conventions are more than two years overdue.

Apart from legally binding treaties, there are other international human rights standards addressing police abuse. The U.N. Code of Conduct for Law Enforcement Officials provides that: "In the performance of their duty, law enforcement officials shall respect and protect human dignity and maintain and uphold the human rights of all persons..." (Article 2) and "Law enforcement officials should use force only when strictly necessary and to the extent required for the performance of their duty" (Article 3).[249] The code also states: "No law enforcement official may inflict, instigate or tolerate any act of torture or other cruel, inhuman or degrading treatment or punishment...."(Article 5).[250] While the code is not binding, it does provide authoritative guidance for interpreting international human rights law regarding policing.[251]

As described above, the U.N. Basic Principles on the Use of Force and Firearms by Law Enforcement Officials, adopted in 1990 by the Eighth U.N. Congress on the Prevention of Crime and Treatment of Offenders provides international human rights standards regarding aspects of policing.[252] Regarding

---

[249] GA resolution 34/169 passed on December 17, 1979.

[250] Ibid.

[251] United Nations Centre for Human Rights, *Human Rights Compilation*, p. 312.

[252] UN Doc. A/CONF.144/28/Rev.1 (1990).

recruitment and training of law enforcement officials, it calls on governments and law enforcement agencies to: "ensure that all law enforcement officials are selected by proper screening procedures, have appropriate moral, psychological and physical qualities for the effective exercise of their functions and receive continuous and thorough professional training. Their continued fitness to perform these functions should be subject to periodic review (Principle 18)....ensure that all law enforcemential officials are provided with training and are tested in accordance with appropriate proficiency standards in the use of force (Principle 19).... give special attention to the issues of police ethics and human rights, especially in the investigative process, to alternatives to the use of force and firearms, including the peaceful settlement of conflicts, the understanding of crowd behaviour, and the methods of persuasion, negotiation and mediation, as well as to technical means, with a view to limiting the use of force and firearms. Law enforcement agencies should review their training programmes and operational procedures in light of particular incidents." (Principle 20).

The Basic Principles on the Use of Force and Firearms by Law Enforcement Officials provide that police officers shall "as far as possible, apply non-violent means before resorting to the use of force and firearms"(Article 4).[253]   The principles also call for proportionality in the amount of force used when required, for the adoption of reporting requirements when force or firearms are used, and for governments to ensure that "arbitrary or abusive use of force and firearms by law enforcement officials is punished as a criminal offence under their law" (Article 7). Similar requirements are found in the Principles on the Effective Prevention and Investigation of Extra-legal, Arbitrary and Summary Executions, adopted by the U.N. Economic and Social Council on May 24, 1989. The principles prohibit extra-legal, arbitrary and summary executions, and call for prompt and impartial investigations and public reporting on the outcome of any investigation.

In his April 1998 report, the UN Special Rapporteur on extrajudicial, summary or arbitrary executions examined cases of police killings in Los Angeles, New York and San Francisco.[254]   He raised concerns regarding the absence of national data concerning killings by the police, the poor quality of some investigations of killings by police, and the low rate of criminal prosecution in cases of police abuse resulting in death. The Special Rapporteur recommended: enhanced training on international

[253]   Ibid.

[254]   *Report of the Special Rapporteur on extrajudicial, summary or arbitrary executions*, submitted pursuant to Commission resolution 1997/61, Mission to the United States of America, E/CN.4/1998/68/Add.3.

standards on law enforcement and human rights; independent investigations of deaths in custody; and the use of special prosecutors.

U.S. Law

The U.S. Constitution provides protections against human rights violations by police officers, primarily under the Fourth, Eighth, and Fourteenth amendments. The Fourth Amendment prohibits "unreasonable searches and seizures;" the Eighth Amendment bars "cruel and unusual punishments;" and the Fourteenth Amendment prohibits any state from depriving any "person of life, liberty, or property, without due process of law."[255]

Under state laws, police officers who use excessive force may be prosecuted on general assault, murder, or other relevant charges. Some states have specific laws under which police officers are charged for acting under "color of law." Individuals may also bring civil lawsuits, claiming constitutional violations by the officer or his or her police department. A court may order injunctive relief, calling on the state to end the violative practice, or, more commonly, monetary relief in the form of compensatory or punitive claims. Civil lawsuits alleging police misconduct are often "settled" by the city, prior to a trial; in most cases, the city and police department admit no liability but pay the plaintiffs to avoid a full trial.

Criminal Prosecution

Under federal law, police officers may be prosecuted criminally under Reconstruction-era (1871) civil rights statutes. A police officer using excessive force is violating civil rights if he or she "under color of any law, statute, ordinance, regulation, or custom, willfully subjects any person in any State, Territory, Commonwealth, Possession, or District to the deprivation of any rights, privileges, or immunities secured or protected by the Constitution or laws of the United States...."[256] A conspiracy charge may also be filed "if two or more persons conspire to injure, oppress, threaten, or intimidate any person in any State, Territory, Commonwealth, Possession, or District in the free exercise or enjoyment of any right or privilege secured to him by the Constitution or laws of the United

---

[255] In 1989, the Supreme Court recognized definitively that police use of excessive force in an arrest is an unreasonable seizure of the person under the Fourth Amendment. *Graham v. Connor*, 490 U.S. 386 (1989).

[256] 18 U.S.C. §242. Until 1988, an abuse by a federal official acting alone, absent a conspiracy, was only a misdemeanor, no matter how serious the injury to the victim. In 1994's omnibus crime bill, civil rights violations became capital crimes.

States, or because of his having so exercised the same...."[257] Violations of the civil rights statutes carry penalties of fines and imprisonment and, in the most serious cases, life imprisonment or the death penalty.

In practice, as described above, local criminal prosecution of officers who commit human rights violations is rare. Local prosecutors are loath to pursue cases against police officers with whom they normally work to prosecute criminal suspects. Although it varies from community to community, many citizens are unwilling to find officers guilty of criminal behavior except in the most extreme cases.

In the case of federal criminal civil rights prosecutions, less than 1 percent of the complaints referred to the Justice Department alleging civil rights violations by law enforcement officials lead to the filing of indictments by federal prosecutors. Reasons for the extremely low rate of prosecution include the Justice Department's passive role in pursuing cases clearly within its mandate, a very high threshold for proving cases (requiring a "specific intent" by the offending officer to deprive an individual of his or her rights) and under-staffing of the Justice Department division responsible for fulfilling this essential function, demonstrating the low priority assigned to prosecuting officers accused of committing abuses.

Civil Remedies

In deflecting criticisms regarding the government's failure to fulfill its obligation to ensure the rights of individuals within the United States are protected, officials often point to civil remedies as the most effective avenue for redress. Although no substitute for prosecutions of officers who commit crimes, civil cases are easier to pursue as an evidentiary matter because they use a lower standard of proof than is required in criminal cases: a preponderance of the evidence, rather than beyond a reasonable doubt. Some reforms in police practices have stemmed from costly lawsuits or the threat of lawsuits; more typically, however, civil remedies have been limited to providing monetary relief to individual victims. And, unlike criminal cases and disciplinary actions against officers, which are pursued by the government, most civil cases must be shouldered by the plaintiff.

Under 42 U.S. Code, section 1983, the relevant federal civil statute, individuals may file lawsuits against the offending officer, department or jurisdiction.[258] It states:

---

[257] 18 U.S.C. §241. The 1994 omnibus crime bill made conspiracy charges a capital offense.

[258] There are also state-level civil statutes that plaintiffs may use to bring abuse lawsuits, but the federal law, Section 1983, is used more frequently.

Any person who, under color of any statute, ordinance, regulation, custom, or usage, of any State or Territory or the District of Columbia, subjects or causes to be subjected, any citizen of the United States or other person within the jurisdiction thereof to the deprivation of any rights, privileges, or immunities security by the Constitution and laws, shall be liable to the party injured in an action at law, suit in equity, or other proper proceeding for redress....[259]

Section 1983 actions are intended to fulfill at least two basic purposes in the police abuse context. First, such actions are designed to compensate victims of police abuse, usually through an award of compensatory damages. Second, such actions are intended to make police officers and departments accountable to constitutionally required standards of conduct.[260]

Although the statute stems from Reconstruction-era civil rights laws, it was only commonly utilized by police abuse victims following a landmark 1978 case, *Monell v. Dept. of Social Services of the City of New York,* which assigned liability to local governments for constitutional violations by their employees.[261] *Monell* thus opened the "deep pockets" of local government.

Civil lawsuits are limited in important respects that undermine their effectiveness in providing a remedy for past violations and in providing protection against future police abuse. Under Section 1983 a victim of police abuse may not win a damage award following a judgment against a police department unless it can be shown that the injury was caused by a municipal "policy" or "custom."[262] In 1989, the Supreme Court imposed a separate "state of mind requirement," so that plaintiffs must prove deliberate indifference to abuse on the part of the municipality in cases involving inadequate training.[263] These requirements create difficult hurdles for Section 1983 plaintiffs to overcome.

---

[259] 42 U.S.C. §1983.

[260] Hoffman, "The Feds, lies, and videotape," *Southern California Law Review.*

[261] *Monell v. New York City Department of Social Services,* 436 U.S. 658 (1978).

[262] Ibid.

[263] *See* report by law firm Piper and Marbury, June 29, 1995, p. 19, regarding the civilian complaint review board in Washington, D.C. citing *City of Canton v. Harris,* 489 U.S. 378, 389 (1989). To be assigned liability, the municipality's policy or custom must directly cause or constitute a "moving force" behind the constitutional deprivation.

Furthermore, individual police officers have immunity from Section 1983 liability unless it can be shown that their conduct violated "clearly established" statutory or constitutional norms of which a reasonable person would have known.[264] In practice, qualified immunity benefits officers accused of using excessive force because while juries are supposed to focus on whether the officer's conduct was objectively reasonable, they may focus instead on what the officer reasonably believed about the facts justifying the force used. As a result, they may find in favor of the officer if the conduct is objectively unreasonable but understandable.[265]

The effectiveness of Section 1983 is further undermined by the sharp limits on the use of civil rights actions to restrain future constitutional violations, especially in the area of police abuse. The *Lyons v. City of Los Angeles* case best illustrates this problem.[266] In *Lyons,* the Supreme Court overturned an injunction issued by a lower federal court prohibiting the use of chokeholds by the LAPD. The use of chokeholds was extremely controversial in large part because more than a dozen people died as a result of their use in Los Angeles, most of them African-Americans, between 1975 and 1980.[267] The Supreme Court reasoned that Lyons had no "standing" to bring a claim for relief against future uses of the chokehold because he could not allege that he was likely to be stopped by the LAPD again and unjustifiably subjected to a chokehold. Because it would always be difficult for almost any person claiming relief from future police abuse to make such a showing, the *Lyons* case has been an insuperable barrier to many suits seeking to challenge ongoing police practices. The damage caused by this ruling was described by former Justice Thurgood Marshall in his *Lyons* dissent:

> Under the view expressed by the majority today, if the police adopt a "shoot to kill" policy or a policy of shooting one out of every ten suspects,

---

[264] *See* Hoffman, "The feds, lies and videotape," *Southern California Law Review.*

[265] Mary Cheh, "Are lawsuits an answer to police brutality," *And Justice for All,* (Washington, D.C.: Police Executive Research Forum, 1995), pp. 233-259.

[266] 461 U.S. 95 (1983). *See* also *Rizzo v Goode*, 423 U.S. 362 (1976)(overturning an injunction issued against the Philadelphia police department).

[267] Of the fourteen city police departments examined by Human Rights Watch, only four (San Francisco, District of Columbia, Los Angeles, and Minneapolis) still allow chokeholds, according to 1993 Law Enforcement Management and Administrative Statistics, 1993, Bureau of Justice Statistics, Washington, D.C., pp. 169-180.

the federal courts will be powerless to enjoin its continuation....The federal judicial power is now limited to levying a [money damage] toll for such a systematic constitutional violation.[268]

In an April 1997 decision in the case of *Commissioners of Bryan County v. Brown*, the Supreme Court ruled that municipalities could not be held liable for the hiring of law enforcement officers with criminal histories indicating violent behavior who then went on to use excessive force.[269] The court ruled that a victim must show that a city or county consciously disregarded the risk of hiring a person and that injuries were a "plainly obvious consequence" of the hiring decision. The majority opinion contended that it must be shown that "this officer was highly likely to inflict the particular injury suffered by the plaintiff."[270] By so doing, the court limited an individual's ability to sue successfully in cases in which screening and hiring procedures and decisions are faulty, and thus whittled away the most frequently used remedy for police abuse in the United States.[271] This is an important, and unfortunate, development, since police abuse experts point to massive hiring periods – and poor background investigations, screening, and training that often accompany such hiring surges – as a key contributor to the recruitment of individuals who become abusive as officers.

The Violent Crime Control and Law Enforcement Act of 1994 included a new statute under which the Department of Justice may enforce the constitutional rights of individuals abused by police officers. Under the new statute, the Justice Department may sue for declaratory and equitable relief if any governmental authority or person acting on behalf of any governmental authority engages in "a pattern or practice of conduct by law enforcement officers...that deprives persons of rights, privileges, or immunities secured or protected by the Constitution or laws of the United States."[272]

---

[268] 461 U.S. at 137.

[269] *Board of the County Commissioners of Bryan County, Oklahoma v. Brown, et al.*, U.S. Supreme Court, No. 95-1100, April 28, 1997.

[270] Ibid.

[271] Municipalities are still held liable for insufficient training and flawed disciplinary policies when these are found responsible for the use of excessive force by individual officers.

[272] "Police Pattern or Practice" 42 U.S.C. §14141.

Police abuse experts had long recommended giving federal authorities power to bring civil actions against police departments engaging in a pattern or practice of misconduct. In April 1997, the Justice Department, relying on this new authority, reached a consent decree to force reforms in Pittsburgh, Pennsylvania's police force and in August 1997 reached a consent decree with the Steubenville, Ohio police force. The department has disclosed that it is closely monitoring at least four other police departments – in Los Angeles, New Orleans, New York, and Philadelphia – to decide whether to proceed with formal injunctive actions to end abuses committed or tolerated by these police departments.

ATLANTA

In Atlanta, the police department and elected leadership boast of low complaint rates of police brutality. Chief Beverly Harvard recently noted to Human Rights Watch that in 1996, out of a total of 288 citizen complaints against the police that the department investigated, only fifty-six involved unauthorized use of force; and in 1997, the department investigated 331 complaints, of which sixty-one involved unauthorized use of force.[1] This is, as the mayor has stated in the past, a very low number of complaints.[2]

What these numbers do not show is the fact that the department chooses which complaints have enough merit to investigate, and its internal affairs unit – the office that carries out the investigations – is widely perceived as biased, while Atlanta has the weakest external review mechanism of any city that Human Rights Watch covered for this report.[3] Moreover, Georgia grants the police special privileges in grand jury proceedings – privileges unique in the United States – such that prosecuting a police officer for crimes relating to the use of excessive force, or any other criminal charge, is even more difficult in this state than in others.

In these circumstances, it is extremely difficult to gauge how prevalent the problem of police abuse really is, though the city's public defender's office reports that many of its clients claim abuse.[4] What can be said is that the complaint-intake

---

[1] Letter from Chief Beverly Harvard, January 27, 1998.

[2] Kathy Scruggs, "Angry Harvard changing policies," *Atlanta Journal-Constitution,* January 11, 1996. In 1996, the department reportedly investigated only fifty-six complaints that alleged the use of unauthorized force. Compare this low rate to the San Francisco Police Department, which had a slightly larger force–in 1996, approximately 2,000 sworn officers with the San Francisco force compared to 1,500 with the Atlanta police. The San Francisco Police Commission's Office of Citizen Complaints receives 1,000 complaints each year, with approximately half of the complainants alleging unnecessary force or unauthorized action by the police. A further comparison: the San Jose (California) Police Department, which had approximately 1,200 sworn officers in 1996, received 198 unnecessary force complaints in 1994 and 122 in 1995. In other words, the San Jose force was 20 percent smaller than Atlanta's but, if Atlanta's official tally is to be believed, receives three times as many unnecessary force complaints.

[3] Providence has no external review mechanism.

[4] Telephone interview, Deputy Director Vanessa Gales, March 4, 1996. Those with physical signs of mistreatment are photographed by the public defender's Office and brought to the attention of the OPS

process is flawed, which discourages even legitimate complaints; the police department resists revealing information about the cases it has received and investigated; and there is no independent agency, commission, or nongovernmental organization that regularly monitors police brutality complaints so as to follow the process and tally the numbers and types of complaints in Atlanta.

During the past several years, Atlanta's police department has received negative publicity for, among other cases, an officer's fatal shooting of an unarmed man in December 1995, five officers caught on videotape beating a motorist in April 1997, and a corruption scandal that revealed how little police officers fear the oversight of the Office of Professional Standards (OPS), the internal affairs unit, with regard to brutality complaints. These cases and others indicate that there is a need for more sustained, forceful independent oversight, to check on the rigor of internal investigations and to ensure that, where complaints are justified, the offending officers are disciplined or charged as appropriate.

On December 7, 1995, suspecting a robbery in progress, plainclothes Atlanta police officer Willie T. Sauls entered a motorcycle shop with his gun drawn and shouting obscenities. An employee thought the police surrounding the store were themselves robbers, and a gunfight ensued. When the shooting stopped, a customer named Jerry Jackson was dead and two others, including Officer Sauls, were wounded.[5]

What was initially reported as a tragically botched raid became a significant scandal when witnesses who viewed some of the incident from a nearby building contacted reporters weeks after the shooting, stating that they had attempted to provide police investigators with their eyewitness accounts but were ignored. The witnesses claimed that police spokespeople quoted in the press were misleading the public because they did not want to acknowledge what the witnesses reportedly had seen: Sauls's partner, Officer Waine Pinckney, shooting Jackson as he lay prone and unarmed on the sidewalk outside the store, apparently posing no risk.[6]

---

[5] One officer, Ivant Fields, was on the scene even though he was under investigation for his second shooting in a sixteen-month period and should have been assigned to desk duty. R. Robin McDonald, "In 16 months, 2 shootings," *Atlanta Journal-Constitution*, February 6, 1996. Fields's presence at the scene raises additional questions since, according to Lt. Scott Lyle of the force's internal affairs unit, the Office of Professional Standards (OPS), officers involved in shooting incidents are removed from situations that may require the use of firearms until investigations are completed. Human Rights Watch telephone interview with Lieutenant Lyle, March 26, 1996.

[6] Ronald Smothers, "Atlanta police face criticism in recent killing by an officer," *Atlanta Journal-Constitution*, December 29, 1995.

The incident exposed a range of problems, from poor training to serious shortcomings in investigative procedures, since eyewitnesses' statements were either not taken or ignored once received.[7] The Jackson shooting also highlighted the absence of any external check on the police department generally, because unlike most U.S. major cities, Atlanta had no functional citizen review mechanism. In the shootings' aftermath the city's Civilian Review Board was re-activated, though unfortunately not with adequate powers.[8]

The review of police brutality complaints is entirely in the hands of the police. According to the department's internal affairs unit, the Office of Professional Standards (OPS), each precinct is allowed a great deal of discretion in deciding which cases are serious enough to submit to the OPS. According to police abuse experts in the city, there is a perception that the internal affairs unit is not interested in pursuing complaints against police officers, resulting in distrust of the OPS in many affected communities. Because victims of police abuse may not believe the OPS will handle their cases properly, many do not file formal complaints. Another important contributing factor in the low number of complaints filed with the OPS may be its requirement that a complainant must file his or her complaint in person, rather than filing a complaint form by mail.

Civilian Review Board

In response to many Atlantans' outrage over the Jackson shooting, Mayor Campbell called for the creation of a civilian review board, apparently without realizing one already existed (thus proving how marginal the pre-existing board had

---

[7] After the seriously flawed investigation into the Jackson shooting, Mayor Bill Campbell promised changes at the Atlanta Police Department. In February 1996, the commander of the homicide section, who was responsible for the Jackson investigation, was transferred to a senior position in the Office of Professional Standards (OPS), the internal affairs unit responsible for reviewing and investigating police misconduct. No official explanation was given for the transfer.

[8] Scruggs, "Angry Harvard changing policies," *Atlanta Journal-Constitution*. According to Lieutenant Lyle of the OPS, his office initiated forty-seven unauthorized- use-of-force investigations in 1995. There were 134 such investigations in 1991; 125 in 1992; eighty-three in 1993; and sixty-one in 1994. In response to a query from Human Rights Watch, Chief Harvard reported that in 1996 the department investigated 288 citizen complaints, fifty-six of which involved unauthorized use of force, and in 1997 the department investigated 331 complaints, sixty-one of which involving unauthorized use of force. Letter from Chief Harvard, January 27, 1998.

become).[9] Once the existence of the board was acknowledged, the mayor signed an administrative order to "continue" the Civilian Review Board (CRB).[10]

The CRB does not receive initial complaints of brutality from the public, has a minimal staff, does not have subpoena power, does not meet in public and does not necessarily make its findings or recommendations available to the public.[11] The review board does "receive reports from the OPS and may receive requests for review from citizens who are dissatisfied with the result of the OPS review."[12] After its "investigation" (without its own investigators), the board recommends to the mayor whether there is "probable cause for [administrative] charges to be brought by the City against the affected officer[s]...."[13] If administrative charges have been proffered against the affected officer(s), the CRB chair alone reviews them to determine whether department policy changes should be recommended. There is no possibility for the CRB to review cases where victims or others protest the leniency of any administrative charges applied.

The CRB is also prohibited from completing its review while any "litigation arising from the complaint against the City, its officers, or employees" is pending.[14] Since the CRB's mandate is limited to allegations of excessive force, serious bodily

---

[9] Charmagne Helton and Lyda Longa, "Mayor appoints board to review killing by police," *Atlanta Journal-Constitution*, January 6, 1996; R. Robin McDonald and Charmagne Helton, "Confusion surrounds review board," *Atlanta Journal-Constitution*, January 25, 1996.

[10] Administrative Order No. 96-1, "An Administrative Order to Continue the Civilian Review Board, Define its Composition and to Establish the Criteria and Scope of Review for this Board," January 5, 1996.

[11] In discussing the CRB's shortcomings, a former CRB member told Human Rights Watch that it was his understanding that the mayor and police administrators are counting on community policing to address the problem of brutality. While community policing may improve relations with affected communities, there is no reason not to pursue both the CRB and community policing initiatives seriously.

[12] Administrative Order No. 96-1. The administrative order does not delineate who may "appeal" an OPS finding.

[13] Ibid.

[14] Human Rights Watch interview with Mike Langford, director of the mayor's Office of Community Affairs, which is responsible for re-starting the CRB, Atlanta, March 4, 1996. *See* Administrative Order, Section 3(d).

injury, and death, nearly all of the cases it is authorized to review will involve civil suits, and some will lead to criminal charges; such delay completely sidelines the CRB, since litigation in these cases may span several years. If the CRB is intended to ease public anxieties following cases like the Jackson shooting, it can have little effect in practice, since, according to its own mandate, it would not be permitted to review the Jackson case until the federal criminal civil rights investigation, now underway, is completed and any civil actions are concluded. Indeed, CRB staff told Human Rights Watch that the board was pulled off the Jackson case after Jackson's mother filed a civil lawsuit.[15]

In explaining why the CRB does not need subpoena power, which would require the Atlanta Police Department and Department of Corrections, over which the CRB has jurisdiction, to provide all relevant files or access to "at-risk" officer tracking systems, the mayor's Office of Community Affairs explained that such power was not necessary because internal affairs (OPS) has always been cooperative.[16] A sergeant in the OPS told Human Rights Watch that he had little knowledge of the review board and stated he "never had any interest in the Civilian Review Board."[17] A former member of the CRB told Human Rights Watch that, at some point, OPS stopped forwarding relevant cases to the board and that recommendations made by CRB members were often ignored by police management.[18] When asked for her views about civilian review generally, Chief Harvard stated, "Civilian review boards can and have played a very useful role in

---

[15] Telephone interview with CRB staff member, May 14, 1997.

[16] This is not a view shared by others interviewed by Human Rights Watch. When the *Atlanta Journal-Constitution* requested OPS's files on forty-four shooting cases, there were delays and the newspaper was not provided with all of the information it requested, as required by state law. Photographs, transcripts of 9-1-1 (emergency) calls, medical examiners' reports and other documents were missing from files. The newspaper was able to ascertain what was missing because OPS did not remove file indices listing the items that should have been in each file.

[17] Human Rights Watch telephone interview with Sgt. Dennis Mullen, OPS, Atlanta, November 1, 1995.

[18] There was unanimous opinion among everyone interviewed by Human Rights Watch that the Civilian Review Board, as it currently operates, is not equipped to make a difference. This was the view of attorneys who represent alleged victims of police brutality, reporters who cover the police, public defenders whose clients have been abused by police, at least one former member of the CRB, and police officers themselves, most of whom did not know the CRB even existed.

the overall picture of police accountability, integrity and community involvement in the disciplinary process."[19] When asked specifically about Atlanta's Civilian Review Board and its impact on accountability, the chief referred to this general statement without commenting on the board.

The absence of any provision for public disclosure of information regarding complaints of abuse or any public access to the hearings that the CRB may hold undermines one of the central goals of civilian review – improving public confidence through enhanced information about police handling of abuse complaints. Despite the appointment of prominent and respected members of the community, this sort of secrecy and the board's staff and mandate limitations, as described above, will not enhance police-community relations in Atlanta. While some in the community derided the CRB as a "paper tiger" when it was "reactivated" in January 1996, that label would suggest that, on paper, the board has powers that it does not have in practice.[20] In fact, its powers as described are hardly impressive; the CRB requires major revisions to live up to its name and stated goal.

As of mid-1997, a CRB staffperson reported that the board had only taken on two cases (the Jackson shooting and an undercover operation shooting) since it was "restructured" in 1995.[21] As mentioned above, the Jackson investigation was halted once a civil lawsuit was filed by his mother. The CRB has published no report on its activities.[22]

Despite the CRB's obvious shortcomings, during 1997 the mayor continued to tout it as an external review option, as in an April 20, 1997 case that attracted a great deal of attention. A police sergeant and four other officers were caught on videotape repeatedly striking an African-American motorist.[23] Mayor Campbell told reporters that the CRB would look at the case, even though the victim's lawyer had announced that he planned to file a civil lawsuit, an internal investigation was ongoing, and both of these circumstances meant – as the mayor knew – that the CRB would be sidelined in dealing with this case of alleged abuse.

---

[19] Letter to Human Rights Watch from Chief Harvard, January 27, 1998.

[20] Helton and Longa, "Mayor appoints board...," *Atlanta Journal-Constitution*.

[21] Telephone interview with CRB staffperson, May 14, 1997.

[22] Ibid.

[23] Kevin Sack, "Police chief says officers violated policy in beating," *The New York Times*, May 13, 1997.

As of August 1997, the CRB reportedly had still not become involved.[24] The case did provoke action from the police leadership, however. According to the alleged victim's attorney, OPS investigated the incident and recommended that all of the officers involved be exonerated, but Chief Harvard disagreed and called for a thirty-day suspension without pay for one of the officers, and an official reprimand for another; the officers were reportedly appealing the disciplinary sanctions to the civil service board.[25]

Police Administration/Internal Affairs

The Office of Professional Standards is the internal affairs division of the Atlanta Police Department; it is divided into units that investigate allegations of corruption, brutality and other serious misconduct. OPS currently has a staff of approximately thirty-five (including civilian support staff, investigators, and supervisors) that is tasked with investigating the 2,300 employees on the police force.

The aftermath of the Jackson case and widespread criticism of the police force emerging from that case coincided with the criminal trial of officers, primarily from Zone 3 (one of six police zones in the city), who were accused of corruption. That trial raised new questions about OPS's effectiveness. One sergeant, in his testimony against another officer, explained that members of the "bad cop ring" did not fear an OPS investigation because they knew how to circumvent it: "As a supervisor, I knew my processes and I knew OPS's processes....It'd be the officer's word versus the citizen's and the officer would win out since there were no witnesses."[26]

At least six officers involved in the corruption scandal had personal experience with OPS procedures and had good reason to believe OPS would ignore or tolerate their criminal behavior, according to an investigation by the *Atlanta Journal-Constitution*.[27] Despite many allegations of brutal treatment or violent behavior, these officers remained on the force until they faced federal corruption charges.

---

[24] Telephone interview, attorney Albert Mitchell, August 18, 1997.

[25] Ibid.

[26] Bill Torpy, "Jailed cop tells of thefts by police," *Atlanta Journal-Constitution*, February 23, 1996.

[27] Bill Rankin, "Badges for sale," *Atlanta Journal-Constitution*, February 18, 1996. In the absence of any other police monitoring group in the city, the *Atlanta Journal-Constitution* has played an unusually active role in obtaining information about police misconduct.

Specific information was produced by the police department as part of the corruption investigation; this unusual glimpse into the department's apparent tolerance of violent behavior is cause for concern.

One of the officers was the subject of five brutality complaints. One complainant alleged that the officer and his partner drove him to a deserted location where the officer reportedly unzipped the man's pants and his partner grabbed the suspect's testicles and squeezed while asking questions; the officers also reportedly kicked and choked the man.[28] Despite similar complaints by other suspects, OPS dismissed all five complaints as unfounded because there were no witnesses other than police officers, who backed the officer.[29]

Another officer, this one from Zone 6, reportedly had a violent past. In July 1991, he was charged with battering his live-in girlfriend, and in March 1993 faced the same charge from another girlfriend.[30] According to newspaper reports, both times he was suspended with pay and reinstated when the women chose to drop the charges.[31]

A leader of the ring was arrested in DeKalb County for allegedly battering his wife, leading to a court-ordered psychological profile, which reportedly stated that he had been in seventy-five fistfights in his lifetime, including some while on duty.[32] His wife recanted, and prosecutors dropped charges against him. After the corruption scandal broke, Atlanta police reopened an internal investigation into the 1993 shooting death of a criminal suspect who was shot five times by the officer after a foot chase, including three times in the back at a distance of two and a half feet. Nonetheless, despite questions about his actions and many complaints from suspects and his supervisors alleging misconduct, the officer was praised by superiors in annual performance reports for his "gung ho" attitude.[33]

Three more officers involved in the corruption ring had been cleared by OPS in a 1993 shooting incident that crippled Sameth Svay. Svay was shot by police during an investigation into illegal gambling. In files turned over to the *Atlanta*

---

[28] Ibid.

[29] Ibid.

[30] Ibid.

[31] Ibid.

[32] Ibid.

[33] Ibid.

Journal-Constitution, Svay's sworn statement about the incident was missing (he had been charged with assaulting an officer and illegal gambling, but charges were later dropped), and the files reportedly show that he was never interviewed by OPS during its inquiry that led to the officers' exoneration.[34]

When Human Rights Watch asked Lieutenant Lyle of OPS how these officers consistently avoided serious disciplinary sanctions or termination for these alleged abuses, Lyle suggested that the brutality complaints helped to spur the federal corruption investigation. If this is the case, it raises an obvious question: Why did brutality complaints lead to a corruption investigation instead of a civil rights probe? This comment may reveal a great deal about the priorities of both federal investigators and the Atlanta Police Department. National statistics suggest that federal prosecutors are much more likely to pursue official corruption cases than civil rights prosecutions. In fiscal year 1996, for example, approximately 40 percent of official corruption cases referred by the FBI to U.S. Attorneys were prosecuted, compared to approximately 4 percent of civil rights referrals.[35]

In another case, a civil lawsuit filed on behalf of Charles Cunningham alleges that the plaintiff was beaten with a flashlight by Atlanta Police Officer Charles Traylor on June 11, 1993.[36] According to Cunningham, he was a bystander during a fistfight outside a nightclub in Atlanta when Officer Traylor arrived at the scene. Officer Traylor allegedly hit another individual with a flashlight, while Cunningham protested from some distance. Officer Traylor then allegedly struck Cunningham with the flashlight. The blow cut completely through Cunningham's lip, requiring an operation.

Traylor reportedly was found psychologically unfit for police work by several psychologists, one of whom warned in 1988 that "persistent demands to cope with

---

[34] Ibid.

[35] Information collected from the Executive Office of the U.S. Attorney's office by the Transactional Research Access Clearinghouse, a private research group.

[36] Civil complaint, *Cunningham v. City of Atlanta, Eldrin Bell (former A.P.D. Chief of Police), Officer Charles Traylor*, U.S. District Court, Northern District (Atlanta Division) 94-CV-1018-RHH, May 1, 1995. Information provided by the American Civil Liberties Union of Georgia, which represents the plaintiff in this case. Peter Mantius, "Brutality lawsuit filed against Atlanta officer," *Atlanta Journal-Constitution*, April 19, 1994.

stressful or demanding situations might lead to outbursts of emotion."[37] Traylor's behavior was attributed to attention deficit disorder, and he was given medication. But, in 1992, a psychologist warned that Traylor was still not fit for full duty.[38]

This was all the more disturbing in that Officer Traylor had been convicted and disciplined for violent behavior in the past. In 1988 he was convicted of simple battery after he fought with another driver over a parking space.[39] In 1989, Traylor fought with another officer after an argument over race relations and was hospitalized for his injuries. That fight resulted in a three-day suspension. Over half a dozen complaints had been filed against the officer, though none of these resulted in discipline. In one startling off-duty incident, Traylor reportedly shot at another vehicle on an interstate highway. He later stated that he thought he saw a revolver in the other vehicle; no firearm was found. As of August 1997, Officer Traylor was still on the force and working out of Zone 6; as part of the settlement with Cunningham, Traylor must remain on desk duty.[40]

The OPS staff who spoke with Human Rights Watch were suspicious of complainants' motives and appeared to give police the benefit of the doubt. An OPS representative told Human Rights Watch during an interview in November 1995, "People make complaints to get out of trouble."[41] When Human Rights Watch questioned the low number of complaints received by the Atlanta police and the OPS's assertion that the sustained rate is very low, OPS asserted, "We don't have a brutal police force here."[42] The same sergeant from OPS was not aware of any brutality case leading to dismissal.

---

[37] *Cunningham v. City of Atlanta, Eldrin Bell (former A.P.D. Chief of Police), Officer Charles Traylor*, U.S. District Court, Northern District (Atlanta Division) 94-CV-1018-RHH, May 1, 1995, quoting Dr. Myrna Burnette.

[38] Ibid., citing Dr. Stephen O'Hagan.

[39] *Cunningham v. City of Atlanta, Eldrin Bell (former A.P.D. Chief of Police), Officer Charles Traylor*, U.S. District Court, Northern District (Atlanta Division) 94-CV-1018-RHH, May 1, 1995.

[40] Telephone interview, Gerald Weber, ACLU of Georgia, April 27, 1998.

[41] Human Rights Watch interview with Sgt. Dennis Mullen, OPS, Atlanta, November 1, 1995.

[42] Ibid. Despite repeated requests, the OPS was unable or unwilling to provide us with a precise, or even estimated, sustained rate for abuse complaints. Sergeant Mullen's statement that the sustained rate is "very low" was the only response provided.

The OPS does maintain an early warning system, but when questioned by Human Rights Watch, Chief Harvard refused to disclose the number of officers who have been reviewed under the system.[43] If three or more maltreatment complaints are filed against an officer in a one-year period, whether or not the complaints are sustained, a review is initiated. Similarly, four firearms discharges by an officer in a five-year period result in a review. Of course, if the review of an officer results in no retraining or counseling (as seems to have been the case with some of the officers involved in the Zone 3 corruption), procedures leading to review may not be sufficient.

Civil Lawsuits

According to the City Attorney's office, the "vast majority" of plaintiffs in civil lawsuits have already filed a complaint with OPS prior to filing the lawsuit, but if they have not done so, the City Attorney's office makes OPS "aware" of a citizen's complaint.[44] It is not clear whether the passing of such information leads to any inquiry on the part of the OPS.[45] Nor is it clear whether civil lawsuits alleging brutality are utilized as part of the early warning system and whether such lawsuits are recorded as part of the subject officer's personnel or disciplinary record. When Human Rights Watch raised these questions with Chief Harvard, the oblique response was that "use of unauthorized force complaints" are part of the early warning system and that "whether an unauthorized use of force complaint does or does not result in a civil lawsuit does not deter the Atlanta police department from taking appropriate action...."[46]

The City Attorney's office does not maintain readily accessible data regarding the amounts paid by the city to settle police brutality lawsuits, revealing an apparent lack of interest in the financial implications of such lawsuits. In response to a 1996 Human Rights Watch request, a helpful staff member in the City Attorney's office pulled together a compilation of settlements and awards for 1994 and 1995 by

---

[43] Letter to Human Rights Watch from Chief Beverly Harvard, January 27, 1998.

[44] Attorneys representing such complainants have stated, however, that they do not always advise their clients to file an OPS complaint prior to proceeding with a civil lawsuit.

[45] Letter from Rosalind Rubens, senior assistant city attorney with the City Attorney's Office to Human Rights Watch, dated August 7, 1997. The City Attorney's office did not answer Human Rights Watch's question regarding whether or not it notified the CRB when a lawsuit is filed alleging brutality.

[46] Letter to Human Rights Watch from Chief Harvard, January 27, 1998.

asking attorneys which cases they remembered. According to this informal poll, Atlanta paid $610,368 in police brutality settlements in 1994 and $67,000 in 1995, a relatively small figure. As a representative from the City Attorney's office notes, the city "litigates aggressively."[47] The 1996 total for the same categories, as provided by the City Attorney's office, was $437,184, with the largest single payout in the amount of $185,000 in the Roderick Stewart case (*See* below).[48] The settlements are paid out of general funds, not by an insurer, which may contribute to the city's interest in fighting such lawsuits vigorously.

In July 1997, the city settled with the Holder family for $750,000, one of the largest single payouts in Atlanta's recent history.[49] The attorney representing the Holder family claimed that the large settlement stemmed, in part, from the affidavit provided by a retired Atlanta police major who stated excessive force was not unusual on the Atlanta police force and that officers often protected one another with a "code of silence."[50]

The lawsuit stemmed from an incident on Christmas Eve, 1993, when three Atlanta police officers from Zone 1 arrived at the home of Zezar Holder, to arrest the man's stepson.[51] The officers had allegedly heard there was a warrant for the stepson's arrest, but had no warrant in hand themselves. When Holder asked to see the warrant, the officers became combative, and one reportedly said to Holder, "I don't have to show you shit, nigger." Holder and the officer were in the kitchen where a physical altercation ensued. At this point, an African-American officer joined the officer fighting with Holder, and reportedly struck Holder in the head twice with his baton.

---

[47] Human Rights Watch telephone interview with June Green, public safety division of the City Attorney's office of Atlanta, April 5, 1996.

[48] Letter from the City Attorneys Office to Human Rights Watch, dated August 7, 1997.

[49] According to attorneys representing Holder, he also received an official apology from the police chief and the mayor. Telephone call from attorney Stephen La Briola, July 8, 1997.

[50] Lolita Browning, "Atlanta Pays $750,000 to settle police-abuse suit," *Fulton County Daily Report*, August 4, 1997.

[51] *Zezar M. Holder, et al. v. The City of Atlanta, et al.*, State Court of Fulton County, Civil Action File No. 95 vs 107983-B, filed December 22, 1995. The stepson did not normally reside at the Holders' home.

The officers later explained the beating by stating that Holder had reached for one officer's gun, and that the white officer was struggling with Holder and screaming, "He's going for the gun" as the other officer entered the house and hit the man; this version reportedly was disputed by another officer in the house. After Holder was cuffed and lying on the floor, the white officer stood over him allegedly taunting him while he bled. The family was arrested (father, mother, daughter, and stepson), and the mother and father were jailed until December 27, for allegedly obstructing justice – charges which were later dismissed.[52] Holder was treated at Grady Hospital for scalp injuries and received stitches. A neurologist stated that he suffered a permanent brain "deficit."

No disciplinary sanctions were forthcoming until the FBI heard about the case a year later and started questioning police officials. Soon thereafter, disciplinary hearings were held and two officers were fired, with another two suspended for six days. The officers who were fired were found to have engaged in excessive force and to have used racial epithets, but the city offered them thirty-day suspensions if they would waive a civil service appeal. They refused and were fired.

Criminal Prosecution

The already difficult task of prosecuting police officers accused of criminal offenses is compounded by Georgia state law that allows special privileges for public officials, including police officers, during grand jury proceedings.[53] Defendant police officers are allowed to be present, with legal counsel, throughout the proceedings. At the conclusion of the hearing, the defendant may make a statement to the jurors, while the prosecutors are not allowed to rebut the officer's account. Experts interviewed by Human Rights Watch stated that these procedures are unique and were unaware of other states in which public officials are granted these privileges.[54]

---

[52] According to the plaintiff's lawsuit, the white officer initially denied to investigators that he used the word "nigger" but when he retold the story, he said that Holder told the officer he could not be in his house using the word "nigger."

[53] Police officers are accorded the same rights as public officials in the Official Code of Georgia Annotated (O.C.G.A.) Title 17-7-52, which refers to Title 45-11-4, describing special grand jury procedures for public officials.

[54] According to the National Association of Criminal Defense Lawyers' grand jury expert David S. Rudolph of Rudolph and Maher, Chapel, South Carolina and Prof. Frederick Lawrence, Boston University School of Law.

Prosecutors dislike the special rules for public officials, and acknowledge that they serve as a barrier in their prosecution efforts.[55] The chief of special litigation of the Georgia Attorney General's office objects to the special treatment and believes it is "outrageous that public officials are given greater rights than those provided to ordinary citizens. It gives them a shot to prevent indictment at a stage when no one else has that right."[56] He believes that public officials might be entitled to a small privilege, but testimony the state cannot rebut "is wrong."[57]

The Fulton County District Attorney's office may share that view, following a grand jury's decision not to indict the officers involved in the Jerry Jackson shooting.[58] The defendants were able to gain the sympathy and support of the grand jurors. Not only did the jurors decide not to indict; one juror told reporters that she thought the officers "should be given medals" for their hard work.[59]

A spokesperson with the Fulton County District Attorney's office, Melvin Jones, told Human Rights Watch that he could recall only three cases, including the Jackson shooting, prosecuted by the district attorney during the past five years.[60] He stated that few excessive-force cases reach the stage of charges being filed

---

[55] Georgia state law does not contain a statute specifically addressing use of force by peace officers. The statutes which address use of force are generic and apply to use of force by any person. O.C.G.A. 16-3-21, 16-3-23 and 16-3-24.

[56] Human Rights Watch telephone interview with Terry Lloyd, chief of special litigation for the state's Attorney General's office, March 29, 1996.

[57] Ibid.

[58] See *The State v. Waine L. Pinckney and Willie T. Sauls*, Murder, felony murder and aggravated assault with a deadly weapon (eight counts) No Bill (no indictment), February 8, 1996, Fulton County Superior Court, NB 003050. Most of Atlanta is part of Fulton County.

[59] Rhonda Cook, "Officers should get medals, says grand juror on case," *Atlanta Journal-Constitution*, March 2, 1996.

[60] Human Rights Watch telephone interview with Melvin Jones, spokesperson with the Fulton County District Attorney's office, April 1, 1996. It is worth noting that the *Atlanta Journal-Constitution* and the OPS have reported that files regarding police shootings sent to the district attorney's office in recent years have been lost, which may help explain the lack of action in such cases.

because they seem to "wash out" with the OPS When asked why he believes the cases do not hold up, Jones stated that it's "the police looking out for themselves."[61]

In another case, Roderick Stewart reportedly sustained a black eye and other injuries after Atlanta police officers stopped his vehicle on the evening of November 5, 1993, following a two-mile chase, because they suspected he was driving under the influence of alcohol; officers also reportedly had seen Stewart push someone from his car in a parking lot. The unusual aspect of this case was that the alleged beating was videotaped by cameras mounted on the police vehicles. After viewing the tape, then-Police Chief Eldrin Bell stated, "The tape shows excessive force was used."[62]

Despite the videotaped beating, a Fulton County grand jury chose not indict the accused officer on an aggravated assault charge. After the grand jury failed to indict the officer, the Fulton County District Attorney stated, "The grand jury just isn't after police officers."[63] In 1996, Stewart received $185,000 from the city in a pre-trial settlement.[64]

In 1996, of the twenty cases decided by federal prosecutors for the federal district containing Atlanta (Northern District of Georgia), four were prosecuted (presented to a grand jury to seek an indictment) and sixteen were declined for prosecution. Between 1992 and 1995, 133 cases were considered and none was prosecuted.[65]

Following the reaction to the Rodney King beating case in Los Angeles, the FBI initiated a four-hour civil rights training course for new and current police

---

[61] Ibid. Human Rights Watch attempted to obtain the number of criminal prosecutions against police officers, but no such tracking was done by the district attorney's office at that time; there were plans to institute a policy of tracking these cases. Telephone inquiry, district attorney's office, August 1997.

[62] Bill Robinson, "2 Atlanta officers face probe after beating is videotaped," *Atlanta Journal- Constitution*, November 11, 1993.

[63] Sandra McIntosh, "Atlanta officer cleared of alleged excessive force," *Atlanta Journal-Constitution*, February 2, 1994.

[64] Telephone inquiry, city attorney's office, September 29, 1997.

[65] According to data obtained by TRAC from the Executive Office of U.S. Attorneys, Justice Department. Cases prosecuted or declined represent only a portion of the total number of complaints alleging federal criminal civil rights violations referred to each district in a given year. Several steps prior to this decision narrow down the number of complaints actually received to those considered worthy of consideration.

officers from throughout Georgia. Jerry Miles of the FBI's Atlanta office noted that four hours are not enough, but stated that police chiefs do not want to lose officers for a full day.[66] While much of the information provided in the course's lesson plan is useful, statements such as "civil rights investigations account for less than one percent of the FBI's investigative efforts" and "historically ninety-five percent of the civil rights allegations made to the FBI are determined to be unfounded," seem intended to reassure police officers that they should not fear investigation or prosecution by federal authorities.[67] Further, while the lesson plan states the FBI is unbiased in such investigations, a section of the plan provides defenses available to officers accused of brutality.

The Holder case, described above, shows the pressure federal investigators can bring to bear on police departments to discipline officers appropriately. According to attorneys representing the Holder family, there was little progress in the internal investigation until federal investigators began asking questions.

---

[66] Human Rights Watch interview, Jerry Miles, Federal Bureau of Investigation, Atlanta, March 1, 1996.

[67] Civil Rights Under Color of Law lesson plan, developed by the FBI and the Georgia Civil Rights Under Color of Law Committee, dated May 18, 1993.

BOSTON

Physical abuse of citizens by a police officer is among the most serious violations of the public trust possible.
– St. Clair Commission Report, 1992[1]

The Boston Police Department was founded in 1854, making it one of the first police departments in the country. Although there have been incidents of serious misconduct and brutality, the department is not a notoriously abusive one. As several observers have stated, Boston's 2,300 sworn officers usually seem to abide by an "unwritten rule" that limits how rough they can get without attracting media attention and community outrage. Furthermore, prompt implementation of the recommendations made in the 1992 St. Clair Commission report improved the operations of the police force's internal affairs unit. Still, the 1995 alleged beating of an on-duty, plainclothes officer by fellow officers, and the code of silence that has thus far blocked efforts by investigators in that incident, indicate that reforms are still needed.

The department received a great deal of scrutiny following door-to-door and street searches of a predominantly African-American housing project, following the October 1989 murder of Carol Stuart, who was white. Her husband – who was suspected to be responsible for the murder – claimed the assailant was an African-American man, leading the police to search and harass scores of alleged suspects.[2] Charges of excessive force were made during the raids, but disciplinary sanctions against officers were light.[3]

Following the Stuart case, then-Mayor Raymond Flynn appointed a commission to examine allegations of brutality against the department and how

---

[1] St. Clair Commission, *Report of the Boston Police Department Management Review Committee*, January 14, 1992 (hereinafter St. Clair Commission report).

[2] Kevin Cullen, "Stuart dies in jump off Tobin Bridge," *Boston Globe*, January 5, 1990; Kevin Cullen and Mike Barnicle, "Probers suspect Stuart killed wife," *Boston Globe*, January 10, 1990.

[3] Telephone interview, Bureau of Internal Investigations Superintendent Ann Marie Doherty, January 30, 1998. Doherty noted that delays in the department's investigations into these abuse allegations made fact-finding more difficult. Doherty headed the Bureau of Internal Investigations (BII), which includes the Internal Affairs Division, for six years before transferring to another bureau in February 1998. William F. Doherty, "Internal affairs had gets transfer," *Boston Globe*, February 7, 1998.

those allegations were handled by the force's Internal Affairs Division (IAD). Flynn appointed attorney James St. Clair to chair the commission, which produced a detailed and critical report about the department's management that was particularly negative about IAD's operations. Since the St. Clair Commission report, the department has addressed the report's recommendations, yet accountability at times remains elusive.

St. Clair Commission Report

The St. Clair Commission report was submitted to Mayor Flynn on January 14, 1992. The commission found "substantial problems in the leadership and management of the Department and recommends major changes" including the resignation of then-police Commissioner Francis Roache. Furthermore, its chair stated:

> Our study revealed an investigative and hearing process characterized by shoddy, halfhearted investigations, lengthy delays, and inadequate documentation and record-keeping. The present Internal Affairs process is unfairly skewed against those bringing a complaint. Given the Internal Affairs Division's ("IAD") failure to routinely provide thorough and timely investigations of alleged misconduct, and the fact that the Department sustains less than 6% of complaints against officers, it is no surprise that the overwhelming majority of community residents we spoke to have little confidence in the Department's ability or willingness to police itself. The IAD reports to the Commissioner and its shortcomings adversely reflect on his performance.[4]

By describing in detail the shortcomings of the department and providing recommendations toward improving it, the St. Clair Commission report became something of a blueprint for police reform efforts in the city.

Racial tensions between minority communities and the predominantly white police force did not begin with the Stuart case, but the overzealous conduct of the police during that period reinforced many communities' belief that the police force was unduly suspicious and disrespectful of African-Americans and other minorities. The St. Clair Commission report found that 50 percent of complainants were black and 9 percent were of other minority groups. African-Americans make up approximately 26 percent of the city's population, with other minority groups

---

[4] St. Clair Commission report, p. iv.

accounting for about 15 percent. As of 1996, 69 percent of the Boston police force was white.[5]

Civilian Review

Although the St. Clair Commission report did not endorse a strong civilian review mechanism, it found that, "...given the disturbing results of our case review and the profound lack of confidence and trust the community expressed in the department's current methods of handling citizen complaints, we believe the public must be given access into the system for it to work properly."[6] St. Clair recommended the creation of a Community Affairs Board (CAB), made up of police officers and community members, to review investigations by IAD and, when warranted, to return the cases for further investigation. The CAB was created in 1992, and it may review IAD investigations and, if requested by a complainant, may review the conduct of a disciplinary hearing when a complaint is sustained by IAD. The CAB has five members representing the community and "police interests," who serve without remuneration. The CAB does not receive initial complaints.

If IAD does not sustain a complaint, the complainant has fourteen calendar days to request a CAB review. The CAB is limited to examining investigative techniques only, and cannot deal with a complaint's substance; it does not investigate complaints, but sends them back to IAD if its members agree with the complainant that an investigation was not thorough. Neither CAB's deliberative meetings nor its findings are made public.

If a complaint is sustained and a disciplinary hearing is held to determine the sanction appropriate for the officer involved, the complainant may appeal to the CAB if he or she believes the disciplinary hearing was conducted in an unfair manner. The appeal request must be submitted within seven days of the conclusion of the hearing. According to a CAB representative, such appeals are rare, and she knew of none since 1995.[7]

---

[5] Boston Police Department, 1996 *Annual Report*, p. 24. The annual report does not provide information regarding the race of complainants.

[6] St. Clair Commission report, p. v.

[7] Telephone interview, Victoria Williams, CAB, October 28, 1997. At least one police abuse expert in the city told Human Rights Watch he believed complainants were not allowed, as a rule, to attend entire disciplinary hearings – making such an appeal unlikely – while a representative of the Bureau of Internal Investigations stated that complainants may attend but often choose not to for a variety of reasons.

In response to pressure from citizens in the Dorchester neighborhood of Boston after misconduct complaints increased in that minority community, and following a mistaken SWAT raid on seventy-five-year-old Rev. Accelyne Williams's home on March 24, 1994, the mayor vowed to make improvements in the CAB's operations. During the raid on the wrong house, officers chased Williams into a bedroom and handcuffed him; he then had a heart attack and died. The mayor and police chief acknowledged a mistake, thus alleviating tensions. On April 23, 1996, the city paid $1 million to the wife of Rev. Williams in a wrongful death suit.[8] People in the community pushed for a new civilian review agency, but Mayor Thomas Menino would only promise an improved CAB. City Councilor Charles C. Yancey stated, "I do not believe community residents are comfortable saying the police can police themselves."[9] Menino offered to hire new people and placed the CAB under the city's Office of Civil Rights. In an attempt to defend the CAB's record, Menino compared it to Washington, D.C.'s failed and backlogged civilian review board. He stated that he was proud that "over the last couple of years more than 30 cases have come before our board."[10] Superintendent Ann Marie Doherty, head of the Bureau of Internal Investigations, which includes IAD, had to correct the mayor and noted that, as of mid-1994, the CAB had heard sixteen cases, not thirty. [11]

The CAB is generally considered irrelevant, or worse, among police abuse experts in Boston. Attorneys who specialize in police misconduct civil cases explain that in order to make a successful appeal, a complainant must have information from IAD files which are not accessible to the complainant or the public. The process is underutilized, with the IAD reporting that the CAB received just twenty-three complaints in its first year, referring three to IAD as needing more investigation. According to IAD, CAB had received only six appeal requests during

---

[8] "Boston to give victim's widow $1 million in wrongful death suit," *New York Times*, April 25, 1996.

[9] Adrian Walker and Chris Black, "Police criticized as Menino vows better oversight,"*Boston Globe,* May 18, 1994.

[10] Ibid.

[11] Ibid.

1995.[12] Internal Investigations Superintendent Doherty agreed that improved community outreach regarding CAB was necessary, and stated that a paid CAB staff position was under consideration.[13] Doherty stated that she opposed enhanced civilian review because the police department should be responsible for setting standards, holding officers accountable, and disciplining those who commit offenses.[14]

Police Administration/Internal Affairs Division

The St. Clair Commission was outraged by the quality of IAD investigations and by the absence of a department-wide performance appraisal system. Since the report, the IAD restructured in 1992 and has doubled its staff, to sixteen. According to the 1996 Boston Police Department's *Annual Report*, it received: 460 complaints of all types in 1990, 447 in 1991, 378 in 1992, 271 in 1993, 221 in 1994, 248 in 1995, and 231 in 1996.[15] In 1997, the department reported receiving 166 complaints.[16] In 1996, 22 percent of the complaints alleged the "use of force," but there are other categories that could include excessive force, including violation of rights and violation of criminal law.[17] According to the 1996 *Annual Report*, 28 percent of the complaints filed in 1996 were sustained (with 23 percent pending), a relatively high sustained rate that may be explained by a significant number of

---

[12] Telephone interview, Victoria Williams, CAB, October 28, 1997. In October 1997, Human Rights Watch attempted to obtain information about 1996 CAB appeals, but the CAB representative said the numbers were not then available and failed to provide them subsequently.

[13] Telephone interview, Bureau of Internal Investigations Superintendent Doherty, January 30, 1998.

[14] Ibid.

[15] Boston Police Department, 1996 *Annual Report*, p. 22.

[16] Telephone interview, Bureau of Internal Investigations Superintendent Doherty, January 30, 1998.

[17] Ibid. and telephone interview, Lt. Kevin Averill, IAD, October 16, 1997. It was unclear why "use of force" is a category for violations, since officers are allowed to use force appropriately.

internally generated complaints, which are typically sustained at a higher rate.[18]
The report does not provide disposition statistics broken down by type of complaint,
or any information regarding disciplinary measures taken against officers named in
sustained complaints. The report does not provide age or race information
regarding complainants or districts from which complaints are initiated.

Because the police and CAB both reveal so little information to the public,
tracking specific cases and thus evaluating the department's disciplinary practices
cannot be done systematically. Anecdotal evidence reinforces concerns about
police department oversight of its officers' conduct, however. For example,
following a 1988 beating of a suspect by thirteen officers after a vehicle pursuit, the
state attorney general's office intervened and claimed the police had "stonewalled"
the investigation.[19] A Superior Court judge noted that the intervention was
necessary, "because police officers are not likely to regulate police conduct...."[20]
The attorney general's office and the police department agreed to penalties for the
officers approved by a judge, including retraining on civil rights issues, on truth-
telling, and on the appropriate use of force, and the department was required to
submit regular reports about the named officers for two years. But, according to
press accounts, the department filed only one report in 1994, despite reminders
from the attorney general's office; meanwhile, some of the thirteen officers have
been promoted.

The St. Clair Commission report found that "IAD files revealed a disturbing
pattern of allegations of violence toward citizens by a small number of officers."[21]
In the random sampling of IAD files reviewed by the commission, 49 percent of
officers with new complaints against them in 1989-90 had previously been the
object of complaints, 17 percent had no prior complaints, and in 34 percent of the
cases this could not be determined (due in part to the poor records kept by IAD).
When incomplete files are excluded, 74 percent of officers accused of abuse had
prior complaints. Among officers with prior records of complaints, the median

---

[18] Boston Police Department, 1996 *Annual Report.*, p. 26. Internally generated
complaints (of undefined types) rose from 11 percent of the total in 1991 to 27 percent in
1996. 1997 figure provided in a telephone interview with Superintendent Doherty, January
30, 1998.

[19] Dick Lehr, "Department unwilling to face brutal facts," *Boston Globe,* December 8,
1997.

[20] Ibid.

[21] St. Clair Commission report, p. iv.

number of prior complaints was three. Of the 134 officers who were the object of previous complaints, thirteen (10 percent) had more than ten previous complaints; this small group of thirteen officers had generated an incredible total of 246 complaints. Very few of these complaints had been sustained.

The St. Clair Commission drew highly critical conclusions from these alarming statistics and that fact that they had been ignored by police managers. The commission's report stated: "The failure to monitor and evaluate the performance of police officers – particularly those with established patterns of alleged misconduct – is a major deficiency in the management of the department and an unnecessarily dangerous situation for the citizens of the City of Boston. No police department and no community should tolerate a situation where officers with long records of alleged misconduct, including some with histories of alleged physical abuse of citizens, remain on the street largely unidentified and unsupervised."[22]

During 1997, three officers received more than three complaints, six had three complaints, and fifteen were the subject of two complaints during the year; 94 percent of the force received no complaints.[23] Under the early intervention system, any officer with three or more complaints during a two-year period, no matter the disposition, is identified.[24] The IAD and the officer's commander discuss complaints, talk with the officer about how he or she is dealing with people, and he or she is urged to stay professional. This type of "consulting" happens with each complaint within the police complaints system thereafter against said officer. Inexplicably, however, complaints reflected through civil lawsuits filed or settled or awarded against an officer are not used as part of the EIS, and do not trigger investigations.[25]

The complaints process, prior to IAD's restructuring in 1992, allowed for too much discretion for district supervisors in deciding whether an allegation is well-founded before giving a report to the commander, who then forwarded it to IAD. IAD also lacked the personnel to carry out investigations of all complaints it

---

[22] Ibid., p. 114.

[23] Telephone interview, Superintendent Doherty, January 30, 1998.

[24] Approximately thirty officers were the subject of two or more complaints during 1996, a decrease from previous years, according to the department's 1996 annual report. According to the 1995 annual report, thirty-eight officers were the subject of two or more complaints during that year. The information provided does not show the overlap between years of "repeat" offenders on the force or the types of complaints.

[25] Telephone interview, Lt. Kevin Averill, October 28, 1997.

received directly from internal sources or the public, so the initial, and sometimes the entire, investigation was handled by the supervisor of the accused officer – a situation problematic on its face, since the supervisor may be personally close to the individual or may not want to reflect poorly on his own supervisory skills by acknowledging misconduct on the part of his or her underling. Furthermore, district supervisors described the process as "awkward" because, if they investigated an officer in their district, they had no power to control the disciplinary sanctions that could arise as a result. In district investigations of misconduct, most claim that the IAD was merely a "rubber stamp" on the district's findings.

IAD received harsh criticism from the St. Clair Commission for biased, shoddy investigations and an unusually low sustained rate: "it appears that the department seldom, if ever, believes allegations of police misconduct by Boston's citizens."[26] The IAD files themselves had incomplete or missing forms, were disorganized with no checklist for file contents, and almost 80 percent of files examined by the St. Clair Commission had no record indicating whether non-police department witnesses or the alleged victim had been interviewed.

Despite the post- St. Clair Commission reforms, complainants contend that the investigations drag on for long periods, with some complainants believing the department just hopes they will give up and drop the complaint over time. Complainants also report that investigators and the department do not advise them about the progress of the investigation or even give details about its outcome. IAD claims it stays in close contact with complainants throughout the process, yet staff acknowledge that the final letter to a complainant does not inform as to what discipline, if any, will be applied to the officer if the complaint has been sustained.

IAD now investigates excessive force allegations, and it reviews all investigations conducted by districts.[27] After its investigation, IAD can find the complaint sustained, not sustained, unfounded, filed (if the complainant fails to pursue the complaint), or exonerate the officer's actions as within policy. If the complaint is sustained, the IAD report to the commissioner notes prior complaints, with findings, against the named officer; only previously sustained complaints can be used in determining appropriate disciplinary sanction. If the commissioner in turn sustains the complaint, the case is referred to the legal advisor's office and to a hearing officer to prepare for a disciplinary hearing. If the hearing officer finds against the officer, the officer has the option of appeal through the civil service system and the courts. If the officer prevails, or if the complainant is unhappy with

---

[26] St. Clair Commission report, p. 115.

[27] Telephone interview, Lt. Kevin Averill, October 16, 1997.

a finding other than sustained, he or she has the option of appealing through the CAB (yet such appeals are rare and unlikely to succeed, as explained above).

The St. Clair Commission recommended that the department have IAD handle all complaints from the outset; maintain a centralized personnel computer system; develop written handbooks in several languages about the way the complaint system works; recruit improved IAD staff, with incentives to include a choice of next assignment; enforce a ninety-day deadline on the investigation and resolution of civilian complaints; conduct hearings, review, and disciplinary sanctions, if warranted, of officers involved in the Stuart abuses; develop the EIS; and formalize the organization of "shooting teams "to investigate shootings involving the police. By 1996, the department claimed it had implemented all of the St. Clair recommendations.[28]

In an interview with Human Rights Watch, Bureau of Internal Investigations Superintendent Ann Marie Doherty stated that police misconduct could be curtailed by more rigorous screening of new recruits, improved supervision, and training that emphasizes good decision-making in situations when some force may be justified.[29] Doherty also noted that officers need to feel comfortable coming forward to report incidents of misconduct by fellow officers. She states that she has also tried to work with the police union to make agreements with some officers to hold discipline in abeyance if there is an underlying problem that would not be addressed by discipline, such as the need for counseling or alcohol or drug treatment. If the officer fails to meet the terms of the agreement to get help, the department will move to dismiss him or her.[30]

The department's efforts at improvement have been questioned in some serious cases, however. One, in 1995, involved the beating of a black police officer in plainclothes and others involve police officers' violent treatment of wives and girlfriends.

Officer Michael A. Cox, who is black, was on duty and in plainclothes when he joined the pursuit of a murder suspect in the early morning hours of January 25, 1995. As Cox chased the suspect, he claimed uniformed officers grabbed him and beat him severely, apparently believing that he was a suspect as well. He was

---

[28] Brian MacQuarrie, "Probe of police belies relatively good record," *Boston Globe,* February 12, 1996. In a January 1998 interview, Superintendent Doherty confirmed that IAD had implemented all of the St. Clair Commission recommendations relating to internal affairs procedures.

[29] Telephone interview, Superintendent Doherty, January 30, 1998.

[30] Ibid.

transported by ambulance from the scene to the hospital and treated for large contusions on his head, lacerations on his face and lips, a concussion, and kidney damage. He reportedly missed six months of work while recovering.[31]

The officers accused of the beating gave wildly inconsistent versions of the incident, initially contending that Cox was either not at the scene or that he was not hurt. The two dozen other officers present at the end of the chase denied seeing Cox at all, or claimed they were not near him at the time of the beating. Some of the officers present passed on the rumor that Cox had sustained his injuries after falling on a patch of ice, yet no original source for this contention was identified.

More than three years after the incident, the officers identified by Cox as the assailants have not been disciplined by police officials or charged criminally.[32] The internal investigation has been widely criticized; for example, the suspect who was chased by Cox has claimed that he saw the other officers beating Cox, yet he had not been questioned by investigators as a witness.[33] Federal and local prosecutors intervened two years after the incident, bringing a perjury indictment against one of the officers who was present during the Cox beating and gave a particularly unbelievable account of the incident; the same officer was also suspended.[34] Cox has filed a civil lawsuit, which is pending at the time of this writing.

---

[31] John Ellement, "Detective files suit vs. fellow officers, *Boston Globe*, December 13, 1995; Dick Lehr, "Years after beating, officer has seen no help from colleagues," *Boston Globe,* December 8, 1997. The *Globe* examined internal investigative files to piece together this incident and the subsequent inquiry.

[32] After these allegations, Officer Cox, who is now a detective sergeant, reports that his car's tires were slashed and that he received repeated hang-up calls at night. He has since been assigned to the internal affairs unit.

[33] The supervising sergeant during the Cox incident, who also filed an inconsistent report, was later transferred to the anti-corruption unit responsible for investigating the case. The internal affairs unit, and the department more generally, have fought efforts to make any information about the Cox case public. Documents requested in a civil lawsuit were not turned over until a federal judge threatened to find the city in default.

[34] Telephone interview, Superintendent Doherty, January 30, 1998. Doherty confirmed that the officer had been indicted on perjury charges.

IAD has also been criticized for its handling of domestic violence complaints filed by the wives and girlfriends of Boston police officers.[35] Superintendent Doherty acknowledged to Human Rights Watch that the most common reason police officers are arrested is for domestic violence and that those cases often do not lead to convictions.[36] Indeed, as part of a review of the department to identify those convicted of domestic violence charges in order to comply with a new federal law, only one or two officers may be dismissed, with six officers on modified duty pending the outcome of investigations into alleged domestic violence.[37]

In response to critics who claim that officers protect each other in these cases, the Bureau of Internal Investigation's Doherty has told the press, "We're [officers are] extraordinarily sensitive to domestic violence, and we deal with it as aggressively on the inside as the outside."[38] Yet she acknowledged to reporters that the department did not know the number of cases of domestic violence because it did not classify the complaints under a single category.[39] Compounding the problem is that a restraining order against a police officer may not be reported to the police department if the officer lives in a community outside the force's own jurisdiction. The officer's superior may not know that an order has been issued.[40] According to an IAD representative, it is not the responsibility of other jurisdictions to report officers involved in domestic violence, but instead such reporting is incumbent upon the involved officer.[41] If the department becomes aware of

---

[35] Sally Jacobs, "Women say their abusers had badges," *Boston Globe*, July 3, 1994. In one case, a sergeant was charged with stalking his former girlfriend and threatening to kill her and her children in June 1994. According to reports, during his fifteen year career, he was the subject of six complaints: two for verbally abusing women, one for alcohol use, and three for excessive force. The harshest penalty was a one-day suspension after a fellow officer complained about his behavior.

[36] Telephone interview, Superintendent Doherty, January 30, 1998.

[37] Ibid.

[38] Jacobs, "Women say their abusers...," *Boston Globe*.

[39] Ibid.

[40] Ibid. and Lynda Gorov, "No unusual trend seen in officers' behavior," *Boston Globe*, March 9, 1993.

[41] Telephone interview, Lt. Kevin Averill, October 28, 1997.

incidents of domestic violence, an investigation may ensue to determine whether the officer was involved in "conduct unbecoming an officer" or other rules violations.[42]

Civil Lawsuits

Human Rights Watch initially requested information about civil lawsuits in a December 1996 letter; after four telephone reminders and a new letter, Human Rights Watch received a response in September 1997. We requested information on the amount of money paid by the city of Boston for the purpose of settling cases alleging police brutality or the use of excessive force. The staff attorney with the Office of the Legal Advisor of the police department responded: "Neither the Department, nor the City of Boston, maintain records in a form responsive to your request, i.e., a list or compilation of the amount of money paid to settle police brutality cases."[43] When asked about this information, the BII superintendent claimed that such data do exist; she did promptly provide judgment award amounts in police misconduct cases, but she did not provide information about settlements, as requested.[44] During 1997, there were two judgments totaling $7,500 against officers whom the city did not represent because they broke departmental rules, and one judgment of $250,000 in a case the city did defend; that case was being appealed as of January 1998.

Human Rights Watch also requested information on procedures: whether an investigation is initiated by the police department once a civil lawsuit is filed, settled, or judged in favor of a plaintiff in a brutality-related case. The legal advisor's response did little to clarify this point; he stated that the city's Law Office may send notification to the police department regarding the filing of a civil action, and an "informational memo" is sent to the department's Bureau of Investigative Services, if there are potential internal affairs implications. It is unclear who decides whether there are such implications or what precisely happens upon receipt of an "informational memo."[45]

---

[42] Ibid.

[43] Letter from Robert E. Whalen, Staff Attorney, Office of the Legal Advisor, to Human Rights Watch, September 16, 1997.

[44] Telephone interview, Superintendent Doherty, January 30, 1998.

[45] Letter from Robert E. Whalen, Staff Attorney, Office of the Legal Advisor, to Human Rights Watch, September 16, 1997. Indeed, according to an IAD representative, his understanding was that it was incumbent upon the officer named in a civil lawsuit to notify his or her commander.

According to the BII superintendent, civil lawsuit awards and settlements are now paid from the police department's budget; this practice began in 1997.[46] She stated that this change has made the department pay closer attention to civil suits.

Criminal Prosecution

IAD claims to work closely with the district attorney's office of Suffolk County. In rare cases, prosecutors initiate investigations into alleged criminal police misconduct, but the D.A.'s office reportedly does not maintain a list of cases involving police officers as defendants.[47]

In 1996, of the eighteen cases decided by federal prosecutors for the federal district containing Boston (Massachusetts), two were prosecuted (presented to a grand jury to seek an indictment), and sixteen were declined for prosecution.[48] Between 1992 and 1995, 102 cases were considered, and one was prosecuted.

The IAD - federal prosecutor relationship is more distant. IAD rarely passes cases to federal prosecutors in the U.S. Attorney's office. The U.S. Attorney generally relies on direct complaints, referrals from the Justice Department, or media coverage of a case.[49] According to a lawyer with the U.S. Attorney's office, the last successful case prosecuted under the federal criminal civil rights statutes in the district was in 1984 from Lynn, Massachusetts.[50] He stated that there are very few complaints coming from the city of Boston. The U.S. Attorney's office has prosecuted cases from surrounding towns, including Falmouth and Worcester.

---

[46] Telephone interview, BII Superintendent Doherty, January 30, 1998.

[47] Telephone inquiry, Suffolk County District Attorney's office, August 6, 1997.

[48] According to data obtained by TRAC from the Executive Office of U.S. Attorneys, Justice Department. Cases prosecuted or declined represent only a portion of the total number of complaints alleging federal criminal civil rights violations in each district in a given year. Several steps prior to this decision narrow down the number of complaints actually received to those considered worthy of consideration.

[49] As described above, federal prosecutors are investigating and prosecuting some of the officers involved in the Cox incident.

[50] *U.S. v. William T. Marler*, U.S. Court of Appeals for the First Circuit, 756 F.2d 206, decided March 8, 1985, decision upholding conviction. Human Rights Watch interview, Theodore Merritt, U.S. Attorney's office, August 9, 1995.

CHICAGO

In 1968, Chicago became a symbol of police brutality as overzealous police officers attacked protesters outside the Democratic National Convention while a national television audience watched. There was no repeat of that level of violence against protesters during the 1996 Democratic National Convention, but in the intervening years Chicago's police have reportedly committed serious abuses, including torture. In November 1997, police Superintendent Matt Rodriguez resigned after reports surfaced that he had maintained a close friendship with a convicted felon, in violation of department policy.[1] A new chief, twenty-nine-year veteran Terry Hillard, was named in February 1998; he told reporters that "misconduct, corruption and brutality will not be tolerated."[2]

Torture

The repeated practice of torture by Chicago police came to light in the late 1980s and early 1990s.[3] One case involved Andrew Wilson, who was accused (and later convicted) of shooting and killing police officers William Fahey and Richard

---

[1] Police Department regulations prohibit police employees from fraternizing with anyone who has been convicted of a crime. Fran Spielman and John Carpenter, "Rodriguez retires as top cop," *Chicago Sun-Times*, November 14, 1997; Steve Mills and Andrew Martin, "Rodriguez bails out," Chicago Tribune, November 15, 1997; "Chicago police official retires," New York Times, November 15, 1997. It was later reported that police officers' unhappiness with the superintendent's treatment of two officers accused of using excessive force in a racially charged September 1997 case played a part in Rodriguez's decision to resign. Stephanie Banchero, "Brutality case, promotions spur police union vote on Rodriguez," Chicago Tribune, November 4, 1997.

[2] Gary Washburn, "Hillard named Chicago's top cop," *Chicago Tribune*, February 18, 1998 and Dirk Johnson, "Popular detective will head Chicago police," *Chicago Tribune*, February 19, 1998.

[3] Torture by police officers is not, strictly speaking, use of excessive force, but is an unjustified and criminal assault. Torture is prohibited by international human rights treaties by which the U.S. is bound, including the International Covenant on Civil and Political Rights and the Convention against Torture and Other Cruel, Inhuman or Degrading Treatment or Punishment.

O'Brien on February 9, 1982.[4] When Wilson was questioned on February 14 at the South Side Area 2 station, he suffered multiple injuries: he claimed that officers supervised by Commander Jon Burge tortured and brutalized him during an interrogation that lasted for seventeen hours.[5] He claimed electric shocks were administered to his head and genitals and that police cranked a "black box" to produce electric currents after clips were attached to parts of his body; Wilson was also allegedly stretched over a hot radiator and burned.[6]

The People's Law Office, an activist firm, conducted an investigation and identified sixty-five suspects who were tortured by Burge or other officers and detectives between 1972 and 1991 in Areas 2 and 3.[7] A report by the police investigatory agency, the Office of Professional Standards (OPS), found that physical abuse "did occur and that it was systematic....[T]he type of abuse described was not limited to the usual beating, but went into such esoteric areas as psychological techniques and planned torture. The evidence presented by some individuals convinced juries and appellate courts that personnel assigned to Area 2 engaged in methodical abuse."[8]

---

[4] Amnesty International, "Allegations of Police Torture in Chicago, Illinois," December 1990 (hereinafter Amnesty International, "Allegations of Police Torture"); Ken Parish Perkins, "The bane of brutality," *Chicago Tribune*, July 4, 1994.

[5] Ibid., John Gorman, "'Police tortured me,' cop killer says at suit hearing," *Chicago Tribune*, February 24, 1989; John Gorman, "'Torture' charged in rights suit," *Chicago Tribune*, February 16, 1989; Ken Parish Perkins, "The bane of brutality," *Chicago Tribune*, July 4, 1994; John Conroy, "Town without pity," *Chicago Reader*, January 12, 1996.

[6] Ibid.

[7] Telephone interview with attorney G. Flint Taylor of the People's Law Office, October 23, 1997; list of sixty-four alleged victims in Affidavit of G. Flint Taylor, *Illinois v. Patterson*, No. 86-C-6091 (Cook County Cir. Ct. filed November 13, 1996); Statement of G. Flint Taylor, before the Congressional Black Caucus, September 12, 1997, p. 2. For a detailed description of many of the torture allegations, *see* Conroy, "Town without pity," *Chicago Reader*; and Conroy, "The shocking truth," *Chicago Reader*, January 10, 1997.

[8] Office of Professional Standards report by investigator Michael Goldston, September 28, 1990 (hereinafter "Goldston Report"), p. 3. Goldston's report listed the names of fifty alleged victims of torture and brutality, the names of detectives who had been involved, and stated: "Particular command members were aware of the systematic abuse and perpetuated it either by actively participating in same or failing to take any action to bring it to an end." Ibid.

After the city settled the claim of thirteen-year-old Marcus Wiggins, who alleged electric shock by Burge's detectives, the attorneys representing Wiggins fought for the release of the department's internal documents related to the case and its investigation, noting that the police are public servants and that issues of public safety and general public interest were at stake. The city and police union had argued to protect the privacy interests of the officers named in the files and a supposed chilling effect that would negatively affect future police internal investigations.[9] The court found in favor of the public's right to know, stating:

> No legitimate purpose is served by conducting [police internal] investigations under a veil of near total secrecy. Rather, knowledge that a limited number of persons, as well as a state or federal court, may examine the file in the event of civil litigation may serve to insure that these investigations are carried out in an even handed fashion, that the statements are carefully and accurately taken, and that the true facts came to light, whether they reflect favorably or unfavorably on the individual police officers involved or on the department as a whole.[10]

Andrew Wilson's first civil case alleging torture by the police resulted in a hung jury; his retrial did not find the officers personally responsible but did find a de facto policy within the Chicago police department to ill-treat certain suspects. After a complicated series of court challenges, Wilson won a judgment of over $1.1 million ($100,000 for damages and $1 million for attorneys' fees).[11] At least three other plaintiffs were awarded damages in civil lawsuits related to the torture allegations for an additional $250,000.[12]

---

[9] The contract between the city and the police union prevents the disclosure of the names of officers under investigation "unless there has been a criminal conviction or a decision has been rendered by the Police Board." Andrew Martin, "Badge shields cops accused of misconduct," *Chicago Tribune*, August 6, 1995. When names of officers are disclosed, they are usually provided by prosecutors' offices.

[10] *Wiggins v. Burge* (Slip Op. At 6,) quoting *Mercy v. County of Suffolk*, 93 F.R.D. 520, 522 (E.D.N.Y.)

[11] Telephone interviews, G. Flint Taylor, October 31, 1997 and January 15, 1998. Wilson's $100,000 was awarded to the estate of one of the police officers he was convicted of killing.

[12] Amnesty International, "Allegations of Police Torture," p. 2 and telephone interview with G. Flint Taylor, October 31, 1997.

In March 1994, the city argued that Burge and other detectives were not acting within the scope of employment when they abused Wilson, and that the city should not have to pay any jury award against those officers; instead the payment should come from the officers themselves. In practice, this would mean that the victim would not be compensated appropriately. The city's court pleading stated, in part, "[I]mmediately following his arrest, plaintiff Wilson was placed in the custody of Chicago police. While in police custody, defendant Burge physically abused plaintiff Wilson by a variety of means including kicking him, electro-shocking and burning him by attaching him to a radiator...."[13]

After the Wiggins case in September 1991, and long after the Wilson allegations of torture, Burge was dismissed and two detectives involved in the Wilson case were suspended by the Police Board.[14] According to insider and press reports, as of 1997, no other detectives or others on the force had been disciplined for any of the other sixty-four cases where torture was alleged.[15] Indeed, several of Burge's colleagues involved in the torture cases had been promoted, commended or allowed to retire with full benefits.[16] OPS investigators reopened twelve of the torture cases and reportedly recommended discipline for several officers, but the

---

[13] *See* para. 11 of the Cross-Claim of the City of Chicago against Officer Jon Burge, *Wilson v. City of Chicago*, No. 86-C-2360 (U.S. District Court, N.D. Ill. filed April 18, 1996). The judge ruled against the city. *See* also Charles Nicodemus, "City appealing brutality award," *Chicago Sun-Times*, January 11, 1997 and Conroy, "The shocking truth," *Chicago Reader*.

[14] The Police Board issued its decision in February 1993; in December 1995, the officers' court appeals were exhausted and the punishments were upheld. Burge was dismissed for participating in and not stopping the abuse of Wilson, and the detectives were suspended for failing to stop or report the abuse. All three were found guilty of failing to obtain medical attention for Wilson. Supt. Matt Rodriguez reportedly attempted to also demote the detectives, but the punishment was overturned because the police union contract allows only one punishment for an infraction. Conroy, "Town without pity," *Chicago Reader*, January 12, 1996.

[15] Taylor, statement before Congressional Black Caucus, p. 3, and Conroy, "Town without pity," *Chicago Reader*.

[16] Taylor, statement before the Congressional Black Caucus, p. 3.

OPS director overruled the recommendations.[17] In the cases of two sergeants identified as abusers involved with Burge, OPS investigators sustained complaints and recommended discipline; instead one sergeant was decorated for valor by the mayor (who also recommended him promoted to lieutenant) while the other retired with full benefits.[18]

No criminal prosecutions were pursued against the officers involved in the torture incidents. The U.S. Attorney's office reportedly learned of the Area 2 torture cases after the five-year statute of limitations for civil rights cases had passed; when it was suggested that conspiracy charges could still be brought against those involved who continued to cover up their involvement, there was still no action toward pursuing the cases.[19] Meanwhile, prisoners remain on death row following confessions forced by Burge and others on the police force through torture techniques.[20] Burge attempted to get reinstated, but his dismissal was upheld in February 1994. The police union expressed outrage when he was not reinstated: "This we feel is a miscarriage of justice.... In this entire case, there is not one shred

---

[17] No investigation was reopened in the Melvin Jones case. Jones alleged that he was electric-shocked by Burge in the presence of several other detectives, and the city of Chicago reportedly admitted in court pleadings that Jones was tortured. *See* Local Rule 12 N Statement of the City of Chicago in Opposition to Plaintiff Andrew Wilson's Motion for Summary Judgment against the City of Chicago, Complaint, *Andrew Wilson v. City of Chicago*, U.S. District Court, Northern District of Illinois, No. 86-C-2360, para. 26, May 15, 1995: "Nine days before plaintiff was abused, defendant Burge electroshocked Melvin Jones on the genitals and thigh with a device in a wooden box and threatened him with a gun, while he was handcuffed....in an attempt to coerce a confession from him...." City's answer: "The city admits the statements contained in para. 26." *See* also G. Flint Taylor, "Two significant decisions in Chicago torture cases," Police Misconduct and Civil Rights Law Reporter, vol. 5, issue 10, July/August 1997, p. 109.

[18] One of those involved in the torture incident, Sgt. Peter Dignan, was promoted to lieutenant in 1995. When questions were raised about Dignan's connection with several allegations of brutality and torture – as established in OPS reports and publicized civil cases against the city – Superintendent Rodriguez told reporters that he was not aware of allegations against Dignan when he made his promotion selections. Charles Nicodemus, "Brutality rap hits merit cop," *Chicago Sun-Times*, March 18, 1995.

[19] Conroy, "Town without pity," *Chicago Reader*.

[20] According to attorney G. Flint Taylor, ten such prisoners remain on death row. A press report placed the number at six. Editorial, "Probe Illinois justice," *Chicago Sun-Times*, July 16, 1997.

of evidence. It's strictly a political victory and that's what this is, political."[21]
Union officials further claimed the dismissal of Burge was an effort to "neutralize
law enforcement."[22]

Incidents

In Chicago, as in most cities, abuse cases often have racial components. The
local National Association for the Advancement of Colored People (NAACP)
reports that its office receives, on average, two complaints of police misconduct a
week involving African-American victims.[23] The NAACP notes that race data are
not collected by the Office of Professional Standards (OPS) – data that could help
identify trends in the treatment of minorities.

Case of Jeremiah Mearday: Racial tensions between minority communities and
the police most recently came to a head in September 1997, when eighteen-year-old
Jeremiah Mearday alleged brutality on the part of officers from the city's West
Side.[24] On September 26, Mearday, who is black, was with friends when two white
officers, James Comito and Matthew Thiel of the Grand Central District, emerged
from their patrol car, one of them reportedly with his gun drawn.[25] Mearday and his
friends claimed the officers started kicking and beating Mearday with flashlights.[26]
Mearday was hospitalized with a broken jaw and head injuries. For their part, the

---

[21] Andrew Fegelman, "Cop firing in torture case upheld," *Chicago Tribune,* February
11, 1994.

[22] Perkins, "The bane of brutality," *Chicago Tribune.*

[23] Telephone interview, Furmin Sessions, Executive Director, Chicago NAACP,
August 24, 1995.

[24] Stephanie Banchero and Flynn McRoberts, "Forces collided to highlight cop-abuse
charges," *Chicago Tribune*, October 13, 1997; Michelle Roberts, "Pols join marchers in
brutality protest," *Chicago Sun-Times*, October 12, 1997.

[25] It was later reported that there was an arrest warrant out on one of the men with
Mearday, but it was unclear whether the men were originally approached in relation to the
warrant.

[26] After the incident, the department reportedly switched to less heavy flashlights.
Steve Mills, "Brutality probe makes case for Mearday, cops," *Chicago Tribune*, December
7, 1997.

officers claimed Mearday resisted arrest and punched Comito.[27] Mearday was charged with resisting arrest and battery; there were no reports of injuries to the officers who were allegedly attacked by Mearday.[28]

In response to community outrage over this and other incidents of perceived police abuse and harassment in the city's West Side, and following the intervention of state and national legislators, the U.S. Justice Department announced it would review the Mearday incident to ascertain whether federal criminal civil rights violations had occurred.   And in an unusually rapid response, the police superintendent suspended the two officers involved in the Mearday beating and sought to have them fired.[29] The department filed disciplinary charges against the officers and claimed that the officers had filed false reports about the altercation. It was reported that Officer Comito was involved in at least one other incident involving the use of excessive force on April 20, 1997, but was not disciplined until the Mearday case attracted attention; the superintendent reportedly was seeking to dismiss him in relation to the April 1997 incident.[30] Fraternal Order of Police officials denied wrongdoing on the part of the officers, with the union's president, William Nolan, telling reporters, "I'm sick and tired of our police officers getting punched and pummeled and kicked," Nolan said. "Some punk gets cracked because he resists arrest, and everybody makes him out to be a hero."[31] In the meantime, the attorney representing Mearday claimed difficulty in obtaining even basic information about the incident from the police department, telling reporters, "The city has taken the position that they don't have to provide anything."[32]

---

[27] Steve Mills, "Brutality probe makes case for Mearday, cops," *Chicago Tribune*, December 7, 1997.

[28] Ibid.

[29] Steve Mills, "Two cops suspended in Mearday beating," *Chicago Tribune,* October 21, 1997.

[30] Ibid. and Steve Mills, "Cop in Mearday brutality case is suspended," *Chicago Tribune,* October 20, 1997. At the time of this writing, the alleged victim in the April 1997 claimed that Officer Comito was not one of the officers who beat him but was present during the incident. Steve Mills, "Beating victim says accused cop not the one," *Chicago Tribune*, February 26, 1998.

[31] Michelle Roberts, "Brutality fall out enrages cop union," *Chicago Sun-Times*, October 11, 1997.

[32] Ibid.

After reports of a disorganized and contentious police board disciplinary hearing, featuring conflicting witness accounts and an apparently substandard OPS investigation,[33] the police board found the officers guilty on administrative charges of using excessive force and of trying to cover it up by filing "blatantly false reports."[34] The police board president reportedly stated the officers' version of events was "simply unbelievable."[35] The officers were fired, but their attorney reportedly planned to appeal the decision. In April 1998, resisting arrest and battery charges against Mearday were dropped.[36]

Following the Mearday case and other incidents of brutality, Mayor Richard Daley stated, "[A]ny officer who commits police brutality will be looking at penitentiary time, and he or she will lose their job. That's plain and simple right there."[37] Then- Police Supt. Matt Rodriguez stated that the department would have a "zero tolerance" policy toward misconduct and reportedly sent a department-wide memo expressing his concern over "serious allegations of excessive use of force and criminal acts [that] have been leveled against members of the department."[38] And the mandate of a task force created in February 1997 to investigate police corruption was expanded to include brutality.[39]

---

[33] Mills, "Brutality probe makes case...," *Chicago Tribune*, December 7, 1997; Steve Mills, "Cops try to turn tables on Mearday," *Chicago Tribune*, December 16, 1997; Mills, "Key Mearday witnesses stumble at hearing," *Chicago Tribune*, December 24, 1997; Mills, "Side issues bog down Mearday hearing," *Chicago Tribune*, January 13, 1998; Mills, "Testimony adds to twists in Mearday beating case," *Chicago Tribune*, January 14, 1998.

[34] Associated Press, "Police board: 2 guilty of brutality," March 13, 1998, [Wire Service]; Michelle Roberts, "Cops who beat Mearday dismissed," *Chicago Sun-Times*, March 14, 1998.

[35] Michelle Roberts, "Board fires 2 cops in Mearday beating," *Chicago Sun-Times*, March 13, 1998; Steve Mills, "2 cops guilty in Mearday case," *Chicago Tribune*, March 13, 1998.

[36] Lorraine Forte, "1st Mearday case dismissed," *Chicago Sun-Times*, April 10, 1998.

[37] Michelle Roberts, "Cop panel takes lumps on brutality," *Chicago Sun-Times*, October 10, 1997.

[38] Michelle Roberts and Basil Talbott, "Feds go after cop brutality," *Chicago Sun-Times*, October 8, 1997.

[39] Ibid.

Case of Eric Holder: In another racially charged case, Eric Holder, a Chicago police officer who is African-American, alleged that he was beaten while off duty on July 10, 1997 by white officers at the scene of a shooting, and that the beating took place despite Holder's identifying himself as an officer.[40] Holder also alleged the officers, from the West Side's Austin District, yelled racial epithets at him. Holder claims that he was attempting to calm the shooting victim's brother when officers told him to leave the scene; when he responded that he was an officer and was taking the man to see his brother at the hospital, the officers reportedly took offense, pushed him to the hood of a patrol car, and hit him. When he fell to the ground, Holder claims he was dragged nearby and beaten with batons and flashlights. The officers reportedly told him, "You're not one of us." Several neighborhood residents reportedly confirmed Holder's account.[41] Holder was arrested and charged with battery and resisting arrest; he told reporters that he was not surprised by the charges, since officers involved in altercations usually charge the individual involved, even when the officers are the aggressors.[42]

In March 1998, Holder was convicted of resisting arrest and sentenced to a form of probation and a work program.[43] He was also stripped of his police duties. According to an OPS investigator, an investigation into Holder's allegations was opened, but she could not disclose additional information about its status.[44] In January 1998, the Justice Department announced that it would open an investigation into Holder's allegations.[45]

Case of Joseph Carl Gould: In another high-profile case, Joseph Carl Gould, an African-American homeless man, was shot and killed on July 30, 1995, by an off-duty white police officer, Gregory Becker. Gould, who washed windshields at red lights and asked for payment from drivers, got into an altercation with Becker. According to press reports, Becker went to his car to retrieve his gun, shot Gould,

---

[40] Steve Mills, "Cops beat me, officer says," *Chicago Tribune*, October 8, 1997.

[41] Ibid.

[42] Ibid.

[43] "Cop gets probation for resisting arrest," *Chicago Tribune,* March 7, 1998.

[44] Telephone inquiry, Investigator Conlis, April 27, 1998.

[45] Steve Mills, "U.S. to probe cop's alleged beating," *Chicago Tribune*, January 10, 1998.

and drove away; he did not report the shooting.[46] Becker was subsequently charged with involuntary manslaughter, but that charge was dismissed by a Cook County Circuit Court judge because of conflicting witness accounts, including Becker's companion's defense of him. A witness who knew neither of the men reportedly said Becker grabbed Gould and shot him.[47] Community activists alleged a weak effort by the Cook County state's attorney, who is a former police officer. Because of sustained community pressure, former officer Becker was subsequently charged with involuntary manslaughter and armed violence, and was convicted in April 1997. In May he was sentenced to fifteen years in prison.[48] Gould's family filed a civil lawsuit against the city that is pending.

Case of Jorge Guillen: On October 3, 1995, Jorge Guillen, who had a history of mental illness and was reportedly threatening his family, died after officers tackled him and one knelt on his back, apparently causing asphyxiation.[49] OPS investigated the case and found that Guillen had been asphyxiated by one officer and that other officers allegedly hit him with a flashlight while he was handcuffed. The officers claimed that Guillen attacked them with a board. After the OPS reportedly recommended that three of the involved officers be suspended, police Superintendent Rodriguez vacated one of the suspensions; the Police Board eventually vacated the remaining two suspensions.[50] The decision was met with community protests, with some calling for the resignation of the Police Board's

---

[46] Don Terry, "Homeless man's life gains currency in death," *New York Times,* September 10, 1995; John W. Ellis IV, "Homeless face death on the streets of Chicago," *Streetwise,* August 16-31, 1995.

[47] Terry, "Homeless man's life...," *New York Times.*

[48] Gary Marx and Flynn McRoberts, "Hard time for cop: Becker gets 15 years," *Chicago Tribune,* May 29, 1997.

[49] Jerry Thornton, "Ruling on cop suspensions sparks protest," *Chicago Tribune,* December 13, 1996; Andrew Martin, "Daley backs officers in death of Honduran," *Chicago Tribune,* February 5, 1998.

[50] Brian Jackson, "Fire cops, says widow of man who died in police struggle," *Chicago Sun-Times,* February 5, 1997.

members and the police superintendent.[51] No criminal charges were brought against the officers following federal and state's attorneys' investigations.[52]

In February 1998, the city reportedly agreed to a settlement of $637,000 for Guillen's family, one of the largest settlement amounts involving police in recent city history.[53] The settlement required City Council and court approval, which were pending at the time of this writing.

Sexual assaults: In August 1993, a Chicago police detective was arrested and charged with kidnaping, criminal sexual abuse, and official misconduct following a twenty-hour standoff with officers attempting to arrest him.[54] Harrison Area Det. John Summerville was accused of committing three sexual assaults over a month and a half beginning in July 1993. He allegedly ordered women into his car at gunpoint, showing his police identification. Summerville had reportedly been the subject of three complaints of alleged brutality, none of which were sustained by IAD.[55] In July 1995, he pleaded guilty to sexually assaulting several women during traffic stops and was sentenced to four years in prison.[56] At least one of the women reportedly filed a lawsuit against the city.[57]

Case of David Arana: On April 29, 1988, off-duty officer Johnny Martin got into an altercation after a fender-bender with David Arana.[58] Arana spoke no

---

[51] Ibid.

[52] Andrew Martin, "Daley backs officers in death of Honduran," *Chicago Tribune*, February 5, 1998.

[53] Ibid.

[54] Lou Carlozo, "Cop facing misconduct, sex counts after standoff," *Chicago Tribune,* August 21, 1993.

[55] Ibid.

[56] "Ex-cop gets 4 yrs. in sex assault," *Chicago Sun-Times*, July 28, 1995; Andrew Martin, "Badge shields cops accused of misconduct," *Chicago Tribune*, August 6, 1995.

[57] "Suit claims officers assaulted woman," *Chicago Tribune*, August 11, 1994.

[58] Florence Hamlish Levinsohn, "A fender bender escalates into a police brutality suit," *Chicago Tribune*, February 12, 1993; interview with Edward Stein, attorney for Arana's family, August 24, 1995.

English, and Martin did not speak Spanish. After Arana failed to produce his license and appeared drunk, Martin fatally shot Arana in the right side of the neck as he drove slowly and as Martin leaned into the car's passenger side window.[59] Arana's autopsy showed bruises on Arana's face and right arm. While Arana was being operated on after the shooting, police charged him with battery, leaving the scene of an accident and negligent driving. A friend of Martin's who witnessed the incident, however, stated that Arana never posed a threat to Martin.[60]

Martin reportedly told the OPS three different stories about what had happened, witness statements taken by a plainclothes officer on the scene were not found in the investigators' files, and relevant tests were not done. Arana's attorney told the press that the OPS investigator never questioned Martin, or any witnesses, or other police officers because, as the investigator explained to the attorney, he knew there was a code of silence.[61] The OPS report said "the shot fired by Officer Johnny Martin was accidental. Officer Martin was justified in having his gun drawn. Officer Martin was in fear of his life because the victim/offender refused to stop his vehicle while a part of Officer Martin's body was hanging out of the car and while the victim/offender punched Officer Martin in the face."[62] Martin, reportedly, was never treated for wounds allegedly received during the confrontation.[63]

The attorney representing Arana's family filed a civil suit against Martin and the city. As the civil trial approached in January 1993, the city settled the case by offering Arana's family about $1 million.

Martin was shot and killed during another off-duty altercation two years later. The Chicago police department gave Martin a hero's funeral, and the City Council proclaimed a "Johnny Martin Day," rather than the typical practice of passing a resolution in honor of the slain officer.[64]

---

[59] Martin had explained that he always carried his gun because, "I never know when I am going to get involved in some type of action that requires police intervention." Hamlish Levinsohn, "A fender bender escalates...," *Chicago Tribune.*

[60] Hamlish Levinsohn, "A fender bender escalates...," *Chicago Tribune.*

[61] Ibid.

[62] Ibid.

[63] Ibid.

[64] Ibid.

The case of Shirley Alejos: On June 10, 1994, Shirley Alejos was arrested by Chicago police officers after she and others reportedly refused to leave an area near Alejos's home.[65] Alejos was taken to the police station, where officers claimed she was uncooperative and would not answer questions about an alleged gang-related disturbance in her neighborhood.[66] Alejos alleges that, once she was at the station house and handcuffed, two Foster Avenue District officers, Ross Takaki and Robert Knieling, beat her; her eyes reportedly were swollen shut afterward, and she was bruised on her face and body.[67] The officers claimed that Alejos injured herself, yet witnesses reported hearing her scream during the beating, and a doctor found that her injuries were consistent with her allegations.[68]

Officers Takaki and Knieling were found guilty of the beating in administrative hearings and were suspended for fifty-five days; they reportedly remained on the force as of October 1997. Alejos also won a $200,000 settlement of a lawsuit against the city. In April 1997, Alejos and her attorney renewed their calls for criminal prosecution of the officers. A spokesmen for the State's Attorney office and the U.S. Attorney's office told reporters that prosecutors would consider the case if Alejos's attorney would provide them with information. It was unclear why the prosecutors were seemingly unaware of a three-year-old case that had resulted in relatively serious disciplinary action against the officers or why the burden to provide information was placed on the victim and her representative when the Police Board had deliberated on the case already and would have key information. The prosecutors' reactions also pointed to a lack of communication between the police department and prosecutors, since this type of case – involving apparent criminal behavior on the part of officers – should have been brought to prosecutors' attention much earlier.

Corruption scandal: As in other cities' police departments, there is often a link between brutality and corruption on Chicago's police force. On December 20, 1996, seven Chicago police officers were indicted in federal court on charges of

---

[65] Telephone interview with Standish Willis, an attorned who works closely with the NAACP, August 24, 1995, and Lorraine Forte, "Beating victim wants cops prosecuted," *Chicago Sun-Times,* April 15, 1997.

[66] Misdemeanor battery and property damage charges against Alejos were subsequently dropped.

[67] Lorraine Forte, "Beating victim wants...," *Chicago Sun-Times.*

[68] Ibid.

extortion after they allegedly stole money from drug dealers.[69] The officers were part of an elite tactical unit, members of which robbed or extorted money from undercover officers posing as drug dealers. The sting operation followed months of complaints by residents of the Austin neighborhood in the city's West Side about the officers, who would also rough up drug addicts and steal their money.[70] Said a community leader, "[M]aybe they thought they were doing some kind of street justice....But that's no excuse. If you can't trust the police, who can you trust?"[71]

Following this police corruption scandal and another in Gresham District, the Commission on Police Integrity (hereinafter "the Commission") was created to examine misconduct in the Chicago police force and ways to avoid future scandals; in November 1997, the commission published its findings and recommendations.[72] While the focus of the report was police corruption, it also described general problems with recruitment, training, oversight and disciplinary systems that are relevant to the issue of police brutality. (See below.)

Office of Professional Standards
The Office of Professional Standards (OPS) was created in 1974. It is part of the 13,500-member police department but is staffed by civilians. The office is headed by a chief administrator who is appointed by the mayor and works for the police superintendent. It has approximately sixty-five investigators who may be ex-police officers but not from the Chicago police department.[73] According to OPS, the police department is required to notify OPS when they receive complaints

---

[69] Don Terry, "7 Chicago police officers indicted in extortion scheme," *New York Times,* December 21, 1996 and Terry, "Worst fears realized with Chicago officers' arrests," *New York Times*, December 30, 1996.

[70] Investigators were also trying to determine whether one of the arrested officers was a high-ranking gang leader, as rumored, and if so, how he became and remained a police officer. Terry, "Worst fears realized...," *New York Times.*

[71] Terry, "7 Chicago police...," *New York Times.*

[72] Office of International Criminal Justice, University of Illinois, Chicago, *Report of the Commission on Police Integrity*, presented to Chicago Mayor Richard M. Daley, November 1997.

[73] Telephone interview with Carmen Cristia, Coordinator of Operations, OPS, October 22, 1997.

directly, and the police stations must be accessible to complainants.[74] All excessive force complaints, shootings by police, deaths in custody and domestic disputes involving officers are investigated by OPS. The department does not have a special team to deal with shootings by officers; homicide detectives work with OPS on shooting investigations (although critics claim OPS often simply adopts the homicide investigation's findings as its own). The OPS files a report with the Police Board monthly, and those reports are available to the public.

The office received more than 3,000 excessive force complaints a year during both 1996 and 1997.[75] This is a high rate of excessive force complaints; for example, New York City's police force is the subject of a similar number of excessive force complaints annually, yet is triple the size of Chicago's. A representative of the department told Human Rights Watch that one explanation for the high rate of complaints is that each complaint made to OPS is counted, whether or not the complainant signs a complaint or submits one in writing at all.[76]

The OPS claims to sustain approximately 10 percent of investigated complaints.[77] The OPS chief administrator reviews investigations and recommends

---

[74] Interview with Gayle Shines, Chief Administrator, OPS, August 24, 1995.

[75] Telephone interview, Carmen Cristia, OPS, October 22, 1997 and OPS memorandum to the police superintendent, dated October 6, 1997. Steve Mills, "Brutality complaints about cops on decline," *Chicago Tribune*, January 13, 1998. That article noted that the number of complaints dropped slightly, from 3,138 in 1996 to 3,115 in 1997.

[76] Telephone interview, Don Zoufal, general counsel, Chicago Police Department, January 22, 1998.

[77] Ibid. According to press reports, the 1996 sustained rate for excessive force complaints was 8 percent. Michelle Roberts, "A heavy burden of proof," *Chicago Sun-Times*, October 9, 1997. Information provided by OPS to Human Rights Watch did not include totals for 1997, as requested, but the 1995 sustained rate provided was also 8 percent. According to press reports, about 10 percent of complaints investigated during 1997 were sustained. Mills, "Brutality complaints about cops," *Chicago Tribune*, January 13, 1998. Police abuse experts contend that the sustained rate includes allegations that are part of excessive force complaints but not directly related to excessive force itself; they further contend that after appeals and arbitration, sustained complaints actually acted upon are much lower than 8 to 10 percent.

discipline up to thirty days' suspension.[78] The police superintendent may order discipline of up to five days' suspension, and the officer may not appeal; when the discipline is six to thirty days' suspension, the officer may appeal to the Police Board.[79] If the discipline is more than thirty days' suspension or dismissal, the Police Board hears the case.[80] In 1992, in response to police-union complaints about the disciplinary charges against Commander Burge (*See* above), who was brought up on charges nine years after he allegedly tortured Andrew Wilson, a five-year statute of limitations on administrative proceedings was established through state legislation.[81]

The Police Board, composed of nine civilians appointed by the mayor, often exonerates officers brought before it for serious disciplinary sanctions, or reduces the penalties against the officers.[82] According to press reports, more than half of the officers the superintendent tried to fire over a five-year period ending in late 1997 were either acquitted or had their sentences reduced.[83] In its own defense, the board contends that it is presented with weak cases that cannot be upheld. In 1996, during which more than 3,000 complaints against the police were filed with OPS, the board decided six cases in which the superintendent sought dismissal based on excessive force charges: in one case a firing was reduced to a suspension, in another the charges were withdrawn (which usually means an officer resigned before a case was

---

[78] Only prior complaints that were sustained are considered in disciplinary recommendations, and five years after investigations are completed OPS purges all non-sustained complaints from its files, in accordance with the police union's contract.

[79] Telephone interview, Don Zoufal, general counsel, CPD, January 22, 1998.

[80] Anything less than dismissal may be arbitrated. Telephone interview, Don Zoufal, general counsel, CPD, January 22, 1998.

[81] Conroy, "Town without pity," *Chicago Reader.*

[82] Steve Mills, "Lax discipline for cop brutality fuels distrust," *Chicago Tribune,* November 12, 1997.

[83] Ibid.

heard), and four officers were found not guilty.[84] The board usually does not explain the reasoning behind its rulings.[85]

For its part, the Police Board blamed former Superintendent Rodriguez for not taking brutality cases seriously enough. The board also blamed OPS for delays. The board's president claimed, "it is so bogged down in OPS that we're losing credibility."[86] And the Commission on Police Integrity found that the disciplinary system was thwarted by long delays between an incident and the imposition of a sanction due to multiple appeals.[87] The Commission called for streamlining this process so that arbitration does not take place years after an incident, thus requiring the department to locate and seek cooperation from witnesses who may have observed an incident years earlier.[88]

Many community activists and attorneys who represent victims of police abuse in civil suits do not hold the OPS in high regard.[89] They claim that the OPS staff is often rude to complainants, conducts sloppy investigations, and places an enormous burden on complainants to prove their cases. Said one attorney who often represents alleged victims in civil lawsuits against the police force, "If the police officer denies it, you're out of luck."[90] There is a perception among community activists that the OPS is biased in favor of the police generally and is particularly vulnerable to pressure by the police union. The code of silence among officers is strong during OPS reviews, as officers routinely claim no knowledge of alleged excessive force.

---

[84] Ibid.

[85] According to press reports, the Police Board members who decide cases do not necessarily hear the case, instead relying on transcripts and help from the hearing officer. Mills, "Cops try to...," *Chicago Tribune.*

[86] Ibid.

[87] Office of International Criminal Justice, University of Illinois, Chicago, *Report of the Commission on Police Integrity*, November 1997.

[88] Ibid.

[89] The OPS's reputation was not helped when an OPS investigator was found guilty of misdemeanor theft in 1996 yet remained employed by the OPS after a thirty-day suspension. The investigator denied stealing items, despite a videotape showing the theft. Steve Mills, "Cop prober's shoplifting conviction disclosed," *Chicago Tribune*, October 21, 1997.

[90] Telephone interview, attorney Standish Willis, August 24, 1995.

The vast majority of cases investigated by OPS are found "not sustained," meaning that the OPS could not determine whether or not the incident took place as alleged by the complainant.[91] OPS Chief Administrator Gayle Shines claims the reason for the small percentage of sustained cases "...is that a lot of these cases are one-on-one."[92] Because cases are so rarely sustained, police abuse experts and even the commander of the Internal Affairs Division have recommended using "not sustained" complaints to gauge whether certain officers against whom repeated complaints are filed should receive training, counseling or other special attention.

OPS does not have subpoena power, does not hold public hearings and, if it makes policy recommendations, they are not made public.[93] The OPS does not publish a detailed report on its work, key findings, or important trends in abuse complaints; the report that it makes public contains only tallies of complaints, investigative findings (unfounded, exonerated, not sustained, or sustained), and disciplinary action recommended (reprimands, suspensions, and separations). The OPS does not provide any information regarding the subject officer or complainant, such as race, age, or gender, or the district where the incident took place or where the officer involved is assigned. OPS staff explain that funding has not been available for computerization of its work, and that everything is done by hand, making a comprehensive public report unfeasible.[94]

Police Administration/Internal Affairs Division

Because of the role assigned OPS, the Internal Affairs Division (IAD) does not play a large role in excessive force cases. The division is responsible for keeping track of complaints against officers, yet efforts to utilize a computerized tracking system that would identify "problem" officers who are the subjects of repeated complaints have been derailed. According to a police abuse expert in the city, approximately 200 to 300 officers (or 2 percent), out of a department of more than 13,000, are the subjects of 20 to 25 percent of brutality complaints.[95]

---

[91] The OPS uses a preponderance of the evidence legal standard.

[92] Roberts, "A heavy burden...," *Chicago Sun-Times.*

[93] Telephone interview, Carmen Cristia, OPS, October 22, 1997.

[94] IAD and OPS will not allow complainants to view investigative files without obtaining a subpoena. Telephone inquiry, IAD and OPS representatives, December 17, 1997.

[95] Taylor, statement before the Congressional Black Caucus, September 12, 1997.

In July 1994, Police Superintendent Rodriguez announced the use of a computer system, called BrainMaker, that would identify officers whose records indicated that they required additional oversight, training, or counseling, with the goal of keeping problem-prone officers from becoming worse.[96] Attorneys representing alleged police abuse victims in civil cases claimed that an IAD sergeant deleted the lists of "problem" officers generated by BrainMaker once attorneys began requesting the lists.[97] The head of IAD disclosed in a deposition that the BrainMaker system was used, and that reports were generated every three months from the beginning of 1995 through mid-1996; it was not clear what, if anything, was done to deal with officers identified in those reports – or what became of the reports themselves, which are now missing.[98] As of late 1997, police officials stated that they were considering utilizing BrainMaker again, but only in close cooperation with the police union; police abuse experts expressed doubt that the system would ever be used as initially intended. When questioned about BrainMaker, the police department's general counsel stated that there has been an early warning system – a behavioral alerts system – in place since 1983.[99] He stated that BrainMaker was not intended to supplant the system that already existed, but acknowledged that the department was unable to implement BrainMaker.[100]

The Commission on Police Integrity report urged the enhancement of the behavioral alerts program to identify at risk officers more consistently.[101] As proof of the need for an improved early warning system, the report noted that the seven indicted officers from the Austin District were the subject of ninety-three

---

[96] Tom Seibel, "Computer profiles to help sniff out crooked cops," *Chicago Sun-Times,* July 4, 1994; Steve Mills, "High-tech tool to weed out bad cops proved a bust," *Chicago Tribune,* October 15, 1997.

[97] Telephone interview with attorney G. Flint Taylor of the People's Law Office, October 23, 1997

[98] Ibid.

[99] Telephone interview, Don Zoufal, general counsel, CPD, January 22, 1998.

[100] Ibid.

[101] Office of International Criminal Justice, University of Illinois, Chicago, *Report of the Commission on Police Integrity,* November 1997.

complaints, with only two sustained.[102] In the Gresham District, three indicted officers were the subject of forty complaints, and only three were sustained. The Commission urged the behavioral alerts program to include non-sustained complaints, since they are neither proven nor disproved. The Commission also urged the department to examine units that have a higher than usual rate of allegations of misconduct, since the report contended that corrupt officers tend to bond together. The report also recommended that the behavioral alerts system include not just complaints, but also other data indicative of potential misconduct, including civil liability judgments.[103]

Police personnel are not always willing to receive complaints and pass them to OPS. One police sergeant interviewed by Human Rights Watch stated that he talks to complainants to determine whether the complaint is good. He contended that many complaints are made by people who are arrested who just want to cause trouble for the officer. He also said that the department does not like one-on-one complaints. He stated that most firings of police officers are related to drug charges or corruption, and rarely to the use of excessive force.[104]

Civil Lawsuits

Between 1992 and 1997, the city reportedly paid more than $29 million to settle 1,657 lawsuits involving excessive force, false arrest, and improper search allegations.[105] Earlier published figures showed that between 1991 and 1994, the city paid $16 million in civil settlements relating to police brutality and false arrest cases.[106] The city's corporation counsel pointed out to reporters that this amount was not an increase, since between 1984 and 1988, Mayor Washington's administration paid $27 million. The corporation counsel did not mention that these

---

[102] Ibid.

[103] Ibid.

[104] During ride-along with Sgt. Lynn Garmon, August 25, 1995, in 7th District/Englewood section.

[105] Martin, "Daley backs officers ...," *Chicago Tribune*. This figure does not appear to include judgments against officers after civil trials. Despite several letters and a half-dozen phone calls over a ten-month period, the corporation counsel failed to provide current figures on police misconduct civil lawsuits to Human Rights Watch.

[106] John Kass, "Watchdog proposed for police," *Chicago Tribune*, January 10, 1995.

amounts could be reduced if police officers refrained from abusive treatment in the first place. Indeed, according to court records examined by an investigative reporter, 230 officers with repeated complaints against them accounted for 46 percent of the $16 million in judgments against the city between 1991 and 1994.[107]

In 1995, a mayoral candidate called for a new post of inspector general to monitor civil suits against the police after reports were published showing large amounts paid by the city in civil lawsuits alleging police brutality and other misconduct. The city's corporation counsel at the time, Susan Sher, stated in response, "There's no need whatsoever for an inspector general."[108] This was not the first time concern about significant civil settlements had been voiced. In 1994, city aldermen balked at authorizing a $500,000 settlement for a man who had suffered brain damage as the result of an alleged police beating, with one suggesting a special council subcommittee to review settlements in more depth.[109] The city is self-insured, and the City Council must authorize any settlement over $100,000.

OPS initiates an investigation when a civil suit is filed against an officer. According to an attorney who frequently represents plaintiffs in police abuse civil cases, he allows OPS to attend depositions rather than interviewing his client separately. He states that OPS will not proceed with an investigation under these stipulations, and that the investigation will be closed instead. An OPS representative disputed this, stating that this situation does not present a problem and that investigators would attend a deposition under these conditions.[110]

According to attorneys who represent alleged victims of police abuse in Chicago, officers are not concerned about these cases because they do not have to pay damages themselves, and their supervisors often do not know about complaints involving their own officers. Advocates believe that an OPS investigation that leads to a not-sustained conclusion should be reopened if the city agrees, or is ordered, to pay the client.

Other attorneys claim that alleged victims are not advised by OPS that their statements could be used against them in criminal trials. Nonetheless, during the

---

[107] Deborah Nelson, "Cops' free rein costs city millions," *Chicago Sun-Times*, January 8, 1995.

[108] Kass, "Watchdog proposed...," *Chicago Tribune*.

[109] Robert Davis, "City may look closer at suit settlements," *Chicago Tribune*, February 8, 1994.

[110] Telephone interview with Carmen Cristia, OPS, October 22, 1997.

last few years some attorneys have begun encouraging complainants to file their complaints with the OPS to put the incident on record.

Criminal Prosecution

Local prosecutions of Chicago police officers accused of criminal acts are rare. According to press reports, the Cook County State's Attorney's office has prosecuted only a handful of cases against officers accused of brutality during the past fifteen years.[111] As in most cities surveyed for this report, the district attorney's office does not acknowledge tracking criminal cases against police officers. The former chief administrator of the OPS, David Fogel, who headed the office between 1984 and 1990, told the press he remembered only one brutality case leading to a criminal conviction during his tenure.[112] Foley also has stated that he believed going to the State's Attorney's office futile, and instead reported cases to the U.S. Attorney's office for federal prosecution.[113] For their part, the State's Attorney's office claims that it counts on the OPS to refer possibly criminal cases but that OPS rarely does so.[114]

One longtime police misconduct attorney told Human Rights Watch he knew of no federal prosecutions of abusive Chicago police officers during the past fifteen years.[115] Attorneys in Chicago do pass suitable cases to federal prosecutors, but few lead to prosecution. According to press reports, the U.S. Attorney's office only learned of the Area 2 torture cases after the five-year statute of limitations for civil rights cases had passed; when it was suggested that conspiracy charges could still be brought against those involved who continued to cover up their involvement, the office still did not act.[116]

---

[111] Conroy, "Town without pity," *Chicago Reader*. Citing a *Chicago Tribune* report, Conroy states that there were only two such prosecutions between 1983 and 1992, and that he surveyed prosecutors for his 1996 article and they were unable to cite any such cases.

[112] Steve Mills, "U.S. police brutality indictments prove rare," *Chicago Tribune*, October 9, 1997.

[113] Conroy, "Town without pity," *Chicago Reader*.

[114] Ibid.

[115] Interview with attorney Edward Stein, August 24, 1995.

[116] Conroy, "Town without pity," *Chicago Reader*.

In 1996, of the eighteen cases involving possible civil rights violations decided by federal prosecutors for the federal district containing Chicago (Northern District of Illinois), none was prosecuted (presented to a grand jury to seek an indictment). Between 1992 and 1995, seventy-nine cases were considered, and six were prosecuted.[117]

---

[117] According to data obtained by the Transactional Records Access Clearinghouse (TRAC) from the Executive Office of U.S. Attorneys, Justice Department. Cases prosecuted or declined represent only a portion of the total number of complaints alleging federal criminal civil rights violations because several steps prior to this decision narrow down the number of complaints actually received to those considered worthy of consideration.

DETROIT

Detroit has a history of racial unrest, expressed in race riots in the 1960s. In the 1990s, racial tensions have been exacerbated by the case of African-American Malice Green, who was reportedly brutally beaten by white officers in 1992 and later died en route to a hospital. Still, police abuse monitors in Detroit report that police brutality within the city is less pronounced than in surrounding, majority white, suburbs where African-Americans are reportedly harassed and mistreated more regularly by the police.

Incidents

Malice Green: On November 5, 1992, Malice Green was questioned by Detroit police officers Larry Nevers and Walter Budzyn, who suspected Green of possessing drugs, as he sat in a parked car.[1] Green allegedly failed to comply with the officers' order to drop something in his hand (which, although disputed, may have been drugs). Budzyn reportedly hit Green's fist and wrestled with him in the front seat of the car. Nevers allegedly hit Green in the head repeatedly with his flashlight during the incident. Another officer placed him on the ground and allegedly kicked him. An Emergency Medical Service (EMS) worker arrived on the scene and sent a computer message to his superiors asking, "[W]hat should I do, if I witness police brutality/murder?"[2] Other officers and a supervisor arrived but did not intervene to stop the beating. Green had a seizure and died en route to the hospital. After the beating, officers reportedly washed blood from their hands with peroxide and wiped blood from their flashlights and Green's car. Then-Police Chief Stanley Knox quickly labeled Green's death a murder and dismissed seven officers who were involved in the incident because of their actions or inaction.[3]

Officer Nevers had reportedly been the subject of twenty-five citizen complaints, and Officer Budzyn was the subject of nineteen; none was substantiated

---

[1] Sean P. Murphy, "Detroit hurts anew," *Boston Globe*, November 23, 1992; Jim Schaeffer and Roger Chesley, "The fatal force case," *Detroit Free Press*, May 29, 1993; Janet Wilson, "Ex-cops get prison," *Detroit Free Press*, October 13, 1993.

[2] Schaeffer and Chesley, "The fatal force case," *Detroit Free Press*.

[3] Ibid. Four of the suspended officers later sued the city, Mayor Coleman Young, and Chief Knox, claiming their dismissals violated due process. In February 1997, the city agreed to pay the officers a total of $3.35 million in an out-of-court settlement. "4 cops win $3.35. million in Green case settlement," *Detroit Free Press*, February 25, 1997.

by investigators.[4] Nevers was also reportedly the subject of three lawsuits the city settled with plaintiffs. In one lawsuit, the city settled for $275,000 in the shooting of a robbery suspect.[5] Green's family was awarded $5.25 million in a civil lawsuit. [6]

In 1993, Nevers and Budzyn were convicted of second-degree murder in the Green case and began serving their sentences at a federal prison in Fort Worth, Texas; Nevers received a twelve- to twenty-five-year sentence, and Budzyn was sentenced to eight to eighteen years in prison.[7] Nevers and Budzyn appealed their convictions, alleging jury tainting, jury bias, erroneous jury instruction, insufficient evidence, and improper denial of a change of venue to lessen pre-trial media impact.[8] In July 1997, the Michigan Supreme Court overturned Budzyn's conviction, finding that the jury had been tainted but that only Budzyn's conviction was affected because the evidence against him was not as compelling as the evidence against Nevers.[9] Budzyn was subsequently freed on bond. Then, in

---

[4] Sean P. Murphy, "Detroit hurts anew," *Boston Globe*, November 23, 1992. The *Free Press* reported that each of the officers had more twenty-five citizen complaints filed against them and that none was substantiated by police investigators. Schaeffer and Chesley, "The fatal force case," *Detroit Free Press*, May 29, 1993.

[5] Ibid.

[6] In another costly lawsuit relating to the Green case, a former assistant Wayne County medical examiner who was pressured to alter his findings by his superiors was awarded $2.5 million by a jury in May 1997. The coroner had claimed that he was dismissed because he refused to state that cocaine contributed to Green's death but stuck by his finding that Green's death was a homicide caused by blunt-force head injuries. "Coroner in Green case gets millions," *Detroit Free Press*, May 16, 1997.

[7] The other officer involved in the Green case, Officer Robert Lessnau, was reinstated in March 1994 after he was acquitted on assault charges, and remained on the force as of October 1997.

[8] Charlie Cain, "State high court to hear appeals of Budzyn, Nevers this week," *Detroit News,* November 11, 1996.

[9] Pete Waldmeir, "O'Hair's decision to retry Budzyn certainly doesn't make a lot of sense," *Detroit News*, August 17, 1997; David Ashenfelter, "Budzyn case prosecutor opts to go for new trial," *Detroit Free Press*, August 15, 1997.

December 1997, Nevers was released from prison.[10] Prosecutors appealed the decision by a federal judge to overturn Nevers' conviction.

In August, the Wayne County prosecutor announced plans to retry Budzyn.[11] In April 1998, Budzyn was convicted of involuntary manslaughter in the Green case and sentenced to four to fifteen years in prison.[12] It appeared that he would not serve additional time in prison because of time already served.[13]

Officer Vernon Gentry: In a case that was developing at the time of this writing, Vernon Gentry, a 5th District officer, was charged along with two other officers in federal court with conspiracy to rob a citizen of $1 million.[14] Gentry reportedly had a troubled history on the force. He was suspended twice and was the subject of brutality lawsuits that were settled by the city. The suspensions stemmed from alleged attacks against his girlfriends. He was acquitted on charges related to fires he had been accused of setting at one girlfriend's house in 1994, but he was suspended for approximately two years while the charges were pending. In 1997 he was again reportedly involved in an assault on a girlfriend, during which he reportedly put a gun to the woman's head and beat her hands with the gun's handle; he was charged with felonious assault, but the charges were dropped when the woman failed to appear in court. Gentry was suspended for two months in the second case.[15]

---

[10] Ron French and David Shepardson, "The partner: Nevers hopeful about outcome," *Detroit News*, March 20, 1998.

[11] Ibid., and Jim Dyer, "Budzyn, Nevers 'not close friends,'" *Detroit News*, February 19, 1998.

[12] B.J. Reyes, "Detroit cop sentenced in beating," *Associated Press*, April 17, 1998, [Wire Service]; "Ex-cop convicted in beating death," *Associated Press*, March 19, 1998, [Wire Service].

[13] "Ex-Cop free in beating death," *Associated Press*, May 20, 1998, [Wire Service].

[14] David Migoya, "10-year cop had history of suits, suspensions," *Detroit Free Press*, January 15, 1998; Suzanne Siegel, "The Southfield raid case," *Detroit Free Press*, January 23, 1998; David Migoya, "Victims' families recall violence by heist suspects," *Detroit Free Press*, January 19, 1998.

[15] Migoya, "Victim's families recall violence by heist suspects," *Detroit Free Press*, January 19, 1998.

At least two lawsuits alleging brutality were filed against Gentry. In 1993, a man filed a lawsuit over a reported beating incident. In 1995 a man sued the city and Gentry, after Gentry allegedly shot the man in the leg; at the time of the incident, Gentry was on suspension in relation to the arson charges but was reportedly carrying his badge and gun when the shooting occurred. The city settled this case for $32,500, according to press reports.

Freddie Vela: Freddie Vela, age eleven, was shot and killed by off-duty Detroit police officer Glenn Price on July 22, 1995.[16] Vela was riding his bicycle near a dispute between Price and another man outside a bar. Price shot twice at the man, but missed and hit Vela, who was riding his bicycle nearby. Price was convicted of second-degree murder charges and sentenced to ten to fifteen years in prison.[17] The Vela killing led the city's Latino minority to decry mistreatment by officers and lack of attention by the media and civil rights groups. Vela's family reportedly filed a wrongful death lawsuit against the police department.

Bobby Fortune: On June 29, 1995, Bobby Fortune was walking in the area of Rangoon and Tireman in Detroit when a police squad car approached and two officers emerged.[18] The officers questioned Fortune, who pleaded with them not to arrest him; Fortune claims that one of the officers told him, "You look like you want to run; go ahead, run."[19] Fortune ran, and the officer chased him, punched him in the face, and knocked him to the ground. Both officers then reportedly proceeded to punch, kick, and stomp Fortune about his head, face, chest, and body and legs. Witnesses to the alleged beating told the officers to stop, and the officers threatened the witnesses and told them to leave. Other officers arrived on the scene, and they brought Fortune to Detroit Receiving Hospital where he was treated for broken ribs, facial lacerations requiring stitches, a fractured nose, and an eye injury, along with

---

[16] Santiago Esparza, "Detroit's Latinos cry out for respect after officer's trial," *Detroit News*, February 25, 1996.

[17] According the Wayne County prosecutor's office, telephone inquiry, October 15, 1997.

[18] *Bobby Fortune v. City of Detroit, Detroit police officers Darryl Brown and Lemuel Wilson, and other officers*, U.S. District Court Case No. 96-72432, filed July 10, 1996, U.S. District Court, Eastern District of Michigan, Southern Division.

[19] Ibid.

various contusions and abrasions. He was released the next day and was not charged with any crime.

On September 20, 1995, Fortune, through his attorney, requested copies of records pertaining to his arrest and injuries. On October 4, 1995, a complaint and warrant were issued against Fortune, resulting in his being charged with resisting and obstructing a police officer, stemming from the June 29 incident.[20] It appeared that charges were only filed against Fortune after his attorney requested records to support a possible civil lawsuit against the officers.[21]

Citizen Review

The civilian Board of Police Commissioners has its own investigative staff, called the Office of the Chief Investigator (OCI), with two civilians and eleven police investigators.[22] The OCI is responsible for receiving and investigating non-criminal citizen complaints, although it only investigates some of the complaints received, allowing supervisors in the involved unit or precinct to conduct their own investigations in some cases.[23] The OCI and precinct misconduct investigations are reviewed and approved by the Board of Police Commissioners. A complainant may "appeal" if he or she believes there was an error or omission in the investigation. Hearings are not provided for, and the OCI does not usually make policy recommendations to the department, although it is permitted to do so. Detroit's procedures are somewhat unusual, because civilians on the board are allowed to impose discipline on officers.[24]

Citizens can complain by letter, phone, in person or through a friend at any precinct, bureau, section or unit of the police department, or with the OCI directly, according to the OCI. According to activists, however, complainants are often

---

[20] Ibid.

[21] Telephone interview with an attorney representing Watson, Michael Haddad of Goodman, Eden, Millender & Bedrosian, October 21, 1997.

[22] Interview with Thomas Eder, then-chief investigator, August 16, 1995 and acting Chief Investigator Odson Tetreault, October 24, 1997.

[23] The Internal Affairs Division investigates possibly criminal misconduct.

[24] August 17, 1995 letter from the OCI to Human Rights Watch stating one of the duties of the board is to "act as final authority in imposing or reviewing discipline of employees of the Police Department."

dissuaded by officers from filing complaints. It also appears local stations have a certain amount of discretion regarding which complaints they pass to the OCI.

Activists also claim that the process is generally too informal, with the complainant receiving nothing in writing when the complaint is initially filed by phone or mail (if filed in person, the complainant receives a copy of the complaint) or as the investigation progresses or ends, from either OCI or the Internal Affairs Division. This is confirmed by IAD, which told Human Rights Watch that it has no standardized complaint form and does not always inform complainants about the conclusion of an investigation, but it does contact the complainant at the outset of an investigation.[25]

According to its 1995 annual report, 901 citizen complaints were made against the police during 1995, up from 819 in 1994; 710 in 1993; and 693 in 1992.[26] Between 1992 and 1995, citizen complaints rose 23 percent, while the police force grew by approximately 2.5 percent.[27]

During 1995, there were 281 "force" allegations. A force complaint involves the use, or threatened use, of force. Since officers are allowed to use force appropriately, the definition does not necessarily mean "excessive" or "unnecessary" force is alleged. The annual report states that 281 force allegations were closed during the year (apparently leaving no backlog), and seven were found to have involved "improper conduct."[28] This is a 2.5 percent sustained rate on force complaints.

If OCI receives a complaint it considers serious, it will pass the complaint to IAD. Technically, the OCI can monitor IAD investigations that began with an OCI complaint, but IAD often investigates without OCI's knowledge.[29] If a civil lawsuit is filed against a police officer, alleging misconduct that would fall under OCI's mandate, OCI may receive a request from the city's Law Department for

---

[25] Telephone interview, Lt. Williams, IAD, August 16, 1995.

[26] City of Detroit, Board of Police Commissioners, *Annual Report: 1995*, pp. 3 and 6. The 1996 annual report was not available as of late September 1997.

[27] Ibid, p. 13.

[28] Ibid, p. 8.

[29] Telephone interview with Lt. Williams, August 16, 1995 and interview with Tom Eder, OCI, August 16, 1995.

information to defend the city, if an OCI investigation has already taken place. Otherwise OCI does not receive notification and no investigation is initiated.[30]

The OCI chief investigator acknowledges that precinct investigations are not of the same quality as OCI's.[31] He reported that the OCI was working on creating an "at risk" database to identify and monitor officers with repeated complaints, yet as of October 1997, no such database was being utilized.[32] The acting chief inspector cited "computerization problems" to explain why the "at-risk" system was not functional.

Then-OCI chief investigator Thomas Eder told Human Rights Watch in August 1995 that Detroit did not have a major police abuse problem. He stated that, more and more, communities were working with the police, and that those making complaints are "not part of the community in a positive way."[33] This is a troubling statement, coming from the individual tasked with overseeing investigation of such complaints in an unbiased manner.[34]

Police Administration/Internal Affairs

The five-member civilian Board of Police Commissioners oversees the nearly 4,100-person police department. Its members are appointed by the mayor and approved by the City Council and serve five-year terms. The board has been criticized in the past for not acting independently of the police department. Said former City Councilman Keith Butler of the commission, during the uproar caused by the Green incident, "It has not acted as an independent commission. They are supposed to watch out for citizens, not be a rubber stamp for the mayor and police department."[35]

As with many internal affairs divisions, the Detroit IAD does not provide much information to the public about its operations or investigations. An IAD

---

[30] Telephone interview with Odson Tetreault, acting Chief Investigator, OCI, October 24, 1997.

[31] Ibid.

[32] Ibid., and telephone interview with Tetreault, October 24, 1997.

[33] Interview with Tom Eder, OCI, August 16, 1995.

[34] Eder has since retired, and, as of this writing there was no permanent replacement.

[35] Zachare Ball and David Ashenfelter, "Detroit police board faulted," *Detroit Free Press,* November 21, 1992.

representative told Human Rights Watch that there are no standardized complaint forms, and the number or type of complaints investigated by IAD are not published. But he did claim a 40 percent sustained rate on complaints handled by IAD.[36] Since no information is provided, there is no way to verify this claim, nor to isolate the sustained rate on excessive force complaints, since the IAD's overall sustained rate includes theft, drug, and other corruption investigations that are typically sustained at a much higher rate than excessive force cases.

The IAD representative confirmed that OCI often has no knowledge of IAD investigations. Furthermore, he stated that IAD does not have access to OCI records on past abuse complaints (nor does OCI have access to IAD data), meaning that significant information about an officer's past misconduct complaints may not be known to investigators.

If a complaint is sustained, we were told, there are internal disciplinary hearings; no civilians are involved, except for an attorney to represent the accused officer. IAD does not recommend disciplinary sanctions, said the IAD representative; these are handled entirely by the chief of police.[37] In late 1997, the police department created a computer tracking system to identify officers who are repeatedly the subjects of civil lawsuits or citizen complaints.[38] Prior to this development, IAD did not have a real tracking system, but maintained "cards" on allegations to look for patterns; it was a judgment call as to whether an officer required attention.[39]

Prior to January 1994, there was a special team to monitor incidents of firearms discharges, but it is now defunct. Only the police homicide division now investigates shootings by police.

A ride-along by Human Rights Watch with two Detroit police officers was instructive regarding officers' attitude about misconduct charges.[40] The two officers were from the 1st Precinct, which covers the downtown area; one of the officers was

---

[36] Telephone interview with Lt. Williams, August 16, 1995.

[37] The Board of Police Commissioners is the final authority in disciplinary matters.

[38] David Migoya, "Police computer will track complaints against officers," *Detroit Free Press*, September 6, 1997.

[39] Telephone interview with Lt. Williams, August 16, 1995.

[40] Ride-along, August 16, 1995.

a man and white, the other a woman and African-American.[41] The male officer told Human Rights Watch that he believed police do not receive enough respect and that citizens have too many rights. He stated that the Malice Green case was a "travesty" – not the alleged abuse, but the way it was handled in court.

The woman officer told of a colleague (also female) who, having witnessed abuse by a fellow officer, was prepared to testify against him at a disciplinary hearing; she was taken off the witness list when superiors learned of her intent. Both officers said that there is a lot of favoritism, so that whether or not you get punished or dismissed for misconduct has more to do with your connections than with the seriousness of the alleged abuse. The woman officer did say that if she sees another officer out of control and becoming abusive, she calls for a sergeant.

Civil Lawsuits

Detroit frequently settles police misconduct lawsuits without much resistance by the city. As a result, those filing lawsuits receive compensation from the city, but little is done to correct problems identified in the suits. According to reports prepared by City Councilman Mel Ravitz, the city spent $72 million on police lawsuits between 1987 and 1994.[42] And between July 1, 1995 and April 1997, the city paid nearly $20 million in cases involving excessive force, wrongful death, vehicle pursuits, and minor accidents.[43] Using court and city records, the press reported that, between 1986 and 1997, the city paid more than $100 million to settle civil lawsuits against the police force.[44] Said former Councilman Keith Butler after the Malice Green beating, "The millions of dollars the city paid out in police lawsuits should have been a real red flag that they need to do something."[45]

---

[41]   The force is divided almost equally between whites and African-Americans.

[42]   Roger Chesley, "Police training program could cut lawsuits," *Detroit Journal,* April 20, 1997; Telephone interview with Brenda Miller, City of Detroit Legal Department, May 8, 1997. These figures include all cases of "police impropriety," while excluding high-speed chase payouts; most amounts relate to wrongful death and excessive force incidents.

[43]   Ibid. During 1997, it was reported that the city paid or was ordered to pay approximately $15 million in lawsuits filed against Detroit's police force for all types of misconduct and mistakes. David Josar, "Cops cost Detroit millions in lawsuits," *Detroit News,* March 9, 1998. Some of the jury awards were being appealed by the city. Lawsuits against the city are paid out of the city's general fund.

[44]   Josar, "Cops cost Detroit...," *Detroit News.*

[45]   Ball and Ashenfelter, "Detroit police board...," *Detroit Free Press.*

Councilman Ravitz has repeatedly urged the police department to develop a risk management program, which the department reportedly did after Chief McKinnon took office in 1994.[46] Even though the program reportedly monitors officers involved in lawsuits or citizen complaints, with one goal being a reduction in police abuse lawsuits, 1997 saw the largest amounts in payouts since 1990.[47]

In response to Ravitz's reports and press attention, Chief Isaiah McKinnon stated in early 1995 that he was trying harder to improve recruiting, supervision, and attitudes on the force so as to try to reduce these lawsuits.[48] And in April 1997, the police department initiated a new field training program so that new officers are paired with veteran officers who are tasked with showing the recruits the proper way to deal with citizens; city leaders believed the programs should have cut down on complaints and lawsuits.[49]

Neither the OCI nor the IAD initiate investigations once a lawsuit is filed alleging excessive use of force or other abuse relating to the agencies' mandates.

Criminal Prosecution

Both OCI and IAD representatives told Human Rights Watch that criminal prosecution of officers was rare, except for very high-profile cases (as described above). The Wayne County prosecutor's office does not record criminal prosecutions of police officers.

Federal prosecution is also rare. Deval Patrick, then assistant attorney general for civil rights at the Justice Department, visited Detroit during public hearings about police abuse held there in February 1996. He was asked to examine abuses, and promised to do so.

In 1996, of the thirty-seven cases decided by federal prosecutors for the federal district containing Detroit (Eastern District of Michigan), one was prosecuted

---

[46] Memorandum from Councilman Ravitz to City Council, January 31, 1995.

[47] Josar, "Cops cost Detroit...," *Detroit News.* Ravitz has also found that, of 1,631 lawsuits against the police during a ten-year period, 106 officers were named in at least two cases, seventy-one were named in at least three, and nine were named in at least five cases.

[48] Dan Holly, "Police lawsuit settlements soar," *Detroit Free Press*, February 1, 1995.

[49] Chesley, "Police training program...," *Detroit Journal.*

(presented to a grand jury to seek an indictment). Between 1992 and 1995, thirty-nine cases were considered, of which three were prosecuted.[50]

The federal prosecution rates must be seen in context; a case in neighboring Monroe County demonstrates the difficulty of getting even the strongest cases prosecuted. The county has been the subject of many abuse complaints, often involving alleged racial bias. Kenneth Watson, an African-American, alleges that in January 1989, after being arrested for leaving the scene of an automobile accident,[51] he was beaten brutally by Monroe County sheriffs' deputies.

He alleges that his mouth was taped and he was beaten while chained to a drain cover on the floor of his cell, bent backward and twisted by his shackles.[52] For several hours – witnessed by other inmates – several deputies hit and kicked Watson, while using racial epithets. He reportedly suffered a broken wrist, a fractured skull, cuts, and bruises. Watson claims the beating only ended when he began vomiting and passed out.

During a deposition in 1992 for Watson's civil case, a deputy reportedly stated that it was common practice to immobilize inmates by cuffing their hands and ankles and shackling them to a drain grate in a basement holding cell; several other deputies reportedly confirmed this practice.[53] When a captain was assigned to look into Watson's allegations, he reportedly told the sheriff he found "nothing out of the ordinary."[54] One deputy who was involved was also implicated in several other brutality cases, including one that was settled for $300,000. In a civil lawsuit (which was settled in Watson's favor for approximately $600,000 in December 1992) Watson's lawyers contended that Monroe County did not take abuse

---

[50] According to data obtained by TRAC from the Executive Office of U.S. Attorneys, Justice Department. Cases prosecuted or declined represent only a portion of the total number of complaints alleging federal criminal civil rights violations in each district in a given year. Several steps prior to this decision narrow down the number of complaints actually received to those considered worthy of consideration.

[51] Watson's car hit a tree and he left it there.

[52] Robin Erb and Gary T. Pakulski, "Violence inside its jail costing Monroe County," *Toledo Blade,* February 21, 1993; Said Deep, "Allegations of brutality rock Monroe," *Detroit News,* March 28, 1993; interview with an attorney representing Watson, Michael Haddad of Goodman, Eden, Millender & Bedrosian, August 16, 1995 and telephone interview with Haddad October 21, 1997.

[53] Erb and Pakulski, "Violence inside its...," *Toledo Blade.*

[54] Ibid.

allegations seriously, and had not disciplined a single deputy.[55] According to press reports, none of the deputies allegedly involved in Watson beating were disciplined, despite the large settlement and serious allegations. Nor did local prosecutors take action.

Thus, in a notoriously abusive sheriffs' department – where in 1992 Watson's civil damages and those of other cases of abuse totaled $1 million, or $10,000 per sheriffs' deputy – local authorities failed to discipline deputies involved, either administratively or through criminal charges.[56] Watson's attorneys made repeated efforts to get federal prosecutors to prosecute the deputies, but no criminal prosecution has taken place at the federal level either.[57]

---

[55] Telephone interview with an attorney representing Watson, Michael Haddad, of Goodman, Eden, Millender & Bedrosian, October 21, 1997.

[56] Said Deep, "Allegations of brutality rock Monroe," *Detroit News and Free Press*, March 28, 1993.

[57] Interview with an attorney representing Watson, Michael Haddad of Goodman, Eden, Millender & Bedrosian, August 16, 1995 and telephone interview with Haddad October 21, 1997. According to press reports, the Justice Department did not find enough evidence to bring charges in the Watson case. "Feds drop probe in civil-rights case," UPI, May 12, 1993, [Wire Service].

INDIANAPOLIS

The Indianapolis Police Department has been at the center of two racially charged incidents since July 1995, one leading to a "mini-riot" and both contributing factors in the resignation of two successive police chiefs, exacerbating what appears to be a leadership problem at the department. The new incidents build on a recent history of unresolved cases of serious abuse, a weak civilian review mechanism, and a problematic attitude exhibited by some police in dealing with minority communities in particular. Many observers believe that the police are overreacting to a perceived increase in crime by harassing African-American youths and treating them all as if they were violent gang members as part of a new program of more aggressive policing. While the high-profile incidents have directly involved only a dozen or so officers, they have tarnished the 1,000-member department's reputation and have increased distrust of the police among minority residents.[1]

On July 25, 1995, Danny Sales was arrested by a police sergeant and allegedly beaten.[2] The next day, Sales went to file a complaint at the North District police station, but was dissatisfied with the officers' response so he started a protest in front of the station at 42nd Street and College Avenue.[3] He was joined by approximately one hundred protesters, and a similar number of police officers responded and attempted to disperse them, using tear gas, K-9 (police dog) units, and armored riot vehicles. The confrontation soon turned violent, with protesters and others looting stores and throwing bricks, rocks and pieces of concrete. Mayor

---

[1] A new scandal was emerging at the time of this writing. In December 1997, a joint federal and local task force was formed to investigate possible corruption in the Indianapolis police department. R. Joseph Gelarden and James A. Gillaspy, "Cottey pulls deputies off joint task force," *Indianapolis Star/News*, January 10, 1998. The task force was formed after an Indianapolis police officer was charged in December 1997 with murdering a suspected drug dealer, and it was believed a group of officers may have been stealing money from drug dealers. "Probe for 'bad officers' widening in Indianapolis," *Chicago Tribune*, December 19, 1997; R. Joseph Gelarden and James A. Gillaspy, "FOP won't pay officer's bills," *Indianapolis Star*, December 20, 1997.

[2] The sergeant reportedly had received a two-day suspension in 1991 as the result of a sustained complaint filed by a woman motorist who claimed the sergeant had pointed his gun at her.

[3] James A. Gillaspy and Sherri Edwards, "Silent protest sparks violence," *Indianapolis Star*, July 27, 1995.

Stephen Goldsmith termed the melee a "mini-riot."[4] Unrest continued for days, at differing levels, with twenty-seven arrested for disorderly conduct; there were also injuries to those pelted with debris.[5]

The FBI reportedly began investigating the Sales altercation a few days later, after the chief requested their assistance. Although Sales did not immediately file a formal complaint with city agencies or with police monitoring groups, friends claimed that he was handcuffed and then beaten by "jump-out boys," described by the friends as officers who jump out of cars and chase black youths who are acting "suspiciously."[6]

Mayor Goldsmith, toward the end of the disturbances, said, "People want officers to be more respectful to those who aren't involved in crime. We want to encourage that....[T]he police aren't completely perfect."[7] Police Chief James Toler resigned as chief soon thereafter, reportedly telling a community leader that his "hands were tied" in dealing with problem officers.[8] The fact that Sales's allegation led to such turmoil seemed to reveal a reservoir of distrust and anger in the minority community toward police.

Just over a year later, nine apparently intoxicated off-duty officers started fights and yelled racial epithets, beat passers-by, and harassed women in a busy downtown neighborhood on August 27, 1996; at least one officer reportedly pulled his gun on the citizens during the melee.[9] The incident received national media attention,

---

[4] Ibid.

[5] "Picking up the pieces of unrest," *Indianapolis Star*, July 29, 1995.

[6] "Police to be out in force," *Indianapolis News*, July 29, 1995.

[7] "Picking up the ...," *Indianapolis Star*.

[8] Judy Pasternak, "Indianapolis wrestles with police melee," *Los Angeles Times*, October 3, 1996.

[9] The officers reportedly were all white members of an elite police unit, and all but one were off duty. Ashley H. Grant, "Police chief quits over fray in Indianapolis," *Washington Post*, September 13, 1996; Pasternak, "Indianapolis wrestles with...," *Los Angeles Times*; James A. Gillaspy, "IPD chief punishes brawling officers," *Indianapolis News*, November 8, 1996; R. Joseph Gelarden, "Prosecutor to probe police brawl," *Indianapolis Star*, August 31, 1996.

leading Police Chief Donald Christ to step down "in the best interest of the department as well as the city."[10]

More than a dozen officers who were present during the altercations were reassigned to desk duty. Four were subsequently indicted on battery, disorderly conduct and other charges relating to the incident, and three others were found to have violated department rules.[11] On October 25, 1997, the four officers' trial ended with a hung jury, and prosecutors indicated they would retry the case.[12] Instead, a deal was struck and two of the officers resigned with some back pay (with officials explaining that they had been suspended without pay beyond the six-month limit and were eligible for back pay) while two others remained on the force.[13] As part of the deal, the officers acknowledged their disorderly conduct and received counseling but no jail time; one of the officers still faced felony charges relating to this and another incident.[14]

Incidents

Michael Taylor: The recent police encounters have exacerbated tensions between the African-American community and the predominantly white police force stemming from earlier cases that were not resolved to the community's satisfaction. In one, sixteen-year-old Michael Taylor was shot in the head while he was handcuffed with his hands behind his back in a police patrol car in September 1987; the police and a coroner contended that it was a suicide.[15] Nonetheless, in a civil

---

[10] Grant, "Police chief quits....," *Washington Post.* It was later disclosed that then-Chief Christ initially failed to tell internal affairs investigators that he was with the officers drinking earlier in the evening. George McLaren, "Police brawl report details earlier deception," *Indianapolis Star/News,* December 12, 1996. In February 1997, Michael Zunk was named as chief.

[11] "7 police officers fired or punished for offensive actions during brawl," *Los Angeles Times,* November 8, 1996.

[12] George McLaren, "Jury hung in brawl case," *Indianapolis Star,* October 26, 1997.

[13] George McLaren, "Brawl case settled," *Indianapolis Star,* November 21, 1997.

[14] Ibid.

[15] Editorial, "Michael Taylor legacy," *Indianapolis Star,* March 23, 1996.

lawsuit a jury awarded Taylor's family approximately $3 million dollars; as of September 1997, the city was appealing the case.[16] After the jury found against the city, the Justice Department said that it would reconsider the case. Because the explanation provided by the police seemed so absurd, many African-Americans were outraged and cited it as an example of impunity, even ten years later.

The case of Leonard R. Barnett: When a white police officer fatally shot an unarmed African-American robbery suspect in July 1990 and then was awarded the police department's medal of valor for his handling of the robbery suspect, some minority residents expressed outrage that the police department would display such insensitivity.[17] On July 9, 1990, Officer Scott L. Haslar shot and killed Leonard R. Barnett after a long car chase that ended in a crash.[18] Barnett's leg reportedly was broken during the crash, yet Officer Haslar claimed Barnett moved quickly from the crashed car and then returned to it, Haslar said he believed, to get a gun; Barnett was then shot, and no gun was found.[19] Haslar was later promoted to sergeant A federal grand jury that examined the case declined to indict Haslar.[20]

The case of Edmund Powell: In an incident that led to one of the largest civil jury awards against the police department, Officer Wayne Sharp, white, shot and

[16]   Susan Schramm, "Officer says teen's death changed his life," *Indianapolis Star,* September 24, 1997.

[17]   "Chief apologizes, says award shouldn't have been given," *UPI*, March 20, 1991, [Wire Service]. A spokesman from the police department confirmed that the award was given for Sgt. Haslar's heroic handling of an armed robbery situation. Telephone inquiry, Lt. Horty, Media/Public Relations office, IPD, May 26, 1998.

[18]   Gillaspy and Edwards, "Silent protest against...," *Indianapolis News.*

[19]   Benjamin T. Moore, "Business as usual in latest police probe," *Indianapolis Star,* January 21, 1998; Editorial, "Michael Taylor legacy," *Indianapolis Star*, March 23, 1996; "Police confrontations," *Indianapolis News*, July 27, 1995.

[20]   Editorial, "Michael Taylor legacy...," *Indianapolis Star.*

killed Edmund Powell, black in June 1991.[21] Powell had allegedly stolen something from a department store, and Sharp chased him into an alley with his gun drawn. Sharp, a veteran officer, claimed the shooting was accidental and that Powell had swung a nail-studded board at him, but according to at least one witness, Powell was lying on the pavement when Sharp shot him at close range.[22]

The Marion County prosecutor brought the case before a grand jury, which declined to indict Sharp.[23] Community activists claimed the shooting was racially motivated, based on Sharp's personal history; Sharp had killed an African-American burglary suspect ten years earlier and was cleared by a grand jury.[24] At that time, Sharp had been removed from street duty because of his alleged "flirtation" with the National Socialist White People's Party, a neo-Nazi group.[25]

Powell's grandmother, Gertrude Jackson, alleged Sharp intentionally shot Powell, and filed a civil lawsuit in 1992; the jury found in favor of Jackson and awarded $465,000 to Powell's family.[26] After the award, the chief litigator for the city, Mary Ann Oldham, stated, "Obviously, we are disappointed by the verdict....Officer Sharp did not do anything wrong;"[27] the city was considering an

---

[21] Erica Franklin, "Witness saw suspect prone before officer shot him," *Indianapolis Star*, April 18, 1995; Erica Franklin, "Officer says he doesn't remember firing gun," *Indianapolis Star*, April 21, 1995.

[22] Ibid.

[23] Sherri Edwards and Erica Franklin, "Jury finds police officer guilty of intentionally killing suspect," *Indianapolis Star*, April 22, 1995.

[24] Ibid.

[25] Ibid.; "FBI probes police shooting," *UPI*, June 20, 1991, [Wire Service]; "Police confrontations," *Indianapolis News*, July 27, 1995.

[26] Howard M. Smulevitz, "Jury award could bust IPD's bank," *Indianapolis Star*, April 25, 1995.

[27] Edwards and Franklin, "Jury finds police officer guilty of intentionally killing suspect," *Indianapolis Star*, April 22, 1995.

appeal.[28] Jackson's attorney asked that Sharp be ordered to pay $50 each week from his paycheck "to make him think about it."[29] According to a public affairs officer with the police department, Sharp was neither disciplined nor retrained following the Powell shooting.[30] In January 1998, in response to a written question posed about Officer Sharp, Police Chief Michael Zunk replied that Sharp had been thoroughly investigated and was subsequently returned to street duty as a detective. According to Chief Zunk, Sharp "has received high accolades and several awards for superior work."[31]

Fatal shooting: On March 24, 1992, a narcotics officer shot a drug suspect in the head, killing him.[32] Working undercover, the officer had just completed a drug buy and started to arrest the suspect and his friend. The officer claims that the suspect reached for his waistband and a gun, so the officer shot him once in the head. According to an attorney for the victim's family in a civil lawsuit, the officer's gun went off accidentally (and the story about the suspect reaching for a gun was made up later to cover the error). Key evidence about the incident was lost when another officer allegedly erased part of an audiotape made during the encounter that, according to the victim's attorney, reportedly recorded the narcotics officer apologizing to the victim's friend for the accidental shooting.[33] A Marion County grand jury declined to indict the officer on criminal charges in 1993. The officer who allegedly erased the tape was suspended for thirty days, but was not charged with obstruction of justice because he had limited immunity for testifying

---

[28] Welton W. Harris II, "Officer loses fatal shooting suit," *Indianapolis News,* April 22, 1995; Sherri Edwards and Erica Franklin, "City may appeal verdict giving slain man's family $465,000," *Indianapolis Star*, April 23, 1995.

[29] Harris, "Officer loses fatal...," *Indianapolis News.*

[30] Telephone inquiry, Lt. Horty, Media/Public Relations office, IPD, May 26, 1998.

[31] Letter to Human Rights Watch from Chief Michael H. Zunk, dated January 26, 1998.

[32] Erica Franklin, "IPD fatal-shooting case dismissed in federal court," *Indianapolis Star*, April 27, 1995.

[33] Ibid.

before the grand jury in the shooting officer's case. As of late 1997, both officers were sergeants on the force.[34]

Civilian Review

The Indianapolis Citizens Police Complaint Office was created by ordinance in 1989 and is part of the city's public safety department. Its board has nine members (three from the police department and six civilians appointed by the city council and mayor) who meet four times a year, and the office has three staff members, but no investigators. The CPC receives complaints by phone or in person. Formal complaints are signed and notarized. The office only investigates non-criminal matters, forwarding possibly criminal matters to the Internal Affairs Division (IAD) of the police department.

According to statistical information contained in the 1996 annual report of the Indianapolis Police Department, the Citizens Police Complaint Office (CPC) received a total of 127 complaints in 1995 and 155 in 1996.[35] In 1996, unnecessary force complaints made up approximately 28 percent of the total (or 84 allegations, since one complaint may include several allegations). As of August 1997, there were ninety complaints received in total for the year, with forty-eight allegations of unnecessary force.

Of the cases resolved during 1995, there was an approximately 8 percent sustained rate (complaints investigated and found to be true) by the IAD; in 1996, the sustained rate of resolved cases was approximately 16 percent, but it was impossible to know from information provided in the annual report which types of complaints were sustained, or whether any were related to excessive force. Human Rights Watch attempted to obtain the sustained rate for excessive force complaints from IAD, but its representative failed to provide this information. Furthermore,

---

[34] According to police department's personnel office, October 3, 1997.

[35] In 1996 and through August 1997, there were "informal" complaints which were roughly the same amount as the complaints "received." An IAD representative explained that these figures indicate a phone call or letter alleging police misconduct that is not followed-up with a "formal" signed, in-person complaint.

by the end of 1996, 40 percent of cases involving complaints received during 1996 were pending.[36]

Because the CPC Office does not have its own investigators, all complaints are investigated by the police – either by IAD or, for less serious complaints, by district-level investigators. The CPC does review the IAD or district investigations of complaints it has forwarded, or if a complainant requests a hearing when a complaint has not been sustained by IAD. If the CPC finds that an IAD complaint was incomplete or biased, the CPC requests that IAD re-open the investigation.

The CPC Office does not produce its own report, but it provides information to the police department, which includes basic statistical information in its annual reports. The reports include no information regarding race, age, gender, or description of the incident.

The CPC maintains a database of complaints against officers, and the CPC believes less than 10 percent of the officers generate most complaints.[37] Since 1991, the CPC has forwarded lists of repeat offenders to IAD but is not notified by IAD about how it deals with the officers on the list. The CPC is not notified about disciplinary sanctions stemming from CPC investigated complaints. The CPC does not make disciplinary or policy recommendations, and there is no obligation for the police department to report to it about disciplinary action taken. According to the CPC Office, proposals are now being considered by the city council that would enhance the powers and staff of the CPC.[38]

In response to a question from Human Rights Watch regarding civilian review, Chief Michael Zunk replied that there was adequate civilian review of the Indianapolis police by the CPC, Civilian Police Merit Board, and grand juries. He also asserts that civilian review boards, to his knowledge, have not reduced claims of police brutality or other misconduct, and that there are reported incidents that

---

[36] The Indiana Civil Liberties Union estimated that it receives at least five complaints involving the Indianapolis police each week, and the Indiana Civil Rights Commission reports receiving one complaint each week of minor to serious race-related police abuse in Indianapolis and other parts of the state.

[37] Human Rights Watch interview with CPC Office director Chris Reeder, August 21, 1995.

[38] Telephone interview with Chris Reeder, September 17, 1997.

have occurred in jurisdictions with very active civilian review boards.[39] The chief believes instead that improved recruit screening, training, code of conduct instruction, and adequate supervision are more important.[40]

Police Administration/Internal Affairs Division

As noted above, the police department has gone through a series of leadership transitions during the past several years. Michael Zunk has been the chief since February 1997. In response to a written question posed by Human Rights Watch, Chief Zunk stated that one main challenge in curtailing abuses by officers is that one-on-one cases – where an alleged victim of abuse is the only witness – are difficult to sustain because the complainants are often accused of criminal activity and "do not make the best witnesses." [41] The other challenge to curtailing abuses, said the chief, is that officers are entitled to full constitutional protections, and their rights must be protected "just as zealously as the rights of other citizens."[42]

The Internal Affairs Division (IAD) investigates, or reviews the district investigations of, all complaints of police brutality or other misconduct.[43] IAD receives complaints from the public, as well as internally generated complaints. According to the CPC, IAD does not provide information to complainants about the status of its investigation.[44] CPC has also noted that IAD reviews the criminal history of the complainant, but does not review the criminal history or prior complaints against the subject officer.

The IAD informs complainants that they have a choice between filing a complaint first with IAD or the CPC Office, and informs them that if they submit their complaint to IAD, they can later request citizen review by the CPC Office, but

---

[39] Letter to Human Rights Watch from Chief Zunk, dated January 26, 1998.

[40] Ibid.

[41] Ibid.

[42] Ibid.

[43] Telephone interview with Lt. Darrell Pierce, IAD, October 3, 1997.

[44] Interview with Reeder, August 21, 1995.

if they file a complaint with the CPC office, they may not have an "appeal" opportunity.[45]

IAD reportedly investigates any unnecessary force allegation, and if it is of a possibly criminal nature, the complaint is forward to the district attorney's office. The CPC is not involved in the most serious investigations, according to IAD.

The IAD's findings on whether a complaint is sustained, not sustained (could not make determination, usually involves one-on-one cases with only officer's and complainant's accounts), exonerated (officer acted within departmental rules), unfounded (incident did not happen as alleged by complainant), or terminated (not pursued for a range of reasons), are sent to the executive assistant to the police chief, who agrees or disagrees with the findings. Not sustained findings are sent to the CPC, and if the CPC disagrees with the findings, the complaint is returned to IAD, which is not obligated to renew the investigation. If the complainant is not satisfied with the IAD's findings, he or she may ask for a hearing, but the hearing request must take place within 180 days of the incident (so that if an investigation is delayed through no fault of the complainant, he or she may not get a hearing).

The department does not yet appear to have an "early warning system" in place to identify officers who are the subjects of repeated complaints, but a system is being established.[46] The program will monitor several factors, including activity, arrests, sick time, and complaints to decide whether the officer deviates from the norm. The officer may then be counseled, receive help (voluntary or mandatory) through the Employee Assistance Program, or be closely monitored to ensure the problem is resolved.[47] Chief Zunk also states that a new Professional Standards Unit has been created to conduct inspections of the entire department's operations,

---

[45] Ibid. The IAD representative stated that this is according to the CPC's guiding ordinance.

[46] Telephone interview with Lt. Darrell Pierce, IAD, October 3, 1997. In a letter to Human Rights Watch dated January 26, 1998, Chief Zunk stated that there is an early warning system, but speaks of it in the future tense. IAD's Lieutenant Pierce told Human Rights Watch in October 1997 that no such system existed yet.

[47] Civil lawsuit information will not be included as part of the early warning tracking system. Telephone interview with IAD's Lieutenant Pierce, October 3, 1997.

and that policies on substance abuse, duties of officers arrested, and improper use of force have been strengthened.[48]

IAD receives notice of tort civil claims against Indianapolis police officers, but an IAD representative reports that the incidents have usually already been investigated by IAD by the time a civil lawsuit is filed.[49]

Civil Lawsuits

Police Chief Zunk states that whenever the city loses a civil lawsuit involving an officer, it leads to a review of policies and procedures, but that the awarding of a large sum of money to a plaintiff "merely serves to give us less resources to use in our battle against crime."[50] According to the city's Office of Corporation Counsel, in Fiscal Year (FY) 1994 there were seven settlements or jury awards paid, totaling $59,380; in FY 1995, there were eleven totaling $581,750, and in FY 1996, there were three totaling $104,294.[51] (In 1996, there was a $3.55 million jury verdict award in favor of the family of Michael Taylor, which is now on appeal.) According to the Indiana Civil Liberties Union, which files civil lawsuits against police officers, there is a usually a high level of sympathy among jurors toward officers, making pre-trial settlements by the city less common.[52]

Criminal Prosecution

Local criminal prosecution of Indianapolis police officers is rare, but the exact frequency is difficult to ascertain because the prosecutor's office does not record

---

[48] Letter to Human Rights Watch from Chief Zunk, January 26, 1998. In a related positive development, Chief Zunk suspended, and began dismissal proceedings, against a veteran sergeant accused of hitting his girlfriend and failing to cooperate with investigators; it was the second time the sergeant had been accused of mistreating his girlfriend. R. Joseph Gelarden, "Police chief suspends IPD sergeant," *Indianapolis Star/News*, March 6, 1998.

[49] Telephone interview with IAD's Lieutenant Pierce, October 3, 1997.

[50] Letter to Human Rights Watch from Chief Zunk, January 26, 1998.

[51] Telephone inquiry with Greg Ray of the Office of Corporation Counsel, July 28, 1997.

[52] Interview with Sheila Kennedy, ICLU, August 18, 1995.

the number of officers prosecuted.[53] According to Chief Zunk, on average just one Indianapolis police officer each year is criminally prosecuted.[54] When questioned about the effect on other officers when a fellow officer is arrested or convicted, the chief responded that this "obviously has an effect on other members of the department, just as the arrest of a family member would have on anyone else."[55] Prosecution of officers on federal criminal civil rights charges is also rare.

In 1996, of the twelve cases decided by federal prosecutors for the federal district containing Indianapolis (Southern District of Indiana) none was prosecuted (presented to a grand jury to seek an indictment).[56] Between 1992 and 1995, sixty-nine cases were considered, and five were prosecuted.

---

[53] According to telephone inquiry, city corporation counsel's office, September 15, 1997.

[54] Letter to Human Rights Watch from Chief Zunk, dated January 26, 1998.

[55] Ibid.

[56] According to data obtained by TRAC from the Executive Office of U.S. Attorneys, Justice Department. Cases prosecuted or declined represent only a portion of the total number of complaints alleging federal criminal civil rights violations in each district in a given year. Several steps prior to this decision narrow down the number of complaints actually received to those considered worthy of consideration.

LOS ANGELES

The problem of excessive force in the LAPD is fundamentally a problem of supervision, management and leadership.
— Report of the Independent Commission on the Los Angeles Police Department[1]

After decades of brutal behavior by officers, poor management by the chief and his deputies, and racist attitudes expressed at all levels of the department in word and deed, the troubled Los Angeles Police Department appears to be, slowly, on the mend. Unfortunately, the department waited until its shortcomings became so overwhelming that building trust in many, particularly minority, communities will require a Herculean effort. Thanks in large part to the blueprint provided by the July 1991 *Report of the Independent Commission on the Los Angeles Police Department* (known as the Christopher Commission report) and consistent pressure from community activists, it has been possible through subsequent reports to measure some progress on the commission's recommendations for reform. Because the 9,500-officer department has received such scrutiny – and because its flaws are mirrored in police departments around the country – what it does to create and maintain a culture of accountability will have important ramifications.[2]

Background
The 1991 videotaped beating of Rodney G. King exemplified so much that was (and in some cases still is) wrong with the LAPD that it bears re-telling.[3] In brief, in the early morning hours of March 3, 1991, King led California Highway Patrol,

---

[1] *Report of the Independent Commission on the Los Angeles Police Department* (hereinafter "Christopher Commission report"), July 9, 1991, p. 32.

[2] It should be noted that many Los Angeles residents and others in Southern California believe the Los Angeles County Sheriff's Department is more abusive currently than the LAPD. Similarly, neighboring cities have been identified as having serious police abuse problems. Because this study focuses on major U.S. cities, the LAPD is receiving our attention at this time. This in no way should suggest that we are not concerned by allegations of abuse in the county and in nearby cities.

[3] See also Paul Hoffman, "The feds, lies, and videotape: the need for an effective federal role in controlling police abuse in urban America," *Southern California Law Review* (Los Angeles) vol. 66, no. 4, May 1993, pp. 1455-1532, and Human Rights Watch, "Police brutality in the United States: A policy statement on the need for federal oversight," July 1991.

Los Angeles Unified School District police, and LAPD officers on a high-speed car chase in the San Fernando Valley. Once he pulled over, he and his friends were ordered out of the car. King was beaten by LAPD officers, as a sergeant directed from nearby, with approximately fifty-six baton strokes; he was also kicked in the head and body and stunned with a Taser stun gun. Some of the beating was captured on an amateur photographer's videotape, a tape that was eventually viewed around the world.[4]

Many components of the King incident are common to less-publicized abuse cases. There was the obvious race factor – the officers involved in the beating were white, and King was black. The beating followed a vehicle pursuit, and once stopped, the defendant was not considered by officers to be compliant enough – a common scenario in police beatings. When the man who videotaped the beating and King's brother, Paul, attempted to report the incident they reportedly were turned away or ignored. Inaccurate reports were filed by police after the incident. Three out of the four officers eventually indicted for the beating had been named in prior complaints of excessive force.[5] In fact, it is likely that, if this incident had not been videotaped and broadcast widely, any complaint about the beating would not have been sustained, since the sustained rate for complaints during that period was approximately 2 percent.[6]

A cavalier attitude was demonstrated after the beating. On a radio transmission, from the LAPD dispatcher to the fire department for an ambulance, a police dispatcher said, "....he pissed us off, so I guess he needs an ambulance

---

[4] The videotaped beating shown on television was edited by a local television station, leaving out a portion of the incident during which King allegedly lunged towards one of the officers. The editing's impact is described in Lou Cannon, *Official Negligence* (New York: Random House, 1997), pp. 23-4, 577-81 .

[5] Officer Laurence Powell, who was an officer trainer, was the subject of several excessive force complaints and at least one civil lawsuit which cost the city $70,000 in a settlement after he broke a man's elbow with baton strikes. Officer Theodore Briseno had reportedly hit and kicked a handcuffed suspect in 1987, which was witnessed by two other officers, and received a sixty-day suspension. Sergeant Stacey Koon was the subject of one excessive force complaint during more than fourteen years on the force, stemming from an incident in September 1986. The complaint was not sustained, but he was suspended for five days for failing to report the incident. The fourth officer, Timothy Wind, was still a probationary officer at the time of the King incident. Cannon, *Official Negligence*.

[6] In a related development, following the King beating and videotape, the use of batons by officers – or the reporting of their use – fell off dramatically, and the use of pepper spray went up. As described in the May 1996 Police Commission report, pp. 7-8.

now....should know better than run, they are going to pay a price when they do that....It's a...it's a ....battery, he got beat up."[7] One of the officers on the scene stated on the car radio, "Oops," and "I haven't beaten anyone this bad in a long time."[8]

The subsequent April 29, 1992 state court acquittal of four officers on assault with a deadly weapon and assault under color of authority charges[9] led to rioting in the city: fifty-four people were killed, 2,383 injured (221 critically), and 13,212 arrested. Property damage was estimated at more than $700 million for the county.[10] There were also violent protests in other cities in response to the verdicts. While some who rioted may have been less concerned with the "not guilty" verdicts than with an opportunity to steal items and destroy property, the explosion of rage reflected the belief that African-Americans could not get justice, even when the crime seemed apparent on tape.

The officers were subsequently tried on federal criminal civil rights charges. Sergeant Stacey Koon and Officer Laurence Powell were convicted of violating Rodney King's civil rights in April 1993 and sentenced to thirty months' imprisonment.

The Christopher Commission Report
In July 1991, some four months after the King beating, the Christopher Commission report was published. The commission, headed by attorney Warren Christopher (who later became U.S. Secretary of State), was created to conduct "a full and fair examination of the structure and operation of the LAPD," including its recruitment and training practices, internal disciplinary system, and citizen complaint system.[11] Its investigation and report was unprecedented, reviewing a

---

[7] Christopher Commission report, p. 15.

[8] Transmission from the squad car of Officers Laurence Powell and Timothy Wind, Christopher Commission report, p. 15.

[9] The jury was deadlocked on one assault charge against Officer Powell; the Superior Court judge dismissed that charge once federal civil rights prosecution was initiated.

[10] James D. Delk, "Fires and Furies: The L.A. Riots," ETC Publications, Palm Springs, CA. 1995. Property damage was estimated to have exceeded $900 million in Cannon, *Official Negligence*, p. 347.

[11] Charge by Mayor Tom Bradley to the Special Independent Commission, April 1, 1991, as included in appendix of Christopher Commission report.

five-year period of internal use of force reports, Mobile Digital Terminal (MDT) transmissions between squad cars and police stations, and eighty-three civil damages cases involving excessive force settled by the City Attorney for more than $15,000. The commission also held hearings and interviewed scores of officials and residents.

The following are, verbatim, some of the commission's findings:

There is a significant number of officers in the LAPD who repetitively use excessive force against the public and persistently ignore the written guidelines of the department regarding force.[12]

The failure to control these officers is a management issue that is at the heart of the problem. The documents and data that we have analyzed have all been available to the department; indeed, most of this information came from that source. The LAPD's failure to analyze and act upon these revealing data evidences a significant breakdown in the management and leadership of the Department. The Police Commission, lacking investigators or other resources, failed in its duty to monitor the Department in this sensitive use of force area. The Department not only failed to deal with the problem group of officers but it often rewarded them with positive evaluations and promotions.[13]

We recommend a new standard of accountability....Ugly incidents will not diminish until ranking officers know they will be held responsible for what happens in their sector, whether or not they personally participate."[14]

The commission highlighted the problem of "repeat offenders" on the force, finding that of approximately 1,800 officers against whom an allegation of excessive force or improper tactics was made from 1986 to 1990, more than 1,400 had only one or two allegations. But 183 officers had four or more allegations, forty-four had six or more, sixteen had eight or more, and one had sixteen such allegations. Generally, the forty-four officers with six complaints or more had received positive performance

---

[12] Christopher Commission report, p. iii and p. 31.

[13] Ibid., p. iv.

[14] Ibid.

evaluations that failed to record "sustained" complaints or to discuss their significance.

Race

Race has often played a role in police abuse cases in Los Angeles, with minority residents believing that white officers (most of whom live in predominantly white suburbs) are overly aggressive and abusive in minority communities.[15] According to the Christopher Commission: "The problem of excessive force is aggravated by racism and bias" within the LAPD. More than one-quarter of 650 officers responding to a survey said "an officer's prejudice towards the suspect's race may lead to the use of excessive force."[16] MDT transmissions – typed messages between patrol cars or stations – revealed racial animosities among some officers. Just as troubling as the content of these messages was the officers' lack of concern that they would be held accountable for hateful and violent messages sent via the MDT system. The LAPD had clear rules about not using certain language or racial/sexual bias on the system and, if the officers had feared any kind of accountability, they would not have boasted of using excessive force against minority suspects.

In addition to the racial attitudes expressed on the MDT system, African-Americans and Latinos have long complained that when they are stopped for even minor traffic infractions, they are "proned out" or forced to lie face down, flat on the ground with their arms outstretched.[17] Whites who are stopped for traffic or other minor violations are rarely subjected to this treatment, according to minority rights advocates.

The 1995 O.J. Simpson trial fueled racial tensions in the city, particularly when Det. Mark Fuhrman, who was eventually convicted on perjury charges, denied using racial slurs while audio-tapes existed on which he used the word "nigger" at least forty-one times. In those tapes, he also claimed to have beaten and framed African-American suspects, and stated that Internal Affairs Division (IAD) investigators knew what he was doing but did not hold him accountable. The Justice Department initiated a review of the allegations in 1995; three years later, federal prosecutors

---

[15] ACLU of Southern California, "From the Outside In," March 1994. According to the OIG, approximately 85 percent of all LAPD employees live outside of the city of Los Angeles. OIG, "Domestic Violence in the Los Angeles Police Department: The report of the Domestic Violence Task Force," July 1997, p. i.

[16] Christopher Commission report, p. 69.

[17] Ibid., p. 75.

determined that the five-year statute of limitations had long passed in relation to the allegations against Fuhrman and decided not to prosecute him.[18]

Another source of racial tension was the LAPD's use of K-9 (police dog) units, which during the late 1980s and early 1990s were concentrated in minority areas and were trained to find suspects and bite them, even when there was no resistance offered by the suspect.[19] Biting was only avoided if the handler called the dog off; in some cases, the dog handlers allowed the dogs to bite suspects who had been subdued. On average, there was one dog bite per day, according to attorneys challenging the policy.[20] In 1992 several civil rights groups presented evidence that the dog handlers had used excessive force and called for a review of the K-9 units' handlers, which, according to attorneys involved in the case, has never taken place.[21] According to attorneys in the case, none of the dog handlers appeared on the list of "problem officers" compiled by the Christopher Commission. Indeed, according to an attorney involved in monitoring the unit, at least four of the K-9 unit's officers have been promoted to sergeant posts.[22] In 1995, the civil case challenging the policy was settled, with the city paying $3.6 million, and the policy was changed from "find and bite" to "find and bark."[23]

Progress Since the Christopher Commission
The Christopher Commission report concluded that, if "faithfully implemented," the report's scores of recommendations would help to avoid a repetition of the abhorrent King incident and others like it. One of the most important recommendations, however, took five long years to implement. This was

---

[18] Ronald Ostrow, Richard A. Serrano, "Justice dept. won't prosecute Mark Fuhrman," *Los Angeles Times*, April 3, 1998.

[19] See January 7, 1992 report submitted by ACLU of Southern California, NAACP Legal Defense and Educational Fund, and other civil rights groups to the L.A. Police Commission.

[20] Ibid.

[21] Telephone interview with attorney Donald Cook, October 20, 1995.

[22] Telephone interview with attorney Donald Cook, March 6, 1998. The four officers reportedly promoted were among those with high "bite-ratios" named in the January 1992 report.

[23] Christopher Commission report, p. 78.

the appointment of an inspector general to review the operations of the Internal Affairs Division: the recommendation was made in July 1991, and the inspector general was hired in July 1996.[24] Along with other problems of implementation, this delay undermined many observers' faith in city and police officials' commitment to the Christopher Commission report.

In the years since the Christopher Commission report, many police abuse monitors in Los Angeles have expressed concern in letters and reports about the lack of progress on the Christopher Commission recommendations.[25] In May 1996, the special counsel to the Los Angeles Police Commission published a report finding that progress, in some areas, toward reforms in the LAPD had been "halting."[26] Further, the report stated,

> [G]iven the five years that have elapsed since the Christopher Report was published, we conclude that the department has not undergone reform to the extent that was possible or required. For the most part, what reform there has been has been more attributable to the acts of dedicated individuals than a coordinated plan or effort....[27]

The report noted progress, particularly in the area of community policing. But it was critical of slow progress in implementing an "at-risk" program. "We have seen no evidence of a meaningful, institutionalized effort by the Department to do work history reviews for officers generating an unusually high number of uses of force or force-related complaints."[28] Similarly, they found that "the LAPD continues to lack a comprehensive system to analyze and manage use of force,"

---

[24] The Inspector General's office existed prior to the appointment of the inspector general, but its activities were limited.

[25] Including the ACLU of Southern California, Police Watch, and the Coalition Against Police Abuse.

[26] Los Angeles Police Commission, "In the course of change: The Los Angeles Police Department five years after the Christopher Commission," May 30, 1996. The special counsel included Mark Epstein and Merrick Bobb; Bobb had monitored the L.A. Sheriff Department's progress following the 1992 Kolts Report describing serious abuses and management problems.

[27] Police Commission report, p. vi.

[28] Ibid., p. 16.

despite the recommendation to this effect by the Christopher Commission.[29] The commission concluded, "the absence of such proactive management (with a few isolated exceptions) five years after the Christopher Report is a matter of substantial concern."[30]

The commission found that citizen complaints were down, and that internal investigations of citizen complaints were more thorough and adjudications appeared more fair than was the case when the Christopher Commission issued its report.[31] Still, the unwritten rule that a police officer's statement is given greater weight than a complainant's (or a "tie goes to the officer") remained problematic. Furthermore, department investigators' definition of "independent witnesses" remained overly narrow, meaning that witness accounts by individuals who knew the alleged victim were disregarded by investigators. The commission also noted that discipline for code of silence-related misconduct was too rare.[32]

The commission examined 130 use of force or ethnic bias cases and found that punishment of excessive force "remains low."[33] The report also noted that there was no "disciplinary matrix" (a standardized scale of punishments) despite much discussion about it.[34] The commission criticized the use of "Miscellaneous Memos," which were used instead of a personnel complaint forms (1.81s) in cases where complaints appear to be baseless and not worthy of a formal investigation. The LAPD justified the use of miscellaneous memos by stating that there should be a category for disposing of allegations that, on their face, disclose no apparent misconduct. The commission found that miscellaneous memos were, in fact, being used in cases where possible misconduct or violation of policy did exist, and that they should have been treated as formal complaints of police abuse. The use of miscellaneous memos made the total count of complaints provided by the

---

[29] Ibid., p. 2. The special counsel found that officers neither increased nor decreased their use of force as a percentage of arrests significantly following the King incident. p. 6

[30] Ibid., p. 6.

[31] Ibid., p. 33.

[32] Ibid., p. 34. The commission also noted poor data collection, resulting in three separate sets of complaints statistics provided to investigators that could not always be reconciled.

[33] Ibid., p. 44.

[34] Ibid., p. 45

department incorrect; the commission concluded that, "for all practical purposes, it is as if the allegations were never made and an investigation never occurred."[35]

Finally, the commission described the status of the forty-four "problem officers" identified in the Christopher Commission report. The commission described the limitations on the department on administering discipline, or firing, the named officers who had already had the complaints against them investigated and adjudicated. The report noted that the department has begun a manual review of personnel complaints and was to provide quarterly reports to managers when an officer under their command has been the subject of three or more complaints.[36] The commission warned, however, that while sophisticated databases will simplify the task, even they will not be useful if "top management does not hold its managers and supervisors strictly accountable for the actions of subordinate personnel."[37] When the U.S. Commission on Civil Rights later held hearings in Los Angeles, in September 1996, Mayor Richard Riordan appeared to agree with this conclusion, and said he believed there had been a great deal of progress, but that more needed to be done to hold supervisors accountable for the actions of their subordinates.[38]

Nearly six years after the Christopher Commission report recommended it, the Police Commission approved a set of discipline guidelines on June 24, 1997.[39] Although not binding, the guidelines would apply the most severe punishments to officers who engage in dishonesty, excessive use of force, abuse of a firearm, or discourteous behavior toward members of the public or the police force, including derogatory, ethnic or racial or sexist remarks or behavior. Prior to the approval of the guidelines, supervisors were allowed broad discretion in the punishments meted out. The guidelines were created by a disciplinary systems task force that included police personnel and members of the public. One of the task force members warned that, "[N]o discipline guide on paper is worth anything unless it is implemented in an intelligent and appropriate way," yet there was widespread agreement that the

---

[35] Ibid., pp.47-48.

[36] Ibid., p. 17.

[37] Ibid., p. 17.

[38] Jim Newton and Abigail Goldman, "Williams, union chief clash before panel," *Los Angeles Times*, September 13, 1996.

[39] Matt Lait, "LAPD board adopts new discipline rules,"*Los Angeles Times*, June 25, 1997.

existence of a disciplinary matrix that highlighted these types of offenses was a significant, and essential, reform development.[40]

After Chief Parks took office in 1997, however, he drafted his own disciplinary guidelines after deciding that the guidelines created by the task force, and approved by the interim chief and Police Commission, were unacceptable.[41] At the time of this writing it was not clear how his guidelines differed from those created by the task force. And although he was within his powers to draft the new guidelines without input from others, his apparent disregard for the work of members of the task force and the Police Commission sent a negative signal.[42] The Police Commissioners, who reportedly favor the task force's disciplinary guidelines, planned to discuss the chief's new rules but the Commissioners' approval is not required.[43]

Civilian Review

Although the Police Commission does serve as civilian oversight of the police department, there is no civilian review board dedicated to receiving and investigating individual citizen complaints against the police. That function is performed by the police department's division commanders and the Internal Affairs Group (IAG), with the Police Commission reviewing the department's findings when there are shootings.[44] It was reported that the Police Commission has proposed reviewing all injury reports stemming from encounters between residents and the police.[45] The Office of the Inspector General does receive initial complaints

---

[40] Ibid.

[41] Telephone inquiry, Cliff Weiss, acting executive director, Los Angeles Police Commission, May 12, 1998.

[42] Matt Lait, "LAPD watchdog commission napping, critics contend," *Los Angeles Times*, May 11, 1998.

[43] Telephone inquiry, Cliff Weiss, acting executive director, Los Angeles Police Commission, May 12, 1998.

[44] The Internal Affairs Division was reorganized and renamed the Internal Affairs Group in 1997. The IAG Commander told Human Rights Watch that the IAG did not conduct all excessive force allegation investigations but that if, for example, an abuse case gets a great deal of press attention, IAG will conduct the investigation itself. Telephone interview, IAG Commander James McMurray, May 8, 1998.

[45] Lait, "LAPD watchdog commission napping," *Los Angeles Times*, May 11, 1998.

from the public, as well as inquiries about the way the internal affairs division dealt with a complaint.[46] The OIG passes initial complaints to the internal affairs group and assists complainants in finding out what became of complaints already filed with internal affairs.

Despite efforts by local advocates since the 1970s to create some sort civilian review mechanism in Los Angeles, the Christopher Commission did not recommend civilian review. Instead, it emphasized the role the civilian Police Commission could play.[47] In addition, the commission called for the complaint, investigation and disciplinary system to be restructured fully, and operation of the system to be open to meaningful public review by a civilian authority.[48] Finally, the commission called for the establishment of an "office of the inspector general within the police commission, with responsibility to audit and oversee the disciplinary process, participate in the adjudication and punishment of the most serious cases, and report to the police commission and its newly created chief of staff."[49]

More than five years later, Katherine Mader was named as the first inspector general, and the office's first report was published in January 1997.[50] Mader is authorized to have complete and unrestricted access to all LAPD documents, to obtain direct and prompt access to any LAPD or Police Commission employee, and to subpoena witnesses and compel the production of any materials. The inspector general is not expected to do independent investigations, but instead is to audit the activities of the police department's investigators and leaders. There are fourteen OIG staffmembers, including two sworn employees.[51]

The purpose of the OIG's reports, to be published every six months, is to describe the police department's progress in implementing the Christopher Commission's and other reform recommendations. The January 1997 report echoed

---

[46] Telephone interview, Inspector General Katherine Mader, April 20, 1998.

[47] There are community police advisory boards that liaise with the eighteen police commanders around the city. While there are differing opinions about the effectiveness of these boards, they do appear able to alert police managers about emerging problems or tensions in their communities.

[48] Christopher Commission report, p. 154.

[49] Ibid.

[50] Her duties were defined in the voter-approved Charter Amendment 3 in 1995.

[51] Telephone interview, Inspector General Mader, April 20, 1998.

several of the concerns raised in the May 1996 Police Commission report (described above), and noted that the police department appeared to be underreporting the number of complaints received by only counting those that the department deemed worthy of investigation, rather than the total complaints received.[52] Chief Williams and other city officials had touted the decrease in the number of complaints, from 717 in 1991 to 496 in 1995, as a sign of progress, so they protested the report's assessment that the LAPD had not been entirely forthcoming.[53]

The report also found that complaints filed against higher-ranking police personnel did not become formal complaints using form 1.81, but instead were processed using miscellaneous memos, which presuppose that the complaint is without merit. The report's analysis showed that complaints against higher-ranking personnel were less likely to be sustained than those against officers with a rank of lieutenant or lower. The report criticized the department for not taking action against officers who lied or covered for colleagues under a code of silence. The OIG noted specifically that there were fewer code of silence investigations in 1996 than in previous years, with fourteen officers disciplined for code of silence violations in 1993, twelve disciplined in 1994, ten in 1995, and none in 1996. Chief Williams took offense at this criticism as well, particularly after he had boasted to the U.S. Commission on Civil Rights of a tougher line on code of silence violations. Said Williams, in response to the OIG findings, "I do take some personal offense that simply because the chief of police makes a statement at a public meeting, that now the inspector general is going to run out and see if we are in fact doing anything about addressing the code of silence."[54] Yet that was an entirely appropriate inquiry for the IG's office to initiate.

In July 1997, the inspector general issued a report highlighting the issue of domestic violence involving LAPD officers and criticizing the department's

---

[52] Los Angeles Board of Police Commissioners, Office of the Inspector General Six-Month Report, January 1997. Complaints received and deemed worthy of investigation are converted into formal complaint forms, then known as "1.81s." Since January 1998, complaint forms have been renamed "1.28s."

[53] Jim Newton, "Williams Disputes Report on LAPD," Los Angeles Times, January 22, 1997.

[54] Ibid.

investigations and punishments for those cases.[55] According to her report, there were 227 domestic violence cases investigated by the LAPD against its employees between 1990 and 1997.[56] The OIG found that "many of the investigations lacked objectivity or were otherwise flawed or skewed."[57] The OIG also found that there were many repeat offenders – thirty employees accounted for seventy-one of the 227 investigations (31 percent), and twenty-nine out of ninety-one sustained allegations (32 percent).[58]

Furthermore, "in more than 75 percent of the sustained cases, the performance evaluations of the employees failed to mention the sustained allegations of domestic violence, and many of the performance evaluations that did mention sustained domestic violence incidents tended to minimize the misconduct."[59] In an example of a sustained excessive force complaint that was ignored in the officer's evaluation, the officer was found to have grabbed a complainant by the hair, forced her to fall down, and punched her in the upper torso with a closed fist. The OIG reported that his performance evaluation made no mention of the incident and stated that the officer had "consistently displayed a calm and professional demeanor even when dealing with the most highly agitated and stressful situations."[60]

In response to the OIG's report, a Domestic Violence Unit within the LAPD was created in mid-1997, and more LAPD officers were arrested in such cases.[61] The increase in arrests of LAPD officers in surrounding communities may have

---

[55] Office of the Inspector General, "Domestic Violence in the Los Angeles Police Department: the Report of the Domestic Violence Task Force," July 22, 1997.

[56] Ibid., p. i. During 1997 there were ninety-four cases reported, and during the first two months of 1998 there were fifteen.

[57] Ibid., p. i.

[58] Ibid.

[59] Ibid., p. ii.

[60] Ibid.

[61] Scott Glover, "Arrests of accused abusers in LAPD soar," *Los Angeles Times*, February 20, 1998. Under a 1996 federal law, individuals convicted of domestic violence charges, including police officers, may not carry firearms. Police departments are required to identify officers with convictions who may not carry guns and, as a result, may be dismissed.

been due in part to a letter sent to those jurisdictions by the department, requesting that LAPD officers not be given special treatment during criminal investigations.[62]

The Fuhrman Report

The May 1997 report by a police task force on LAPD Det. Mark Fuhrman also provided important insights into the operation of the LAPD. The report was prompted by statements that Fuhrman made as a witness in the 1995 murder trial of football player O.J. Simpson. In contrast with its handling of most internal investigations into alleged officer abuses, the department chose to release an edited version of its investigation to the public, claiming that Fuhrman's statements had already brought the issues into the public domain. The report states, "[I]n this *very* unusual situation, the Department has determined that its efforts to investigate Fuhrman's allegations of systemic brutality, racism, perjury and evidence planting within the Los Angeles Police Department require a public accounting."[63]

In investigating Fuhrman's claims of brutality and harassment of female officers, the department found that many of the brutality incidents did not take place as he had described or were impossible to confirm due to failed memories and flawed record-keeping. The report did confirm, and express outrage, that there was institutional harassment of women on the force that was ignored by police officials.[64] By delving into Fuhrman's claims, the department's investigators also acknowledged serious shortcomings in the way it investigates and adjudicates complaints alleging abuses by officers, with many of its findings and recommendations echoing those of the Christopher Commission and subsequent reports.

The May 1997 report concludes that command officers are not held accountable when egregious or systemic misconduct is found within a command. In describing the Department Manual, the report states, "[N]owhere does it spell out a command officer's responsibility to deal with systemic misconduct and to establish sufficient detection systems to ensure command awareness of activities

---

[62] Ibid.

[63] LAPD report of the Mark Fuhrman task force, executive summary, as edited for public release, May 5, 1997. Emphasis in original.

[64] Harassment of co-workers for any reason is not within the scope of this report, yet the systemic nature of the problem that was repeatedly ignored by police officials for at least ten years is alarming and must be addressed.

which have the potential to become systemic."[65] The report urges that a series of unresolved complaints making similar allegations should be investigated, and that lying by officers in any context should be punished severely.

The investigators found that victims frequently were not interviewed during internal investigations of the use of force, that supervisors who were actively involved in use of force incidents conducted the investigation into the incident, and that record-keeping was so poor that it needed to be reorganized. The report called for improved record-keeping by the City Attorney's office, including all civil lawsuits against officers, whether stemming from their on-duty employment or off-duty conduct which is regulated by the department (such as off-duty employment). Although Fuhrman was the subject of seven civil lawsuits during his career, the city was found to have no record of three of the suits.[66]

One of the explanations for Fuhrman being allowed to stay on the force was this: "He knew exactly where the disciplinary line was, and he avoided creating any significant pattern of misconduct."[67] This point assumes that there is such a line and implies that a high level of abuse was permissible within its bounds. In the absence of a functioning early warning system, the observation illustrates the need for oversight of police conduct that looks beyond the latest incident to a pattern that may span years and may manifest itself in a variety of ways, in contrast to an officer who hits someone in the same situation in incident after incident. Repeating one of the major findings of the Christopher Commission investigation, the report concludes, "[T]he Department must identify problem officers so investigations of this sort are not necessary in the future."[68]

One negative effect of the investigation into Detective Fuhrman's allegations was the backlog it created in the Internal Affairs Division because so many IAD resources reportedly were expended on the Fuhrman probe.[69] Because there is a one-year statute of limitations on internal investigations, beyond which the maximum disciplinary sanction for an officer is a reprimand, regardless of offense, officers who may have engaged in serious abuse were not being punished

---

[65] LAPD report of the Mark Fuhrman task force, p. 66.

[66] Ibid., p. 4.

[67] Ibid., p. 61.

[68] Ibid., p. 65.

[69] Beth Shuster, "Fuhrman case adds to delays of LAPD probes," *Los Angeles Times*, February 18, 1997.

appropriately. In one case reported in the press, an officer was given a reprimand rather than a five-day suspension recommended by his supervisors because the limitations period on his case had run out. Attorneys representing alleged victims in these cases claimed the delays were a way for the department to avoid the difficult task of disciplining officers, while police union representatives complained that they were not allowed sufficient time as cases reached the end of the year period and needed to be adjudicated in a hurry, and that accused officers were not permitted to work while cases against them are pending (although they are usually suspended with pay). As a result of the backlog, the department requested thirty-eight new IAG detectives in the 1997 budget request.

Incidents

Once the list of forty-four "problem" officers was published, many of those officers did not appear in the news again. Two of the named officers, however, subsequently made news in violent incidents resulting in two fatalities. In July 1995, one officer who appeared on the list yet was assigned to a confrontational anti-gang unit, shot and killed a fourteen-year-old in July 1995.[70] The officer claimed the young man pointed a weapon at him, but the weapon was later found on the opposite side of a fence several feet from the suspect. In June 1996, the Police Commission cleared the officer of any wrongdoing, no local criminal prosecution took place, and federal prosecutors wrote in a January 1997 letter that they were "unable to authorize investigation."[71] The second officer shot and killed a man who had a plastic toy gun in his rear waistband.[72] The officer had been sued for two previous, serious abuse incidents – in one case, he allegedly beat a suspect with his fists, and in another he fatally beat a suspect on the head with his flashlight; the city reportedly paid more than $400,000 after juries found in favor of plaintiffs in both cases. The LAPD ruled the shooting justified. The officer resigned and went to work as a jail guard in California.[73]

---

[70] Alan Abrahamson, "What has happened to the 'LAPD 44'?" *Los Angeles Times*, October 15, 1995.

[71] "Officer cleared in fatal shooting of 14-year-old," *Los Angeles Times*, June 8, 1996. Telephone interview with attorney Luis Carrillo, August 27, 1997 and January 2, 1997 letter from Deval Patrick, Civil Rights Division, to Antonia Tellez.

[72] Abrahamson, "What has happened to the 'LAPD 44'?" *Los Angeles Times*, October 15, 1995.

[73] Ibid.

Media attention and policy reviews followed a three-day period in March 1996 when three men in vehicles were shot and killed by LAPD officers in three separate incidents in west San Fernando Valley.[74] In two of these incidents, officers who were apparently not properly trained to deal with fleeing suspects, put themselves in harm's way and then shot the men. In one case, William Betzner, age forty-three, was stopped by officers on March 9 and fled to his car to drive away.[75] An officer reached into the car, and Betzner continued driving; the officer reportedly shot Betzner to make him stop the car. According to the autopsy reports Betzner was under the influence of drugs. In another case, officers patrolling on bicycles in Canoga Park attempted to question twenty-nine-year-old Eduardo Hurtado and the passengers in his car on March 11, 1996.[76] Officers claimed the front-seat passenger reached for his waistband, and an officer reached into the car. Hurtado reportedly drove off with the officer holding onto the vehicle, and the officer shot Hurtado as he drove. Hurtado, who according to the autopsy report was intoxicated, died from a single gunshot to his head.[77]

In another case, police attempted to stop Jaime Jaurequi, age twenty-three, when he led them on an hour-long chase on March 9, 1996.[78] He was reportedly not armed and not involved in the crime they attempted to question him about. Officers stated that it was when he attempted to back into one of the patrol cars, after he drove onto a dead-end street, that officers opened fire, shooting twenty-three times and hitting him ten times in the shoulder, back, chest and arms.

All of the shootings were ruled "within policy," although police officials acknowledged that officers are trained not to reach into vehicles, as officers did in

[74] Beth Shuster, "LAPD panel to review 3 fatal March shootings," *Los Angeles Times*, June 1, 1996; Beth Shuster, "In wake of four shootings, lengthy internal reviews are underway," *Los Angeles Times*, March 17, 1996; John Johnson and Beth Shuster, "Police to review use of rookies in wake of shootings," *Los Angeles Times*, March 15, 1996.

[75] Ibid.

[76] Ibid.

[77] Shuster, "LAPD panel to review 3 fatal March shootings," *Los Angeles Times*, June 1, 1996; Telephone interview with attorney Luis Carrillo, September 4, 1997.

[78] Ibid.

two of the March 1996 incidents.[79] And in the Betzner case, the two officers involved had less than three years' experience between them. Police officials and one City Council member expressed concern that a high rate of resignations and retirements, combined with a hiring push, had led to inexperienced officers being paired with other rookies. Said one unnamed LAPD captain, "[I]t's almost like the blind leading the blind."[80] And LAPD Lt. Anthony Alba told reporters, "[W]e don't have enough training officers to go around."[81] Civil lawsuits are known to be pending in the Jaurequi and Hurtado cases.

In a January 1997 letter from the Justice Department to attorneys concerned about police abuse of Latinos, it was disclosed that the Civil Rights Division was investigating the Hurtado case. The same letter stated that the Justice Department would not initiate an investigation into the Jaurequi case.[82]

The Special Investigations Section (SIS)

The SIS was formed in 1965 as a surveillance unit to apprehend robbers and burglars. The SIS developed a practice of standing by during criminal activities, when individuals were being victimized by armed robbers or others, and then apprehending the suspects as they left the scene.[83] The SIS, which typically has about twenty members, killed twenty-eight suspects between 1965 and 1992, an extraordinarily high number.[84] In defending the unit's methods, then-commander

---

[79] Although not clear from press reports, it does not appear that the passenger in Hurtado's car who allegedly "reached for his waistband" was armed.

[80] John Johnson and Beth Shuster, "Police to review use of rookies in wake of shootings," *Los Angeles Times*, March 15, 1996. The same captain estimated that 40 percent of the force has less than four years' experience.

[81] John Johnson and Beth Shuster, "Police shootings raise questions about '3 Strikes' *Los Angeles Times,* March 13, 1996.

[82] January 2, 1997 letter from Deval Patrick, Civil Rights Division, to Antonia Tellez.

[83] Jerome Skolnick and James Fyfe, *Above the Law*, (New York: The Free Press, 1993), pp. 146-164, and Paul Chevigny, *Edge of the Knife,* (New York: The New Press, 1995) pp. 48-9.

[84] *Above the Law*, p. 146. During the same period, one SIS detective was shot and killed in an accidental shooting by a fellow officer. Estimates vary regarding the number of individuals shot by SIS officers during the past fifteen years, with the LAPD claiming that eighteen people have been killed and sixteen wounded during confrontations with the SIS,

of the SIS, Capt. Dennis Conte explained, "Public safety is a concern, but we have to look beyond that because if we arrest someone for attempt [sic], the likelihood of a conviction is not great."[85] The SIS reportedly does not inform local police units about its activities, adding to the danger and confusion at the scene of crimes.

Police abuse experts who have reviewed the tactics of the SIS have found the unit's actions alarming. Paul Chevigny, author of *Edge of the Knife* has described the shootings by SIS as unnecessary and as violations of international human standards, which require that officers only use force or firearms if non-violent means are unavailable.[86] In his book, Chevigny warned that members of the SIS unit may have become a "law unto themselves."[87] And an author of another book that highlighted the SIS shootings, *Above the Law*, noted that the unit's tactic of trapping and blocking suspects' cars after robberies makes shootings virtually inevitable. The author, James Fyfe, told Human Rights Watch that in most cases SIS agents know the identities of the suspects prior to the robberies, meaning that they could be apprehended while unarmed.[88] If the SIS is able to identify the suspects before these crimes are committed, it would appear that non-violent alternatives to its tactics would be possible and preferable.

In one of the unit's highest-profile cases, several suspects were under surveillance for allegedly robbing McDonald's restaurants in Sunland, a suburb northwest of Los Angeles. On February 12, 1990, a McDonald's was robbed by four individuals while the SIS monitored the events but did not intercede as the restaurant workers were held at gunpoint. Once the suspects left, the SIS blocked their car, claimed to see a gun, and opened fire, shooting twenty-four shotgun rounds, each containing nine pellets, and eleven .45 caliber rounds for a total of 227

---

and an attorney representing the victims and their families claiming a much higher number of fatalities. Patrick McGreevy, "$500,000 more ok'd for police unit's lawyers," *The Daily News of Los Angeles*, April 26, 1997, and Thao Hua and Matt Lait, "Police fire on robbery suspects, wound 2" *The Los Angeles Times*, April 25, 1997.

[85] As cited in *Above the Law*, p. 146.

[86] Principle 4 of the U.N. Basic Principles on the Use of Force and Firearms by Law Enforcement Officials states, "[L]aw enforcement officials, in carrying out their duty, shall, as far as possible, apply non-violent means before resorting to the use of force and firearms. They may use force and firearms only if other means remain ineffective or without any promise of achieving the intended result." UN Doc. A/CONF.144/28/Rev.1 (1990).

[87] Paul Chevigny, *Edge of the Knife*, (New York: The New Press, 1995), pp. 48-49.

[88] Telephone interview, Prof. James Fyfe, May 20, 1998.

projectiles.[89] One of the men attempted to run away and was shot nineteen times in the back. SIS agents claimed the man, Hector Burgos, had a gun in his hand, but according to a pathologist, the nature of a gunshot wound in his hand showed he could not have been holding a gun. In the end, three of the robbers were killed and one seriously injured; the suspects had fired no shots.[90] According to a police abuse expert who examined the photographs and evidence from the scene, none of the men were shot in the front, and they appeared to have been in "duck and cover" positions.[91]

All of the men in the car allegedly possessed weapons at the time of the robbery, but the guns the men possessed were empty pellet guns, and the shooting survivor said that it was their practice to place the guns in their car's trunk after robberies and that they had done so in this case. Some of the crime scene photographs reportedly showed no guns, others had clean guns on top of glass and other debris, leading to speculation that they had been placed there after the shootings.[92]

In a subsequent civil lawsuit, the families of the dead men were awarded $44,000 to be paid by the SIS officers themselves and by Daryl Gates, the former chief.[93] The city, not the individual officers and Chief Gates, ultimately paid the amount after indemnifying the officers, and in November 1996, a federal appeals court in San Francisco – in a judgment relating to the SIS case – upheld the right of the Los Angeles City Council to shield officers from punitive damages awarded in excessive force cases.[94] The court ruled that the City Council is entitled to indemnify officers for punitive damages if the council reviews the case and if the employee was acting within the course and scope of duty, in good faith without malice, and in the public's best interest.

---

[89] *Above the Law,* p. 159.

[90] Ibid.

[91] Telephone interview, Prof. James Fyfe, May 20, 1998.

[92] *Above the Law.,* pp. 146-164. According to one of the book's authors, James Fyfe, he saw the photographs from the crime scene, and the guns were not in the first photos taken, but appeared in subsequent photos. Telephone interview, Prof. James Fyfe, May 20, 1998.

[93] Ibid., p. 164.

[94] Henry Weinstein, "Council can pay damages for police officers, court rules," *Los Angeles Times,* November 2, 1996.

The police department found the shooting justified, and the D.A.'s office closed its investigation in May 1995. In February 1995, federal prosecutors decided there was insufficient evidence to pursue civil rights charges against the SIS officers involved in the Sunland shooting. In August 1995, federal prosecutors ended their investigation of possible perjury by members of the SIS.[95] Reacting to the various investigations of the SIS, a police union representative commented, "[I]t's like a witch hunt....[W]e're talking about crippling law enforcement."[96]

During at least three shootouts involving the SIS and armed robbery suspects between June 1995 and April 1997, four suspects were shot and killed, four were wounded, one bystander was shot and wounded, and two SIS detectives were shot and wounded.[97]

At the time of this writing, an attorney representing victims and victims' families in civil actions against the SIS and the city, in relation to several of the SIS shootings, appeared to have argued successfully to obtain federal grand jury transcripts for use in his civil cases.[98] Disclosure of grand jury transcripts to plaintiffs' attorneys in civil proceedings is highly unusual. He had argued, however, that he needed the transcripts to identify discrepancies in officers' accounts. He had also contended that the SIS's tactics violated shooting victims' civil rights.

Police Administration/Internal Affairs

The Board of Police Commissioners (Police Commission) is made up of five civilians, appointed by the mayor and approved by the City Council; the

---

[95] Ann W. O'Neill, "No perjury indictments due in probe of Sunland shootings," *Los Angeles Times,* August 4, 1995.

[96] Ann W. O'Neill, "U.S. panel probes testimony on 1990 LAPD shootings," *Los Angeles Times*, May 5, 1995.

[97] Mack Reed, "2 LAPD detectives, suspect recovering from shootout," *Los Angeles Times*, June 29, 1995; Beth Shuster, "Shooting reignites furor over LAPD unit," *Los Angeles Times*, February 27, 1997; Beth Shuster and Andrew Blankstein, "FBI opens probe of police shooting," *Los Angeles Times*, February 28, 1997; "Suit seeks damages over raid, calls for SIS unit to be scrapped," *Los Angeles Times*, April 10, 1997; Andrew Blankstein, "Sole survivor of gun battle described as informant," *Los Angeles Times*, October 24, 1997; Jim Newton, "Anti-LAPD attorney to question mayor about police shootings," *Los Angeles Times*, January 8, 1998.

[98] Greg Krikorian, "Court refuses to block release of transcripts in suit against LAPD," *Los Angeles Times*, February 27, 1998. The same attorney has deposed the city's mayor to determine his knowledge of SIS's tactics.

commissioners serve on a part-time basis. Its president, Edith R. Perez, has served on the board since 1992. The police chief, also appointed by the mayor, serves under the supervision of the Police Commission for a five-year term that must be approved and may be extended by the commission.[99] In August 1997, Bernard C. Parks was appointed the new chief.[100] Katherine Mader is the first inspector general, and was hired in July 1996; the inspector general reports to the Police Commission.[101] Human Rights Watch requested an interview or a response to written questions from Chief Parks, Commission President Perez, and Inspector General Mader. After a delay there was a response from the Internal Affairs Group commander, on behalf of Chief Parks, and Inspector General Mader was interviewed by Human Rights Watch. There was no response from Commissioner Perez.[102]

Internal Investigations

The Christopher Commission found that only forty-two of 2,152 allegations of excessive force from 1986 to 1990 were sustained – or less than 2 percent.[103] According to the Christopher Commission "... the complaint system is skewed against complainants."[104] The majority of investigations at that time were done by division staff, not IAD, and the commission found this seriously problematic

---

[99] As required by the voter-approved Charter Amendment F in 1992.

[100] Parks, who joined the force in 1965, has a reputation for dealing appropriately with officers who use excessive force or who are involved in other misconduct. According to the Inspector General, he is a stronger disciplinarian than his predecessor. Telephone interview, Inspector General Mader, April 20, 1998.

[101] The inspector general serves at the pleasure of the police commissioners and may be removed if three out of five commissioners vote to replace him or her. Telephone interview, Inspector General Mader, April 20, 1998.

[102] At the time of this writing there were press reports describing increasing tensions between the Police Commission and the Office of the Inspector General. It was suggested that the Police Commission had become protective of Chief Parks and some of its members were not pleased with the criticisms of the department put forth in the OIG's reports. Critics of the commission also told reporters that it had become a "rubber stamp" for the new chief. Lait, "LAPD watchdog commission napping," *Los Angeles Times*, May 11, 1998.

[103] Christopher Commission report, p. 35.

[104] Ibid., p. xix.

because division investigators often failed even to interview or identify witnesses. The commission found similar problems with IAD investigations, although they were generally of a higher quality than those carried out by the divisions. As described above, the LAPD's May 1997 report regarding former Det. Mark Fuhrman concluded that internal investigations were still flawed. The Fuhrman report noted that victims frequently were not interviewed during internal investigations of the use of force, that supervisors who were actively involved in use-of-force incidents were permitted to conduct the investigation into the incident, and that record-keeping was so poor that it needed to be reorganized.

Punishment for sustained complaints, the Christopher Commission also found, was more lenient than it should be, with one deputy chief telling the commission that there was greater punishment for conduct that embarrassed the department, such as theft or drug use, than for conduct that reflected improper treatment of citizens, like excessive force (which apparently was not seen as damaging). The less than 2 percent sustained rate for excessive force allegations tends to support this contention. The commission called for an overhaul of the disciplinary system, and the inclusion of the inspector general in the disciplinary process.[105] The Police Commission, it said, should hold the chief responsible for applying appropriate disciplinary sanctions. Given the flaws in the process, it was evident to the commission that the problem went beyond the forty-four officers that the commission had identified. The commission noted that, despite the large number of use of force incidents, complaints or shootings, those forty-four officers had received very positive performance evaluations.[106]

Intake of complaints against LAPD officers has long been criticized by civil rights groups an community activists who claimed that complaint forms were not always being used, and that police personnel were often logging complaints improperly or not at all. In her January 1997 report, the inspector general reported improvements in this area, stating that public information programs had been instituted, that residents had a better idea about how to file complaint, and that 1.81 complaint forms were being used by police personnel. The exception to this improvement, according to the inspector general, was the continued use of miscellaneous memos (*See* above). As of early 1998, the inspector general reported

---

[105] Ibid., p. 171

[106] Ibid., p. 40. According to press reports, as of October 1995, three of the forty-four had been fired, ten had quit, and nine had been promoted. Two reportedly killed suspects while on duty, and one was accused of falsifying evidence in a murder trial. Alan Abrahamson, "What has happened to the 'LAPD 44'?" *Los Angeles Times*, October 15, 1995.

that the police department had provided complaint forms displays in many precincts so that complainants do not have to ask for a form.[107]

Because not all complaints reached the formal stage, the inspector general noted in her January 1997 report that the total number of complaints was not available. The only numbers available were totals representing the number of cases assigned a "1.81" designation that are closed during a given year. In other words, police personnel may choose not to transform a complaint into a formal 1.81 and instead log it elsewhere, not at all, or as a miscellaneous memo, as described above. IAD numbers of total 1.81 adjudicated complaints, as follows, are therefore no more than a base-line. Those in parentheses were citizen-generated complaints, with the remainder internally generated.[108]

1991: 2,051 (717)[109]
1992: 2,359 (944)
1993: 2,017 (787)
1994: 1,529 (642)
1995: 973 (496)

In 1996, there was a total of 1,706 complaints, including 208 alleging unauthorized force, with most of those complaints coming from citizens; a breakdown of internally-generated complaints was not available. In 1997, there was a total of 1,912 complaints, including 219 alleging unauthorized force.[110]

In response to complaints over incomplete statistics regarding the total number of complaints received alleging misconduct by the LAPD, the department changed its procedures. Beginning in 1998, each complaint, no matter its merit or nature, is now being recorded in one place and investigated. It is expected that in 1998 there will be a dramatic increase in the number of complaints as a result of the new procedures.[111]   Indeed, during the first two months of 1998, there were

---

[107] Telephone interview, Inspector General Mader, April 20, 1998.

[108] In order to file an internal complaint, police department personnel are required to have a supervisor's approval. Telephone interview, Inspector General Mader, April 20, 1998. This requirement may inhibit complaints against officers' superiors or complaints the officer wishes to keep confidential.

[109] As described in the Los Angeles Board of Police Commissioners, Office of the Inspector General Six-Month Report, January 1997, pp. 11-12.

[110] 1996 and 1997 figures provided by the Inspector General's office, April 20, 1998.

[111] Telephone interview, Inspector General Mader, April 20, 1998.

approximately 800 complaints logged – at that rate, the department would receive nearly 5,000 complaints by year's end.[112] There were concerns that by investigating each complaint, whether or not it is clearly frivolous, a significant backlog is likely for all cases. Others contend the new system is similar to those used in other cities, such as Chicago, where each complaint is counted. When asked about the anticipated increase in citizen complaints against the police, IAG's commander predicted that nuisance complaints, rather than abuse complaints, would increase.[113]

IAG, which was called the Internal Affairs Division until it was reorganized in 1997, is now divided into three offices: the administrative services division (which compiles complaint statistics and analyzes complaint trends, among other duties), the investigations section, and the advocate's office (which conducts boards of rights hearings).[114] There have been repeated calls for increasing IAG's staff because its responsibilities have increased. Expansion of IAD staff was also a key recommendation of the Christopher Commission, which recommended that field police stations no longer conduct excessive force and improper police tactic investigations.[115] Yet in September 1996, Mayor Riordan defended his budget team's decision to cut back the proposed expansion of internal affairs.[116] As described above, following the Fuhrman investigation, there were renewed calls for additional internal affairs personnel. Such increases in staffing, of course, are no substitute for improved diligence and thoroughness in IAG's work. Yet the failure to staff IAG up to the requirements suggested in the Christopher Commission report and by experts since, is troubling.

Complaints alleging officer misconduct can be classified as sustained, not sustained, unfounded, or exonerated.[117] Officers found responsible for misconduct

---

[112] Matt Lait, "New LAPD complaint-logging system makes mark," *Los Angeles Times*, February 25, 1998.

[113] Telephone interview, IAG Commander James McMurray, May 8, 1998.

[114] Telephone inquiry, internal administrative services, April 30, 1998.

[115] Christopher Commission report, p. 174.

[116] Newton and Goldman, "Williams, union chief clash before panel," *Los Angeles Times*, September 13, 1996.

[117] According to the IAG's Commander, the biggest barrier to curtailing abuses and finding a complaint sustained is the lack of witnesses, both from inside the department and in the community. Telephone interview, IAG Commander McMurray, May 8, 1998.

can receive a warning, admonishment, official reprimand, suspension, or be dismissed. As noted above, there is a one-year statute of limitations requiring that any action by the chief to suspend or remove an officer must be initiated within a year of the action giving rise to the complaint.[118] A board of rights hearing takes place if an officer requests it after receiving notification of a disciplinary action against him or her, or if the action involves a suspension of more than twenty-two days. Until revisions in the 1992 Charter Amendment were implemented, the names of six officers of a rank of captain or above were drawn at random to serve on the board of rights. The accused officer then chose three of the officers, from the six randomly drawn. Now, the board of rights is made up of three members: two command officers and one civilian, with the civilian picked by the Police Commission.[119] The Charter Amendment revisions, however, did not eliminate the charged officer's ability to select any two of a list of four command officers provided to serve on the board.[120]

The Christopher Commission had called for an early warning system to track officers "at risk" of committing abuses. No such system exists yet. The May 1996 Police Commission report found that the Training Evaluation and Management System (TEAMS) is a "far cry from an automated tracking system that permits management to make informed decisions about officers or to identify and manage at-risk employees as envisioned by the Christopher Commission."[121] And in November 1997, the Office of the Inspector General released a report focusing on "high-risk" officers and found that the tracking system was still inadequate.[122]

The OIG's November 1997 report found that the police department could not comprehensively identify employees who were the defendants in civil lawsuits because of the City Attorney's policies. It provided an example of an August 1997 settlement with four plaintiffs in the amount of $125,000 stemming from alleged excessive force used by officers. During the incident, a man was rendered unconscious from a chokehold and his fourteen-year-old son was allegedly struck

---

[118] Christopher Commission report, p. 157.

[119] A representative from the Inspector General's office may also be present during board of rights hearings.

[120] May 1996 Police Commission report, p. 44.

[121] Police Commission report, p. 59.

[122] Office of the Inspector General, "Status update: management of LAPD high-risk officers," November 1997.

in the face with the butt of a gun and lost a tooth.[123] The OIG found that the department had no record of the lawsuit or settlement, there was no department personnel complaint investigation, and that the involved officers' supervisors knew nothing of the lawsuit or settlement.[124]

The OIG reported that the department lacked adequate policies to inform sergeants and lieutenants about potential high-risk officers under their command and that there were no written procedures mandating the circulation of information about high-risk officers to those who are accountable for the reduction and control of abusive behavior.[125] When OIG staff asked the chief and a deputy chief about the use of quarterly reports describing potential high-risk officers, they were told that the lists were never intended to circulate to employees below the rank of captain.[126] Therefore, direct supervisors of officers who are the subjects of repeated complaints are not necessarily aware of the allegations or the trends in such complaints. When asked about this criticism, IAG's commander stated that it was the responsibility of supervisors to check on the officers they supervised, and that they should do so in a proactive manner. He also stated, however, that many of those supervisors do not have direct access to the tracking systems and would need to submit names of their subordinates to a training sergeant who would have access.[127]

The OIG also called for the elimination of the list of forty-four allegedly at-risk officers identified in the Christopher Commission because the list is outdated.[128] The report notes that none of the officers on the list appeared in the October 1, 1997

---

[123] Ibid., p. 4.

[124] Ibid.

[125] Ibid., p. 12.

[126] Ibid. The OIG report also revealed that there was a ten-month period (between November 1996 and October 1997) during which the department failed to provide quarterly reports of employees with three or more personnel complaints

[127] Telephone interview, IAG Commander McMurray, May 8, 1998.

[128] Ibid., pp. 13-14.

quarterly report. The OIG suggested that instead of monitoring the list of forty-four, the department should better monitor those who are currently "high-risk."[129]

The LAPD has reportedly received funding from the Justice Department to create an enhanced TEAMS system to track at-risk employees, but it will not be operational for several years.[130] The new system would compile all personnel information in one place; currently investigators need to obtain some information from computers and other information from paper files in separate locations. The OIG's November 1997 report also expressed concern that, on the advice of the City Attorney's office, an officer's litigation history has not been included as part of the TEAMS system, thus making it less effective.[131]

In addition to calling for an early warning system, the Christopher Commission had recommended correcting several procedural anomalies in the LAPD's internal investigations. In shootings involving officers, the commission found that officers were interviewed as a group, allowing them to "get their stories straight."[132] Their statements were not recorded until after a pre-interview; the district attorney's office was not allowed to interview the involved officer or witnesses until the police department had concluded its investigation; and by compelling an officer's statement in these internal interviews, the department's procedures meant the statements could not be used in any criminal prosecution. Said the commission, "Other law enforcement agencies have successfully conducted shooting and other investigations without resorting to these techniques. The commission perceives no legitimate reason why the LAPD continues to engage in these practices."[133]

The district attorney's office used to send a representative to the scene of any police-involved shooting in Los Angeles, but the "roll-out" team (staff assigned to

---

[129] Ibid., p. 13. The report also describes the failure of the department to track employees facing criminal charges or who are on criminal probation, and noted that the department lacks standards and policies to determine whether these officers should continue to perform field duties. Further, the department also lacks adequate policies or standards to appropriately assign officers with recent sustained administrative discipline for integrity-related offenses.

[130] Telephone interview, Inspector General Mader, April 20, 1998.

[131] Office of the Inspector General, "Status update," November 1997, p. 14.

[132] Christopher Commission report, p. 161. According to the IAG Commander, this practice was discontinued around the time of the Christopher Commission report. Telephone interview, IAG Commander McMurray, May 8, 1998.

[133] Ibid., p. 161-162.

this duty) was discontinued in 1995. In an August 16, 1995 letter from District Attorney Gil Garcetti's office to an attorney representing the victim of a Los Angeles Sheriff's Department shooting, Garcetti explained: "[T]he department has suffered budget cuts....[O]ur rollout program has been discontinued because of this financial shortfall....[W]e can no longer send attorneys or investigators to shooting scenes. Additionally, as of September 1, 1995, we will discontinue our review of all officer involved shootings, unless the police agency involved believes that their officers have committed some criminal act and have submitted their reports to us with a request for a criminal filing....We deeply regret...we are forced to discontinue our traditional role as independent investigator for the community in officer involved shootings."[134] Even before this, however, according to press reports, district attorney review of shootings had not made much of a difference. Between 1990 and the first half of 1994, the district attorney's office reviewed 284 LAPD shooting investigations, and prosecutors brought charges only once.[135]

IAD is still notified when there is an officer-involved shooting, and its investigators may go to the scene of the shooting, as does the Robbery/Homicide Division, which handles all shooting investigations; Robbery/Homicide is also responsible for investigating any in-custody death.[136] When Robbery/Homicide investigates, the involved officer is compelled to cooperate or may be dismissed. Because the statement is compelled, it cannot be used in civil or criminal trials. Whether the investigation is by IAD or by Robbery/Homicide, officers involved in shootings do not have to speak with any investigator until they have consulted with an attorney. Around the same time that the D.A.'s roll-out team was suspended, the Police Protective League (the police union) created a roll-out team for officers involved in shootings, when an officer shoots and hits someone, and for cases in which someone dies in custody in a non-suicidal situation. This means that D.A. investigators are not on the scene, but attorneys to defend the involved officer are always available. According to IAG's Commander, the union attorneys do not play

---

[134] Letter from District Attorney Garcetti to Attorney Luis A. Carrillo, August 16, 1995.

[135] Eric Lichtblau, "LAPD officers faulted in 3 of 4 shooting cases," *Los Angeles Times*, August 14, 1994. In a positive development, the inspector general's office now reviews all officer-involved shootings.

[136] Telephone interview, Lt. Donald Hartwell, Robbery/Homicide Division, August 28, 1997.

a constructive role and often prolong an investigation unnecessarily by advising an officer not to provide an account about what took place.[137]

A Robbery/Homicide Division representative told Human Rights Watch that there was a total of 111 weapons discharges in 1994; 106 in 1995, and 122 in 1996.[138] In 1994, forty-one suspects were killed or injured in shootings, forty-four were killed or injured in 1995, and fifty-one were killed or injured in 1996. The Robbery/Homicide representative told Human Rights Watch, however, that it has been "many, many" years since an on-duty shooting has been ruled "out of policy."[139] And according to the IAG Commander "the vast majority" of shootings are found "within policy."[140]

The Christopher Commission highlighted the problem of the department's "code of silence" as inhibiting investigations into excessive force cases.[141] "When an officer finally gets fed up and comes forward to speak the truth, that will mark the end of his or her police career. The police profession will not tolerate it, and civilian authorities will close their eyes when the retaliatory machinery comes down on the officer."[142] Said former Assistant Chief Jesse Brewer, officers will not report excessive force when it happens, and if it later comes out, "they try to save themselves by saying, 'I don't know,' or 'It didn't happen' because if it comes out that they knew it happened and did nothing about it, then they would be subject to a personnel complaint for failing to take appropriate action."[143] The commission concluded, "Police officers are given special powers, unique in our society, to use force, even deadly force, in the furtherance of their duties. Along with that power, however, must come the responsibility of loyalty first to the public the officers

---

[137] Telephone interview, IAG Commander McMurray, May 8, 1998.

[138] Ibid., 1996 figures come from the Internal Affairs Division.

[139] Ibid.

[140] Telephone interview, IAG Commander McMurray, May 8, 1998.

[141] Christopher Commission report, p. 170.

[142] Former LAPD Officer Brenda Grinston, *Los Angeles Times*, July 2, 1991, as cited in Christopher Commission report, p. 170.

[143] Ibid., p. 169.

serve. That requires that the code of silence not be used as a shield to hide misconduct."[144]

After the commission's report, the department instituted code-of-silence violation prosecutions; the January 1997 inspector general's report criticized the dwindling number of such prosecutions in recent years. This is a serious concern. It may be partially offset, however, by a concurrent development, noted above, that should lead to more serious and consistent disciplinary sanctions against officers engaged in abuses.

Civil Lawsuits

The Police Commission is notified when civil lawsuits are filed against LAPD officers, and the inspector general is tasked with tracking the suits. Between 1991 and 1995, the city paid approximately $79.2 million in civil lawsuit judgments and awards and pre-trial settlements against police officers (not including traffic accidents).[145]

1991: approx. $14.6 million
1992: $19.7 million
1993: $10.6 million
1994: $8.7 million
1995: $13.5 million
1996: $12.1 million

In February 1997, the city agreed to pay gay rights demonstrators $87,000 in a settlement for police misconduct in a 1991 incident, while admitting no wrongdoing; the settlement also required LAPD officers to identify themselves to anyone seeking their names or badge numbers.[146] The settlement stemmed from an incident during which gay rights protesters were allegedly shoved and beaten by officers.[147]

In October 1992, additional staff were brought into the City Attorney's office as part of a new unit to handle lawsuits against the police, and a legal counsel's

---

[144] Ibid., pp. 170-171.

[145] Office of the City Attorney, data provided November 22, 1996 and updated September 4, 1997. No breakdown was provided regarding the precise types of complaints in each lawsuit. The city is self-insured.

[146] Bettina Boxall, "City settles policy brutality suit over incident at a gay rights protest," *Los Angeles Times*, February 7, 1997.

[147] Ibid.

office was created within the police department to coordinate responses to the lawsuits but not to investigate the underlying claims.[148] Prior to 1992, the city was reportedly overwhelmed with the number of lawsuits and settled quickly for fear of losing larger amounts if cases went to trial.

Until 1998, the IAG would receive a copy of civil lawsuits that are filed and, after deciding whether there is possible misconduct, IAG or the division where the subject officer was stationed would do a preliminary investigation.[149] Only if it was determined that misconduct may have been involved, and after the preliminary investigation was reviewed, a formal personnel complaint investigation, or 1.81, was opened.[150] In early 1998, this pre-screening was eliminated; now, every claim that is filed against LAPD initiates an internal investigation.[151] Yet according to the IAG Commander, if there is a civil jury verdict against the officer, no information about it will be entered into the officer's records unless the police department also finds the officer administratively guilty of the offense that generated the civil lawsuit.[152] He also said the department's tracking system would only list that there was a claim filed against the officer, but not the outcome.[153]

The OIG's November 1997 report reviewed 561 civil claims for damages involving department employees forwarded from the City Attorney's office to the department in 1995.[154] The department had not sustained a single allegation of misconduct against a sworn employee, of the 561 claims reviewed. While the City

---

[148] Telephone interview with civil liability office of the Legal Affairs Office of the LAPD, August 27, 1997.

[149] Telephone interview with Lt. Peter Trilling, IAD, August 27, 1997.

[150] Ibid.

[151] Telephone interview, Inspector General Mader, April 20, 1998. The IG's November 1997 report blamed the City Attorney's office for not providing information to the police department regarding lawsuits filed against police personnel. IAG's Commander told Human Rights Watch that lawsuits, which may be filed after a claim is denied by the city, rather than initial claims, now trigger an investigation. Telephone interview, IAG Commander McMurray, May 8, 1998.

[152] Telephone interview, IAG Commander James McMurray, May 8, 1998.

[153] Ibid.

[154] Office of the Inspector General, "Status update: management of LAPD high-risk officers," November 1997, pp. 6-7.

Attorney's office does notify the department when a claim is filed in state court, the OIG found that there has been no procedure in place for the City Attorney to notify the department of federal lawsuits.

In a previous survey of civil lawsuits alleging excessive or improper force, the Christopher Commission examined eighty-three successful lawsuits involving a payment by the city of at least $15,000 each and found: "...[A] majority of the cases appeared to involve clear and often egregious misconduct resulting in serious injury or death to victims, although some of the cases involved accidental or negligent conduct. The LAPD's investigation of these 83 cases was flawed in many respects, and discipline against the officers involved was frequently light or nonexistent. Moreover, the LAPD does not have adequate procedures in place to review or learn from the results of this litigation."[155] IAD had investigated twenty-three of the eighty-three incidents, and fifty-two were investigated by the Robbery/Homicide unit because they involved shootings, and others were investigated by the relevant divisions; fourteen were not investigated at all.[156] Only 21 percent of the officers involved in the eighty-three incidents were disciplined, only three officers (or 6 percent) were terminated. Forty-two percent of the officers named in lawsuits had been promoted as of 1991, and 84 percent received positive overall ratings in performance evaluations.[157]

Criminal Prosecution

Criminal prosecution of police officers for alleged brutality is extremely rare in Los Angeles. According to the IAG's Commander, at most one officer a year is prosecuted for an on-duty abuse-related incident, while prosecutions are "common" for other types of charges, such as drunk driving or domestic violence.[158] The district attorney's office does not specifically track or tally cases in which police officers are defendants.[159]

The January 1997 report by the inspector general provided one explanation for the low number of prosecutions. IAD (later IAG) supervisors claimed that

---

[155] Christopher Commission report, p. 55.

[156] Ibid., p. 57. The totals overlap because some investigations were conducted by more than one entity.

[157] Ibid.

[158] Telephone interview, IAG Commander McMurray, May 8, 1998.

[159] Telephone inquiry, district attorney's office, August 1997.

prosecutors frequently objected to reviewing anything but "good cases."[160] As a result, only about half of unauthorized force complaints that were sustained by internal affairs were being sent to prosecutors.[161] IAD, therefore, was choosing which cases they believed warranted prosecution rather than leaving prosecutorial decisions to the city or district attorney and ignoring the LAPD manual, which states: "Department entities completing personnel complaint investigations, which establish prima facie evidence of the commission of a criminal offense within the City by Department employees, shall submit the completed investigation to Internal Affairs Group for presentation to a prosecuting agency."[162] In response to this criticism, the IAG reportedly became more consistent in passing prima facie cases to the district attorney's office.[163]

Regarding federal prosecution of officers on civil right rights charges, the Office of the U.S. Attorney in Los Angeles told Human Rights Watch that between 1993 and 1995, besides the four officers involved in the King beating, there had been two other prosecutions of LAPD officers (Officers Dana Patrick Hansen and Steven Wayne Pollack).[164]

In 1996, of the twelve cases decided by federal prosecutors for the federal district containing Los Angeles (Central District of California), one was prosecuted (presented to a grand jury to seek an indictment). Between 1992 and 1995, thirty-nine cases were considered, of which twelve were prosecuted.[165]

The Justice Department's special litigation section of the Civil Rights Division reportedly continues to review the Los Angeles Police Department under its new powers to bring civil injunctions against police forces engaging in a "pattern or

---

[160] OIG report, January 1997, p.45.

[161] Telephone interview, Inspector General Mader, April 20, 1998.

[162] Ibid., Manual Section 3/837.30.

[163] Telephone interview, Inspector General Mader, April 20, 1998.

[164] Telephone interview with Carol Levitsky, U.S. Attorney's office, October 19, 1995.

[165] According to data obtained by the Transactional Records Access Clearinghouse from the Executive Office of U.S. Attorneys, Justice Department. Cases prosecuted or declined represent only a portion of the total number of complaints alleging federal criminal civil rights violations in each district in a given year. Several steps prior to this decision narrow down the number of complaints actually received to those considered worthy of consideration.

practice" of misconduct. The review was acknowledged by a Justice Department representative testifying at the September 1996 U.S. Commission on Civil Rights hearings in Los Angeles.[166] He refused to state that federal officials would not intervene in Los Angeles, "[W]e [DOJ] will stay engaged as long as we need to stay engaged."[167] In October 1996, the Justice Department turned its informal probe into an expanded investigation of the department's operations, police brutality, and racially motivated abuse.[168] The Police Protective League's representative shrugged off the federal probe, however, claiming, "It's all a big political game....they won't find anything. Racism and sexism has [sic] not been rampant in the LAPD."[169]

There may be particular pressure for the federal authorities to apply in Los Angeles because the LAPD traditionally receives more federal funding than any other city for the hiring of new officers and to enhance communications and technological capabilities. According to press reports, between 1993 and 1997, the LAPD received more than $141 million in federal grants.[170]

Unions

Until recently, the Police Protective League's employee representative was William B. Harkness, who himself was on the list of "forty-four problem" officers in the Christopher Commission report.[171]

Civil rights advocates have long contended that the police officers' "bill of rights," which provides protections for officers accused of abuse, including human rights violations, is too strong, and that it is a barrier to accountability, and have

---

[166] Steven Rosenbaum of the special litigation section of the Civil Rights Division; Newton and Goldman, "Williams, union chief clash before panel," *Los Angeles Times*, September 13, 1996; Ostrow and Serrano, "Justice dept. won't prosecute Mark Fuhrman," *Los Angeles Times*, April 3, 1998.

[167] Ibid.

[168] Pierre Thomas, "U.S. widens investigation L.A. police," *Washington Post,* October 4, 1996.

[169] Ibid.

[170] Human Rights Watch attempted to obtain these figures directly from the Justice Department, but the funds come from several different departments, and no total is compiled by the agency.

[171] Richard A. Serrano, "'They hit me, so I hit back,'" *Los Angeles Times*, October 4, 1992.

urged its repeal.[172] As mentioned above, the PPL has a roll-out team of attorneys to help officers involved in shootings, where officers are sometimes interviewed as groups by the union.[173]

At the September 1996 U.S. Commission on Civil Rights hearing in Los Angeles, the PPL's president complained that training has suffered: good trainers, he said, were being passed over due to an over-emphasis on complaint histories. During 1996, the PPL supported two bills in the state legislature that would have removed complaint records from the reach of managers, making it more difficult for them to re-train and discipline officers appropriately. The inspector general, the Police Commission, and the police chief, among others, opposed the bills. Governor Pete Wilson vetoed one of the bills that would have allowed officers across the state to delete unfounded complaints from their personnel files, but he did allow the deletion of "frivolous" complaints.[174]

---

[172] §§3300, 3311 Cal. code, public safety officer "bill of rights."

[173] Telephone interview, IAG Commander McMurray, May 8, 1998.

[174] Vetoed bill was S.B. 282; Passed bill was A.B. 3434, now Chapter 1108, Statutes of 1996.

MINNEAPOLIS

There was a problem and continues to be a problem of excessive force in this community. I'm not going to deny that. I grew up here.
— Minneapolis Mayor Sharon Sayles Belton, 1994

As crime in Minneapolis is perceived as more serious and its police department has been confronted with more violent criminals, some observers claim it has overreacted to the crime threat by at times harassing members of minority groups and committing abuses. When Police Chief Robert K. Olson took over the 960-member force in 1995, he emphasized respect for human rights and made clear he would not tolerate abuses by police officers. He set out a disciplinary matrix, allowing officers to know exactly what to expect if they break the rules, and he emphasized that sergeants and lieutenants were responsible for knowing about, and appropriately dealing with, officers who commit abuses. As a result, he has earned high marks among police abuse experts in the city, although his department's record has not been perfect.[1]

Minneapolis's police force has a history of using excessive force. Said former police chief Tony Bouza (1980-88): "Police will abuse their power....They feel themselves leashed. They want to be free to 'thump,' free to handle assholes. When someone gives them lip, they want to be able to kick their ass[es], and when you don't let them, they feel shackled. I do not let them [the police officers] 'handle' assholes."[2] Bouza says the force was "damn brutal, a bunch of thumpers," when he took over as chief in 1980.[3] Bouza was followed as chief by John Laux, who made fighting the crack-cocaine trade a priority. In officers' zeal to pursue drug traffickers, raids were sometimes conducted on the wrong houses. In a mistaken raid in January 1989, a stun grenade – designed for use in hostage situations – caused a fire at an elderly African-American couple's home, killing

---

[1] To his credit, Chief Olson agreed to be interviewed by Human Rights Watch. He was the only head of fourteen police departments who responded directly to our interview request.

[2] "Drug Enforcement in Minority Communities: The Minneapolis Police Department," Police Executive Research Forum/National Institute of Justice, 1994, p. 7. Hereinafter PERF study.

[3] Ibid.

235

them.[4] Gleason Glover of the Urban League stated at the time: "The whole issue of police brutality is nothing new to the city of Minneapolis. It almost gives the impression that if you are black and poor, it doesn't really matter if you lose your life. The police did not say 'we are sorry.' There was no remorse at all! It was just a cold thing. It happened, that's the way it is sometimes. I hate to say this, but I just don't see that happening to a white couple."[5] Just after the botched raid, there was a police raid at a hotel where black college students were having a party, and party-goers were reportedly roughed up by officers. The minority community (African-Americans, Native Americans, Latinos and Asians made up about 14 percent of the city's population in the early 1990s) demanded improved accountability for the police, leading to the creation of the Civilian Police Review Authority (CRA) in 1990, as described below.

Race
        Fifty-four percent of complaints to the CRA in 1994, 58 percent in 1995, and 61 percent in 1996 were made by people of color, although they constitute just one-quarter of the city's population.[6] A representative of the Minneapolis Urban League, which receives complaints primarily from the African-American community, told Human Rights Watch that his office receives approximately fifty complaints a month alleging police misconduct.[7] As cited in a 1994 study about drug enforcement in minority communities in Minneapolis, the Urban League said:

> The issue is essentially that the black African-American citizen continues to be deprived of the same civil liberties as those offered to the white Anglo suburbanite. The black citizen is caught in an unenviable dilemma. They must depend on the police to provide basic services, yet do not trust the police to provide the service fairly and equitably. There is a basic distrust for the police and the black African-American feels that any time

---

[4] Ibid., p. 17.

[5] Ibid.

[6] 1994, 1995 and 1996 Annual Reports issued by the Minneapolis Civilian Police Review Authority.

[7] Interview with Roger Banks, Urban League, August 30, 1995.

the police will turn on them and they will be the one incarcerated. If we are to make any progress, this basic distrust must be overcome.[8]

This distrust, on both sides, came to the fore when Minneapolis Police Officer Jerry Haaf was shot and killed on September 25, 1992, and the suspects were African-American.[9] One of the suspects in the shooting alleged brutality by the Hennepin County sheriff's deputies detaining him.[10] And after the shooting, the racial climate remained tense. Several African-American young men alleged police brutality in unrelated cases. In one, Larry Dent said he was beaten badly and was called "nigger" by several white officers in front of onlookers;[11] Dent suffered several injuries to his jaw, eyes, and mouth, and lost two teeth.[12] When asked about excessive force problems, then-Chief Laux acknowledged there were occasional problems but that "you got to factor in [Officer] Jerry Haaf's murder, you got to factor in the frequency [sic] officers take away guns and the senseless murders that are happening."[13]

Incidents
Officers Marvin Schumer and Michael Lardy: On April 17, 1993, Officers Michael Lardy and his partner Officer Marvin Schumer of the 4th Precinct encountered Charles Lone Eagle and John Boney, Native Americans who were apparently intoxicated and sleeping in front of an apartment building.[14] According

---

[8] PERF study, p. 5.

[9] Suzanne P. Kelly, "Shooting further polarizes race relations," *Minneapolis Star Tribune*, September 29, 1992.

[10] Neal Gendler, "Haaf killing suspect accuses deputies," *Minneapolis Star Tribune,* January 28, 1993.

[11] Patricia Lopez Baden, "Black motorist alleges police beating," *Minneapolis Star Tribune*, December 25, 1992.

[12] Ibid.

[13] Tatsha Robertson, " Officers say citizens don't realize law allows some use of force," *Minneapolis Star Tribune*, October 24, 1993.

[14] *Charles Lone Eagle and John Boney v. Minneapolis, Marvin Schumer, and Michael Lardy*, Hennepin County District Court, No. 94-00083, a civil complaint filed on December 30, 1993. Randy Furst, "Marchers protest police treatment of Indians," *Minneapolis Star*

to the plaintiffs' civil complaint, the officers called for an ambulance and then canceled their request and dragged the men to the squad car. The men were then allegedly handcuffed and thrown in the trunk of the squad car; the trunk was closed on Lone Eagle's leg, injuring it.[15] The two men in the trunk claimed that the ride to the hospital, which was only three blocks from where the men were picked up, took an unreasonably long time, and that the car's driver drove erratically, causing injuries. The officers later claimed that they used the squad car because they were worried about the well-being of the men and wanted to get to the hospital quickly, yet the dangerous and menacing confinement in the vehicle's trunk undermines this claim.

At the time of this incident, Officer Schumer had reportedly been the subject of thirteen complaints, and at least two were sustained. He was accused of picking people up and taking them to deserted areas near the Mississippi River, where he would allegedly beat and question them. Schumer reportedly told internal affairs investigators that it was his practice to take "troublemakers" out of downtown areas to secluded spots.[16] In 1989, Schumer was reportedly suspended for six days for taking two men to the river to intimidate them, and an internal affairs investigator warned him that similar misconduct in the future would be grounds for further discipline, including dismissal.[17] The incident of Charles Lone Eagle and John Boney involved serious misconduct. Officer Schumer, nonetheless, remains a member of the Minneapolis police force.[18]

Charles Lone Eagle and John Boney filed a lawsuit against the city of Minneapolis, alleging civil rights violations, and the city paid approximately

---

Tribune, May 20, 1993.

[15] A third man accompanying Lone Eagle and Boney was placed in the back seat of the car.

[16] Furst, "Marchers protest police treatment," *Minneapolis Star Tribune*, May 20, 1993.

[17] Randy Furst, "Officer accused of mistreating Indians has record," *Minneapolis Star Tribune*, April 30, 1993.

[18] Telephone interview, Chief Olson, January 23, 1998. The police department's personnel office also confirmed that Officer Lardy remains on the force. Telephone inquiry, April 22, 1998.

$100,000 each to Charles Lone Eagle and John Boney as the result of a civil trial jury verdict in October 1995.[19]

Officer Michael Ray Parent: In the early morning hours of August 5, 1994, a woman motorist was stopped by Officer Parent, who asked her whether she had been drinking.[20] She acknowledged she had been drinking, and he put her in the back seat of his squad car and told her she was under arrest for driving under the influence. He then stood over her, with his waist at her eye level, and asked her if she could think of anything she could do to avoid being arrested. She did not respond, so he tried again, this time warning her that the arrest would cost her $1,500 and three days in jail. Then he said, "You mean a pretty girl like you doesn't know what to do?" while stroking her arm. He started fondling one of her breasts, then took her to a more remote area. She began crying. He reportedly forced her to have oral sex with him, and he told her this was better than going to jail and having some woman have her way with her. He also let her know there was no record of his having pulled her over. Indeed, there was no record, but his notes contained her phone number and address, and his clothing tested positive for sperm.

After the incident was reported, investigators reportedly found several complaints about Parent involving inappropriate sexual conduct while on duty, even though he had only been on the force for a year and a half prior to the August 1994 case; he was accused of a sexual incident during his probationary period on the force, when dismissals of officers who commit abuses are much easier, but was not dismissed. In learning about Parent's behavior, Mayor Sharon Sayles Belton stated "as a woman who lives in the city of Minneapolis, I am horrified."[21] She wanted Parent fired immediately, but the county prosecutor convinced her to hold off until the criminal proceedings were completed. In April 1995, Parent was convicted in state court on kidnaping and rape charges and sentenced to four years in prison.[22]

---

[19] Telephone inquiry, Larry Warren, city solicitor's office, October 28, 1997. A total of $448,000 was reportedly paid in the case, with $248,000 provided for attorneys' fees. Telephone interview, attorney Larry Leventhal, October 28, 1997.

[20] According to criminal complaint filed by Hennepin County, *State of Minnesota v. Michael Ray Parent*, District Court, Hennepin County, September 1, 1994, No. 94-3037.

[21] Pat Pheifer, "Minneapolis officer held on charges of assault," *Minneapolis Star Tribune*, September 2, 1994.

[22] Burl Gilyard, "Al Berryman cops an attitude," *Twin Cities Reader*, August 30 - September 5, 1995.

Lt. Mike Sauro: After midnight on January 1, 1991, Lt. Mike Sauro was working off duty in uniform, at a club for a New Year's Eve party, when he arrested and handcuffed Craig Mische, then a twenty-one-year-old student at the College of St. Thomas, during a rowdy event. Mische claims he was kicked and beaten by Sauro in the club's kitchen while his hands were cuffed behind his back. Witnesses testified that they saw Mische being hit by Sauro, while officers contended that Mische was the aggressor.[23]

In September 1992, federal prosecutors decided not to pursue the case, explaining, "We do not believe there's a reasonable likelihood that a jury would find [Sauro] guilty beyond a reasonable doubt."[24] Local prosecutors also reportedly decided not to prosecute Sauro in relation to the alleged Mische beating. Mische filed a police misconduct civil lawsuit, and the city council decided against settling with Mische for $415,000, and instead went to trial.[25] Their decision followed Sauro's campaign on television and radio news shows, defending his record and convincing the public and the council that the city would win if they went to court.[26]

Sauro was wrong, and his conduct and the department's indifference cost the city $700,000, the largest civil award in a police misconduct case in the city's history; with attorneys' fees the case would cost the city over $1 million.[27] The jury found the city liable for "maintaining a custom of deliberate indifference to complaints about excessive force in the department."[28] At the time of the civil trial, Sauro had in his nineteen-year career reportedly been the subject of thirty-two internal affairs complaints, many alleging excessive force; none were sustained, and

---

[23] Mark Brunswick, "Lt. Thomas denies using brutal tactics during '90s New Year's Eve bar fracas," *Minneapolis Star Tribune*, June 30, 1994.

[24] Associated Press, "No indictment against officer," *Minneapolis Star Tribune*, September 11, 1992.

[25] Kevin Diaz, "City will go to court over claim of brutality," *Minneapolis Star Tribune*, May 14, 1994.

[26] Diaz, "Officials concerned by implications of Sauro verdict," *Minneapolis Star Tribune*, July 15, 1994.

[27] Ibid.

[28] Diaz, "Minneapolis won't appeal judgment in Sauro case," *Minneapolis Star Tribune*, July 23, 1994.

he was promoted through the ranks.[29] In the Mische case, the department reportedly decided not conduct an internal affairs investigation at all because its findings could have had a detrimental effect on the city's attempts to defend itself in the civil trial.[30]

Sauro had been the defendant in an excessive force lawsuit that was settled for $350,000 in 1991. And in 1996, the city agreed to pay $300,000 to another plaintiff in relation to an alleged beating by Sauro on the same night as the Mische incident.[31] In December 1996, the city settled for $25,000 with yet another plaintiff alleging excessive force used by Sauro in a September 1992 incident.[32] While a sergeant, Sauro led the 1989 mistaken raid on the home of an elderly couple who were killed in a fire set off by the officers' use of a "flash bang" grenade – an incident that reinforced distrust of the police in the black community and led to the creation of the CRA.[33] *(See* above.)

Despite the large civil jury award and two attempts to fire him, Lieutenant Sauro has successfully fought efforts to have him removed from the force. In July 1997, an appellate court upheld an arbitrator's ruling that Sauro had been fired improperly in 1995 and should be reinstated with seniority and back pay.[34] Sauro's lawyers had argued that the complainant's injuries were not consistent with his testimony and that the mayor's attempt to rescind a suspension ordered by the

---

[29] Mark Brunswick, "Minneapolis liable in Sauro case," *Minneapolis Star Tribune*, July 15, 1994; Kevin Diaz, "Sauro stands by his record, profession, *Minneapolis Star Tribune*, April 15, 1997.

[30] Kevin Diaz, "City will go to court over claim of brutality," *Minneapolis Star Tribune*.

[31] David Channen, "Judge confirms ruling favoring Sauro," *Minneapolis Star Tribune*, August 15, 1996.

[32] "Minneapolis City Council approves $25,000 Sauro settlement," *Minneapolis Star Tribune*, December 14, 1996.

[33] Wayne Wangstad, "Grenade use suspended after fatal raid/fire," *St. Paul Pioneer Press Dispatch*, January 27, 1989.

[34] "Lt. Mike Sauro: another blow to public confidence," editorial, *Minneapolis Star Tribune*, July 7, 1997. Mayor Sayles Belton fired Sauro, overruling then-Chief Laux, who had ordered a twenty-day suspension. The arbitrator eventually upheld the twenty-day suspension.

police chief and to instead dismiss Sauro constituted double jeopardy.[35] Sauro was fired a second time by Chief Olson in July 1996 after an internal investigation into another incident. Chief Olson reportedly found Sauro's conduct, "incompetent, unprofessional and inappropriate, at best. At worst it constituted criminal assault." The dismissal was subsequently reversed by an arbitrator who cited the alleged victim's inconsistencies and lack of credibility.[36] Lieutenant Sauro was again reinstated with rank and back pay.[37] In an interview with Human Rights Watch, Chief Olson stated that the arbitration system was perhaps the greatest barrier he faces in his efforts to hold police officers accountable for misconduct.[38]

Sgt. William Hannan: In January 1995, Sgt. William Hannan's ex-girlfriend accused him of throwing her down two flights of stairs, banging her head into a concrete wall, and sexually assaulting her while he held her captive in his home in Olmstead County.[39] He faced criminal sexual conduct, kidnaping and assault charges, but the charges were dismissed in June 1995 after the alleged victim refused to cooperate with prosecutors.[40] Hannan had a history of complaints; he had been suspended from the force three times and fired once (the firing was later reversed by the Civil Service Commission). In April 1992, he was charged with fifth-degree assault and other charges when he called his estranged wife and threatened her and her boyfriend. Former Chief Laux suspended him after he was convicted on all of those charges in October 1992, but he returned to duty and remains on the force today.[41]

---

[35] Kevin Diaz, "Judge sends Sauro case to arbitration," *Minneapolis Star Tribune*, May 16, 1995; Blake Morrison, "Mike Sauro must be re-hired," *St. Paul Pioneer Press*, April 2, 1997.

[36] Kevin Diaz, "Credibility was key factor in Sauro's latest victory," *Minneapolis Star Tribune*, April 3, 1997.

[37] Telephone interview, Chief Olson, January 23, 1998.

[38] Ibid.

[39] Incident as described in *State of Minnesota v. William James Hannan*, January 31, 1995, Hennepin County, District Court, No. 95-0427.

[40] Margaret Zack, "Rape, assault charges against policeman dropped," *Minneapolis Star Tribune*, June 2, 1995.

[41] Telephone inquiry, MPD personnel office, May 13, 1998.

Civilian Review

The Minneapolis Civilian Police Review Authority (CRA) was established by ordinance on January 26, 1990 to receive, consider, investigate, and make determinations regarding complaints brought by the public against the Minneapolis Police Department.[42] The board has seven members (four appointed by the City Council, three by the mayor), an executive director, three investigators (two of the three current investigators are ex-police officers but not from Minneapolis), and three administrative staff. In Fiscal Year 1997 the CRA had a budget of approximately $470,000. The board does not have subpoena power, but its founding ordinance requires that the police department cooperate with the CRA. It has no role in investigating shootings involving police; it does investigate incidents arising from off-duty employment. The CRA can make public the name and rank of an officer named in a complaint, the status of the complaint, and any disciplinary action taken by the chief at the end of the process. There is no linkage between the city attorney's office, when it receives or settles a lawsuit alleging police misconduct, and the CRA.

The CRA's creation was opposed by the then-police chief and police unions, among others. It had a rocky first few years, criticized for being slow, ineffectual, and for having a lower sustained complaint rate than the Internal Affairs Division (IAD) of the police department.[43] IAD sustained about 17 percent of citizen's "most serious" complaints prior to CRA's creation, while the CRA had a sustained rate below 5 percent during its first two years.[44]

The CRA, which is not part of the police department, has a broad mandate, and can look at allegations of excessive force, language, harassment, discrimination, theft, and failure to provide adequate or timely police protection. The CRA reports that only about 10 percent of inquiries by phone or mail result in the complainant filing a formal complaint. Complaints must be filed within a year of an alleged

---

[42] Interview with CRA Executive Director Patricia Hughes, August 30, 1995 and CRA annual reports. The CRA handles only allegations that are not criminally prosecutable.

[43] David Peterson, "Study: Civilian board upholds fewer police complaints," *Minneapolis Star Tribune*, July 22, 1993, describing study conducted by the University of Minnesota's Center for Urban and Regional Affairs.

[44] Ibid. The CRA claims that the comparison was unfair because the CRA was just beginning and did not have strong leadership initially. It was also unclear at what stage the IAD considered a complaint to have been formally lodged, investigated, and sustained, making its sustained rate meaningless. In other words, the sustained rate may be a percentage of the complaints investigated, rather than a percentage of the total number of complaints citizens attempted to file.

incident of officer misconduct. Within thirty days of receipt of a signed complaint, the executive director decides whether to recommend the case for mediation (a discussion between the complainant and officer involved in the incident, leading to a mutually agreeable resolution), dismiss the case, or forward it for investigation. If the complaint is investigated, the investigation must be completed within 120 days of the date the complaint was signed.

Investigators make recommendations to the executive director about whether there is probable cause that misconduct occurred, and the executive director then makes a probable cause determination.[45] If probable cause is found, the matter is usually sent to a three-member panel of the board. The executive director then serves as the complainant's representative at the evidentiary hearing, while the officer's attorney represents him or her, and witnesses are called for both sides. After the hearing, the panel deliberates privately and makes factual findings about what actually occurred, then makes a finding as to whether the complaint is sustained, using a "clear and convincing" standard in reviewing cases.[46] The board's panel does not make disciplinary recommendations to the police chief but simply refers the case as sustained or not sustained. The chief is then required to provide his reasons, in writing, for disciplinary actions to the mayor and CRA.[47]

In June 1997, the City Council created a "redesign team" to analyze the CRA's performance and structure, and in November 1997, the task force released its report.[48] After holding focus group meetings, conducting a mail survey, and consulting with experts, the task force made findings and recommendations to improve the CRA's operation. Among the report's findings: many people in the community do not understand what the CRA does, and those with an understanding of the CRA's procedures criticized the lack of openness during the CRA's hearing

---

[45] 1996 *CRA Annual Report*, pp. 4-5.

[46] Under state law, the CRA's proceedings are considered part of the disciplinary process, and thus are not public.

[47] The CRA gives Chief Olson higher marks than his predecessor for his handling of disciplinary sanctions in cases investigated by the CRA. The CRA was also behind the push for a disciplinary matrix because former chiefs had done too little with CRA-sustained complaints.

[48] Redesign team, "Minneapolis Civilian Police Review Authority," November 1997. The task force was made up of six individuals representing the police department, police federation, CRA board, city attorney's office, and the city's Department of Civil Rights; it was chaired by the city coordinator.

process. The focus groups and survey respondents also stated that the CRA board needed additional training to better understand police procedures and asked for clearer and more detailed explanations to complainants about why the board or chief reached their conclusions.[49] Generally, the task force called for no radical changes to the CRA, but its review did highlight issues of concern to the community and police.

Also in November 1997, voters approved a measure that subjects the police department to the jurisdiction of the city's Commission on Civil Rights; the police department was previously exempt. As a result, complainants alleging discriminatory treatment by police officers may file a complaint with the commission. The CRA redesign team noted this change and called for improved communications among the CRA, the Commission on Civil Rights, and the police department's IAD to coordinate investigations and share relevant information.

The CRA tracks complaints, sending a report every three months to the chief, IAD, and the relevant supervisor about officers with records of repeated complaints.[50] The CRA retains complaints indefinitely, with no set time period for purging files.[51]

In its 1995 annual report, published in March 1996, CRA reports receiving 146 signed complaints, with 49 percent citing excessive force as the primary characteristic, and in 1996 there were 129 signed complaints, with 44 percent alleging excessive force.[52] (The CRA only counts complaints that are formally submitted, not those made in phone calls or informally.) Probable cause of wrongdoing is found in about 10 percent of the cases; in two-thirds of the cases no probable cause is found, with the remainder dismissed, mediated or withdrawn by the complainant. This means that of 129 signed complaints in 1996, approximately fifty-six (or 44 percent) alleged excessive force, and approximately five or six of these would be found as having sufficient merit and would proceed to a hearing. More than 80 percent of cases found to have sufficient merit that go to a hearing are sustained, so perhaps five excessive force complaints would be sustained and

---

[49] Chief Olson generally expressed support for the CRA, but agreed with the review's findings that its board members should receive better training. Telephone interview, January 23, 1998.

[50] Although it is of public interest, there is no information about this reporting in the 1996 *Annual Report*.

[51] Interview with Hughes, August 30, 1995.

[52] In 1994, 58 percent of the 150 signed complaints alleged excessive force.

submitted to the chief. Unfortunately, the CRA report does not break down its probable cause or sustained rate by type of complaint (such as excessive force), so it is difficult to ascertain whether the number of excessive force cases sustained differs from other types of complaints.

In fact, disciplinary action by the police chief following an allegation of excessive force submitted in a signed CRA complaint is rare. For example, between March 1995 and February 1997 (the first two years of Chief Olson's term) only eighteen cases were sustained – two involving excessive force. In one case, an officer was disciplined with a one-day suspension without pay, and in another involving excessive force, language and harassment, an officer received a five-day suspension without pay. No further information is provided about the incidents leading to the discipline. In the same two-year period, there were 127 complaints of excessive force. Although the complaints filed during this two-year period are not necessarily the same submitted to the chief, it would appear that few complaints result in disciplinary action.

Police Administration/Internal Affairs Division

The Internal Affairs Division investigates possibly criminal misconduct or internally generated complaints, and monitors any case when a civil lawsuit is filed against the police.[53] It does not work with the CRA.[54] For the past two years, the city attorney's office has notified IAD when an excessive force or misconduct lawsuit is filed against the police. According to a representative of the police department's legal advisor's office, the department is proactive on these cases; it will open an investigation even if that means acknowledging the facts of the lawsuit.[55] The department claims that it wants to get rid of the "bad" officers so that they will only have to pay damages involving them once, avoiding future claims alleging willful or deliberate indifference to abuse complaints, as in the Sauro case. (*See* above.) As an example of this proactive stance, the legal advisor's office described a recent case in which, she said, the chief fired an officer absent any

---

[53] In its fiscal year 1997 budget, the IAD had a total of seven staff members, five of whom were investigators. According to Chief Olson, the practice of initiating preliminary investigations following the filing of civil lawsuits against police officers began in March 1995 and was directly related to the "deliberate indifference" finding in the Sauro case. Telephone interview, January 23, 1998.

[54] Telephone interview with Alison Baskfield, Legal Advisor's Office, Office of the Police Chief, January 27, 1997.

[55] Ibid.

complaint or lawsuit, on the basis of a videotape showing the officer kicking a rape suspect who was in handcuffs.[56] The department does not utilize an "early warning system" to identify officers who are the subject of repeated complaints, but does compile a "top ten" list of officers who are the subject of the most complaints.[57]

The chief's office acknowledged a flaw with tracking officers because "use of force reports," which must be filed anytime an officer uses more than a "come-along" touch, are so vague that they are rendered useless.[58] The reports name all of the officers on the scene, regardless of whether they used force, so pinpointing a particular officer with repeated "use of force" reports is made nearly impossible; clearly, this flawed system needs to be corrected.

IAD does not publish public reports regarding its activities relating to possibly criminal, internally generated, or civil lawsuits alleging police misconduct.[59]

In March 1995, Chief Olson developed a clear disciplinary matrix – a necessary tool in holding officers accountable. He also made statements emphasizing respect for human rights. Still, some observers contend that there is a small percentage of officers who should have been dismissed long ago and who serve as "role models" to some newer recruits.

Civil Lawsuits

Minneapolis is self-insured, and settlements and awards against the police are paid out of the police department's budget according to the city solicitor's office, although there are plans to change the current system.[60] Payments are made following authorization from the City Council, which usually agrees to settlements rather than going to trial. A representative from the city solicitor's office told Human Rights Watch that any improvements at the police department stem from big lawsuits.

---

[56] Ibid.

[57] Telephone interview, Chief Olson, January 23, 1998.

[58] Telephone interview with Alison Baskfield, Legal Advisor's Office, Office of the Police Chief, January 27, 1997, and telephone interview with Chief Olson, January 23, 1998.

[59] In October 1997, Human Rights Watch submitted questions to the IAD about its activities, but as of this writing there has been no response.

[60] Telephone interviews, Larry Warren, city solicitor's office, December 5, 1996 and October 28, 1997.

In lawsuits alleging excessive force and/or false arrest, the total amount for settlements and judgments in police misconduct cases were, by calendar year: $570,000 in 1993; $1,367,680 in ten cases (involving eight on duty officers and two while working off duty as security guards) for 1994; and $1,390,000 in nine cases (seven on duty, one off duty, and one off duty working in a security capacity) in 1995.[61]

Criminal Prosecution

Local criminal prosecution against police officers does occur in Minneapolis, where the Hennepin County prosecutors have a reputation for pursuing such cases. According to the Hennepin County attorney's office, an "informal" file is kept of police defendants by the adult prosecution division.[62]

The U.S. Attorney's office told Human Rights Watch that it would need Justice Department authorization before the office could provide information. An attorney in the U.S. Attorney's office did speak to Human Rights Watch "on background" and stated that federal prosecutors were not very active in Minneapolis because local prosecutors do, in fact, prosecute police.[63]

In 1996, of the six cases decided by federal prosecutors for the federal district containing Minneapolis (Minnesota), none was prosecuted (presented to a grand jury to seek an indictment). Between 1992 and 1995, twenty-six cases were considered, and six were prosecuted.[64]

Unions

The Police Federation is very strong in Minneapolis, and its president, Al Berryman, has a very high profile in the city. When asked why he defends officers who commit abuses, Berryman told a reporter, "People don't seem to realize that

---

[61] Telephone interviews, Larry Warren, city solicitor's office, December 5, 1996 and October 28, 1997. At the time of our request in late 1997, 1996 figures had not been compiled.

[62] Telephone inquiry, Hennepin County attorney's office administrator, May 19, 1997.

[63] Telephone interview, U.S. attorney's office staff person, August 31, 1995.

[64] According to data obtained by TRAC from Executive Office of U.S. Attorneys, Justice Department. Cases prosecuted or declined represent only a portion of the total number of complaints alleging federal criminal civil rights violations referred to each district in a given year. Several steps prior to this decision narrow down the number of complaints actually received to those considered worthy of consideration.

[my] job is to defend members and guarantee them due process until the moment they are convicted of a criminal offense."[65] Yet after Minneapolis police officer Kent Warnberg was convicted in Wisconsin for fourth-degree sexual assault, for fondling a female National Guard private in 1993, Berryman publicly supported Warnberg's reinstatement with the Minneapolis police department, arguing, "We all make mistakes. It's a matter of degree of mistakes and the ability to accept responsibility for the mistakes."[66] After the Sauro settlement, Berryman stated, "We do a very good job of policing ourselves."[67] Sauro had been active in the federation, according to press reports.[68]

The federation has opposed enhanced civilian review of the police. Said Berryman, "There's got to be a limit to even what the public wants as scrutiny. A small portion of the public is never going to be happy until they've got police officers all strung up. But the majority of the public just wants competent law enforcement."[69]

---

[65] Gilyard, "Al Berryman cops an attitude," *Twin Cities Reader,* August 30 - September 5, 1995.

[66] Ibid., and Anne O'Connor, "Minneapolis officer won't be fired for sexual assault," *Minneapolis Star Tribune,* February 7, 1995. The incident was also reported as having occurred in 1992.

[67] Diaz, "Officials concerned by implications of Sauro verdict," *Minneapolis Star Tribune,* July 15, 1994.

[68] Ibid.

[69] Diaz, "Civil rights review sought for some police brutality complaints," *Minneapolis Star Tribune,* July 10, 1992.

NEW ORLEANS

The New Orleans Police Department has been rocked by successive scandals during the past several years: an officer was convicted in April 1996 of hiring a hit man to kill a woman who had lodged a brutality complaint against him and another officer was convicted in September 1995 for robbing a Vietnamese restaurant and shooting, execution style, a brother and sister who worked there, as well as an off-duty officer from her precinct working as security at the restaurant. In addition, at least fifty of the 1,400-member force have been arrested for felonies including homicide, rape, and robberies since 1993.[1] As astutely noted by police abuse expert Prof. James Fyfe, some cities' police departments have reputations for being brutal, like Los Angeles, or corrupt, like New York, and still others are considered incompetent. New Orleans has accomplished the rare feat of leading nationally in all categories.[2]

The U.S. Justice Department, hardly an overeager interloper, has been so alarmed by the corruption that it has assigned two FBI agents to work at the department to help reform its internal affairs division, while the Justice Department's civil rights division is conducting an investigation under its new civil powers, allowing the Justice Department to bring civil actions against cities and their police departments if they engage in a "pattern or practice" of rights violations.[3] New Orleans also had the highest ranking of citizen complaints of police brutality in the country, according to a 1991 Justice Department report.[4] Yet, despite its abysmal record, the police department has avoided the widespread community protests or other sustained external pressure that are often necessary for reforms to take hold permanently.

Beginning in early 1997, the city began implementing "quality of life" policing tactics, as implemented in New York City and elsewhere around the country, by

---

[1] Paul Keegan, "The Thinnest Blue Line," *New York Times Magazine*, March 31, 1996, pp. 32-35. According to Maj. Felix Loicano, head of the police department's Public Integrity Division, a total of eighty officers received court summonses, were arrested or indicted between 1995 and 1997. Telephone interview, Maj. Felix Loicano, January 27, 1998.

[2] Keegan, "The Thinnest Blue Line," *New York Times Magazine*, March 31, 1996.

[3] See introduction's legal section.

[4] The statistics stem from a 1991 Justice Department report, described in the overview above.

focusing on more minor offenses.[5] During 1995 and 1996, the crime rate began to drop in some categories, and this drop continued in 1997, with murder and armed robbery rates dropping dramatically. Police abuse experts in the city, however, are concerned that implementation of the "quality of life" plan will result in complaints of harassment and an increase in abuse complaints, as it has in other cities where it has taken effect; there is particular uneasiness about instituting "aggressive policing" by a police force like New Orleans' with its brutal track record. Indeed, police abuse experts in the city noted an increase in complaints during the summer of 1997, following the implementation of the new zero-tolerance program.[6] According to the department's own statistics, citizen complaints against the police rose by 27 percent between 1996 and 1997.[7]

Recent History

After a white officer was killed in November 1980, mobs of police officers went on a rampage in Algiers, a black section of town, killing four and injuring as many as fifty residents. Some of the victims were tortured, including two who were dragged to swamps where the officers carried out mock executions. The violence led to the resignation of the police superintendent, an outsider hired to reform the department – a departure welcomed by many department insiders opposed to reform.[8] Three homicide detectives were convicted on federal criminal civil rights charges.

History repeated itself on March 22, 1990, when Adolph Archie, an African-American, was accused of killing a white officer, Earl Hauck, during a shootout downtown. On the way from the scene of the shooting to the hospital, the police transporting Archie, who had been injured during the incident, took twelve minutes to travel seven blocks. When they arrived at the hospital, approximately one hundred officers were waiting for them after hearing that Hauck had died. During this period, officers were broadcasting death threats against Archie over police radios. Those transporting Archie, including a close friend of Hauck's, stated later

---

[5] As in New York, "aggressive policing" is coupled with the use of computerized monitoring of criminal activity, allowing officers to concentrate on certain areas of the city where certain crimes are common, and to track their progress.

[6] Telephone interview with police abuse expert and attorney Mary Howell, September 5, 1997.

[7] Report by Superintendent Pennington to the City Council, January 22, 1998.

[8] Allan Katz, "Policing an atypical city," *New Orleans*, June 1990, p. 39.

that they thought there could be a lynching at the hospital where the officers continued to threaten Archie. The officers transporting Archie decided not to enter the hospital, but instead of following department policy and taking him to another hospital, they drove him to Hauck's police station. At the station, officers claimed there was a scuffle with Archie, and that he slipped and fell. The station's sergeant denied ever seeing the officers or Archie and did not raise questions about the bloodstains that appeared on the floor; instead he simply ordered a trusty to clean them up.[9]

By the time Archie got to a doctor, he had been beaten severely, yet no officer was held accountable then or later.[10] Once they got to the hospital, events became more confused. Some of Archie's hospital x-rays, showing his injuries, reportedly vanished. Medical staff were unable to determine Archie's name or his background (even though officers knew his name) and injected him with iodine for a medical test, to which he was allegedly allergic, leading some to conclude this had killed him. Two pathologists said he was beaten to death, and it was reported that he had exacerbated his condition by pulling out tubes in his throat at some point and that the injuries to his throat prevented breathing without them. His death was ultimately called a "homicide by police intervention" by the coroner's office.[11]

In a settlement with the city, Archie's family was paid $333,000, with one-third designated for the family of Officer Hauck.[12] According to all reports, no officers were criminally prosecuted or administratively sanctioned; in fact, within hours of Archie's death, then-Superintendent Warren Woodfork cleared all the involved officers of any departmental violations.[13] It was also reported that the rookie officer

---

[9] Russell Miller, "The big sleazy," *Sunday Times Magazine* (London), October 8, 1995; Letter from Dr. Michael Baden, NY State Police, forensic pathologist retained by the FBI, June 25, 1990; Christopher Cooper, "Archie tale doesn't explain it all," *Times-Picayune*, August 8, 1993.

[10] Ibid.

[11] Bob Herbert, "Disgracing the Badge," *New York Times*, September 18, 1995; letter from attorney Mary Howell to Attorney General Janet Reno, March 30, 1993, citing Orleans Parish Coroner's office.

[12] Bill Voelker, "Settlement split with kin of slain cop," *Times-Picayune*, May 20, 1994.

[13] Ibid.; Howell letter, March 30, 1993; and Herbert, September 18, 1995.

who initially apprehended Archie and did not shoot him on the spot, was vilified by fellow officers for his restraint.[14]

In a May 1993 report requested by then-Mayor Sidney Barthelemy – one of several reports detailing problems in the police department and recommending changes that were ignored until subsequent, high-profile cases – the advisory committee on human relations found that some officers behaved brutally and that the department's efforts to control them were "halfhearted and ineffectual."[15] The committee found a relatively small percentage of bad officers, but its chairperson noted: "[T]he police department itself helps to cover up such people through the code of silence, and anyone who rats on another guy will find himself never promoted. Those signals come from the top and work their way down."[16] Among its scores of recommendations, the report called for: public, quarterly reports containing the number of complaints and type, race of all parties, final disposition and reasons; civilian involvement in disciplinary decisions; stricter rules regarding off-duty employment; and publication of the number of civil lawsuits and how they were resolved.[17]

Mayor Marc Morial – who was elected in 1994, in part to clean up the department – appointed former Washington, D.C. assistant chief of police Richard Pennington as an outsider reformer. In discussing the task he faced in fighting police corruption and abuse, Pennington noted, "[I]t took years for the department to get to the point it was when I arrived, and it is going to take years to change the ingrained culture."[18] The superintendent did fire or reprimand scores of officers, called for improved background checks on recruits (ending the practice of hiring known criminals), instituted an early warning system to spot repeat offenders[19] on

---

[14] Allen Johnson, Jr., "Dead men do tell tales," *Gambit*, October 17, 1995.

[15] The Mayor's Advisory Committee on Human Relations, "Report on police use of force," May 19, 1993, p. 3.

[16] Susan Finch, "NOPD told to put stop to brutality," *Times-Picayune*, May 20, 1993.

[17] In 1991, the International Association of Chiefs of Police recommended the creation of an early warning system, another recommendation ignored by the police department until quite recently.

[18] Miller, "The big sleazy," *Sunday Times Magazine* (London).

[19] When an attorney reviewed IAD's files covering 1987 until March 1990, she found that approximately 8 percent of officers were the subject of 38 percent of all complaints.

the force, and placed limits on off-duty employment. In general, the superintendent gets high marks from police abuse experts in the city, but some worry that his reform efforts are linked to him personally and may mean little if he leaves the force. And despite positive actions by Superintendent Pennington, the U.S. Attorney for New Orleans has warned, "There has been a change to some degree in that culture of tolerance of corruption. But as long as there are some officers who are holdovers from the previous regime, then I think we still have a problem."[20]

Incidents

Officer Len Davis: Former Officer Len Davis, reportedly known in the Desire housing project as "Robocop," ordered the October 13, 1994 murder of Kim Groves, after he learned she had filed a brutality complaint against him.[21] Federal agents had Davis under surveillance for alleged drug-dealing and recorded Davis ordering the killing, apparently without realizing what they had heard until it was too late. Davis mumbled to himself about the "30" he would be taking care of (the police code for homicide) and, in communicating with the killer, described Groves's standing on the street and demanded he "get that whore!" Afterward, he confirmed the slaying by saying "N.A.T.", police jargon for "necessary action taken."[22] Community activists reported a chilling effect on potential witnesses or victims of brutality considering coming forward to complain following Groves's murder.

According to a partial list of complaints and disciplinary action against Davis, obtained by an attorney, he was the subject of at least twenty complaints between 1987 and 1992, most involving brutality and physical intimidation; in most cases the complaints were not sustained, but in one case he was suspended for fifty-one days for hitting a woman in the head with his flashlight.[23] One officer told a reporter, "He's got an internal affairs jacket as thick as a telephone book, but

---

[20] Comments of U.S. Attorney for the Eastern District of Louisiana on National Public Radio program, February 4, 1998.

[21] Complaints are supposedly confidential, but it was widely believed that this complaint was leaked by Internal Affairs Division or another department branch.

[22] James Varney, "Trust in police vanishes as horror stories unfold," *Times-Picayune,* December 14, 1994; Michael Perlstein, "Officer had a history of complaints," *Times-Picayune,* December 7, 1994; Jesse Katz, "Corrupt cops: the big sleazy?" *Los Angeles Times,* March 8, 1995.

[23] Attachment to letter from attorney Mary Howell to Mayor Morial and Superintendent Pennington, December 6, 1994.

supervisors have swept his dirt under the rug for so long that it's coming back to haunt them."[24]

On November 6, 1996, Davis was sentenced to death in federal court, on federal criminal civil rights charges, for ordering Groves's slaying.[25] And on December 18, 1996, Davis was sentenced to life plus five years in federal court for his involvement in the cocaine ring.[26] Along with Davis, a half-dozen other former New Orleans police officers were convicted on drug trafficking charges, all stemming from the same FBI sting operation.

Officer Antoinette Frank: At 1:00 a.m. on March 4, 1995, New Orleans police officer Antoinette Frank and an accomplice entered a Vietnamese restaurant in east New Orleans, shot the off-duty police officer moonlighting as a security guard, and then executed a brother and sister who worked at their family's restaurant as they knelt on the floor praying and begging for mercy. The victims' brother and sister hid in a cooler and witnessed much of what transpired. Frank, who did not disguise herself, knew the family and had moonlighted as a security guard at the restaurant before, and even responded to their call for help after the incident, as though she knew nothing about what had transpired. She was quickly convicted and sentenced to death in September 1995.[27]

Frank had been hired as an officer in February 1993; after failing the civil service psychiatric evaluation, she had hired her own physician to find her fit. Following the department's rules, the two contradictory evaluations were then

[24] Perlstein, "Officer had a history...," *Times-Picayune.* An internal affairs "jacket" means file.

[25] Bill Voelker, "Ex-officer gets life for role in coke ring," *Times-Picayune,* December 19, 1996.

[26] Ibid.

[27] Christopher Cooper and Walter Philbin, "NOPD didn't see red flags, records say," *Times-Picayune,* March 7, 1995; Cynthia Sanz, "A killer in blue," Miller, "The big sleazy," *Sunday Times Magazine* (London); "Unthinkable horror," Commentary, *Gambit,* March 14, 1995.

evaluated by a second civil service psychiatrist, who found her suitable.[28] Concerns of fellow officers about her behavior were ignored.[29]

   Lt. Christopher Maurice: Lt. Christopher Maurice was charged with two counts of simple battery by the district attorney's office on August 10, 1994, after allegedly assaulting two motorists during separate traffic stops on Interstate 10.[30] In one of the cases, Maurice allegedly slammed the head of radio personality Richard Blake (known as Robert Sandifer), against his police car's hood after Blake was pulled over on June 22, 1994. Blake reportedly suffered facial lacerations. The altercation began when Blake yelled at Maurice, who was in an unmarked car, to slow down after he tailgated then quickly passed Blake's car; after the incident, Blake did not get a ticket. In November 1995, Maurice was convicted on battery charges in relation to this incident and sentenced to one year of probation and ordered to seek help from a stress management clinic.[31] After a panel of Criminal District Court judges overturned the conviction, the 4th Circuit Court reinstated the conviction in December 1996.[32] According to press reports, the district attorney's office only took up the case against Maurice involving Blake after a government watchdog group pressured the prosecutors to review the case.[33]
   Prior to this incident, Maurice reportedly had been the subject of more than a dozen discourtesy and brutality complaints.[34] According to civil service records,

---

[28] Cooper and Philbin, "NOPD didn't see red flags," *Times Picayune.*

[29] Ibid.

[30] Perlstein, "Radio exec: cop hit me," *Times-Picayune;* "Cop faces battery charges," *Times-Picayune,* August 11, 1994. Also in June 1994, Maurice was served a warrant for a battery charge against a cable company worker in St. Tammany parish. Perlstein, "N.O. cop accused of abuse in past," *Times-Picayune,* July 2, 1994.

[31] Michael Perlstein, "Former officer wants old job," *Times-Picayune,* October 11, 1996.

[32] Walt Philbin, "Ex-officer's battery conviction is reinstated," *Times-Picayune,* December 5, 1996.

[33] Perlstein, "DA's office takes up cop probe," *Times-Picayune,* August 6, 1994.

[34] Just after the incident involving Blake, Maurice was found in violation of department rules for getting into an argument and nearly a fistfight with a fellow officer in early 1994. A two-day suspension was ordered, but Maurice was already suspended because of the

Maurice had been reprimanded twice between 1985 and 1994, and suspended once.[35] The suspension stemmed from an argument with a neighbor in which he allegedly brandished his gun.[36] And in a 1991 civil lawsuit, the city paid a $25,000 settlement to a man who claimed Maurice hit him in the head with his police radio.[37] Despite his record, Maurice served as the commander in charge of enforcing the internal rules of the department.[38] The civilian review agency, the Office of Municipal Investigation, had reviewed several of the complaints against Maurice, but none had been sustained. Commented one officer about Maurice's job to enforce internal rules, "Having him in that position is ridiculous....Here's a guy with a history of complaints and it's like he's being rewarded for it."[39] Maurice is no longer on the police force.[40]

Civilian Review

The Office of Municipal Investigation (OMI) was created in 1981 and is staffed by civilians. It has five investigators, two clerical staff, and a director; three investigators are former New Orleans police officers.[41] The OMI investigates complaints against all city employees, with complaints against the police making up more than half of its caseload. During 1995 and 1996, the office received approximately 250 complaints alleging police misconduct (including incidents involving forty weapons discharges), down from 300-400 received in previous years; as noted above, there was then an increase in complaints during much of

---

Interstate 10 altercation described above. Perlstein, "Accused cop broke rules, sources say," *Times-Picayune,* June 25, 1994.

[35] Michael Perlstein, "Radio exec: cop hit me," *Times-Picayune,* June 24, 1994.

[36] Ibid.

[37] Michael Perlstein, "DA's office takes up cop probe," *Times-Picayune,* August 6, 1994.

[38] Perlstein, "N.O. cop accused of abuse in past," *Times-Picayune,* July 2, 1994.

[39] Ibid.

[40] Maurice was dismissed in November 1995 after he was convicted in the Sandifer case. Philbin, "Ex-officer's battery conviction is reinstated," *Times-Picayune,* December 5, 1996.

[41] Telephone interview with Peter Munster, director, OMI, September 5, 1997.

1997.[42] The OMI retains the more serious cases (but sends possibly criminal allegations to the Public Integrity Division) with minor discourtesy allegations sent to the police district to handle; it does not investigate off-duty misconduct. It has subpoena power and considers itself "an honest broker."[43]

Complaint intake at the OMI is imperfect. Police stations, where most individuals attempt to file complaints, reportedly refer cases to the Public Integrity Division (PID), not to the OMI. The OMI does little community outreach and relies upon high-profile cases and mention of the OMI in the press to inform the public of its existence. Even if it learns of a serious violation, it is prohibited from proactively launching an investigation in the absence of a complaint.

In the cases where it does receive a complaint and the OMI investigator sustains it, the investigator's findings are sent to the OMI's Chief Administrative Officer (CAO), and if the CAO agrees, it is sent to the police superintendent or his designee, who has thirty days to respond in writing regarding what, if any, action has been taken by the department. The OMI is prohibited from making disciplinary recommendations.[44]

The OMI publishes an annual report. As of April 1998, the 1996 report was still not available.[45] During 1995, approximately 200 complaints were either investigated by OMI or referred to the police department for investigation. That year, fifteen complaints against the police were sustained, but the OMI's reports do not distinguish between sustained complaints alleging brutality or more minor offenses.[46] The OMI representative did not know the sustained rate for police misconduct complaints, but noted that it is more difficult to sustain complaints against officers than other city employees because they always have legal

---

[42] Munster stated that the number of complaints in 1996 was similar to those in the 1995 OMI report; no 1996 report was available as of September 1997.

[43] Interview with Peter Munster, October 26, 1995.

[44] June 12, 1984 Chief Administrative Office Policy Memorandum No. 50, Sec. VI (B)] The OMI can also accept "appeals" from citizens who believe a PID investigation was incomplete or flawed. Although the OMI told Human Rights Watch that it can review PID investigations, a PID representative stated this was not the case. Interview with Lt. Charles Schlosser, PID, October 27, 1995.

[45] Telephone inquiry with OMI, April 9, 1998.

[46] This number includes cases investigated or complaints filed from previous years.

representation.[47] According to the OMI's report, of the fifteen sustained complaints of all types against the police, one resulted in a fifteen-day suspension, one in a letter of reprimand, one officer resigned, and in twelve cases the department did not provide information to OMI, in apparent violation of policy. OMI's reports lack racial, age, gender or district breakdowns of parties involved in incidents. They do not describe trends or any policy recommendations made by the office.

The City Attorney's office uses OMI files when it needs to defend officers in civil lawsuits. OMI does a background check of the complainant when it receives a complaint, although it is unclear why a criminal or other background should affect investigation of a complaint. OMI staff are sent to every police shooting but are not involved in determining whether a shooting was justified.

Despite the troubled state of the police department, when a Human Rights Watch investigator visited the OMI office on a weekday afternoon in late 1995, the office was absolutely silent, no phones were ringing, and some staffers were playing computer video games. Although this was a random visit and may not reflect the typical operations of the office, the stillness of the office seemed out of sync with the investigations that would seem necessary in the city.

Police Administration/Internal Affairs

New Orleans is a very poor city, with more residents living in poverty than in any other large U.S. city except Detroit.[48] In recent years, police officer salaries started as low as $18,000. The starting salary began to increase in 1995, but when pay was very low, some observers believed that officers were particularly vulnerable to temptations of more lucrative, corrupt practices. A generally accepted estimate is that about 10-15 percent of the department is corrupt, with some observers putting the percentage much higher.[49] The U.S. Attorney for the Eastern

---

[47] Telephone interview, OMI director Peter Munster, September 5, 1997.

[48] 1990 Census statistics.

[49] Keegan, "The Thinnest Blue Line," *New York Times Magazine*; Miller, "The big sleazy," *Sunday Times Magazine* (London); interviews by the Metropolitan Crime Commission as described in James Varney, "District known for bad cops," *Times-Picayune*, December 9, 1994. Major Loicano of PID has suggested that this percentage has decreased in recent years and may be closer to 5 percent. He notes that many officers have been dismissed or have resigned while under investigation for misconduct; fifty-four were dismissed between 1994 and 1997, and seventy-three resigned.

District of Louisiana, which includes New Orleans, stated that corruption in the police department is "pervasive, rampant, [and] systemic...."[50]

As part of the reform efforts following high-profile abuse and misconduct cases, the Internal Affairs Division was revamped and renamed the Public Integrity Division (PID) in February 1995.[51] When he announced the changes in name and staffing, Superintendent Pennington stated, "No longer will we take complaints and put them in a file cabinet."[52] Pennington replaced the former IAD commander, Maj. Richard Reeves; a state court judge had reportedly ruled that Reeves had ordered the altering of a police brutality report to protect the city from litigation.[53]

Prior to the changes, an outside attorney reviewed internal affairs files and found that the files were disorganized and that the department was using an incorrect standard of proof in deciding whether to sustain complaints: the criminal "beyond a reasonable doubt" standard instead of that of a preponderance of the evidence.[54] She also found a sustained rate of about 1-2 percent for excessive force complaints filed against officers by civilians. The low sustained rate was explained by the criteria through which PID investigators considered almost any witness "involved" and therefore discredited their accounts.[55] She also found that a small percentage of officers were responsible for more than one-third of all complaints. She noted that, in light of the historically lax investigations by the internal affairs unit, many community activists and attorneys who bring civil lawsuits against allegedly abusive police officers do not bother filing formal complaints.

---

[50] Rick Bragg, "New Orleans is hopeful about police overhaul," *New York Times*, January 29, 1995.

[51] The PID staff consists of Major Felix Loicano, two captains, three lieutenants, eighteen investigators, and four civilians.

[52] Christopher Cooper, "Internal affairs unit open for business," *Times Picayune*, February 11, 1995.

[53] "Internal affairs," Commentary, *Gambit*, February 14, 1995. Major Loicano of PID confirmed to Human Rights Watch that it was his recollection that Reeves had been responsible for misconduct during an investigation.

[54] IAD files between 1987 and March 1990 were reviewed by attorney Mary Howell. The May 1993 Advisory Committee report noted the same flaw regarding the standard of proof, p. 19.

[55] Interview with attorney Mary Howell, October 27, 1995.

At a civil trial in 1995, a public administration expert who had studied one hundred police departments around the country found that the New Orleans police department was the worst "in terms of responsiveness to deficiencies."[56] For example, despite scandals, it was reported by other sources that there were no unsatisfactory personnel evaluations given by department managers between September 1992 and September 1995.[57] Clearly, the department had a long way to go when reform efforts began in 1995.

A PID representative explained that districts investigate minor cases, and the PID reviews those investigations and explores possibly criminal behavior by officers.[58] PID takes the lead in investigating any weapon discharge by an officer if no one is injured or killed, with the homicide division responsible for investigating shootings resulting in injury or death. The district attorney's office also reviews any shooting resulting in injury or death.[59]

Although for several months PID failed to respond to repeated requests by Human Rights Watch for statistics on its activities, PID's Maj. Felix Loicano did agree to an interview in January 1998 and provided some of the statistics we had requested.[60] According to Loicano, PID received a total of 589 citizen complaints against the police in 1994, 662 in 1995, 341 in 1996, and 433 in 1997.[61] According to Loicano, there were 509 abuse complaints in 1995, 301 in 1996, and 319 in 1997.[62] Loicano could not estimate sustained rates for abuse complaints, because

---

[56] Johnson, "Dead men do tell tales," *Gambit*, October 17, 1995, referring to testimony in a federal civil trial by Dr. Jim Ginger.

[57] Bob Herbert, *New York Times*, September 15, 1995, citing the Metropolitan Crime Commission.

[58] Interview with Lt. Charles Schlosser, October 27, 1995.

[59] Shootings by police appear to have steadily decreased during the past several years. In 1992, there were sixty-six shootings, with thirty-two leading to injury or death, but by 1997 there were thirty-eight shootings, with eight leading to injury or death. Report by Superintendent Pennington to the City Council, January 22, 1998.

[60] Telephone interview, Major Loicano, PID, January 27, 1998.

[61] Ibid. The figures exclude complaints considered without merit. These figures also appear in a report to the City Council by Superintendent Pennington, January 22, 1998.

[62] Ibid. The City Council report does not define "abuse."

sustained rates are not broken down by type of violation.[63] Generally, he noted, complaints made against officers by supervisors are sustained at a much higher rate than those made by citizens.[64] According to another PID representative, a complaint is not sustained if it is a one-on-one "swearing contest" between an alleged victim and an officer.[65] He described an independent witness as someone else getting a ticket, someone on a corner, with no interest in the incident – thus apparently using a higher standard than in a criminal case.

Even if a complaint against an officer is sustained, appropriate discipline is not always applied.[66] According to Major Loicano, even if PID sustains a complaint and punishment is ordered, the officer in question may avoid discipline. In many cases, he noted, the officer will appeal to the civil service commission and, if the complainant or witnesses fail to appear for the hearing, PID investigators are not able to present their case against the officer fully and the officer will often prevail.

An early warning system to detect officers with repeated complaints, called the Professional Performance Enhancement Program (PPEP), was initiated in mid-1995. Major Loicano of PID considers the PPEP the division's "best success story."[67] Officers selected for the program are picked by collecting information about complaints filed against them, use of force and shooting incidents, and other relevant information that may show that the officer requires additional training, supervision, or counseling.[68] The PID selects groups of officers once or twice a year, and the officers' commanders receive a report from PID about the officers picked. The commander is allowed two weeks to agree to placing the officer in the six-month PPEP program or objecting to the officer's inclusion.

---

[63] Ibid.

[64] Ibid.

[65] Interview with Lt. Charles Schlosser, PID, October 27, 1995.

[66] Unfortunately, disciplinary data provided by Superintendent Pennington in a report to the City Council in January 1998 were too limited and did not include enough information to allow the reader to understand their significance. For example, the data did not describe the type of complaint leading to disciplinary action.

[67] Telephone interview, Maj. Loicano, January 27, 1998.

[68] Ibid. OMI cases, unless sustained, are not included in the selection decision, nor are civil lawsuits alleging brutality or other misconduct.

According to Loicano, the first group of twenty-five officers selected for the PPEP program were collectively the subject of ninety-seven complaints during a twelve-month period ending in mid-1995.[69] During the two years following their participation in the PPEP monitoring program (during which two of the officers were dismissed and one retired), the twenty-two remaining officers received thirty-seven complaints. The subsequent groups of officers placed in the program have shown similar reductions in complaints according to Loicano.[70]

In April 1995, as a bill to forbid officers from purging complaints from their records made its way through the Louisiana legislature, hundreds of officers tried to get their files quickly expunged.[71] The officers were notified of the legislative effort in a letter from the Fraternal Order of Police, which urged officers to "immediately purge all non-sustained and seven-year-old sustained complaints from their files.....[T]his may be your last chance."[72] The letter reportedly included a stock form that officers could use to request the purge.

Civil Lawsuits
There is no linkage between the filing of a civil lawsuit alleging police brutality or other misconduct and the initiation of an investigation by OMI or PID, according to OMI and PID staff. According to the City Attorney's office, the superintendent of police and the PID are notified when the City Attorney's office receives notification of a lawsuit; notification of PID began in 1995.[73] The City Attorney's office claims that "in the vast majority of cases" PID has received a complaint long before a lawsuit has been filed (yet, this is not always the case). The City Attorney's office ignored Human Rights Watch's question as to whether it notifies OMI when a lawsuit alleging police misconduct is filed or resolved.

---

[69] Ibid.

[70] Ibid.

[71] Louisiana R.S.40:2533, allowed officers to demand destruction of records relating to complaints found to be not sustained, unfounded or exonerated.

[72] Christopher Cooper, "N.O. cops rush to purge files," *Times Picayune*, April 29, 1995.

[73] Letter from Chief Deputy City Attorney Franz Ziblich to Human Rights Watch, June 2, 1997.

Civil lawsuits usually have little impact on the subject officer, since the city pays any settlement with the plaintiff. There is also little impact on the department's practices, even when there are significant payouts.[74]

After a dozen telephone calls, repeated written requests, and finally threats to sue under the state's public records act, in June 1997 the City Attorney's office provided Human Rights Watch with information about total amounts paid by the city in police misconduct cases. According to that material, the city paid $619,146 in claims involving excessive force or wrongful death in calendar year 1994, $171,267 for excessive force claims in 1995, and $232,450 in excessive force claims in 1996.[75] Two significant civil lawsuits alleging police brutality on behalf of Kim Groves's survivors (her murder was ordered by then-Officer Len Davis), and the Vu family (a sister and brother were killed by then-Officer Antoinette Frank) were pending.

Criminal Prosecution

Despite the New Orleans police force's reputation as abusive, local prosecution of officers accused of human rights violations is rare. Morris Reed, a 1996 candidate for the district attorney post, stated "If [incumbent District Attorney Harry] Connick was prosecuting rogue cops effectively, a police officer like Len Davis, who had 20 complaints in his dossier, would not have been around to issue a [murder] contract."[76] Possibly criminal acts by officers, when pursued, are presented to grand juries, which are traditionally lenient toward police defendants. Officers are almost always cleared, while the public has no access to the proceedings, nor can outsiders monitor or evaluate their degree of vigor. When indicted, officers usually waive their rights to a jury trial and instead go before a judge. When Connick has been questioned about the lack of prosecutions, he has

---

[74] According to the Office of Risk Management office, the city is self-insured. Telephone inquiry, May 6, 1997.

[75] According to a local attorney, civil suits filed in state court and settled or awarded in favor of the plaintiff have not been paid since April 1995. And several lawsuits involving substantial sums, including a $2 million award in a shooting case, resolved in 1995, were not included on the list and presumably were being appealed by the city.

[76] Susan Finch, "Murder case heats up Connick-Reed forum," *Times-Picayune*, October 5, 1996. For his part, Reed was criticized for his acquittal, as a judge in a non-jury trial in July 1996, of Officers Shepack and Munguia. Michael Perlstein, "Coalition takes aim at Reed," *Times-Picayune*, October 9, 1996. Federal prosecutors have since charged the officers (*See* below).

blamed the police department for the troubled force.[77] In one recent, positive change, the district attorney's office has agreed to provide legal opinions on possible cases against officers before arrests are made. Evaluating the activities and effectiveness of the district attorney's office is not easy; when Human Rights Watch requested from it a list, or total, of police officers prosecuted, they reported that they do not compile such statistics.[78]

Although a Justice Department study showed that New Orleans residents lodged more complaints with federal officials about police abuse than residents in any other U.S. city, federal criminal civil rights prosecutions do not reflect those concerns. In 1996, of the eighty cases decided by federal prosecutors for the federal district containing New Orleans (Eastern District of Louisiana), none was prosecuted (presented to a grand jury to seek an indictment). Between 1992 and 1995, 819 cases were considered, of which nine were prosecuted.[79]

The OMI representative interviewed by Human Rights Watch in late 1995 reported that he knew of no federal criminal civil rights case in a dozen years and, put more bluntly, the federal prosecutors "don't do a damn thing with these cases."[80] (The Len Davis prosecution took place after this interview.) One attorney who represented Adolph Archie's family in their civil case repeatedly urged U.S. Attorney General Richard Thornburgh, and then his successor Janet Reno, to investigate that case, but no federal grand jury was convened.

---

[77] For example, when asked in 1995 whether he was aware of the extent of the problems with the police department, Connick – who had been the district attorney for twenty-one years – told the *Sunday Times Magazine* (London), "Absolutely! I complained about it all the time. There were individuals in the department involved in criminal activity....it made it difficult for us to get convictions [using officer testimony against accused criminals]...." Miller, "The big sleazy," *Sunday Times Magazine* (London).

[78] Telephone inquiry, district attorney's office, August 1997. From another source, Human Rights Watch did obtain such a list, apparently compiled by the district attorney's office for years prior to 1996.

[79] According to data obtained by the Transactional Records Access Clearinghouse (TRAC) from the Executive Office of U.S. Attorneys, Justice Department. Cases prosecuted or declined represent only a portion of the total number of complaints alleging federal criminal civil rights violations because several steps prior to this decision narrow down the number of complaints actually received to those considered worthy of consideration.

[80] Interview with Peter Munster, October 26, 1995. As noted above, in November 1996, Len Davis was convicted on federal criminal civil rights charges.

After a period during 1992 and 1993 when there was no U.S. Attorney in the Eastern District of Louisiana, in 1994 Eddie Jordan, Jr. became the first African-American U.S. Attorney in Louisiana's history. He pledged to stop police brutality: "We must see that police officers who are guilty of those abuses of power are brought to justice."[81] Through several telephone calls, Human Rights Watch attempted to obtain information directly from the U.S. Attorney's office regarding its activities, to no avail.

In at least one publicized recent incident, however, there was reason to believe the U.S. Attorney's office may be taking a more proactive approach in dealing with allegations of police brutality. According to press reports, two New Orleans police officers were indicted on federal civil rights charges on January 22, 1998 for allegedly beating two handcuffed men in custody.[82] (The same two officers, Richard Munguia and James Shepack, had previously been acquitted on state battery charges relating to the same July 1995 incident; Shepack was also indicted on federal civil rights charges relating to a June 1994 alleged beating incident.) One of the officers allegedly pistol-whipped the men while the other allegedly kicked at least one of them; both men were hospitalized, one with a broken jaw. According to press reports, Superintendent Pennington brought the case to the attention of federal prosecutors. U.S. Attorney Jordan told reporters, "Neither my staff nor I will tolerate police brutality in any of its forms, and we will remain relentless in bringing those police officers to justice."[83]

Under new civil powers, the Justice Department can file injunctions against police departments, or specific units, with a "pattern or practice" of abuses or for failing to deal with abuses or misconduct. In the first exercise of this authority in dealing with a police department, the Justice Department initiated a wide-ranging civil investigation into misconduct in the New Orleans police department in 1996 to find out whether the department had adopted adequate procedures to deal with officers who commit abuses. In August 1996, the Justice Department requested all ordinances, policies and procedures dealing with complaints of police misconduct,

[81] "La.'s first black U.S. attorney has eye on the street," *Times-Picayune*, August 16, 1994.

[82] Michael Perlstein, "Two cops face federal charges in beating case," *Times-Picayune*, January 23, 1998.

[83] Ibid.

including documents from the PID and OMI, as part of its investigation.[84] City and department officials complained that the inquiry was unnecessary in light of reforms since Superintendent Pennington's arrival in October 1994. The review is still in progress at this writing. If the New Orleans police department fails to satisfy federal investigators, the Justice Department could force changes through court orders.[85]

---

[84] James Varney and Mark Schleifstein, "Justice asks for reams of NOPD records," *Times-Picayune*, August 24, 1996.

[85] Christopher Cooper, "NOPD probe set in motion," *Times-Picayune*, July 4, 1996.

NEW YORK

We'd just beat people in general....to show who was in charge.
— Former NYPD officer Bernard Cawley (nicknamed "The Mechanic"
for tuning people up, or beating them, frequently) at Mollen Commission
hearings.

New York is enjoying a dramatic drop in violent crime, with some attributing
it to the police department's emphasis on more minor, "quality of life," crimes, such
as graffiti, squeegee windshield washing, and subway turnstile-jumping, pursued as
a way to demonstrate control of the streets and to apprehend individuals who may
have outstanding arrest warrants against them.[1] Civil rights advocates in the city
note, however, that there has been a cost to the new strategy, revealed by steady
citizen complaints against more aggressive NYPD officers during the past several
years and continuing impunity for many officers who commit human rights
violations despite the recent reorganization of both the civilian review board and the
police department's internal affairs bureau. Police abuse experts have wondered
why, if the police leadership is eager to stop crime by aggressively pursuing minor
criminals and crimes, it is failing to demonstrate the same aggressiveness in dealing
with officers before they commit more serious offenses.   In August 1997,
after the alleged torture of Haitian immigrant Abner Louima by police officers made
national headlines and outraged city residents, the anti-crime record of the mayor
and police department was tarnished. In uncharacteristic fashion, Mayor Rudolph
Giuliani and Police Commissioner Howard Safir condemned the officers implicated
in the incident as well as those who reportedly did nothing to stop it or report it.[2]
These were welcome condemnations, but conflicted with the mayor's persistent and
seemingly automatic defense of officers accused of abusive treatment – even when
he lacked a factual basis to do so – in his first term. Following the Louima incident,
Commissioner Safir repeatedly stated that the alleged attack was not police brutality

---

[1] The "quality of life" tactics are combined with the use of a computerized monitoring
system, known as "Compstat" to focus on problem crime areas and evaluate the department's
performance.

[2] Mayor Giuliani also announced the creation of a task force to deal with community
relations between police and residents.

but instead was a crime, thus failing to recognize that brutality that is not of the notoriety of torture is a crime as well.[3]

There is often a racial or ethnic component to police abuse cases in New York City, with many incidents also fueled by language barriers and miscommunication in the culturally diverse city. In the city's Civilian Complaint Review Board's (CCRB) semiannual report for the first half of 1997, African-Americans and Latinos filed 78 percent of complaints against the police.[4] The police force is 68 percent white.[5] According to 1990 census figures, African-Americans made up 28.7 percent of the city's population and Hispanics made up 24 percent.[6]

The CCRB is, on paper, one of the strongest civilian review mechanisms in the country. In practice, however, the review board had only a 4 percent average substantiation rate between July 1993 and December 1996.[7] Even when it does sustain complaints against officers, it has no power to ensure that appropriate disciplinary actions are taken, because that power is left entirely with the police department, which may or may not choose to accept and act upon the board's findings. During the independent CCRB's first three-and-a-half years, only 1 percent of all cases disposed of led to the disciplining of a police officer, and out of 18,336 complaints, there has been just one dismissal of an officer stemming from a CCRB-substantiated case.[8] Preliminary data regarding the first six months of

---

[3] For example, during a television interview, Commissioner Safir stated, "...it is a crime committed by criminals. I mean, it's criminals who happen to be wearing police uniforms. But this is, for my view, this is not police brutality. I mean this goes far beyond the place of police brutality...." *ABC Good Morning America*, August 18, 1997.

[4] CCRB semiannual report, January - June 1997, pp. 61-62.

[5] Statement of Police Commissioner Howard Safir before the New York Advisory Committee to the U.S. Commission on Civil Rights, October 29, 1997.

[6] In December 1997, a study describing the 1996 racial and ethnic composition of New York City found that Hispanics made up 26.6 percent of the city's population, and that blacks made up 26.2 percent.

[7] New York Civil Liberties Union (NYCLU) report: a fourth anniversary overview of the Civilian Complaint Review Board, July 5, 1993 - July 5, 1997.

[8] Ibid.

1997 indicated an increase in fully investigated complaints and a higher substantiation rate.[9]

Traditionally, the department has also been unwilling to acknowledge shortcomings and instead dismisses any criticisms as unfounded or as merely "anecdotal." For example, when Amnesty International published a detailed report about serious abuses and structural flaws in dealing with misconduct and brutality in the NYPD in June 1996, the official response was that it was "not a real analysis....short on facts," because it relied on the accounts of victims, their attorneys and press accounts.[10] The accounts of victims, however, cannot be so easily disregarded; and if official data were lacking, this was because the department as a general rule refuses to release information about police misconduct and disciplinary response.

Even when the mayor himself asked a task force to review police-community issues following the alleged beating and torture of Abner Louima, he immediately criticized the task force's majority report: "Some of the things [recommended] we've already done. Some of the things I've opposed in the past, I'll continue to oppose them. And some of the things are unrealistic and make very little sense."[11] Among the recommendations in the majority report were the elimination of the forty-eight hour delay allowed for officers under investigation; the creation of an auditor position to review the performance of the CCRB and to improve cooperation by the police department with the CCRB; enhanced screening of police recruits; bi- or multi-lingual receptionists in precincts that have a large number of residents who do not speak English; and requiring officers to live in the city in an effort to improve diversity, and cultural awareness, on the force. The mayor complained that the task force had ignored the drop in crime in the city. Later, the mayor softened his response somewhat, but his reaction appeared to be extremely counterproductive and may have lost him support from the task force – made up of

---

[9] NYCLU report, September 1997, p. 7.

[10] Clifford Krauss, "Rights group finds abuse of suspects by city police," *New York Times,* June 26, 1996.

[11] Dan Barry, "Giuliani dismisses police proposals by his task force," *New York Times,* March 27, 1998. There was also a minority report, authored by three, of the thirty-one, members of the task force who reportedly believed the task force's majority report was inadequate. Among other recommendations, the minority report called for the creation of an independent special prosecutor's office.

activists, clergy members, community leaders and attorneys – who had made an effort to provide the mayor with useful recommendations.[12]

Department and city leaders also respond to any criticism by stating that, in a force the size of New York's, 38,000 strong, you will always have some officers who do not follow the rules. This utterly misses the question most human rights activists pose: How does the department deal with officers who commit human rights violations, and those likely to commit abuses? If the studies by civil rights groups and the Mollen Commission are any indication, officers who commit abuses are not being dealt with adequately.

Background

As with most major U.S. cities, New York's police department has gone through cycles of scandal involving corruption and the use of excessive force. A widely respected reformer, Police Commissioner Patrick Murphy, attempted during the early 1970s to hold supervisors responsible for the abuses of officers under their control and to implement an early warning system to help identify officers who have committed human rights violations. His efforts followed the 1972 Knapp Commission report exposing major corruption. Yet many of the reforms he instituted – and the accountability goals he articulated – faded after his departure in 1973.

The department soon returned to its notoriously self-protective ways, with officers involved in misconduct often intimidating bystanders and witnesses. Crowd control situations, such as the Tompkins Square Park encounter between protesters and police in August 1988, were often handled with excessive force. In that incident, after protesters allegedly threw items at mounted police officers attempting to clear the park, police reacted by beating anyone nearby with their nightsticks, including uninvolved restaurant patrons and business owners. The encounter was captured on videotape, forcing officials to acknowledge that the police behavior was "appalling."[13] But, even though more than 120 civilian complaints were filed about the incident, the police department's CCRB faced great difficulty in pursuing charges against the involved officers because it was met with a wall of silence. In the end, administrative charges were presented in seventeen cases, with officers disciplined in thirteen of them.

---

[12] Ibid., Alan Finder, "At the heart of report on police, some modest proposals," *New York Times*, March 28, 1998; John Marzulli, "Mayor, Safir ready to fulfill some cop task force wishes," *New York Daily News*, April 16, 1998; Nat Hentoff, "Police brutality and the mayor," *Village Voice*, May 5, 1998.

[13] Paul Chevigny, *Edge of the Knife* (New York: The New Press, 1995), p. 76.

Many of the Knapp Commission's issues of concern resurfaced again in the early 1990s, as a new corruption scandal emerged. Officers primarily from the 30th, 9th, 46th, 75th and 73rd precincts were caught selling drugs and beating suspects.[14] To look into the allegations, Mayor David Dinkins appointed a commission, headed by Judge Milton Mollen. During hearings in 1993-94, officers came forward to acknowledge that they had become something of a vigilante squad with financial motives. Officer Bernie Cawley was asked if the people he acknowledged beating were suspects and he replied, "No. We'd just beat people in general."[15] Cawley reportedly said he had used his sap gloves (lead-loaded gloves), flashlight, and nightstick as many as 400 times just "to show who was in charge."[16] If victims expressed interest in complaining, he would tell them that it would take three hours to type their complaint. Another officer testified that some officers kept guns seized during raids and used them as "throwaway" guns to plant on a suspect in the event of a questionable arrest or police shooting to make it appear the suspect was armed.[17] Concluded Cawley, "They [residents] hate the police. You'd hate the police too if you lived there."[18]

The Mollen Commission report, published in July 1994, described an internal accountability system that was flawed in most respects. It also described the nexus between corruption and brutality, and urged a plan to combat both problems.

> When connected to acts of corruption, brutality is at times a means to accomplish corrupt ends and at other times it is just a gratuitous

---

[14] The corruption scandal reportedly resulted in nearly one hundred convictions against seventy defendants being thrown out due to police perjury. With approximately fifteen lawsuits still pending, the city has already paid $2 million in civil settlements to perjury victims. David Kocieniewski, "Man framed by police officers wins payments," *New York Times*, February 12, 1998.

[15] Commission to Investigate Allegations of Police Corruption and the Anti-Corruption Procedures of the Police Department, July 7, 1994, hereinafter "Mollen Commission report," p. 48. The Mollen Commission report cited hundreds of acts of brutality claimed by Cawley, yet only one complaint from a citizen, and none from fellow officers, was ever filed. Ibid.

[16] Malcolm Gladwell, "Ex-policeman says he attacked people," *Washington Post*, September 30, 1993.

[17] Mollen Commission report, p. 28.

[18] Ibid; Tom Hays, "Commission told rogue officers kept guns to plant on suspects," *Associated Press*, September 29, 1993, [Wire Service].

appendage to a corrupt act....[C]ops have used or threatened to use brutality to intimidate their victims and protect themselves against the risk of complaints.[19] We found that officers who are corrupt are more likely to be brutal....[20]

Officers also told us that it was not uncommon to see unnecessary force used to administer an officer's own brand of street justice: a nightstick to the ribs, a fist to the head, to demonstrate who was in charge of the crime-ridden streets they patrolled and to impose sanctions on those who "deserved it" as officers, not juries, determined. As was true of other forms of wrongdoing, some cops believe they are doing what is morally correct – though "technically unlawful" – when they beat someone who they believe is guilty and who they believe the criminal justice system will never punish.[21]

What emerged was a picture of how everyday brutality corrupted relations among police officers and city residents. The Mollen Commission heard from officers who admitted pouring ammonia on the face of a detainee in a holding cell and from another who threw garbage and boiling water on someone hiding in a dumbwaiter shaft. Another officer allegedly doctored an "escape rope" used by drug dealers so they would plunge to the ground if they used it, and the same group also raided a brothel while in uniform, ordered the customers to leave, and terrorized and raped the women there.[22] Mollen found: "...[B]rutality, regardless of the motive, sometimes serves as a rite of passage to other forms of corruption and misconduct. Some officers told us that brutality was how they first crossed the line toward abandoning their integrity."[23] Officer Michael Dowd testified, "[Brutality] is a form of acceptance. It's not just simply giving a beating. It's [sic] the other officers begin to accept you more."[24] Officers Cawley and Dowd described hundreds of acts

---

[19] Mollen Commission report, p. 45.

[20] Ibid., p. 46.

[21] Ibid., p. 47.

[22] Ibid.

[23] Ibid.

[24] Ibid.

of brutality they had engaged in; yet apparently no fellow officer had filed a complaint about either one of them.[25]

"As important as the possible extent of brutality," noted the commission's report, "is the extent of brutality tolerance we found throughout the Department....[T]his tolerance, or willful blindness, extends to supervisors as well. This is because many supervisors share the perception that nothing is really wrong with a bit of unnecessary force and because they believe that this is the only way to fight crime today."[26] Internal review was equally corrupted. The Internal Affairs Division was not helpful in identifying problems, and removed especially sensitive cases and placed them in a "tickler file," making each problem appear an aberration. Despite many officers' criminal behavior, their personnel files repeatedly showed that they had "met standards," and they thus avoided scrutiny altogether. Officers who were caught lying were not disciplined and were taught by supervisors how to present false testimony in court.

In reaction to the Mollen Commission report, then-Police Commissioner William Bratton stated that if officers behaved properly, he would back them absolutely, but if they used unnecessary force, "all bets are off."[27] Yet, when Walter Mack, a civilian deputy commissioner in charge of internal affairs, pushed for the creation of a special anti-brutality unit that would be available twenty-four hours a day to investigate allegations promptly, and also took a tough stance on police perjury, he was forced out of the department in 1995.[28]

As of early 1998, Mollen Commission recommendations relating to recruiting, scrutiny during probation, integrity training, and improved supervision have

---

[25] Dowd reportedly had been the subject of more than twenty citizen complaints, some alleging excessive force, in the four or five years prior to his criminal charges, but the complaints were found "not sustained" by the CCRB. Affidavit of James J. Fyfe, Ph.D., April 2, 1997, in *United States of America v. City of Pittsburgh, Pittsburgh Bureau of Police, and Department of Public Safety*, USDC Western District of Pennsylvania, Civil No. 97-0354, April 16, 1997.

[26] Mollen Commission report, p. 49.

[27] Editorial, *New York Times*, May 5, 1994.

[28] Clifford Krauss, "Bratton Assailed on Ouster of Top Official," *New York Times*, January 29, 1995; Leonard Levitt, "Cop monitor out," *New York Newsday*, January 28, 1995. At the time, Commissioner Bratton claimed Mack was being dismissed because he was not a good administrator.

generally been implemented.[29]   The police unions continue to oppose stricter disciplinary measures and the commission's call for changes in the police union's response to allegations of corruption and brutality, such as emphasizing integrity, reportedly have not been heeded.

Race/Ethnicity

There is often a racial or ethnic component to police abuse cases in New York City, with many incidents also fueled by language barriers and miscommunication in the diverse city.[30]   In the CCRB's January - June 1997 report, African-Americans and Latinos filed more than 78 percent of complaints against the police, while 67 percent of the subject officers were white.[31]   A NY1 News local television channel poll released in February 1997 found that 81 percent of blacks and 73 percent of Hispanics believe police brutality is a serious problem in the city.[32]

Racial tensions were exacerbated after the August 1994 shooting of an undercover officer Desmond Robinson, an African-American, by white off-duty officer Peter Del Debbio during confusion after a shot was fired on a subway train.[33]

---

[29]   According to police abuse expert Prof. James J. Fyfe, who has studied the department's reform efforts. Several botched police raids during 1998 raised serious questions about improved training and about the department's stated efforts to improve courtesy, professionalism, and respect. The officers apparently raided the wrong apartments and humiliated their occupants by using racial epithets and dressing a man in woman's clothing before taking him to a station house and, in another case, handcuffing a woman who was eight months pregnant and only partially dressed; she was so frightened by the experience that she reportedly urinated but the officers did not allow her to put on dry clothes for two hours. Bob Herbert, columns, "Day of humiliation," March 8, 1998; "A cop's view," *New York Times,* March 15, 1998.

[30]   For example, the Committee Against Anti-Asian Violence (CAAAV) reports that are few officers who speak Chinese or other Asian languages, yet there are a million New York City residents of Asian descent.

[31]   CCRB Semiannual Status Report, January - June 1997, p. 60.

[32]   Error margin of plus or minus 3 percent. Grant McCool, "New York officer fired on brutality charge," *Reuters,* February 21, 1997, [Wire Service].

[33]   In another similar case in November 1992, African-American Derwin Pannel, an undercover transit police officer, was shot and wounded by three white police officers as he was arresting a turnstile-jumper in a Brooklyn subway station; the other officers allegedly mistook him for an armed mugger. Amnesty International, "Police brutality and excessive

Del Debbio allegedly thought Robinson was involved in a crime because he had a gun; Del Debbio reportedly shut his eyes and shot, hitting Robinson five times, including two or three shots that allegedly were fired as the wounded officer was falling or on the ground. Del Debbio was convicted on second-degree assault charges.[34] Minority-group activists claimed that the shooting demonstrated racial bias because the white officer assumed the black officer was a criminal.

On June 13, 1996, another racially charged shooting, this one fatal, led to protests in East Flatbush, Brooklyn.[35] According to press reports, Aswan Watson, an African-American, was shot eighteen times by plainclothes officers as he sat in a stolen car; he was unarmed. (Police later learned that Watson was wanted in connection with a murder.) The officers blocked Watson's car with theirs and approached his car with their guns drawn. Officers contended that he reached for something under his seat, and they believed he was reaching for a gun, and then opened fire; no gun was found. After the shooting, crowds of several hundred people protested through the night, and many protested during the following day.

In May 1997, a grand jury declined to indict the officers.[36] But it took the unusual step of making recommendations regarding training and supervision of plain clothes officers. Commissioner Safir responded by stating that most of the recommended measures were already in place; the department also released statistics showing a decrease in police shootings.[37]

Civilian Complaint Review Board
When former New York Mayor David Dinkins supported an independent civilian complaint review board in September 1992, police protested violently and

---

force in the New York City Police Department" (hereinafter Amnesty International, "Police brutality,") pp. 50-51.

[34] Clifford Krauss, "Subway chaos: Officer firing at officer, *New York Times*, August 24, 1994; Clifford Krauss, "Cop shoots cop, prompting questions of racism," *New York Times*, August 28, 1994; David Kocieniewski, "Officer shot in subway is arrested," *New York Times,* May 5, 1996.

[35] Charisse Jones, "Protesters dispute police version of a shooting," *New York Times*, June 15, 1996.

[36] "Grand jury exonerates 2 killer cops," *Associated Press*, February 13, 1998, [Wire Service].

[37] Ibid.

engaged in actions, according to a police department report, that were "unruly, mean-spirited and perhaps criminal."[38] An officers' protest, sponsored by the police union, involved thousands of officers demonstrating at City Hall, blocking traffic to the Brooklyn Bridge, and shouting racial epithets; current Mayor Rudolph Giuliani participated in the protest.[39]

Some officers involved in the protest's offensive acts were disciplined, and the police commissioner stated that the nature of the demonstration "raised serious questions about the department's willingness and ability to police itself."[40] If further evidence of violent propensities were needed, an incident right after the City Hall protest provided it. As police were leaving the protest, several off-duty officers, all in civilian clothes, assaulted a man on the subway who had stepped on one of the officer's feet. The man claimed that when he attempted to apologize, the offended officer tried to punch him, and that in self-defense he then pulled out a razor and cut the officer's face. Six officers then reportedly beat and kicked him, and he suffered a broken jaw; several witnesses went directly to the police station to complain. In this case, the department did provide some accountability. Two of the officers were charged with felony assault, leading to one conviction on a misdemeanor charge that led to the officer's dismissal.

In July 1993, the CCRB was reorganized and made independent from the police department. Members of the thirteen-person board, including its chair, are appointed and approved by the mayor: five members are designated by the mayor; five representing the five boroughs are designated by the City Council; and three are designated by the police commissioner.[41] The CCRB investigative staff is made up entirely of civilians. The board has the authority to compel witness testimony. As of fiscal year 1997, it had a staff of approximately 128 (including approximately eighty investigators), with a budget of approximately $5.2 million to monitor all types of misconduct allegedly involving members of the 38,000-strong NYPD.[42]

---

[38] George James, "Police dept. report assails officers in New York rally," *New York Times,* September 29, 1992.

[39] Ibid. and Chevigny, *Edge of the Knife,* pp. 64-65.

[40] Ibid., p. 65.

[41] The three named by the police commissioner are the only ones allowed to have law enforcement backgrounds. CCRB Status Report, January-June 1996, p. 6.

[42] NYCLU, July 1996 report; and Jane H. Lii, "How to Complain," *New York Times,* May 18, 1997.

In September 1997, Mayor Giuliani, while continuing to disagree with the mission of the CCRB, agreed to provide an overdue budget increase of $1.5 million and to increase its staff.[43]

The CCRB publishes reports with statistical data on the number, type and disposition of complaints. It is prohibited from making its findings public regarding individual cases under confidentiality laws.[44] CCRB complaint forms are only in English, although informational brochures are available in several languages (Creole, Spanish, Chinese, and Korean). CCRB staff report that they engage in extensive community outreach to inform residents of their rights and about the CCRB's operations.[45]

When the CCRB receives a complaint, the complainant is given the name and telephone number of the investigator handling the case, and is told that he or she can call at any time. In a recent change, the CCRB now assigns an investigator to each case for its duration, so the investigation is not passed from one to another without any knowledge of the background.[46] The CCRB claims this new practice has expedited investigations. The CCRB also reports that it sends a letter after ninety days have passed, advising complainants of the status of the investigation, or whenever there is a change in the status of the complaint. If a criminal investigation has begun, the CCRB defers to the relevant district or U.S. attorney.

Once CCRB investigators complete a full investigation, the findings are reviewed by a case review panel, made up of three board members or the full board. Review panels or the full board also review truncated investigations (cases in which a full investigation is truncated due to a variety of reasons), and alternative dispute resolution cases. The latter are cases that are not investigated or kept on the subject officer's record but where the subject officer is required to discuss the complaint with a CCRB staff member who instructs the officer about proper procedures.

---

[43] Michael Cooper, "Giuliani to aid police-monitoring agency he had fought," *New York Times,* September 17, 1997.

[44] CCRB Semiannual status report, January - June 1996, p. 15.

[45] Telephone interview with Sherman Jackson of the CCRB, January 29, 1997. Jackson said that in a six-month period beginning in July 1996, CCRB made presentations to about forty groups, distributed signs, and brochures, and also used Public Service Announcements.

[46] Ibid.

Fully investigated complaints made up approximately 25 percent of the cases disposed of by the CCRB between July 1993 and December 1996.[47] During the same period, truncated cases (when the CCRB found complainants "uncooperative" or "unavailable") or administratively closed cases (when complainants fail to arrange or appear for an interview) made up approximately 61 percent of the cases; and alternative dispute resolution (such as conciliation) made up approximately 9 percent.[48]

In 1996, there were 5,596 total complaints received by the CCRB, and 5,716 complaints were disposed of during the year (including some from 1996 and previous years). The board substantiated 259 complaints during the year, for an approximately 4.6 percent substantiation rate.[49]

The CCRB's regular reports contain information about officers who have been the subject of repeated complaints. For example, there were 126 police officers with four or more complaints lodged against them from July 1, 1995 to June 30, 1997.[50] The report notes that about 40 percent of those officers are assigned to Brooklyn commands, with officers assigned to the 75th Precinct making up 8 percent of all officers receiving four or more complaints during this time period.[51]

The system of oversight breaks down most notably at the discipline stage. The board uses a "preponderance of the evidence" standard of proof. The board forwards its recommendation to the police commissioner, who is not bound by the CCRB's findings. If the CCRB recommends disciplinary sanctions against an officer, the police commissioner must report back to the CCRB on the action taken.[52] The CCRB receives a monthly report from the police department, advising the board about police action on CCRB referrals. Outside police-abuse experts

---

[47] NYCLU report, September 1997, p. 6.

[48] Ibid., Table II.

[49] Ibid., Table II.

[50] CCRB Semiannual status report, January - June 1997, p. 41.

[51] Ibid.

[52] Without providing an explanation, the CCRB stopped making recommendations in most substantiated cases during 1994-1995, but has since resumed making them. The CCRB's January-December 1996 report, states, "[S]ince October 1996, the Board has made recommendations in virtually all cases that have been substantiated." CCRB Semiannual status report, January - December 1996, p. 14.

have expressed concern that the internal police department procedures have all but guaranteed that even cases sustained by the CCRB do not lead to adequate discipline, or any at all. (*See* IAB section, below.)

Nor is there oversight of CCRB's own competence. If a complainant is dissatisfied with the outcome of a CCRB investigation, he or she can "appeal" only by providing new information or witnesses. There is no procedure by which a complainant can question the thoroughness of the CCRB's investigation. It is up to the board to determine whether its own investigation was complete.

One significant criticism of the CCRB's operations relates to the way it notifies a complainant about the final status of his or her complaint. In many cases, one complainant may file a complaint detailing more than one allegation against an officer. For example, a complainant may allege an officer used excessive force and a racial epithet. When the CCRB responds, it may merely state that the complaint has been substantiated "in part" without noting which part was sustained. Further, while the police department must notify the complainant of the final outcome of the complaint, it provides no information about whether or how the officer was disciplined when the board has substantiated the complaint.[53]

The CCRB claims that it investigates each complaint it receives, but there are several situations in which complaints are resolved or shelved without full investigation. Complaints are reviewed by an investigator when the complaint is initially filed, with some less serious complaints resolved at that time.[54] Some complaints are resolved by conciliation, a process criticized by civil liberties advocate as an unacceptable way to handle the board's backlog. In this process, the accused officer simply meets briefly with a CCRB senior staff member who instructs the police officer as to the nature of the complaint and the proper conduct expected under police department guidelines.[55] Cases are not fully investigated if the complainant fails to appear for a face-to-face interview with the investigator; those cases are considered administratively closed. Cases are also closed prior to a full investigation if the complainant withdraws his or her complaint, or if a complainant fails to appear or arrange for an interview within ten days of written notice from the CCRB.

---

[53] Dan Barry, "Independent agency isn't policing the police, critics say," *New York Times,* July 13, 1997.

[54] CCRB is reportedly developing a mediation program using outside mediators to discuss complaints with complainants and officers to resolve less serious cases.

[55] CCRB Semiannual status report, January - June 1997 pp. 9-10.

The CCRB reports that CCRB and the police department's Internal Affairs Bureau (IAB) investigations are often concurrent. And, although not frequently, the CCRB states that it does refer cases to local or federal prosecutors.[56] In the CCRB's periodic reports, however, there is no mention of such referrals.

CCRB is entirely complaint-driven. It will not pursue a case unless a complaint is filed with the board. It does not receive notification from the City Attorney's office or from court when a civil lawsuit is filed against a police officer or when one is settled or judged in favor of the plaintiff, and no investigation is initiated as a result. There is no provision for the CCRB to respond to particularly serious complaints made in such lawsuits on its own initiative where the complainant's inaction or withdrawal of the complaint with the CCRB has led to its closure.

Since the CCRB became independent from the police department in 1993, the total allegations (and total excessive force allegations) received are as follows:[57]

1993: 5,487 (excessive force: 2,173)
1994: 7,648 (excessive force: 3,079)
1995: 8,776 (excessive force: 3,528)
1996: 8,869 (excessive force: 3,139)
1997: 7,183 (excessive force: 2,626)[58]

Between the initiation of more aggressive policing policies in 1993 and 1996, complaints against the police rose by 56 percent.[59] In response, Police Commissioner Howard Safir initiated a program promoted as teaching courtesy, professionalism and respect ("C.P.R."). During the first five months of 1997, complaints dropped by 21 percent, leading the commissioner to credit the C.P.R.

---

[56] Telephone interview with Sherman Jackson of the CCRB, January 29, 1997.

[57] Each complaint may contain several allegations. 1993-1995 figures compiled in NYCLU July 1996 report, Table V, from CCRB reports.

[58] According to CCRB's community outreach coordinator, telephone inquiry, March 16, 1998.

[59] Jane H. Lii, "When the saviors are seen as sinners," *New York Times*, May 18, 1997. City officials claim that effective, aggressive policing was the cause of the increase in complaints. But the last time statistics were provided in this regard by the independent Civilian Complaint Review Board (CCRB), 88 percent of complaints came from individuals who were neither arrested nor ticketed (cited for some minor violation). It would appear that many of the people filing complaints are not engaged in criminal conduct, but that "aggressive" policing may involve the harassing and questioning of individuals who later file complaints. CCRB statistics since 1995, however, exclude these data and according to local advocates, the CCRB has never explained why it stopped providing this information.

program – which attempts to hold police commanders responsible for citizen complaints – for the drop. In response to the reported drop in complaints during first months of 1997, critics claimed that residents were not filing complaints because information about the oversight procedure's ineffectiveness had been made public by civil rights groups.[60]   Others explain the drop by questioning the transparency of the complaint process – pointing out that as soon as citizen complaints were to be included in reports on captains' performances (as part of the Compstat data-management program) beginning in the second half of 1996, the number of complaints recorded as received at police stations and forwarded to the CCRB dropped dramatically.[61]   In 1995, the NYPD received 1,955 civilian complaints during the year; in 1996, the number dropped to 1,349. During the same period, the CCRB directly received a total of 3,544 civilian complaints in 1995, with the number increasing in 1996 to 4,228.

Following the August 1997 Louima incident, there was a sharp increase in the number of citizen complaints filed with the CCRB. The number of complaints was initially undercounted by the CCRB due to a "clerical error," with the actual, higher number discovered a week after the November elections. The apparent confusion over the number of complaints stemmed from a February 1997 change in procedures that led to confusion between the CCRB and the police department.[62] The CCRB claims that its staff misunderstood the procedure and believed that the IAB's written reports about complaints were duplicates of calls recorded as received by the CCRB, thus undercounting the total. The IAB explains that it changed its procedures to allow senior officers to review all allegations and to decide which ones were serious enough to warrant an IAB investigation. Of course, even with the decrease in total reported complaints during 1997, as compared to

---

[60] Michael Cooper, "Complaints About Police Fell 21 Percent in Year's First Five Months," *New York Times*, June 20, 1997.

[61] Wayne Barrett, "Brutal Reality," *Village Voice*, September 16, 1997. During 1996, the number of complaints reported as received by the NYPD dropped during the second part of the year, with 945 complaints recorded in the first six months, and just 404 during the second six months.

[62] Michael Cooper, "Undercount found in civilian complaints about NYC police," *New York Times*, December 11, 1997; Cooper, "Error in counting complaints prompts steps by police review board," *New York Times*, December 12, 1997.

1996, complaints are still being filed at a higher rate than in the four years prior to the initiation of more aggressive policing tactics.[63]

The New York Civil Liberties Union was instrumental in the push for, and creation of, an independent CCRB, but it has since made some of the most detailed and scathing criticisms of the CCRB's operations. In July 1996, the group reviewed the CCRB's first three years as an independent entity and found it had "largely failed in its mission." Among the reasons cited were inadequate funding, insufficient staff, and mismanagement.[64]

Since the CCRB became independent from the police force in 1993 until December 1996, it received 18,336 complaints against police officers, yet only one officer was dismissed as a result of a CCRB investigation.[65] According to press reports, of 972 cases of alleged brutality and other misconduct since 1993 confirmed by the Civilian Complaint Review Board, the department disciplined just 215 of the officers (only one resulting in the officer's dismissal).[66]

City and police officials have expressed a lack of confidence in the CCRB. NYPD Commissioner Howard Safir has explained the department's inaction in CCRB-substantiated cases by stating that the CCRB investigations are of a low

---

[63] NYCLU July 1996 report, Table V.

[64] If the difficulty in interviewing CCRB members and getting information from the agency is any indication, it may be understaffed; it was, for whatever reason, uncooperative with Human Rights Watch. CCRB staff would not meet with Human Rights Watch, and CCRB staff denied that the 1996 annual report was available long after its release. Human Rights Watch submitted questions to the board in writing, but it took more than four months and many phone calls to obtain even oral answers to some of the questions, and no response by mail, as promised, has been forthcoming as of this writing.

[65] NYCLU report: a fourth anniversary overview of the Civilian Complaint Review Board, July 5, 1993 - July 5, 1997; Dan Barry, "Independent agency isn't policing the police, critics say," *New York Times*, July 13, 1997. In that case, Officer Stephen Morrissey reportedly used unnecessary force in a February 1994 encounter with a garage manager. Dan Barry, Deborah Sontag, "New York dismisses police, but rarely for brutality," *New York Times,* October 6, 1997.

[66] David Kocieniewski, "The trial room; system of disciplining police assailed from inside and out," *New York Times*, December 19, 1997.

quality.[67] Mayor Giuliani apparently shares that view, stating in July 1997, "[A]n independent body has a very hard time effectively investigating an organization of 38,000 people that is expert at investigating itself....A much better way to improve the Police Department is to get it to investigate itself."[68]

Following the Louima case, the City Council held hearings on the CCRB in August 1997. City Council members reportedly criticized the CCRB as inefficient and ineffective.[69] The CCRB's executive director acknowledged some of the shortcomings, yet neither he nor the board's chairman were able to answer basic questions posed by the council. The executive director stated that the CCRB's record-keeping system was not as "sophisticated as you or I would hope."[70] The councilmembers urged the CCRB leaders, in the face of police department resistance to accepting and acting on the board's findings, to at least provide information about patterns and trends in violations around the city. Yet, according to press reports, neither CCRB leader put forward ideas about how to make the police department take the CCRB's findings more seriously or how to complete more thorough investigations; they did ask for additional funding, however.

Many police-abuse experts in New York City believe the mayor has too much control over the CCRB's composition and, as a consequence, may unduly influence its performance. Citing this lack of independence, they note that the current city administration often appoints ex-prosecutors and others who may be biased in favor of police officers and skeptical of complainants' allegations. Others note that many investigators are ex-police who are not always trusted by victims or witnesses. According to these observers, CCRB contact with complainants, in practice, is sporadic at best.

The board's internal politics also affect its performance. The CCRB has long been disrupted by political disputes among board members and between board

---

[67] The commissioner made this observation on a Black Entertainment Television talk show, August 18, 1997. In a written statement submitted to the New York Advisory Committee to the U.S. Commission on Civil Rights, he wrote that CCRB investigations referred to the department have been "very old, typically 15 months old or older, and they have contained serious deficiencies." Statement dated October 29, 1997.

[68] Randy Kennedy, "Giuliani favors internal police inquiries over review board's," *New York Times*, July 14, 1997.

[69] Randy Kennedy, "Civilian police review unit is criticized as ineffectual," *New York Times*, August 29, 1997.

[70] Ibid.

members and investigators. Board members, executive directors and investigators have periodically resigned in protest when cooperation has not been forthcoming within the CCRB or from the city's administration. And there have been disputes over investigators' findings in high-profile cases. Hector Soto, executive director of the CCRB until February 1996, reportedly left his post due to disputes with the police department and CCRB's chair over high-profile cases. Zornow, in turn, reportedly left his position after receiving inadequate support from the Giuliani administration.[71] In mid-1996, a senior investigator and others reportedly left the CCRB after they found an officer responsible in a high-profile fatal shooting but the board did not substantiate the case.[72] According to some reports, the head of the investigative team was fired, and others quit in solidarity.[73]

Other problems include the eighteen-month statute of limitations from the time of the incident until commencing disciplinary proceedings. The Mollen Commission called for extending the statute of limitations to three years, and Mayor Giuliani has backed this revision.[74] In 1995 and 1996, a total of sixty-three cases were not pursued because the statute of limitations had expired.[75]

Some police abuse experts in the city have suggested that the NYPD's Advocates' Office, responsible for administratively prosecuting officers accused of serious abuses investigated and substantiated by the CCRB at departmental trials, should be abolished.[76] They note that the office has traditionally failed to uphold many of the CCRB-sustained cases and question whether its role is necessary or helpful. These observers believe that the CCRB's findings should be submitted directly to the police commissioner and that CCRB staff should prosecute the case, thereby eliminating the Advocates' Office budget and providing it to the CCRB.

---

[71] Clifford Krauss, "Head of Complaint Board Quietly Resigns," *New York Times,* June 13, 1996.

[72] *See* below, Carasquillo case.

[73] Juan Gonzalez, column, *New York Daily News*, August 27, 1996.

[74] Mollen Commission report, p. 143; Michael Cooper, "Giuliani to aid police-monitoring agency he had fought," *New York Times,* September 17, 1997.

[75] NYCLU report, September 1997, Table III, citing CCRB's 1995 and 1996 annual reports.

[76] See, for example, Joel Berger, attorney, speech to the Staten Island NAACP, October 1996. Berger is a former senior litigator with the New York City Law Department.

In any case, these same observers believe that disciplinary sanctions should be made public with descriptions of cases and explanations for sanctions, while maintaining only the required privacy protections for the individual officers.

In September 1997, the City Council voted to create a five-member independent review board with subpoena power and investigators intended to investigate systemic problems within the police force, including corruption and brutality.[77] The bill's sponsors hoped officers would use the new review board to report corruption in the police ranks. After the new board was approved, the mayor vetoed the bill, but the City Council overrode the veto; the mayor reportedly has threatened to go to court over the bill.[78]

Incidents

Case of Abner Louima: In the early morning hours of August 9, 1997, police officers arrested Abner Louima, a legal Haitian immigrant, outside a Brooklyn nightclub following altercations between police and clubgoers.[79] During the trip to the station house, officers allegedly stopped twice to beat Louima, who was handcuffed. At the 70th Precinct station house, two officers, Justin Volpe and Charles Schwarz, allegedly shouted racial slurs and Volpe allegedly shoved a wooden stick (believed to be the handle of a toilet plunger or broom) into Louima's rectum and mouth. Volpe reportedly borrowed gloves from another officer and walked through the station house with the wooden stick, which was covered with blood and excrement; the gloves were recovered, but the wooden stick was not found on the scene. Louima was placed in a holding cell, where other inmates complained that he was bleeding. An ambulance was eventually requested to take him to a hospital, but he was held for three hours in the cell bleeding following the

---

[77] Vivian S. Toy, "New police review board approved by city council," *New York Times*, October 1, 1997.

[78] Vivian S. Toy, "Veto of police review board overridden," *New York Times*, November 26, 1997.

[79] David Kocieniewski, "Man says officers torture him after arrest," *New York Times*, August 13, 1997; Dan Barry, "Precinct chief is transferred in torture case," *New York Times*, August 15, 1997; Garry Pierre-Pierre, "New York Haitians sensing betrayal in a land of refuge," *New York Times*, August 18, 1997; Michael Cooper, "2nd officer gives account of sex assault of Haitian," *New York Times*, August 18, 1997; Ian Fisher, "Residents wary of police at 70th precinct," *New York Times*, August 15, 1997; David Kocieniewski, "2 more officers disciplined in Louima case," *New York Times*, February 19, 1998.

alleged beating and torture.[80] Once at the hospital, doctors confirmed Louima's serious internal injuries were consistent with his allegations; internal organs were ruptured, and his front teeth had been broken. For the first three days of his two-month hospitalization, Louima was reportedly handcuffed to his bed.[81]

It appears that no officer at the station formally reported the alleged attack, and in the months following the incident, only two officers came forward to provide useful information.[82] One of the officers who provided information was transferred out of the 70th Precinct and reportedly provided with security in case of retaliation by fellow officers. According to reports, eleven NYPD members of various ranks were facing disciplinary sanctions for failing to provide information, or lying, to investigators.[83]

A nurse at the hospital where Louima was treated reportedly called the Internal Affairs Bureau to report the serious injuries later on the day he was hospitalized – the same day the incident took place – yet her complaint was not logged properly or submitted to the district attorney's office, as required.[84] The first officially logged complaint was thirty-six hours later, when Louima's family reported the alleged attack to the IAB. IAB reportedly did not go to the 70th Precinct station house until more than forty-eight hours after the alleged attack.[85]

---

[80] David Kocieniewski, "Precinct silence on Louima is still unanswered question," *New York Times*, February 27, 1998.

[81] According to Mayor Giuliani on ABC News Nightline, February 26, 1998.

[82] Dan Barry, "Officers' silence still thwarting torture inquiry," *New York Times*, September 5, 1997. One officer reportedly did anonymously call a newspaper columnist about the incident. ABC News Nightline, February 26, 1998. And the U.S. attorney and Bronx district attorney claimed that "numerous"officers had cooperated with the federal investigation without describing whether more officers from the station house in question came forward. Joseph Fried, "U.S. takes over the prosecution of New York officers in beating," *New York Times*, February 27, 1998.

[83] David Kocieniewski, "2 more officers disciplined in Louima case," *New York Times*, February 19, 1998.

[84] John Kifner, "Early tip was mishandled in torture case, police say," *New York Times*, August 23, 1997.

[85] "What happened on the morning of the beating and the days afterward," *New York Times*, August 26, 1997.

After the incident, the commanding and executive officers of the 70th Precinct were reassigned, and another fourteen officers reportedly were placed on modified assignment or suspended.[86] According to the NYCLU, the fourteen officers who were either arrested, suspended, transferred or placed on desk duty in the week following the alleged torture of Louima had been accused, among them, of eleven prior unsubstantiated excessive force complaints and of another five misconduct complaints that had been ruled inconclusive or resolved through conciliation.[87]

On August 18, 1997, U.S. Attorney Zachary W. Carter announced that the Justice Department would initiate a preliminary "pattern or practice" civil investigation of the police force.[88] Carter described the incident: "...[O]ne or more officers are alleged to have committed an act of almost incomprehensible depravity within the police precinct and with the apparent expectation that they could get away with it."[89] One of Louima's attorneys initially filed a $55 million lawsuit against the city, which was later reportedly amended to seek $155 million.[90]

Volpe and another officer were charged in state court with aggravated sexual abuse and first-degree assault. Two other officers were charged with beating Louima during the drive to the police precinct, and racial bias charges were subsequently added against all four.

In February 1998, federal prosecutors took over the case, indicting the four officers named in the state indictments and a sergeant accused of attempting to

---

[86] David Kocieniewski, "Man says officers tortured him after arrest," *New York Times*, August 13, 1997, Dan Barry, "Officer charged in torture in Brooklyn station house," *New York Times*, August 14, 1997, "New York police shakeup after alleged attack," Blaine Harden, "Civil rights investigation targets N.Y. police," *Washington Post*, August 19, 1997.

[87] NYCLU report, September 1997, p. 11.

[88] *See* legal section.

[89] Blaine Harden, "Civil rights investigation targets N.Y. police," *Washington Post*, August 19, 1997.

[90] Joseph P. Fried, "In a brutality case, a legal dream team and questions of overkill," *New York Times*, November 9, 1997. There were also reports that the Louima was seeking $450 million in damages. Dale Russakoff, "U.S. indictment broadens New York police assault case," *Washington Post*, February 27, 1998.

cover up the incident.[91] The sergeant and Volpe were also indicted on charges relating to the alleged beating of another Haitian immigrant who was a bystander near the nightclub on the same night; the sergeant was accused of attempting to cover up the beating.[92] Federal control of the case makes longer sentences possible, but if the federal case is unsuccessful, the New York constitution does not allow the state to retry the implicated officers.

Officer Francis X. Livoti: On December 22, 1994, Anthony Baez, age twenty-nine, was playing football with family members at the Baez home in the Bronx.[93] When the ball hit a parked police car more than once, one of the officers in the car, Francis X. Livoti, reportedly became angry and arrested Anthony's brother, David Baez, for disorderly conduct. When Anthony Baez told Livoti to calm down (Livoti later claimed Anthony pushed him), Livoti allegedly used a chokehold, resulting in Baez's death. During his administrative disciplinary hearing, Livoti admitted becoming annoyed with the way David Baez was standing, "daring me to take some action."[94] Also in his administrative hearing, Livoti claimed that he attempted to handcuff Anthony Baez and they fell to the ground together. Asked if his arm ever touched Anthony Baez's neck, Livoti replied, "I'm sure that it must have at some brief period of time."[95] The city's chief medical examiner, Dr. Charles S. Hirsch, found that Baez died of asphyxiation and suffered large bruises on his neck and burst blood vessels around his eyes and larynx. Hirsch found Baez's asthma a minor contributing factor to his death and noted that his case was a textbook example of a death cause by a chokehold.[96] Of the fourteen city police departments

---

[91] Fried, "U.S. takes over," *New York Times*, February 27, 1998; John J. Goldman, "5 New York officers charged in torture case," *Los Angeles Times*, February 27, 1998; Russakoff, "U.S. indictment," *Washington Post*, February 27, 1998.

[92] Ibid.

[93] Michael Cooper, "Officer gives his account in Bronx death," *New York Times*, January 16, 1997; Amnesty International, "Police brutality," pp. 29-30.

[94] Cooper, "Officer gives his account," *New York Times*, January 16, 1997.

[95] Ibid.

[96] Ibid. Chokeholds were banned by the NYPD in October 1993 after the deaths of several suspects in custody from apparent asphyxia. See NYPD Interim Order No. 29, dated October 20, 1993.

examined by Human Rights Watch, only four (San Francisco, Washington, D.C., Los Angeles, and Minneapolis) still allow chokeholds.[97]

Livoti reportedly had been the subject of at least eleven brutality complaints over an eleven-year period.[98] He had been in the force's monitoring program because of these complaints, but then was removed from the program.[99] Livoti was the PBA union delegate for the 46th Precinct. A PBA lawyer said of Livoti, he is "what you want more of in the Police Department: an honest, dedicated, decent young man."[100]

Livoti was acquitted of "criminally negligent homicide" charges in a judge-only trial ending in October 1996. Acting State Supreme Court Justice Gerald Sheindlin explained, "I do not find that the defendant is innocent," but he believed that the prosecution had not proven its case.[101] In referring to conflicting officer testimony, the judge referred to a "nest of perjury" within the department.[102] In September 1997, the Bronx District Attorney's office announced it would reopen its perjury inquiry involving fifteen officers of the 46th Precinct; the inquiry was to focus on what took place at the station house after Baez died.[103]

After his acquittal on criminal charges in the Baez case, Livoti was prosecuted administratively to ascertain whether he broke departmental rules by applying a

---

[97] According to *Law Enforcement Management and Administrative Statistics, 1993* (Washington, D.C.: Bureau of Justice Statistics, September 1995), pp. 169-180.

[98] Clifford Krauss, "Case casts wide light on abuse by police," *New York Times*, April 15, 1995 and Cooper, "Officer gives his account," *New York Times*, January 16, 1997.

[99] Krauss, "Case casts wide light," *New York Times*, April 15, 1995.

[100] Ibid.

[101] David M. Herszenhorn, "Judge assails but acquits officer in man's choking death," *New York Times*, October 8, 1996; Matthew Purdy, "NY judge explains acquittal of officer in choking death," *New York Times*, October 9, 1996; Jan Hoffman, "When is homicide criminally negligent," *New York Times*, October 8, 1996

[102] The one officer who gave an account that contradicted the other officers on the scene, Officer Daisy Boria, was reportedly transferred out of the 46th Precinct.

[103] Neil MacFarquhar, "Possibility of police perjury is the focus of new inquiry," *New York Times*, September 19, 1997.

chokehold and whether he falsely arrested David Baez.[104] In February 1997, Livoti was fired for breaking department rules by using a chokehold, which is prohibited. In discussing the dismissal, Police Commissioner Safir stated, "[T]his department will never tolerate an officer who is abusive or brutal," but also stated he would "certainly not pretend that there are not others [officers] out there who might act inappropriately."[105] The dismissal reportedly stripped Livoti of his pension benefits.

In January 1998, Livoti was indicted by a federal grand jury on charges of assault and causing bodily harm in the Baez case.[106] Baez's family reportedly filed a $48 million lawsuit against the city.[107]

One complaint against Livoti that eventually was substantiated by the CCRB involved the September 1993 non-lethal choking of a sixteen- year-old, Steven Resto, who was allegedly detained for riding a go-cart recklessly.[108] On October 1, 1997, Livoti was convicted on charges of reckless endangerment and assault in the Resto case and sentenced to seven and half months in prison.[109] According to Resto's mother, the CCRB did not contact her or her son until the Baez case

---

[104] Department lawyers attempted to keep the hearing closed to the public, claiming that it might adversely affect the federal criminal civil rights probe underway, but Baez's family and others contended it was just an effort to keep embarrassing information from the public.

[105] "Officer acquitted in slaying is fired for 'aggressiveness,'" *Washington Post*, February 23, 1997; Grant McCool, "New York officer fired on brutality charge," *Reuters,* February 21, 1997, [Wire Service].

[106] David W. Chen, "Federal jury indicts NYC officer in choking death," *New York Times*, January 14, 1998.

[107] Leonard Levitt and Graham Rayman, "The verdict: acquittal," *New York Newsday*, October 8, 1996.

[108] Ibid.

[109] Barbara Stewart, "Ex-police officer receives jail term in choking case," *New York Times*, November 8, 1997, Neil MacFarquhar, "Ex-officer, acquitted in earlier death, guilty of choking," *New York Times*, October 3, 1997. At the time of this writing, he remained free on bail pending an appeal. "Ex-officer indicted in choking," *New York Times*, January 14, 1998.

received press attention some fifteen months after the Resto incident involving Livoti.[110]

Transit Officer Paolo Colecchia:[111] On July 4, 1996, Nathaniel Levi Gaines, Jr., was shot in the back and killed by Officer Colecchia on a Bronx subway platform after Gaines had been frisked and Colecchia knew he carried no weapons. The victim was black, the officer was white. Colecchia waited two days before providing his account of what had taken place.[112] Colecchia had a history of complaints – three for excessive force in 1994; all had been found unsubstantiated, though he was found to have given false statements to superiors investigating the complaints.[113]

He was indicted on August 15, 1996 on charges of first-degree manslaughter and was suspended from the force while the case was pending. Even Mayor Giuliani, who generally has defended police officers when they have been accused of brutality, stated, "There does not appear to be an explanation for it."[114]

---

[110] Stewart, "Ex-police officer receives jail term," *New York Times*, November 8, 1997.

[111] In early 1995, the transit and housing police were merged into the NYPD.

[112] Officers are permitted to wait forty-eight hours to obtain and confer with counsel before providing information if a serious violation is alleged or if sufficient justification is present although the alleged violation is minor. Patrol Guide procedure 118-9 as described in a letter to Human Rights Watch from John P. Beirne, Deputy Chief, Office of Labor Relations, NYPD, May 15, 1998. In practice, the officer is often allowed more than forty-eight hours because an investigator must request an interview before the forty-eight hour clock begins, and weekends are not counted. For example, after the December 25, 1997, fatal shooting of William Whitfield by a Brooklyn police officer, investigators did not immediately request an interview and the officer was interviewed at least six days after the shooting. Robert D. McFadden, "Police officer has yet to give his account of fatal shooting," *New York Times*, December 28, 1997.

[113] Rachel L. Swarns, "Policeman is indicted in killing of unarmed man in subway," *New York Times*, August 16, 1996.

[114] Clifford Krauss, "Tests raise doubts about justification of shooting," *New York Times*, July 10, 1996.

On May 29, 1997, Colecchia was convicted on second-degree manslaughter charges, and on July 21, 1997, he was sentenced to one and one-half to four and one-half years in prison; his attorney said he planned to appeal the conviction.[115]

Officer Francisco Rodríguez: In April 1993, Edward Domínguez was the passenger in a friend's car that broke down in the Bronx as a police squad car followed it. Officers reportedly suspected Domínguez and his friends had stolen the car. Domínguez was arrested though never charged. During the arrest, Officer Rodríguez allegedly kicked Domínguez in the testicles; later, one testicle had to be surgically removed due to the injury. At the station house, Domínguez repeatedly complained to a sergeant that he had been injured, and the sergeant, while placing his hand on his gun, reportedly responded by telling him that he had fallen down and had not been hurt by an officer.

After the case received attention, when the district attorney's office brought charges against Rodríguez, police officials all expressed outrage over his conduct. Yet, before the case was noticed by the district attorney, a departmental disciplinary trial in 1994 showed a much more lenient attitude. The same officials had recommended only a loss of thirty days' pay and departmental probation after he was found guilty of using physical force.[116]

When the Bronx district attorney learned of the case, he prosecuted Rodríguez for second-degree assault and the sergeant for intimidating a witness. Rodríguez was acquitted in a non-jury trial on March 10, 1998, and the sergeant, who has since retired, was acquitted by the same judge.[117] It was expected that Rodríguez would be reinstated.

Detectives Patrick Brosnan and James Crowe: The killings of Antonio Rosario (age eighteen) and Hilton Vega (age twenty-two) undermined the reputation of the CCRB when its findings were repudiated by the police department. On January 12,

---

[115] Randy Kennedy, "Cop sentenced for shooting unarmed man in the back," *New York Times*, July 22, 1997.

[116] Jim Dwyer, column, "Police dept goes soft on its brutes," *Daily News*, October 10, 1996; Dan Barry and Deborah Sontag, "Disrespect as catalyst for police brutality," *New York Times*, November 19, 1997; Joel Berger, attorney, speech to the Staten Island NAACP, October 1996; David M. Halbfinger, "Officer cleared in kicking incident," *New York Times*, March 12, 1998.

[117] Halbfinger, "Officer cleared in kicking incident," *New York Times*, March 12, 1998. The judge cited inconsistencies in medical records and in Domínguez's testimony.

1995, Rosario and Vega were shot dead by 46th Precinct plainclothes detectives inside a Bronx apartment.[118] A third target, Freddie Bonilla (age eighteen) was shot by the detectives and survived. There are several accounts of what transpired prior to the shootings. The police were reportedly called to the home of a couple because the couple stated that they feared they would be robbed, while the young men were reportedly attempting to obtain payment in relation to a marriage scam involving illegal immigrants.[119]

The detectives reportedly shot at the men between twenty-three and twenty-eight times. Rosario, Vega and Bonilla were armed but there were conflicting reports about whether any of them drew their weapons.[120] According to reports citing the Medical Examiner's report, Vega was hit with eight bullets – in his back, buttocks, back of the head and front left forearm. Rosario was hit with fourteen bullets – eight in his back or buttocks, two in his side, two in his right arm, one in his hip, and one in his armpit.[121] Bonilla's left ankle was shot. According to a pathologist hired by one of the victims' families, the men were lying on the floor as they were shot. And according to the account provided by Bonilla to a newspaper columnist, the men had followed the officers' instructions to surrender and lie prone on the ground when the officers shot them.[122]

The CCRB found that the detectives had used excessive force, but when its report was sent to the police commissioner, he ignored the CCRB's substantiation of the charges.[123] This undermined the CCRB by exposing its lack of power. Detective Brosnan was allowed to retire – without facing departmental charges – with benefits, including a disability pension after he claimed hearing damage

---

[118] David Stout, "Failed robbery tactic led to fatal shootout in Bronx," *New York Times*, January 14, 1995; interview with Richie Perez, National Congress for Puerto Rican Rights, August 23, 1996.

[119] Matthew Purdy and Garry Pierre-Pierre, "Police barrage still resounds," *New York Times*, August 20, 1995.

[120] Ibid.

[121] Ibid.

[122] Juan Gonzalez, column, *Daily News*, August 31, 1995.

[123] On the advice of their lawyers, neither of the detectives were interviewed by the CCRB. Garry Pierre-Pierre, "Board says 2 officers used excessive force on suspects," *New York Times*, July 28, 1995.

suffered during the shooting of the young men.[124] The CCRB's executive director, Hector Soto, resigned soon after this and another disputed case. The families filed a civil lawsuit, a grand jury declined to indict the detectives, and federal investigators reportedly reviewed the case.[125]

Officer Michael J. Davitt: The shooting of William Whitfield on December 25, 1997 by Officer Michael J. Davitt uncovered the disturbing fact that an officers' records on shooting incidents had not previously been tracked or subject to review. Officer Davitt reportedly shot and killed Whitfield, who was unarmed.[126] Officers were responding to a report of shots being fired when Whitfield, who reportedly was uninvolved in the incident to which the officers were responding, did not obey the officers' orders to stop and entered a store. Officer Davitt claims he believed the keys or hat Whitfield was holding were a gun and shot him.

After the incident, it was discovered that Davitt had been involved in more shootings than any other officer on the city's force, shooting nine times in fourteen years.[127] Davitt reportedly had also been the subject of twelve unsubstantiated complaints.[128] After Davitt's shooting record was made public, Commissioner Safir announced that officers' shooting incidents would now be tracked and reviewed, surprising police abuse monitors and others who assumed such tracking was routine. *(See* below.) At the time of this writing, the shooting was being investigated by

---

[124] Brosnan had previously worked as a bodyguard for Mayor Giuliani. Purdy and Pierre-Pierre, "Police barrage still resounds," *New York Times*, August 20, 1995. David Kocieniewski, "The trial room," *New York Times*, December 19, 1997.

[125] When Human Rights Watch inquired about the status of the federal inquiry, the U.S. Attorney's office would not provide information about whether the investigation continues or has been closed. Telephone inquiry, May 13, 1998.

[126] David Kocieniewski, "Police's use of deadly force in New York is low for nation," *New York Times*, January 2, 1998.

[127] Ibid. The first shooting took place while Davitt was off-duty and still on probation in 1983. David Kocieniewski, "Officers facing added scrutiny over shootings," *New York Times*, January 1, 1998.

[128] Kocieniewski, "Officers facing added scrutiny," *New York Times*, January 1, 1998.

IAB, and the district attorney's office and was under review by federal prosecutors.[129]

Police Administration/Internal Affairs Bureau[130]

Despite public pronouncements that the department is taking allegations of excessive force seriously, it appears that officers are still not being disciplined by the police department after the CCRB has substantiated complaints. During 1996, the police department disposed of 187 CCRB-substantiated complaints; there were only six guilty findings after a departmental trial, with ten found not guilty.[131] There were far fewer departmental trials in 1995 and 1996 as compared to earlier years, with many more complaints dismissed prior to trial for lack of prima facie evidence or the expiration of statutes of limitations. For example, in 1994 there were seventy trials, but in 1995 and 1996 combined, there were only thirty-three.[132] Critics of the police department claim this decline reflects police officials' efforts to ignore the CCRB's findings altogether.

Human Rights Watch attempted to obtain information from the Internal Affairs Bureau through interviews and correspondence. No high-ranking official agreed to meet with Human Rights Watch as requested in August 1996, though a sergeant, George Tom (hereinafter "IAB representative") was able to answer some of our questions.[133] A letter requesting very basic information about the operations of the IAB was sent to IAB in September 1996; a copy of the letter was sent again in November, and the same request was submitted in June 1997 to the Deputy Commissioner for Public Information. Human Rights Watch also made repeated calls to obtain answers to the questions posed in the letter. In late June 1997, Chief Charles V. Campisi of the IAB provided a partial response to the letter that was

---

[129] Ibid., and "US investigates shooting of unarmed man by police," *New York Times*, February 3, 1998.

[130] Following the Mollen Commission report, the Internal Affairs Division was reorganized and renamed the Internal Affairs Bureau.

[131] CCRB semiannual status reports, January - June 1996, pp. 37-38; and January - December 1996, pp. 45-46.

[132] NYCLU report, September 1997, Table III.

[133] Telephone interview, January 28, 1997.

originally sent to him in September 1996.[134] According to police-abuse experts in the city, the difficulty Human Rights Watch encountered in obtaining information is typical.

Although the IAB representative told Human Rights Watch in January 1997 that the size of the IAB staff is not public information, Chief Campisi replied to this question, stating that there is a staff of 615 in the IAB, with 487 internal investigators.[135] Campisi explained that the IAB handles both criminal and administrative inquiries, with its investigations often serving as the primary criminal investigation of officers.

According to police department figures, there has been a decrease in the number of shootings by officers, and the city's force shoots suspects less than in many other large police departments. In 1996, there were 254 incidents of on-duty shootings and sixty-three off-duty shootings; seventy-four suspects were shot, thirty fatally.[136] In 1997, there were 253 incidents (on- and off-duty combined).[137] Twenty individuals were killed by shots fired by officers in 1997.[138]

After a December 1997 fatal shooting by an officer who was involved in more shootings than any other officer on the force (See Whitfield case, above), the department began monitoring officers involved in shootings.[139] It was reported that 250 officers involved in three or more shootings would be more closely monitored; seven officers reportedly have been involved in six or more shootings.[140]

---

[134] Letter to Human Rights Watch from Chief Charles V. Campisi, Internal Affairs Bureau, June 24, 1997.

[135] The police commissioner stated publicly on August 18, 1997 that there were 700 IAB investigators.

[136] Sixty-four of seventy-four suspects who were shot were black or Hispanic, according to police figures; twenty-three of thirty fatalities were of minorities. Kocieniewski, "Police's use of deadly force in New York is low for nation," New York Times, January 2, 1998.

[137] The figure includes officers shooting accidentally and shooting at dogs.

[138] "Grand jury exonerates 2 killer cops," Associated Press, February 13, 1998, [Wire Service]; Kocieniewski, "Police's use of deadly force...," New York Times.

[139] David Kocieniewski, "Officers facing added scrutiny," New York Times, January 1, 1998.

[140] Ibid.

Commissioner Safir and civil rights activists in the city reportedly were surprised that the department's firearms discharge board did not already monitor officers involved in multiple shootings.[141]

In response to a Human Rights Watch inquiry about deaths in custody, Campisi reported that the IAB only began tracking deaths in custody in 1996, and that there were forty-four cases that year; as of late June 1997, twenty cases in 1997 had been investigated by IAB.[142]

The linkage between civil lawsuits and the initiation of an IAB investigation is unclear. According to the New York City Law Department, "...[C]oncerning notification procedures where a lawsuit alleges police misconduct, the Law Department does not have a formal procedure for notifying IAB or the CCRB of such lawsuits."[143] It appears that any such notification is indirect, at best. In correspondence with Human Rights Watch, the IAB's chief states that, "in situations where an officer is served court papers for civil litigation involving excessive force, the officer must submit to his or her commanding officer a request for indemnification by the City of New York. This request triggers an investigation by the commanding officer concerned and 'conferral' with the Internal Affairs Bureau."[144] The IAB did not respond to Human Rights Watch's questions regarding whether civil lawsuits against officers are compiled as part of the department's officer monitoring system to identify "at-risk" officers, but according to other

---

[141] Kocieniewski, "Police's use of deadly force in New York is low for nation," *New York Times*, January 2, 1998.

[142] Letter to Human Rights Watch from Chief Charles V. Campisi, Internal Affairs Bureau, June 24, 1997. The police department spokesperson has provided deaths-in-custody statistics in the past, however. According to a June 1996 *New York Newsday* article, there were twenty-four deaths in custody in 1994 and twenty-one in 1995. Graham Rayman, "Report sees brutality in NYPD," *New York Newsday*, June 27, 1996. Deaths in custody may not involve misconduct by police officers.

[143] According to a November 8, 1996 letter from the Assistant Corporation Counsel Michael Sarner, of the city's Law Department to Human Rights Watch.

[144] Letter to Human Rights Watch from Chief Campisi, June 24, 1997. It appears that the purpose of this investigation is to decide whether the officer acted within the scope of duty and should, therefore, covered financially by the city; in the vast majority of cases the city does find accused officers' actions within the scope of duty.

sources, few lawsuits are even recorded in an officer's personnel records or are disciplined, while taxpayers cover the cost of misconduct.[145]

For example, sixteen-year-old Yong Xin Huang was shot and killed by an NYPD officer in Sheepshead Bay, Brooklyn in March 1995.[146] Huang and two other boys were playing with a pellet gun; a police officer put his 9 millimeter Glock semi-automatic on or near the boy's head, and the gun allegedly discharged accidentally. There were also impact wounds to the top of Huang's head, face and forehead that may have resulted for his head being pushed into a glass door. In May 1995, a grand jury concluded that no criminal charges should be filed against the officer involved, and the officer was not disciplined. The Committee Against Anti-Asian Violence included the case as part of a March 1996 report presented to U.S. Attorney Zachary Carter regarding police violence against Asian-Americans, but they received no response and do not believe any federal investigation or prosecution took place on the case.[147] In March 1996, the city agreed to pay $400,000 in damages to the family in an out-of-court settlement.

The IAB representative told Human Rights Watch that he believed the CCRB only handles "low-level" discourtesy allegations or ethnic/racial slurs, and that IAB does not share information with the CCRB at all.[148] He stated that allegations of domestic violence and "bar fights" involving officers were of a "less serious" nature and would be dealt with at the bureau level, explaining that IAB only deals with firing offenses and possibly criminal allegations; if the IAB investigates an incident and it is not prosecuted criminally, the IAB will use the information to pursue the case administratively.

According to press reports, in an eighteen-month period Commissioner Safir dismissed 106 officers; only eight dismissals were related to excessive force charges, and three of those were tried on criminal charges in highly publicized

---

[145] Section 50(a) of the Civil Rights Law of New York State makes police personnel records confidential; they can be made public only with the authorization of the subject officer or a court order. Amnesty International, "Police brutality," p. 22.

[146] *The CAAAV Voice*, vol. 8, no. 2; Amnesty International, "Police brutality," p. 46.

[147] Committee Against Anti-Asian Violence, "Police violence in New York City's Asian American Communities," Submitted to U.S. Attorney Zachary Carter, March 12, 1996. Telephone interview with Hyun Lee, August 26, 1997.

[148] Telephone interview, Sgt. George Tom, January 28, 1997.

cases.[149] For two of the three tried – Paolo Colecchia and Frank Speringo – dismissal was mandatory under state law following their convictions for fatal shootings. Officer Livoti was the third officer dismissed after standing trial, although he was acquitted.[150] In an October 1997 statement submitted to the U.S. Commission on Civil Rights, however, Commissioner Safir claimed that he had dismissed thirty-five officers because they had committed excessive or "unnecessary" acts of force – most were dismissed following internal investigations rather than following a CCRB referral.[151]

According to Commissioner Safir, there are several monitoring systems that should hold officers who commit abuses accountable.[152] A Force Monitoring Program utilizes computer tracking capabilities to identify officers who seem to be using excessive force repeatedly. A Civilian Complaint Reduction Program notifies commanders when an officer has generated a high number of complaints, and a Resisting Arrest Charge program highlights officers who lodge a high number of "resisting arrest" charges. Remedies under these programs include counseling, reassignment, training, heightened evaluations, and "special" monitoring, in which termination is likely. And in February 1997, a police committee was formed to examine officers with six or more civilian complaints during a five-year period.

There is no disciplinary sanction available between thirty days suspension and dismissal. The Mollen Commission recommended a new range of penalties, including fining officers found guilty of misconduct.[153] In June 1995, the mayor and

---

[149] Dan Barry, Deborah Sontag, "New York dismisses police, but rarely for brutality," *New York Times,* October 6, 1997.

[150] Ibid.

[151] Statement of Police Commissioner Howard Safir before the New York Advisory Committee to the U.S. Commission on Civil Rights, October 29, 1997. No definition was provided for what constitutes unnecessary acts of force. According to the Legal Affairs Bureau of the police department, the term "unnecessary" is not an official term used in department policies, but, as used in the commissioner's statement, meant force that was used when no force was justified at all, as opposed to "excessive" force used when force was justified. He was unable to provide a breakdown between the two types of force. Telephone inquiry, Sgt. Tom Tuffey of the legislative affairs unit of the Legal Affairs Bureau, April 22, 1998.

[152] Statement of Police Commissioner Howard Safir before the New York Advisory Committee to the U.S. Commission on Civil Rights, October 29, 1997.

[153] Mollen Commission report, p. 143.

police department agreed with the proposal, but it was never enacted, even though it reportedly requires only an amendment to the administrative code.[154] In September 1997, a "Police Disciplinary Bill" was pending in the state legislature that would allow the police commissioner to suspend without pay – for more than thirty days – officers charged with criminal offenses who have not been administratively investigated and disciplined; as it is, they can only be suspended for thirty days, after which they must be paid and are usually placed on desk duty pending the administrative investigation.[155] The bill would also remove provisions allowing officers to wait up to forty-eight hours before providing their statements to investigators when they have been accused of misconduct.[156]

In one case, the department did not punish an officer but the city argued that it should not have to represent the same officer in a civil lawsuit stemming from a beating by the officer's partner because the officer had broken departmental rules by providing false statements and other misconduct relating to the beating. Officer Frank Bolusi was Officer Gerard Pitti's partner when Pitti encountered Victor Medina and his friends in Brooklyn in February 1992.[157] Officer Pitti allegedly grabbed Medina and beat him with a nightstick, a radio and his fists. When Medina's friend yelled at the officer to stop beating him, the friend was briefly handcuffed. No one was arrested, and the friend wrote down Pitti's badge number. Medina went to the hospital with one ear hanging off and a collapsed lung. Pitti was later convicted by a jury on assault charges for the beating but was not sentenced to jail time; at the time of sentencing, the judge mentioned that the

---

[154] Berger paper, citing city's administrative code, Section 14-115.

[155] Michael Cooper, "4 officers accused in brutality case will not be allowed to return to duty," New York Times, September 8, 1997. The thirty-day rule meant that the officers accused in the Louima case, see above, had to begin to receive their salaries after thirty days because administrative actions had been on hold pending criminal prosecution of the officers. Because the commissioner did not want the officers to return to work, they were paid for not working.

[156] Some police abuse experts have suggested that the forty-eight hour delay in obtaining statements from the target officer may be unhelpful because department investigators are able to pull together the facts before compelling the officer to provide information which would not be admissible in court.

[157] Jim Dwyer, "Brutality is a crime oft ignored," New York Daily News, August 17, 1997; Dwyer, "The lies that bind police hurt us all," New York Daily News, October 13, 1996; "Officer convicted of hitting Brooklyn man," New York Times, February 1, 1995.

supportive presence at the hearing of several local politicians was a factor in the sentencing.[158]

Pitti's partner, Officer Bolusi, testified at the trial that he never saw Medina, even though he was in the squad car with an open window.[159] He claimed he was "catching up on paperwork" during the beating. As of late 1997, Bolusi had not been departmentally disciplined even though the city argued that it should not have to defend and indemnify Bolusi in the civil lawsuit stemming from this incident because he had broken departmental rules requiring him to testify fully and truthfully, to report any unusual occurrence while on patrol, and prohibiting him from making false statements.[160] In the opinion of the judge presiding over the criminal case against Officer Pitti, Officer Bolusi had provided an "astounding" account of the incident.[161]

As described in the Mollen Commission report, the code of silence is thoroughly ingrained in the NYPD. "Officers who report misconduct are ostracized and harassed; become targets of complaints and even physical threats; and are made to fear that they will be left alone on the streets in a time of crisis."[162] Officer Bernard Cawley testified to the Mollen Commission that he never feared that fellow officers might turn him in:

> ...it was the Blue Wall of Silence. Cops don't tell on cops. And if they did tell on them, just say if a cop decided to tell on me, his career's ruined. He's going to be labeled as a rat....And chances are if it comes down to it, they're going to let him get hurt.[163]

---

[158] Berger paper, p. 19.

[159] Dwyer, "The lies that bind," *New York Daily News*, October 13, 1996.

[160] The court found that the city was not obligated to defend Bolusi even though the police department had not disciplined him for breaking departmental rules because the city's Corporation Counsel has authority regarding which officers it chooses to represent. "City has no duty to defend officer who sat by as partner assaulted man," *New York Law Journal*, January 17, 1997.

[161] Jim Dwyer, "The lies that bind police hurt us all," *New York Daily News*, October 13, 1996.

[162] Mollen Commission report, p. 53.

[163] Ibid., pp. 53-54, from hearing transcript, p.138.

The inculcation of complete loyalty begins at the police academy, according to some officers. Said one, before the Mollen Commission, when asked when officers learn about the code of silence, "[I]t starts at the police academy and it just develops from there...It starts with the instructors telling you never to be a rat, never to give up your fellow officer...."[164]

In December 1996, the Commission to Combat Police Corruption, an independent agency created in 1995 by a mayoral executive order, studied how the NYPD disciplines its members who make false statements.[165] That commission examined over one hundred cases processed through the NYPD's disciplinary system. The commission studied cases in which officers made false statements to avoid the consequences of an illegal search or the use of excessive force, or to cover up off-duty misconduct; the commission called these types of false statements "routine," in contrast to lies to cover up widespread financial corruption, as examined by the Mollen Commission. It found, "[T]he punishments traditionally meted out for false statements have been inadequate," and called for tougher punishments.[166] Commissioner Safir did implement a policy change in December 1996 allowing him to dismiss officers if a police administrative judge finds that they have lied.[167] But in an October 1997 *New York Times* article, Commissioner Safir's claim that he had dismissed eighteen officers for making false statements was undermined by internal police documents showing that few officers were dismissed for that offense alone; most who were dismissed faced other charges as well.[168]

In addition to officers' silence about individual cases, the department as a whole is unnecessarily secretive. In February 1997, two young men were shot and

---

[164] Ibid., p. 55.

[165] Commission to Combat Police Corruption, *The New York City Police Department's Disciplinary System*, December 12, 1996.

[166] Ibid., p. 2 and 11.

[167] Kocieniewski, "2 more officers disciplined in Louima case," *New York Times*, February 19, 1998.

[168] Dan Barry, Deborah Sontag, "New York dismisses police, but rarely for brutality," *New York Times,* October 6, 1997.

seriously injured by officers in upper Manhattan.[169] Eighteen-year-old Robert Reynoso and seventeen-year-old Juval Green were shot after plainclothes officers say they heard shots fired and saw the young men running; the officers fired at the men, hitting both, but no weapons were found in their possession or on the scene afterward. Another bystander may have been shot and grazed by a stray bullet. He reportedly told a police officer he believed he had been shot, but was taken to the 30th Precinct station house and held overnight instead of being taken to a hospital. His trousers, which allegedly had a hole in them that would support his contention that he had been shot, were confiscated.

The names of the officers involved were kept secret, even from the young men's lawyer, and the department reportedly refused to disclose any information for at least two weeks following the shooting. A *New York Times* columnist obtained an internal memo that included the names of the officers who discharged their weapons and other information.[170] The D.A.'s office was investigating, and the FBI was reportedly monitoring that investigation; no grand jury had been convened as of mid-May 1998.[171]

Civil Lawsuits

According to press reports, the city paid about $70 million in settlement or jury awards in claims alleging improper police actions between 1994 and 1996.[172] The New York City Law Department reports that police misconduct, described as assault/excessive force, assault and false arrest, shootings by police, and false arrests (as categorized by the city's Law Department), cost city taxpayers more than $44 million for fiscal years 1994-95; this works out to an average of almost $2

---

[169] Bob Herbert, columns, *New York Times,* February 28, 1997 and March 3, 1997; David Kocieniewski, "Police criticized in teen-agers' shooting," *New York Times*, March 1, 1997.

[170] Ibid.

[171] Telephone interviews, attorney David Eskin, who is representing Green and Reynoso, August 19, 1997 and May 11, 1998.

[172] Matthew Purdy, "What does it take to get arrested in New York City? Not much," *New York Times*, August 24, 1997. In April 1998, a jury awarded $76.4 million to a man who had been shot by police in 1998; he was paralyzed by the shooting. The city planned to appeal the ruling, and experts predicted the judgment would be reduced dramatically if paid. David Rohde, "$76 million is awarded to man shot by police and paralyzed," *New York Times*, April 9, 1998.

million a month for police misconduct lawsuits alone.[173] And it represents an increase over the three previous years, when the city reportedly paid a total of $48 million in these types of cases.[174] In addition to an increase in amounts paid in recent years, the number of brutality claims has tripled in a decade, to 2,735 between June 1996 and June 1997, according to city Comptroller statistics.[175]

Between June 1996 and June 1997, the city settled 503 police misconduct cases, taking only twenty-four to court, where it won sixteen.[176] Yet, as far as reforms are concerned, settlements provide little public information about incidents of police misconduct and there are few repercussions for an officer who is the subject of such a lawsuit, for which the city pays.

Payments come from the general city budget, not directly from the NYPD. As noted above, the Law Department states that, "...concerning notification procedures where a lawsuit alleges police misconduct, the Law Department does not have a formal procedure for notifying IAB or the CCRB of such lawsuits."[177] Stated more bluntly by City Comptroller Alan Hevesi, "[T]here is a total and complete disconnect....there is a small percentage [of officers] who are habitually macho and violent and they have to deal with that."[178] In approximately 90 percent of the lawsuits, according to press reports, the city's Law Department and the police department determine that the officer was acting within the scope of his or her duty, and the lawsuit is not recorded in the officer's personnel file.[179] The city does not

---

[173] Figure does not include traffic accidents. Letter to Human Rights Watch from the Law Department's Corporation Counsel Michael Sarner, November 8, 1996.

[174] Ibid.

[175] Deborah Sontag, Dan Barry, "Using settlements to measure police abuse," *New York Times*, September 17, 1997.

[176] Ibid. A litigator with the city's Law Department stated that settling a case does not mean the officer did anything wrong, but that the city feared a jury would find the plaintiff sympathetic.

[177] Letter to Human Rights Watch from the Law Department's Corporation Counsel Michael Sarner, November 8, 1996.

[178] Sontag, Barry, "Using settlements to measure police abuse," *New York Times*, September 17, 1997. Hevesi also recommends that the police department pay half of the settlement amounts.

[179] Ibid.

represent about 10 percent of officers named in lawsuits, who face disciplinary proceedings.

Lawyers bringing civil lawsuits against police officers told Human Rights Watch that they often do not recommend that their clients file a complaint with the IAB because the information provided is often used against the client. Officers themselves do not have to pay personally in civil lawsuits; the city almost always indemnifies the officer and pays. In the rare case in which the city has not covered the officer, the PBA usually has done so.

In 1984, the city agreed to pay into a police union "civil legal defense fund." It now pays $75 per year for each officer in the union, meaning that taxpayers may be charged three times for officers who commit abuses: for their legal defense, for their salaries, and for civil settlements or jury awards. When the police department fails to take appropriate disciplinary actions against these officers and repeat offenders, there is an additional cost in terms of public confidence. Juries in civil cases are increasingly willing to believe plaintiffs seeking damages (leading to settlements by the city and large awards when cases do go to trial); and, in separate criminal cases against civilians, the public is increasingly unwilling to believe the police. The true cost of poor accountability for violent police officers is far more than that of the settlements or awards provided to the alleged victims.

Because the police department is secretive regarding how it handles allegations of police misconduct, and the CCRB does not provide specific information about individual cases, the disclosure of information during civil trials in New York would be a large step toward accountability. Even though there is often no connection between disciplinary or prosecutorial action against the officer and the awards following civil trials, information that would otherwise by suppressed may reach the public domain through civil lawsuits. Still, civil suits are brought only in a minority of cases, and if they are settled before trial – as the vast majority are – little information is disclosed. Moreover, the civil suits filed represent just a portion of allegations of police misconduct made by individuals seeking legal representation, since many lawyers who represent victims in police misconduct suits are overwhelmed with requests for help and will only pursue the strongest cases involving the victim's hospitalization or death.

Two of the largest amounts paid during this period followed verdicts in June 1994, one costing $6.5 million (victim Gerard Papa) and another costing $1 million, after a verdict for plaintiff James Rampersant, Jr. who was involved in the same incident.[180] Papa and Rampersant, Jr. were reportedly shot at and beaten by police in Bensonhurst, Brooklyn in March 1986. The police mistakenly believed the men

---

[180] Jim Dwyer, column, *Daily News*, October 10, 1996, and Amnesty International, "Police brutality," pp. 51-52.

to be suspected purse-snatchers, and after the attack charged the men with attempted murder, criminal mischief, resisting arrest and other offenses; the charges were later dropped. After the incident, the Patrolmen's Benevolent Association (PBA) attorney reportedly advised the officers involved not to cooperate with investigators, and the officers apparently were never disciplined, despite costing the city at least $7.5 million.[181]

In another case demonstrating that large civil lawsuit payouts may not correspond to appropriate disciplinary or criminal actions against officers, Carlton Brown, a twenty-eight-year-old African-American was apprehended by officers for allegedly having a suspended license in August 1992. He was handcuffed and taken to the 63rd Precinct in Brooklyn, and he alleges the officers involved beat him and pushed him through a double-paned glass door, shattering it. After he went through the door, the officers kept his handcuffs on, despite his injuries, and added a charge of resisting arrest. Brown sustained spinal cord injuries, was hospitalized for more than three years, and was permanently paralyzed.[182]

In 1995, the city paid Brown what was then the largest pre-trial settlement amount in its history. Brown received $4.5 million in the settlement, but with added annuities, $16.6 million was to be paid.[183] After public protests, the two officers were indicted on assault charges and placed on restrictive duty, but a judge acquitted them. According to press reports, the officers were never disciplined.[184]

Off-Duty Incidents

According to information provided by the NYPD to the *New York Times,* ten officers were dismissed for gun-related, off-duty incidents in an eighteen-month period between January 1996 and July 1997.

Off-duty incidents frequently have racial overtones. In an October 3, 1996 incident, off-duty NYPD officer Richard D. DiGuglielmo and family members got into an altercation with Charles C. Campbell in Westchester County. DiGuglielmo is white, and Campbell was black. Campbell parked his car in front of

---

[181] Ibid.

[182] Amnesty International, "Police brutality," pp. 17-18.

[183] Sontag, Barry, "Using settlements," *New York Times*, September 17, 1997, Joseph P. Fried, "In a brutality case, a legal dream team and questions of overkill," *New York Times,* November 9, 1997, and information provided by the New York City Law Department to Human Rights Watch, dated November 8, 1996.

[184] Sontag, Barry, "Using settlements," *New York Times*, September 17, 1997.

DiGuglielmo's family-run delicatessen, and a physical altercation ensued between Campbell, DiGuglielmo, his father and his brother-in-law. Campbell retrieved a baseball bat from his car and reportedly hit the father in the leg and then backed away, according to at least one witness, while the DiGuglielmos contend that Campbell posed a threat to the elder DiGuglielmo. Officer DiGuglielmo then returned from the family's store with a gun and fired at Campbell three times, killing him.[185] The Westchester County district attorney charged Officer DiGuglielmo with second-degree murder, and his father and brother were charged with second-degree assault. In October 1997, a jury found Officer DiGuglielmo guilty, and in December he was sentenced to twenty years to life in prison; he was fired after the conviction.[186]

In another off-duty incident, Det. Constantine Chronis allegedly took part in the beating of Shane L. Daniels while drinking with friends at a nightclub in Westhampton Beach, Long Island in May 1996.[187] Chronis is white, and Daniels is African-American. According to reports, Chronis and his friends uttered racial epithets at Daniels and his friends, leading to a violent confrontation.[188] Chronis allegedly held Daniels's friends at bay with a handgun as Daniels was beaten with a metal steering wheel lock by Chronis's friend; the attack left Daniels in a coma for weeks, with a three-inch hole in his skull. Daniels survived, with a plastic plate in his skull impaired vision.

A Suffolk County grand jury indicted Chronis on assault, "menacing," and official misconduct charges after he left the scene without reporting the incident. He resigned from the police force in August 1996. Detective Chronis did not have

---

[185] David Kocieniewski, "New York officer charged in murder," *New York Times*, October 5, 1996.

[186] "Rage cited in officer's killing of man over parking space," *New York Times*, September 19, 1997; Jim Fitzgerald, "Jury convicts NYC cop of murder," *Associated Press*, October 25, 1997, [Wire Service]; "Ex-officer is sentenced for parking-space killing," *New York Times,* December 16, 1997.

[187] Dan Barry, "Beating was racial clash, witnesses tell police," *New York Times*, May 31, 1996, Dan Barry, 2d man is charged in L.I. bar beating, *New York Times,* June 13, 1996, and Barry, "The charge is assault in a beating at an L.I. bar," *New York Times*, June 21, 1996; John McQuiston, "Man beaten outside nightclub is back home," *New York Times*, July 12, 1996; John McQuiston, "Man held in beating outside L.I. club is to be freed on bail," *New York Times,* April 17, 1997.

[188] McQuiston, "Man beaten outside nightclub is back home," *New York Times*, July 12, 1996

an extensive physical abuse complaint record, but did have CCRB complaints regarding his use of racially or ethnically offensive language. According to reports, this was one of five off-duty NYPD-officer-related incidents on Long Island during the summer of 1996. At the time of this writing, Chronis's trial was expected to take place in mid-1998.[189]

Unions

The 29,000-member Patrolmen's Benevolent Association and other police unions and fraternal organizations in New York City enjoy a great deal of power but have been unwilling to use their strength to support reforms that would lead to a more professional, and less brutal, police force. In fact, the unions have often been the primary obstacle to efforts to implement reforms. In its statements and lobbying against reform efforts, the PBA has consistently opposed accountability. In doing so, it claims that it merely attempts to protect the rights of its members.[190]

The Mollen Commission report noted that "police unions and fraternal organizations can do much to increase professionalism of our police officers....Unfortunately, based on our own observations and on information received from prosecutors, corruption investigators, and high-ranking police officials, police unions sometimes fuel the insularity that characterizes police culture."[191] The report identified a conflict of interest for the unions, which protect the interests of individual officers and promote the larger interests of their members, finding that, ironically, the PBA "does a great disservice to the vast majority of its members who would be happy to see corrupt cops prosecuted for their crimes and removed from their jobs."[192]

The report was also critical of the police unions' reaction to the commission: "At the outset, we were disappointed at the negative reaction that some police unions had toward the Commission's work. Instead of seeing the Commission as a possible vehicle for reform for the benefit of their members, some unions automatically saw it as a threat and a device of partisan politics."[193] The report

---

[189] John T. McQuiston, "2 years after brutal assault, trial is to begin," *New York Times*, February 17, 1998.

[190] See above, regarding resistance to independent civilian review.

[191] Mollen Commission report, p. 66.

[192] Ibid., p. 67.

[193] Ibid., p. 66.

notes that the Captains Benevolent Association (the union for police captains) initiated a lawsuit to dissolve the commission that sent a negative message to its members about efforts to fight corruption and to the public about the insularity of the force. The report notes that the CBA reaction was "particularly egregious coming from the union representing the highest-ranking members of the Department."[194]

Regarding the PBA's role and the code of silence, the report found that "...past and current prosecutors and Department officials told us in informal interviews that PBA delegates and attorneys help reinforce the code of silence among officers who have committed or witnessed corrupt acts....[B]y advising its members against cooperating with law enforcement authorities, the PBA often acts as a shelter and protector of the corrupt cop rather than as a guardian of the interests of the vast majority of its membership, who are honest police officers."[195]

The PBA itself has been the focus of a federal corruption probe. In February 1997, a federal grand jury subpoenaed ten years of the union's financial records dealing with various union accounts holding more than $100 million in assets, including the legal defense fund.[196] Two of the lead partners of the law firm managing the union funds were indicted in January 1997 on racketeering charges in relation to a "kickback" scheme involving the former Transit Police Benevolent Association.[197]

---

[194] Ibid., p. 66.

[195] Ibid., p. 67.

[196] Matthew Purdy, "NYC police union subpoenaed for records on finances," *New York Times*, February 7, 1997, and Purdy and Kocieniewski, "PBA Funds are the focus of an inquiry," *New York Times*, February 9, 1997.

[197] Ibid.

Criminal Prosecution

Only three city officers have been convicted for on-duty killings since 1977.[198] Most close observers believe that, if district attorneys were more aggressive in these cases, they could win and set important examples. Each borough's district attorneys are quite different in their approach to police brutality cases, with some district attorneys much more likely than others to bring a case against an accused police officer, leading to an arbitrary application of the laws block-by-block in the city.

As in many cities, grand juries often decline to indict officers accused of brutality-related charges, choosing to believe officers' accounts of events. For example, a grand jury chose not to indict an officer who shot and killed Anibal Carasquillo, age twenty-one, in Brooklyn on January 22, 1995. Carasquillo was reportedly looking through the windows of parked cars and was unarmed. Police officials claimed Carasquillo faced the officer who shot him and took a "gun stance," but the city's medical examiner found that he was shot in the back.[199] In another case, the D.A. failed to bring a case against an officer accused of shooting and killing fifteen-year-old Frankie Arzuega, who was a passenger in a vehicle approached by three officers in Brooklyn. The driver of the car, according to the police, attempted to drive off as an officer questioned him, allegedly dragging the officer along. Another officer fired through the back window of the vehicle, killing Arzuega. No weapons were found in the car. The shooting was not recorded in the police department's log of major incidents and was only acknowledged three days later, after Arzuega's family spoke with reporters.[200] The district attorney

---

[198] Former Transit Officer Paolo Colecchia, who had been convicted for second-degree manslaughter for fatally shooting Nathaniel Levi Gaines, Jr. in July 1996, was sentenced to one and one half to four and one half years in prison in July 1997. A New York housing authority officer was convicted of criminally negligent homicide in August 1995, for a fatal shooting that occurred in March 1992, before the housing authority merged with the NYPD. In 1977, Thomas Ryan was convicted of criminally negligent homicide for the beating death of Israel Rodriguez in July 1975; the Ryan homicide conviction was the first recorded in the city of an on-duty policeman. Judith Cummings, *New York Times*, November 6, 1977.

[199] Amnesty International, "Police brutality," p. 44; Leonard Levitt, "NYPD's legacy of distrust," *Newsday*, April 14, 1997.

[200] Amnesty International, "Police brutality," p. 43, and interviews with Richie Perez of the National Congress for Puerto Rican Rights, August 23, 1996 and August 26, 1997.

reportedly said there was only one story – that of the three officers; he disregarded witnesses' statements and did not present the case to a grand jury.[201]

In the state of New York, defendants may waive their right to a jury trial for charges other than first-degree murder.[202] This is a common practice when police officers are accused on criminal charges, because officers know some judges are particularly sympathetic toward the police, while juries may contain local residents who are less so.

In early 1998, federal prosecutors announced their intent to pursue Livoti and the 70th Precinct officers involved in the Louima case. But these were exceptions; federal civil rights prosecutions are rare in New York, even though advocates report serious cases to the U.S. Attorney's office and have also helped federal investigators in identifying "problem" precincts.[203] The CCRB may refer cases to local or federal prosecutors, but the CCRB's reports do not mention such referrals so there is no way to assess their frequency or effect.

In New York City, of the twenty-two cases decided by federal prosecutors for the federal districts containing New York City (Eastern and Southern districts of New York), five were prosecuted (presented to a grand jury to seek an indictment) in 1996.[204] Between 1992 and 1995, ninety-four cases were decided, with nineteen leading to prosecutions.

The U.S. attorney for the Eastern District of New York announced on August 18, 1997 that the Justice Department would initiate a "pattern or practice"

---

[201] *See* Yong Xin Huang, Vega/Rosario cases above as other examples of failure to indict.

[202] New York State Consolidated Laws, Criminal Procedure, Article 320.10.

[203] In New York, as in other cities, a case can be tried by federal prosecutors if local prosecution is not initiated or fails, but the New York State Constitution does not allow the reverse, so if a case goes to federal court and the officer is acquitted, state prosecutors may not try it. *See* Louima case, above.

[204] According to data obtained by the Transactional Records Access Clearinghouse from the Executive Office of U.S. Attorneys, Justice Department. Cases prosecuted or declined represent only a portion of the total number of complaints alleging federal criminal civil rights violations in each district in a given year. Several steps prior to this decision narrow down the number of complaints actually received to those considered worthy of consideration.

investigation of the NYPD under new federal civil powers.[205] This announcement was later modified by Attorney General Janet Reno to an investigation to decide whether to open a "pattern or practice" investigation.[206] The scope of the investigation was not known at the time of this writing, but the investigation should certainly include police precincts renowned for abusive and corrupt behavior. The CCRB's semi-annual reports provide detailed information about each precinct's rate of complaints. In the January-June 1996 report, for example, the CCRB ranked precincts using the location of the incident and found that (adjusting for the uniform personnel at each precinct) the 44th Precinct in the Bronx, the 120th Precinct in Staten Island, and the 75th and 71st Precincts in Brooklyn ranked in the top ten in complaints per officer in both 1995 and the first half of 1996.[207] During the first six months of 1997, the 79th, 67th, and 73rd precincts ranked highest for location of incident.[208]

---

[205] Blaine Harden, "Civil rights investigation targets N.Y. Police," *Washington Post*, August 19, 1997.

[206] Justice Department press release, dated August 26, 1997.

[207] CCRB, January-June 1996, p. 29.

[208] CCRB, January-June 1997, pp. 100-101.

PHILADELPHIA

When the police are indistinguishable from the bad guys, then society has a serious problem.
— Philadelphia District Attorney Lynne Abraham[1]

Philadelphia's police are grappling with the latest of the corruption and brutality scandals that have earned them one of the worst reputations of big city police departments in the United States. The persistence and regularity of the cycles indicate that between the front-page news stories the city and its police force are failing to act to hold police accountable. The result is an undisturbed culture of impunity that surfaces and is renewed with each successive scandal, as each new generation of police officers is taught through example that their leadership accepts corruption and excessive force. As a result, police officers who should not have remained on the force have unlawfully injured and killed citizens, the city has paid enormous sums in settlements and awards to victims of police misconduct, and many minority communities are distrustful of police officers who too often act like criminals. The shortcomings of the department are reinforced by a police union that tirelessly defends officers accused of human rights violations and fights efforts at independent oversight.

The latest scandal, which emerged fully in 1995, involves officers primarily from the 39th District. As of mid-1997, five had been convicted on charges of making false arrests, filing false reports, and robbing drug suspects.[2] Officers raided drug houses, stole money from dealers, beat anyone who got in the way and, as a judge trying one of the ringleaders stated, generally "squashed the Bill of Rights into the mud."[3] Due to exposure of the officers' actions, thousands of drug convictions were under review as of the end of 1997, with between 160 and 300 cases already overturned because the suspects were arrested by officers known or

---

[1] Don Terry, "Philadelphia shaken by criminal police officers," *New York Times*, August 28, 1995.

[2] Michael Kramer, "How cops go bad," *Time* magazine, December 15, 1997.

[3] Mark Fazlollah, "From prison, ex-cops call offenses routine," *Philadelphia Inquirer*, May 12, 1996.

believed to have been involved in misconduct.[4] Following the revelations in the courtroom and press, staff in the police department's Internal Affairs Division (IAD) were transferred, apparently as punishment. No supervisors, and no one from the district attorney's office (which ignored warnings from the city's public defender's office, as early as 1989, that the fabricated justifications given by the officers to enter homes and conduct drug raids were identical in case after case), was held accountable.[5] In fact, the district attorney acknowledged in a January 1997 deposition that, "We have changed nothing in the office with respect to trying to guarantee that police officers are all going to be credible."[6]

The only positive aspect of this recent round of exposure of abuse is that Philadelphia finally agreed to major reforms. Because the city was faced with paying millions of dollars in civil settlements as a result of the 39th District scandal, it agreed to work with attorneys and local police abuse experts to reform the police department. On September 4, 1996, in a far-reaching court-monitored agreement, Philadelphia agreed to changes that, if implemented, could make the city's police department a role model for accountability. Although the overdue reforms were only agreed to under the threat of a class-action lawsuit, it is possible that the agreement will prevent serious abuse from recurring. An FBI official warns, however, "The history of these kinds of scandals is that cops go right back to acting as they always have when the dust settles, because the pressure they most feel is the pressure to produce results, the constant demand to get the job done."[7]

The September 4, 1996 Agreement

After six months of negotiations, an agreement was reached between the city of Philadelphia and civil rights organizations threatening to file a federal "pattern

---

[4] Mark Fazlollah, "Phila. ordered to report on police," *Philadelphia Inquirer*, March 28, 1997; Christopher McDougall, "Law and Disorder," *Philadelphia Weekly*, June 18, 1997. *Time* magazine reported the figure of one-hundred and sixty. Kramer, "How cops go bad, *Time* magazine, December 15, 1997.

[5] Interview with Brad Bridge, city public defender's office, August 20, 1996, and Ibid.

[6] McDougall, "Law and Disorder," *Philadelphia Weekly*.

[7] Michael Kramer, "How cops go bad," *Time* magazine, December 15, 1997.

and practice" class-action suit.[8] The agreement is based on an understanding that if the city fails to implement it, the class-action suit will go forward. The agreement, under the jurisdiction of U.S. District Court Judge Stewart Dalzell, provides for a two-year monitoring period by the court and lawyers from the involved groups. Mayor Edward Rendell, while insisting there was no "systemic" problem in the police force, acknowledged that the agreement was "the most ambitious anti-corruption program undertaken by the Philadelphia Police Department in its history."[9]

After a delay, the police department complied with part of the agreement, providing the plaintiffs' counsel with piles of documents related to police accountability, including abuse complaints. As of this writing, the attorneys were reviewing the information and preparing a database for further analysis. It is anticipated that the information will be made available to the public in some form.[10]

Among the agreement's other reforms, the city created an anti-corruption task force to review systemic problems in training, Internal Affairs Division (IAD) procedures, and internal discipline. The members of the task force had been appointed and were meeting informally as of this writing. The task force reportedly does not have subpoena power, but police officials have been instructed to comply with requests for information and documents.

The agreement called for the creation of an Integrity and Accountability Officer (IAAO), similar to an inspector general, to monitor and audit IAD and the Ethics and Accountability Division (EAD). In October 1996, James B. Jordan, former deputy city solicitor, was named to the new post. Jordan submitted his first report to the judge monitoring the agreement in November 1997 and gave a generally positive assessment of the IAD's reform progress.[11] He stated that there had been

---

[8] "An agreement to combat police corruption," *NAACP, Philadelphia Branch and Police-Barrio Relations Project, on behalf of themselves and their members v. City of Philadelphia,* Civil action no. 96-6045, September 4, 1996. The U.S. Justice Department is reportedly conducting an investigation into whether there is a "pattern or practice" of abuse by Philadelphia's police force. *See* introduction.

[9] Mark Fazlollah, "Major police reforms announced," *Philadelphia Inquirer,* September 5, 1996 and Ibid.

[10] Telephone interview, William Gonzalez of the Police-Barrio Relations Project, August 11, 1997.

[11] Mark Fazlollah, "Conduct report praises police," *Philadelphia Inquirer,* November 20, 1997; Joseph R. Daughen, "IAD gets high marks," *Philadelphia Daily News,* November 20, 1997.

"dramatic improvement[s] in the qualify of IAD investigations" and found that IAD's investigations were "meaningful and thorough."[12] He noted continuing deficiencies, including the IAD's failure to complete investigations within the seventy-five-day limit and long delays in implementing an off-duty policy, noting that "improper conduct and abuse of authority by off-duty police officers has been a significant problem...."

As part of the agreement, attorneys also submitted a report to the judge monitoring the pact in September 1997, and their assessment of the IAD's performance was less positive.[13] They gave the IAD a "C" grade – passing but not good. One of the attorneys stated, "[T]here are significant shortcomings in too many of the investigative files that we reviewed." He added that IAD investigators were "justifying the officers' actions where an independent analysis would find misconduct."[14]

The IAAO was tasked with helping to establish an "at-risk" officer list – identifying officers with repeated or serious citizen complaints and high numbers of use-of-force reports, in an effort to identify officers who repeatedly commit abuses and establish a system of retraining, psychological assistance and intensive supervision – but as of late 1997 the "at risk" system had not been created.[15]

The 1996 plan requires all police personnel to accept citizen complaints and notify IAD regardless of apparent merits or sources, thus removing the discretion exercised by some officers who choose not to accept some complaints.[16] IAD must also set up a hotline for anonymous complaints and make allegations by fellow officers a high priority, the agreement stated, "the department should commend, support and protect officers who truthfully report misconduct or corrupt activities of other officers."[17] There was not full agreement about whether IAD should

---

[12] Fazlollah, "Conduct report," *Philadelphia Inquirer*, November 20, 1997.

[13] Mark Fazlollah, "Police get a 'C' for reviews of citizen complaints," *Philadelphia Inquirer*, September 30, 1997.

[14] Ibid.

[15] Fazlollah, "Conduct report praises police," *Philadelphia Inquirer*, November 20, 1997.

[16] This new requirement was criticized by Jordan, who stated that it contributes in delays in investigating meritorious complaints. Ibid.

[17] September 4 Agreement, point 5.

investigate all cases where officers have used significant force; the city only agreed to have IAD investigate cases involving citizen injury leading to hospitalization, or in cases where the officer files a report after using a blackjack (a hand weapon typically consisting of a piece of leather-enclosed metal with a strap or springy shaft for a handle), baton, pepper spray or firearm. (This provision is imperfect, because officers do not always file use of force reports.) The agreement also instructs, or reminds, the IAD to use a "preponderance of evidence" standard when reviewing complaints. IAD is also instructed to complete investigations within sixty days and, where officers on probation are the subjects of complaints, within the probationary period. If this guideline were followed consistently, it would represent an enormous change from the lengthy investigations of the past – which typically ranged from three months to a year.[18]

The agreement also requires the department to revise its use of force reporting guidelines to require reports on the use of sprays or shocks, batons, fists, feet, the drawing or display of firearms, the use of carotid holds, neck grips, discharge of firearms, and any other degree of force resulting in visible or reported injuries to suspects or others. The attorneys also proposed eliminating the use of blackjacks, but the city ignored that recommendation in its response.[19]

After the agreement was announced, the Fraternal Order of Police, forever out of step with the concept of reform, stated that agreement was part of "ACLU's efforts to keep their boot on the throat of the police."[20]

Police Advisory Commission

The Police Advisory Commission (PAC), the city's external review agency, was created by an executive order issued by Mayor Rendell, under significant City Council pressure, on October 29, 1993, to investigate and publicly report on individual allegations of police misconduct and abuse, and broader issues of policy

---

[18] According to Prof. James J. Fyfe, who examined 277 complaints against PPD officers during 1989 and 1992, the mean time for IAD closure was 136 days. He also examined the time it took to complete investigations into five complaints against PPD Officer Michael Jackson; one was completed within the time limit (which was then seventy-five days), but the mean time for four earlier complaint investigations (during 1995 and 1996) was 326 days.

[19] According to the Bureau of Justice Statistics, only a handful of police departments, of any size, currently use blackjacks. Facsimile dated August 15, 1997.

[20] Michael Matza and Mark Fazlollah, "Measures get mixed reviews," *Philadelphia Inquirer*, September 5, 1996.

and procedure. PAC handles complaints alleging physical abuse, and verbal abuse that is related to ethnicity, race, or sexual orientation. The fifteen-member PAC is selected by the mayor and meets once a month; it had three investigators and two support staff as of August 1997.[21] In April 1998, its Executive Director Charles Kluge was fired amid criticism of the PAC's inadequate community outreach efforts and its focus on minor allegations in recent years, since the DeJesus case.[22] As noted in its fiscal year 1996 annual report, the PAC investigators have an average caseload of over thirty cases at any given time – more than double the caseload for Internal Affairs Division investigators.[23] The PAC is permitted to hold public hearings, subpoena witnesses and review police documents. It can recommend disciplinary action or departmental policy changes.

Unfortunately, the PAC has become the battleground between the Fraternal Order of Police and police reform advocates. As explained by City Councilman Michael Nutter, who backed the creation of the PAC, the reaction has been that if you support the PAC, you are against the police.[24] As part of this dynamic, the PAC has been forced to fight repeated lawsuits filed by the Fraternal Order of Police. In early 1995, in *FOP v. Commission,* the FOP claimed that PAC was illegally created and that it impermissibly interfered with the police department; the FOP later voluntarily dismissed its lawsuit. In the fall of 1995, seven of nine officers involved in the DeJesus case (*See* below) filed suit in state court to enjoin (or prohibit) the compulsion of their testimony at PAC public hearings in *DiPasquale v. City of Philadelphia, et al.*[25] The parties agreed to a compromise: the officers received a letter from the police commissioner stating that they were compelled to testify about the incident, thus obtaining immunity from their testimony being used in any

---

[21] Telephone interview, PAC Executive Director Charles Kluge, August 19, 1997.

[22] Mark Fazlollah, "City police advisory panel dismisses its director," *Philadelphia Inquirer,* April 14, 1998.

[23] PAC Annual Report, Fiscal Year 1996, p. 5.

[24] Interview, August 20, 1996.

[25] As described in PAC Annual Report, Fiscal Year 1995, pp. 21-22.

subsequent criminal proceedings against any of the officers.[26] The FOP again filed suit, this time against the city, calling for it to dismantle the PAC.

Over a two-year period, between July 1, 1994 and June 30, 1996, the PAC received 256 citizen complaints; 197 of the complainants were African-American or Latino, roughly 77 percent.[27] Physical abuse or abuse of authority was the claim in 186 of the complaints.

The PAC operates with a six-month statute of limitations, which unreasonably limits complainants' ability to utilize the commission. Many victims of police abuse have been abused during an arrest and may face criminal charges (including "cover charges" such as resisting arrest or assaulting an officer often used by officers who commit violations). Most attorneys will advise alleged victims of abuse not to file an abuse complaint until criminal charges are disposed of, which can take much longer than six months. The statute of limitations thus prevents complainants from filing a complaint with the PAC. Advocates have suggested revising the deadline by adding a stipulation that a complaint may be filed up to "thirty days after the criminal case is completed." The FOP's local president, Richard Costello, in response to this suggestion, reportedly stated, "This whole commission [the PAC] is a felony in progress."[28]

The second PAC report (the first report described police stress problems) created an enormous stir in examining the death of Moises DeJesus.[29] On August 21, 1994, 25th District officers were called to the 3600 block of North Third Street to subdue a large, allegedly drug-crazed man, DeJesus. DeJesus was placed in a lieutenant's car, then moved to another squad car. Witnesses claimed it seemed he could not breathe, so he kicked out a window and put his hand outside; his hands were hit with an officer's baton. Then he allegedly put his head out the window and was hit by Officer Donna Young. Accounts vary, but he got out of the car somehow, and was allegedly hit again by Officer Young. He was finally handcuffed

---

[26] During the DeJesus hearing, about 300 FOP members reportedly shouted "Kangaroo! Kangaroo!" "Kangaroo courts" are tribunals disregarding or parodying existing principles of law. Paul Maryniak, "Philadelphia's story," *Pittsburgh Post-Gazette,* April 21, 1996.

[27] According to the 1990 federal census, African-Americans make up nearly 40 percent of Philadelphia's population, and Hispanics of any race make up about 5.5 percent.

[28] Michael Matza, "Police panel time limit is assailed," *Philadelphia Inquirer,* September 13, 1996.

[29] PAC report on DeJesus case, December 19, 1995, PAC. NO. 94-0015.

and put in a police wagon and taken to Temple University Hospital; he never regained consciousness and died three days later. PAC members agreed with the city medical examiner who found that drugs were the main cause of death but that excessive force was another, or the "straw that broke the camel's back."[30]

The PAC found that Young had used excessive force and lied, and it recommended a thirty-day suspension for lying. For five other officers – Nicholas DiPasquale and Chris DiPasquale (brothers), William Suarez, Raul Malviero, and Michael Page – the PAC recommended a fifteen-day suspension for "lack of candor." The PAC found the investigations by East Division detectives and the IAD inadequate. For example, when IAD had questioned the officers involved, its investigators allegedly allowed the officers' lawyers to respond to questions directed at the officers themselves, and failed to ask for details or pose follow-up questions. According to the PAC report, "[T]he interviews before Internal Affairs in this case were not calculated to exact the details concerning what had happened but constituted an effort by Internal Affairs to accept the officers' version without question or doubt rather than gather the facts....The investigation by Internal Affairs of this incident was totally inadequate."[31]

Although the police commissioner's report in response to the PAC findings missed the deadlines required in the PAC's charter, he and Mayor Rendell strongly rebuked both PAC and its report once they did respond.[32] The police commissioner disagreed with PAC's conclusion that excessive force was used or that any force used contributed to DeJesus's death, and stated, "I'm going to disregard the findings of the Police Advisory Commission."[33] The FOP called for federal prosecutors to investigate PAC, alleging it had failed to provide some of its witness statements to the police department.[34] The PAC acknowledged its investigation was not perfect, since it was the first major case it had handled, but stood by its findings.

---

[30] Ibid., p. 16.

[31] Ibid., p. 17. One member of the PAC dissented from the report's findings.

[32] Response to Police Advisory Commission, in re: Moises DeJesus, No. 94-0015, April 29, 1996.

[33] Jeff Gammage, Mark Fazlollah and Richard Jones, "8 city officers suspended in DeJesus case," *Philadelphia Inquirer*, April 30, 1996.

[34] According to police abuse expert Prof. James J. Fyfe, the police department's own investigations do not usually include witness statements but instead contain investigators' paraphrased accounts of what witnesses are alleged to have told investigators.

Police Commissioner Neal did acknowledge that officers were not truthful with the PAC; medical experts found that DeJesus had been hit in the head, yet none of the officers on the scene had admitted to witnessing any blows. Neal stated, "I will not, however, condone a lack of candor or 'code of silence' for any reason, even for the purpose of protecting a fellow officer."[35] The police commissioner handed out ten-day suspensions to eight officers for "lack of candor" – reportedly the least severe penalty for failing to cooperate – which the officers appealed.[36] According to the PAC, this is the first time Philadelphia police officers had been disciplined for following the code of silence.[37] In reaction to the penalties, FOP lawyer Jeffrey Kolansky rejected the notion that there is a code of silence but declined to answer a reporter's questions on the topic.[38] In February 1997, DeJesus's family received $250,000 from the city in a settlement; the city officially admitted no wrongdoing but acknowledged possible flaws in training.

Following the DeJesus case, the PAC began convening lower-profile panels hearings, with five such hearings taking place between February and September 1997.[39] PAC staff note that responding to the FOP's legal challenges and holding hearings in each case has resulted in a backlog of cases. They also assert that the PAC's mandate, which calls for broader policy investigations and reports, cannot be fulfilled with current staffing levels.[40]

There is no linkage between the City Solicitor's office (when a civil lawsuit against the police is handled) and the PAC, with the city solicitor's staff claiming that there is no notification because the PAC is an "independent" office.[41]

---

[35] Response to PAC report, p. 47.

[36] Sec. 1.11 of Police Disciplinary Code, cited on p. 48 of response.

[37] PAC annual report, Fiscal Year 1996, p. 2.

[38] Jeff Gammage, "Code of Silence: A barrier to truth in investigations of police," *Philadelphia Inquirer*, May 5, 1996.

[39] PAC Annual Report, Fiscal Year 1996, p. 2, and telephone interview with PAC Executive Director Charles Kluge, August 19, 1997.

[40] Ibid.

[41] Telephone interview with Shelly Smith, City Solicitor's office, January 27, 1997. Smith was contacted by telephone after correspondence from Human Rights Watch went unanswered; she stated she would respond in writing, but no letter has been received.

Incidents

Philadelphia police, like many other police forces around the country, has earned the reputation of having a very tough attitude toward suspects, responding with violence to what officers perceive to be disrespect. As the PAC executive director told Human Rights Watch, "You cannot talk back to Philly cops."[42] Many human rights abuses stem from this attitude, as verbal sparring quickly turns into physical attacks by police.

Officer John Baird: One product of the flawed internal affairs system was John Baird. In his deposition relating to the 39th District scandal, Baird stated, "I never feared an IAD investigation....[T]he way things were done, I mean, unless there is [sic] a whole lot of witnesses against you and a whole lot of pressure, you're not ever going to get found guilty of anything."[43] Baird had been the subject of more than twenty complaints prior to pleading guilty to robbery, obstruction of justice and conspiracy to violate civil rights charges, yet received perfect job ratings throughout his career.[44] In fact, investigations into Baird's actions, and those of other officers from the 39th District, only took place after one of the victims, Arthur Colbert, pursued his brutality and other complaints with the assistance of the public defender's office and, eventually, the U.S. Attorney's office.[45] Colbert was stopped by Baird and another officer in February 1991 and allegedly beaten and threatened with death if he did not provide information about his drug stash, even though there was no indication that he was dealing drugs.[46] The investigation and prosecution

---

[42] Interview, August 20, 1996.

[43] In the U.S. District Court, for the Eastern District of Pennsylvania, re: 39th Police District, Civil Action Nos. 95-1575, etc..

[44] Mark Fazlollah, "Flawed reviews give top ratings to rogues," *Philadelphia Inquirer*, April 21, 1996; Joseph A. Slobodzian, "2 ex-officers plead guilty to corruption," *Philadelphia Inquirer*, March 31, 1995.

[45] Michael Kramer, "How cops go bad," *Time* magazine, December 15, 1997; Stephen Braun, "Scandal rocks Philadelphia cops over corruption, planted evidence," *Chicago Sun-Times*, October 23, 1995. Several other suspects also alleged that Baird beat them. Ibid.

[46] Colbert filed a civil lawsuit against the city and settled for $25,000.

of the officers proceeded only when one of the accused officers in the 39th District provided key information, and indictments soon followed.[47]

In his deposition, Baird claims an internal affairs detective told him he was not interested in doing civil rights cases because they are difficult. He claimed that he would never deny hitting people to IAD investigators. "On my brutality complaints, if I hit them, I usually hit them. I didn't deny if I hit them."[48]

Officer Rodney Hunt: Even though the city believed Officer Rodney Hunt was unsuitable to serve as a police officer, he remained on the force due to an arbitrator's decision. In two off-duty incidents in 1990 and 1991, Hunt shot and killed two men and wounded a woman bystander.[49] On November 4, 1990, Hunt shot Sean Wilson several times after intervening in a bar fight; the bar was known as a drug trafficking and gambling center. Witnesses said that Wilson, who had shot at Hunt as the argument escalated, was shot while he was lying face down on the ground. According to a police abuse expert who examined the physical evidence, the witnesses were supported by the evidence: nine shots hit Wilson in the back, buttocks, and the back of the upper thigh, and forensic examination reportedly showed that at least one bullet hole in Wilson's jacket was made by a gun held right next to Wilson's body.[50] Two of the exit wounds indicated that

---

[47] Kramer, "How cops go bad," *Time* magazine, December 15, 1997. It was reported that the officer only cooperated because he had retired and thus did not have access to a union representative. McDougall, "Law and Disorder," *Philadelphia Weekly.*

[48] May 23, 1996 deposition.

[49] Jeff Gammage and Mark Fazlollah, "Arbitration offers a route back to work," *Philadelphia Inquirer,* November 21, 1995; U.P.I., "Off-duty officer involved in second fatal shooting," March 25, 1991; and case files of off-duty actions provided to Prof. James Fyfe by IAD, who compiled case studies entitled "Philadelphia police off-duty actions: Complaints and Shootings," May 23, 1994. According to the police counsel with the deputy city solicitor, IAD is responsible for investigating off-duty incidents "in the same manner as any other investigation. A complete investigation is conducted and an analysis and conclusion on the substance of the complaint is made. It is reviewed by supervisors and a final determination is made by the Police Commissioner." Letter to Human Rights Watch from David Domzalski, police counsel, deputy city solicitor, November 6, 1996.

[50] According to case files of off-duty actions provided to Prof. James Fyfe by IAD, who compiled case studies entitled "Philadelphia police off-duty actions: Complaints and Shootings," May 23, 1994.

Wilson's body was pressed against a hard surface, such as the ground, when the bullets exited his body.[51]

Hunt had been the subject of other complaints, including one in 1990 claiming that when at a restaurant at 2:45 a.m., he and another officer got into a verbal dispute with other patrons.[52] Hunt arrested a man at the restaurant for allegedly possessing a knife (it is unclear whether the knife existed); one of the complainants was convicted for disorderly conduct, and the complaint against Hunt was not sustained even though he allegedly pointed a gun at one of the complainants.

After the Sean Wilson shooting, Hunt was allowed to keep his gun. On March 24, 1991 – as a grand jury was investigating Wilson's death – Hunt killed another person in an off-duty dispute at a party.[53] At a party at 3:00 a.m., Hunt shot a man and wounded a woman bystander after intervening in a fight. He claims two men had guns (one of the men admitted firing at him), so he shot fourteen times at them. In July 1991, Hunt was indicted for the Wilson shooting and dismissed from the department. (Prior to the indictment, he had perfect performance ratings.) He was acquitted of the murder charges, but Wilson's mother received $900,000 from the city in a settlement.[54] He challenged his dismissal by arguing that it was a political reaction to publicity over the shooting and that the shooting was justified.[55] An arbitrator agreed, and Hunt was reinstated in 1994 with back pay; as of August 1997, he was working in the 2nd District.[56]

---

[51] Ibid.

[52] IAD 90-058.

[53] Gammage and Fazlollah, "Arbitration offers a route back to work," *Philadelphia Inquirer*, November 21, 1995; U.P.I., "Off-duty officer involved in second fatal shooting," March 25, 1991; and case files of off-duty actions provided to Prof. James Fyfe by IAD, who compiled case studies entitled "Philadelphia police off-duty actions: Complaints and Shootings," May 23, 1994.

[54] According to press reports, the City Solicitor's office warned in a memo recommending the settlement, that "facts in this case are potentially horrendous" and that Wilson's wounds would "shock and appall" any jury. Gammage and Fazlollah, "Arbitration offers a route back to work," *Philadelphia Inquirer*, November 21, 1995.

[55] Ibid.

[56] Telephone inquiry, August 11, 1997.

Officer Christopher Rudy: On November 20, 1993, Rudy was on duty but visiting friends and drinking alcohol at a warehouse.[57] There had been a dispute between the warehouse owner and Frank Schmidt, who was accused of stealing items from the warehouse. Rudy, who was friendly with the owner, was at the warehouse when Schmidt telephoned about the dispute. Schmidt said he was afraid of the owner, but Rudy told him to come to the warehouse to talk about the theft. Said Rudy, "I'm a cop. Ain't nothing going to happen."[58]

Schmidt reportedly told internal affairs investigators that once he arrived, the warehouse gates were locked behind him, he was beaten, and the warehouse owner put gun to his head as Rudy watched and poured beer over Schmidt.[59] Then Rudy started beating Schmidt in the face. Schmidt was threatened throughout the ordeal; the warehouse owner allegedly said he would cut his hands off with a knife and threatened to have warehouse workers rape him. Schmidt reported the incident to the police, but Rudy was not questioned for seven months, and he denied everything. While at the warehouse with Schmidt, Rudy had ignored police calls, including one "officer needs assistance." Rudy got a twelve-day suspension for failing to take police action, inflicting physical abuse, providing false statements, and conduct unbecoming a police officer, and was returned to active duty.[60]

Officer Carl Holmes: On January 5, 1992, Holmes saw a man urinating in an alley. He tackled him and, IAD confirmed, stepped on his groin, kicked him, slammed him into a car, and hit the man on the head.[61] Commissioner Neal suspended Holmes for twenty days, but Holmes appealed and got the punishment

---

[57] Mark Bowden, "Major offenses by Philadelphia cops often bring minor punishments," *Philadelphia Inquirer,* November 19, 1995; off-duty case information provided to Professor Fyfe.

[58] Bowden, "Major offenses by Philadelphia cops," *Philadelphia Inquirer*, November 19, 1995.

[59] Ibid.

[60] Ibid.

[61] Bowden, "Major offenses by..." *Philadelphia Inquirer* and Fyfe files. The man had just had a kidney transplant and needed to urinate frequently.

reduced to five days. According to the Philadelphia police department's personnel office, he has since been promoted to lieutenant.[62]

Holmes had at least one other complaint against him, in 1990.[63] When he was a new recruit with nineteen days on the force, he was at a bar at 1:30 a.m. and got into a fight with another bar patron. The complainant alleged that Holmes (6'3" and 290 lbs.), grabbed him by the throat and slammed his head into a car. The complainant was treated at a hospital and had a small abrasion on the back of his head and on his neck. The complaint was not sustained, in part because the complainant had been drinking, but it was reported that investigators apparently asked no questions about Holmes's drinking the same evening.[64]

Police Administration/Internal Affairs Unit

The Philadelphia Police Department has approximately 6,000 officers. The police commissioner is only allowed to appoint a handful of the top commanders; the rest of the force is made up of civil service employees. Some analysts conclude that the police commissioner lacks total control because it is difficult to fire anyone in the department, because the rank and file members are backed by civil service laws.

In March 1998, John F. Timoney became Philadelphia's police commissioner. Timoney, who is a veteran of the New York City Police Department, has a mixed record on dealing with police abuse.[65] Timoney reportedly stated that the Mollen Commission, which looked into police corruption and brutality in New York, made officers ineffectual in their duties and opposed criminal prosecution for perjury of officers involved in the 30th District scandal.[66]

The department's internal affairs units were reorganized in 1998, with the Internal Affairs Division, the anti-corruption Ethics Accountability Division, and the Headquarters Investigative Unit all becoming part of the Internal Affairs

---

[62] Human Rights Watch telephone inquiry, August 11, 1997.

[63] Fyfe files, "Philadelphia police off-duty actions: Complaints and Shootings," May 23, 1994.

[64] Ibid.

[65] Mark Fazlollah and Henry Goldman, "New police chief out to repeat success," *Philadelphia Inquirer*, March 8, 1998.

[66] Ibid.

Bureau.[67] Human Rights Watch was advised that IAD's staffing levels are "considered confidential."[68] It was anticipated that the September 1996 agreement would lead to an increase in IAD personnel. Its complaint form is in many languages, including Spanish, English, Korean and Chinese.

The Internal Affairs Division has often, in effect, protected officers who committed human rights violations by failing to properly handle abuse complaints. A November 1995 investigative series in the *Philadelphia Inquirer*, for example, found that Internal Affairs sustained only a small percentage of complaints, but that even when there was punishment, it was minimal; and in rare cases where officers were fired, they often got their jobs back through arbitration. Similarly, a June 1993 task force report looking into allegations of brutality at a September 1991 demonstration found that the IAD investigation was "structurally and systemically slanted against persons complaining of police abuse."[69] And in a more recent review of IAD files, police abuse expert and Temple University Prof. James Fyfe looked at internal investigations of off-duty incidents of shootings, beatings, and domestic violence. Fyfe found the files were very disorganized, items were missing, and IAD's findings were often flawed.[70]

In 1996, the Internal Affairs Division reported that it received a total of 221 citizen complaints alleging physical abuse.[71] Ninety-three investigations of physical abuse were completed during the year (from previous years and 1996), resulting in eighteen complaints sustained. In 1995, Internal Affairs Division reports that it received a total of 223 citizen complaints alleging physical abuse, with eleven sustained.[72] In 1994, there were 170 citizen complaints alleging physical abuse. Of

---

[67] Mark Fazlollah and Thomas J. Gibbons, Jr., "Timoney hires a special counsel," *Philadelphia Inquirer*, April 3, 1998.

[68] Letter to Human Rights Watch from David Domzalski, police counsel, deputy city solicitor, November 6, 1996.

[69] "Final report of the Citizens' Advisory Group," June 1, 1993, p. 1.

[70] Human Rights Watch interview, August 19, 1996.

[71] The Police Advisory Commission and IAD may receive the same complaints and may investigate them concurrently.

[72] Prior to 1996, information regarding completed investigations by category of allegation were not provided.

the investigations into physical abuse allegations completed during 1994, seventeen were sustained.

The IAD reports contain racial breakdowns, showing that African-Americans and Latinos make up a disproportionate percentage of complainants, but complainant information is not provided for each type of complaint. Of the total of 577 citizen complaints of all types in 1996 (including physical abuse, abuse of authority, harassment, verbal abuse, lack of service, criminal and other misconduct), African-American and Latino men and women made up 67 percent of complainants.[73] IAD does not provide breakdowns by police district, and no information is provided to the public, including the complainant, regarding what disciplinary sanctions, if any, were applied in sustained cases.

When a complaint against an officer is sustained, he or she may appeal to the Police Board of Inquiry, a three-officer panel that can overturn the IAD finding. And if that appeal is unsuccessful, an officer may submit the case to arbitration, which often leads to the overturning or lessening of a disciplinary sanction.

Beginning in 1993, IAD maintained a secret "at risk" officer list to monitor officers who were the subjects of repeated complaints or civil lawsuits alleging abuses.[74] The list contained the names of twenty-one officers, who together had accumulated 180 complaints and had been responsible for actions resulting in about $2 million in lawsuit settlements against the city. The "monitoring" appears to have been entirely passive, yet the FOP protested it anyway, saying that it was used against Officer Leo Ferreira to deny him a promotion. Ferreira reportedly had been the subject of twenty civilian complaints during a nine-year career – more than any other officer on the force. Only one of the twenty had been sustained, after the complainant passed a lie-detector test. The sixteen-year-old complainant reported that Ferreira banged his head into a pole, dragged his face across the sidewalk, and slammed his face into a car. Ferreira was suspended for two days and appealed the penalty. In 1994, the city paid $50,000 in a civil lawsuit to a lawyer who alleged Ferreira beat him after the lawyer won dismissal of charges against a suspect the officer had arrested. In his defense, Ferreira says, "I have a wall with commendations on it."[75]

---

[73] According to 1990 census figures, African-Americans and Latinos made up approximately 45 percent of Philadelphia's population.

[74] Mark Fazlollah, "Police track 'at risk' officers," *Philadelphia Inquirer*, December 31, 1995.

[75] Ibid.

Another name on the same "at risk" list was Willie Robinson, who had thirteen complaints, with one sustained. He was suspended for four days in March 1995 after allegedly putting a gun to the heads of North Philadelphia residents after someone threw water at his patrol car. Robinson allegedly kicked several residents in the head, neck and back while they were on the ground. Robinson unintentionally left his radio on during the incident and was recorded on tape telling one of the men he would "blow his fucking brains out." He appealed his suspension.[76] Also on the list was Detective Kenneth Rossiter, who allegedly had nine complaints, four of which were sustained (the high rate indicating very strong proof of abuses). Despite his record, he was promoted just after a 1990 incident during which he allegedly beat a seventeen-year-old; the complaint against him in this case was reportedly sustained in 1993.[77]

The IAD is notified by the City Solicitor's office when a civil suit is filed alleging police misconduct, and the IAD allegedly "monitors" the lawsuit's progression. Yet the filing of a civil suit alleging excessive force, or even the settlement or award in favor of the plaintiff, will not necessarily lead to an IAD investigation. The City Solicitor's office claims that if a very egregious case is settled, IAD might investigate.[78]

IAD findings, when against the officer, are often not used in performance reviews of officers. The often superficial reviews, known as "the halo effect" (a phrase used by the police, apparently indicating angelic behavior), rarely mention brutality charges against the officer, even if sustained. A *Philadelphia Inquirer* article reported that between 1990 and 1995, the police department fired eighty-two officers it found had committed robbery, rape, extortion, drug trafficking and other offenses. One was convicted of murder. Until they were fired, seventy-nine of the eighty-two officers received top performance ratings.[79] In the first report by the anti-corruption czar James B. Jordan, he noted that the performance evaluation system was "a joke."[80] He reportedly examined the files of one hundred officer who had been fired and found that all but one had previously received top ratings.

---

[76] Ibid. No further information regarding his appeal was available.

[77] Ibid.

[78] Telephone interview, City Solicitor's office, Shelly Smith, January 27, 1997.

[79] Fazlollah, "Flawed reviews give..." *Philadelphia Inquirer*, April 21, 1996.

[80] Fazlollah, "Conduct report praises police," *Philadelphia Inquirer,* November 20, 1997.

John Baird, of 39th District scandal fame, reportedly received perfect job ratings for fourteen years during which he allegedly beat and robbed suspects, planted drugs and gave perjured testimony.[81] Undeserved perfect ratings undermine efforts by the department to fire officers, since they are able to win reinstatement, in part, by referring to their glowing records.

In another case, Officer Michael Jackson received satisfactory performance ratings and a "[K]eep up the good work" comment in his October 1996 written evaluation.[82] Yet during the previous year, Jackson had been the subject of three outstanding citizens' complaints (one leading to a civil lawsuit), had been told his conduct was insubordinate, and had been suspended for thirty days for being absent without leave.[83]

In fact, city officials maintain it is nearly impossible to get rid of problem officers in the rare instances when the department gets tough with them. Since 1992, punishment imposed by the department has been lessened or reversed two-thirds of the time or in fifty-two of seventy-eight cases that went to arbitration; in twenty of the fifty-two, the arbitrator completely reversed the department's punishment.[84] Police Commissioner Neal stated that it is "frustrating to no end, these people who are being fired are people who should not be part of the department."[85] Said Mayor Rendell, "We will fire them and fire them and fire them."[86] An FOP lawyer, Thomas Jennings, told a reporter that beating the city in arbitration, where, as of 1995, paralegals often represented the city, was "like taking

---

[81] Ibid.

[82] From report on Officer Jackson by Professor Fyfe as part of *Greene v. Jackson, et al,* U.S. District Court, Eastern District of Pennsylvania, 2:97-cv-03931, filed June 9, 1997. There was a settlement in this case, for an undisclosed amount, which was entered into in February 1998. Telephone inquiry, U.S. District Court Clerk, May 19, 1998.

[83] The same sergeant who gave the good performance evaluation was the superior who warned Jackson that he was insubordinate.

[84] Gammage and Fazlollah, "Arbitration offers a route back to work," *Philadelphia Inquirer,* November 21, 1995.

[85] Ibid.

[86] Ibid.

candy from a baby."[87] And an attorney who represents the city in these cases said the city devotes little in the way of legal expertise and allows itself to be "outgunned" by the FOP lawyers.[88]

Civil Lawsuits

In the absence of other means of accountability, civil lawsuits have been relied upon by victims of police abuse, and the city has paid huge amounts in settlements and awards during the past several years. During a twenty-eight-month period ending in November 1995, the city paid $20 million; at least another $7 million was paid in a three-week period in July and August 1996, according to press reports.[89] (Human Rights Watch requested these figures directly from the City Solicitor's office in a September 1996 letter and in several phone calls, yet as of November 1997, and despite promises, no figures were forthcoming. A September 19, 1997 letter from the deputy city solicitor states that the information would be "forwarded to you as soon as that information is compiled.") The city is self-insured, so it puts aside a reserve in case of suits against police in each year's budget. They have exceeded the reserve in the past, requiring "local legislation" to supplement the funds.[90]

During 1996, the city paid approximately $13 million, reportedly enough to pay for 250 officers for a year.[91] And in January 1997, the city paid a $1 million settlement to the estates of two men killed during the May 1985 police fire-bombing

---

[87] Mark Fazlollah, "Repeated efforts at reform have gone little beyond paper," *Philadelphia Inquirer*, November 23, 1995.

[88] Gammage and Fazlollah, "Arbitration offers a route back to work," *Philadelphia Inquirer*, November 21, 1995.

[89] Mark Fazlollah, "Philadelphia settles or loses $20 million in lawsuits," *Philadelphia Inquirer*, November 17, 1995. In August, a fifty-four-year-old grandmother falsely imprisoned for three years as a result of one of the 39th District raids received a $1 million settlement. A man falsely imprisoned for three and one-half years – including fourteen months on death row – after police framed him for two murders (and he was prosecuted by former prosecutor Edward Rendell, now mayor of Philadelphia) received $1.8 million from the city. Mark Fazlollah, "A wrongful jailing costs the city a million," *Philadelphia Inquirer*, August 16, 1996.

[90] Telephone interview, Shelly Smith, City Solicitor's office, January 27, 1997.

[91] Mark Fazlollah, "Bill soars on police claims," *Philadelphia Inquirer*, November 21, 1996.

of the homes of black activists who were members of the group MOVE.

The civil suits, and threats of even more costly suits, have been the one available tool to force the city to address police accountability problems seriously. The suits have also, through the years, revealed important information about abuses by officers and the shortcomings of IAD. Unfortunately, they have had little effect on individual officers. Former Officer Baird said in his deposition that he had no idea what happened in any of the civil cases alleging abusive treatment by him, except for one that went to trial; he estimated that he had been sued about six times. The case that went to trial resulted in an award to the victim of $50,000.[92]

Criminal Prosecution

Criminal prosecution of police officers accused of using excessive force is rare in most cities, and Philadelphia is no exception. Advocates claim that the district attorney's office relies too heavily on flawed IAD investigations when deciding whether to prosecute a case, rather than interviewing involved parties. In the DeJesus case, for example, the district attorney reportedly chose not to prosecute based on statements taken by IAD, not through her office's own inquiry. And the district attorney reportedly was notified by the public defender's office in the late 1980s about possibly fabricated evidence by 39th District officers, yet apparently ignored the reports.

Just as disturbing as the 39th District scandal is the apparent unwillingness on the part of the district attorney's office to revise clearly flawed practices. The district attorney has reportedly refused to meet with local advocates to discuss ways to prevent another police scandal, and the city has failed to create a special unit within the D.A.'s office to deal with corruption and brutality.[93] The D.A.'s office, like most we investigated, does not even acknowledge tracking cases against officers and reportedly cannot tell the public how many officers have been indicted or convicted for on- or off-duty crimes.[94]

D.A. Lynne Abraham explains that the problem with criminal prosecution of bad cops is that if they are acquitted, they almost always win their jobs back through arbitration. For this reason, her office looks for rock-solid cases.[95]

---

[92] Baird deposition, May 23, 1996.

[93] McDougall, "Law and Disorder," *Philadelphia Weekly.*

[94] Telephone inquiries, district attorney's office, August 1997 and May 26, 1998.

[95] Gammage and Fazlollah, "Arbitration offers a route..." *Philadelphia Inquirer.*

Federal prosecution is also rare. In 1996, of the two cases decided by federal prosecutors for the federal district containing Philadelphia (Eastern District of Pennsylvania), none was prosecuted (presented to a grand jury to seek an indictment). Between 1992 and 1995, fifty cases were considered, of which thirty were prosecuted.[96]

The Justice Department is also considering "pattern or practice" civil injunctions against certain police departments or units within certain police departments (as mandated by in the 1994 crime bill). When a "pattern or practice" investigation of the NYPD was announced in August 1997, press reports indicated that Philadelphia had already been investigated by the Justice Department.[97] As part of its "pattern or practice" powers, the Justice Department may investigate certain districts or precincts with a disproportionate number of complaints or a pattern of abuse. Several advocates in Philadelphia noted that certain districts receive a disproportionate number of complaints, such as the 24th, 25th, and 26th districts, according to PAC reports, and may be deserving of a "pattern or practice" investigation.

Unions

The Fraternal Order of Police is exceptionally powerful in Philadelphia – some say it has more control of the police than the Police Commissioner does. As described above, the FOP has persistently opposed the creation and operation of the PAC.

Yet footing the bill for accused officers has threatened to bankrupt the FOP's legal fund.[98] As a result of the flurry of allegations and cases against Philadelphia officers, and the accompanying expense, the FOP announced on February 1, 1996 that it would no longer pay legal fees for "crooked" officers.[99] The fact that the

---

[96] According to data obtained by the Transactional Records Access Clearinghouse (TRAC) from the Executive Office of U.S. Attorneys, Justice Department. Cases prosecuted or declined represent only a portion of the total number of complaints alleging federal criminal civil rights violations because several steps prior to this decision narrow down the number of complaints actually received to those considered worthy of consideration.

[97] Blaine Harden, "Civil rights investigation targets N.Y. Police,"*Washington Post*, August 19, 1997.

[98] Richard Jones and Mark Fazlollah, "FOP will no longer pay legal bills for rogue officers," *Philadelphia Inquirer*, February 2, 1996.

[99] Ibid.

FOP has now declared that it has drawn some limits in its defense of officers involved in serious misconduct and abuse is a positive development.

But the FOP has also opposed the creation of an "at risk" or early warning system for officers against whom many complaints are lodged. The FOP has claimed, "We're not opposed to the concept [of an early warning system] at all, not in the least....There are bad cops and we are not out to protect bad cops."[100] Yet its position on early warning is similar to its actions relating to the PAC, in which challenges to the PAC's existence and operations coincide with assertions that FOP is not opposed to some sort of civilian review.

Union lawyers accompany officers to virtually every major disciplinary hearing, with their fees drawn from a city-funded legal services plan among the most generous in the nation. A spokesman of the FOP, who did not wish to be named, told Human Rights Watch that in 90 percent of disciplinary challenges, FOP wins after a finding that the officer was "improperly dismissed."[101] In many cases, the city is paying several times to support problem officers. Taxpayers fund the officers' legal services plan, they pay for enormous civil lawsuits lodged against police officers who are poorly trained, supervised or disciplined, and they pay the officers' salaries, while the worst officers are not doing legitimate or useful police work at all.

[100] Fazlollah, "Police track ..." *Philadelphia Inquirer.*

[101] Telephone interview, August 21, 1996.

PORTLAND

Portland has been touted by some as a community policing model, and its civilian review agency functions better than most examined by Human Rights Watch. Problems do remain, however. Its police force – the Portland Police Bureau – has at times violated the rights of its citizens, and accountability for officers who commit abuses has been lacking in some cases.

The department has made some progress in the past few years. During the 1980s and early 1990s, a lack of trust in the police department developed among minority communities; the department's records on internal review and training were poor and civilian review was ineffectual. In 1985, two Portland officers were reinstated by an arbitrator after they were fired for selling "Don't Choke 'Em, Smoke 'Em" t-shirts on the day of the funeral of Lloyd "Tony" Stevenson, who reportedly had been killed by a police chokehold. In 1990, the internal affairs unit had a unique record in dealing with complaints of excessive force – of seventy-eight complaints, the division found in favor of the officer involved in every case. The next year, two cases were upheld – out of seventy-six – a sustained rate of less than 3 percent.

During the same period, the civilian review board (the Police Internal Investigations Auditing Committee, or PIIAC) was singled out by national police abuse experts as an example not to follow in creating review boards. Members of the PIIAC resigned in protest because of the committee's ineffectiveness. Said one, "[I]t's a failure because it's not meant to do anything.... It's totally ineffective. It's absolutely ignored."[1]

According to press reports, between mid-1989 and mid-1991, training was canceled by police officials because they did not want to take officers off the streets.[2] There was no training on firearms or on tactics in dealing with combative subjects. Police officers went fourteen months without firearms qualification tests, even as the department switched to high-capacity semi-automatic weapons. The more advanced weaponry was supposed to be used in response to violent gangs in the city, but instead some officers used the guns on the mentally ill and drug suspects who did not comply with their commands.[3]

---

[1] John Snell and Phil Manzano, "Police watchdog lacks bite?" *Oregonian*, April 28, 1992, quoting Sandy Herman, who resigned from PIIAC in 1990.

[2] John Snell and James Long, "Deadly force," *Oregonian*, April 26, 1992.

[3] Ibid.

Incidents

Officer George Fort: The career of Portland police officer George Fort illustrates almost every aspect of poor police management.[4] He was hired in 1981 in Multnomah County and transferred into the Portland Police Bureau, even though his job application showed a history of the use of excessive force and disrespect for authority in previous law enforcement jobs. The city paid large civil settlements because of his behavior, he had a large number of complaints, other officers believed he had problems with racial minorities, and he earned a reputation among fellow officers as overly aggressive. Still, he remained on the force for years before retiring in 1996.

According to personnel records made part of a civil lawsuit filed against Fort, his application for employment with the Multnomah County Sheriff's Department listed his reason for leaving the U.S. Marshal's Service after five months: "I didn't go along with the marshal's favoritism and the job itself was...Boring!"[5] He said he could not remember his immediate supervisor's name. He did acknowledge that in 1971 he was asked to resign from the Bryan (Texas) Police Department, stating, "Police chief considered my use of force in an arrest excessive and asked me to resign; I was later exonerated and found out that I was used as a scapegoat to appease the 'Raza Unida' Party's charges against the BPD."[6]

In 1982, a woman sued Fort for using excessive force after a November 1981 incident in Multnomah County when Fort pulled her vehicle over. She asked not to be put in his squad car in front of her neighbors, and he allegedly twisted her arm behind her back, pushed her to the pavement, shoved her face into the ground, and yanked her to her feet using her handcuffed wrists.[7] She was charged with resisting arrest – charges that were later dismissed – and the civil jury found that Fort had falsely arrested the woman.[8] She received a $36,892 award from Multnomah

---

[4] Maureen O'Hagan, "Good cops, bad cop," *Willamette Week,* May 31 - June 6, 1995; civil complaint, *Mary Verghies v. George Fort and City of Portland,* Civil No. 93-1306-ST, filed October 19, 1993, U.S. District Court, District of Oregon.

[5] O'Hagan, "Good cops, bad cop," *Willamette Week,* May 31 - June 6, 1995; employment application attached to civil complaint, *Mary Verghies v. George Fort and the City of Portland.*

[6] Ibid.

[7] Ibid.

[8] O'Hagan, "Good cops, bad cop," *Willamette Week,* May 31 - June 6, 1995.

County. Fort, along with many others, was then transferred to the Portland Police Bureau, without review, after the city annexed a portion of Multnomah County.

Once with the Portland police, Fort was reportedly the subject of twelve citizen complaints, most of them involving allegations of excessive force; the department did not investigate some of the complaints, but three complaints alleging rude behavior were sustained (one of which was filed by fellow officers and paramedics).[9] In January 1993, Fort and his trainee stopped Mary Verghies's vehicle and she alleged abusive treatment by the officers in a civil lawsuit.[10] According to Verghies's court documents, Fort had attacked detainees in a consistent way since at least 1988, twisting and at times breaking arms, dragging detainees on the ground, or using abusive language in five different incidents.[11]

Still, the public information officer at the time, C.W. Jensen – who later became the head of the internal affairs unit – noted that Fort had received twenty commendations during his career with the bureau.[12] A sergeant who worked with Fort had a different opinion. He stated that, "[H]is [Fort's] own peers have complained about him....about the way he deals with the public."[13] The same sergeant stated that another sergeant asked that Fort not be transferred to a traffic unit, because his officers told the sergeant that "there's a real problem with George that way," apparently meaning that he frequently became violent during traffic stops and that "he knows how to work a supervisor....[H]e's extremely con-wise in that nature. He'll agree to anything during counseling session and then go do any...do what he wants."[14]

---

[9] According to the affidavit of expert witness D.P. Van Blaricom, witness for the plaintiff, attached to civil complaint, *Mary Verghies v. George Fort and the City of Portland.*

[10] Civil complaint, *Mary Verghies v. George Fort and City of Portland.* According to the city's Risk Management office, Verghies lost her civil case against Officer Fort in 1996. Telephone inquiry, April 27, 1998.

[11] Civil complaint, *Mary Verghies v. George Fort and City of Portland;* O'Hagan, "Good cops, bad cop," *Willamette Week,* May 31 - June 6, 1995.

[12] O'Hagan, "Good cops, bad cop," *Willamette Week,* May 31 - June 6, 1995.

[13] According to the affidavit of expert witness Donald Van Blaricom, witness for the plaintiff, attached to civil complaint, *Mary Verghies v. George Fort and the City of Portland,* quoting Sgt. Al Akers of the PPB.

[14] Ibid.

Fort was sued repeatedly for alleged abuse.[15] The city paid one plaintiff $500,000 in 1998 after Fort allegedly broke her arm in 1989; the civil jury found that he had falsely arrested the woman.[16] Fort's behavior should have triggered a command review, and may have in 1990, but there is no record of what happened, if anything. Jensen commented, "We haven't been documenting the reviews as well as we could."[17] During the deposition for one of his civil cases, Fort was asked if the police department had ever given him attention, training, or psychological assistance after complaints and he said they had not.[18] Fort chose to retire in August 1996.[19]

Officer Douglas Erickson: On July 19, 1993, two officers shot twenty-seven times at Gerald Frank Gratton as he fled from a bus in North Portland; the bus driver had complained that Gratton and his brother were acting unruly.[20] He was struck by the bullets in the back and the arm, and a bullet grazed his head; he survived. Gratton, an African-American, had a gun in his waistband, but did not pull the gun or use it during the incident.

The case demonstrated how difficult it can be to dismiss officers from the police force. Police Chief Charles Moose dismissed one of the officers, Douglas Erickson, who had reportedly fired twenty-three of the shots, after determining that he had broken department rules because Gratton was not endangering anyone when Erickson opened fire. It was reportedly the first time the department had disciplined

---

[15] According to civil complaint, *Mary Verghies v. George Fort and the City of Portland.*

[16] O'Hagan, "In the end it was George Fort's mouth, not his muscles, that got the Portland police officer in trouble,"*Willamette Week*, February 25, 1998.

[17] O'Hagan, "Good cops, bad cop," *Willamette Week*, May 31 - June 6, 1995

[18] According to Fort's deposition in civil complaint, *Mary Verghies v. George Fort and the City of Portland.*

[19] According to the Portland Police Bureau's personnel office, Human Rights Watch telephone inquiry, December 8, 1997. According to an IAD representative, because Fort was originally hired by the county, his retirement was probably not affected by his record while on the Portland force, and presumably he enjoyed full benefits and pension. Telephone interview, Capt. Bill Bennington, IAD, January 23, 1998.

[20] John Snell, "Moose fires policeman for extreme use of force," *The Oregonian*, October 9, 1993.

any officer for his or her role in a shooting.[21] But in May 1995, Erickson was reinstated by an arbitrator, who found that Erickson was justified in using deadly force because the suspect had a gun and was acting in a threatening manner, even though Gratton was shot while running away and never shot the gun that was in his waistband.[22] Erickson remains on the force.[23] The major Portland daily newspaper wrote in an editorial: "The arbitrator's conclusion that faulty tactical judgment by a police officer does not justify his dismissal on grounds of unjustified use of deadly force demonstrates extraordinary legalistic tunnel vision. The ruling screams for reanalysis of the rules by which police performance is judged in this city."[24]

A grand jury reviewed the shooting and declined to indict Erickson on any criminal charges. The jurors did take the unusual step of asking the district attorney to write to the police chief, expressing the jurors' concern about Erickson's behavior which, they found, "was not consistent with the high standards we expect the Portland Police Bureau to maintain."[25]

Erickson had been the subject of citizen complaints before the shooting. On March 4, 1992, he allegedly broke Charles VanMeter's nose and cheekbone after kicking him twice in the face during an arrest. VanMeter filed a complaint with the bureau, and Erickson's commander (who was Charles Moose before he became chief) sustained the excessive force complaint; his finding was overturned by then-Chief Tom Potter.[26]

Fatal shootings of mentally ill women: In August 1994, two mentally ill women were shot and killed by Portland and suburban police officers in two

---

[21] Ibid.

[22] Editorial, "Setback for police, public," *Oregonian*, May 5, 1995.

[23] Telephone inquiry, PPB information office, April 22, 1998. According to Portland's Copwatch, a citizen police accountability advocacy group, Erickson's arbitration cost the police union approximately $100,000.

[24] Editorial, *Oregonian,* May 5, 1995.

[25] John Snell, "City to fire officer in shooting," *Oregonian*, October 9, 1993..

[26] Ibid.

incidents, because they allegedly posed a threat.[27] One wielded a knife and the other pointed a fake handgun. Following the shootings, there was a debate over the absence of nonlethal, intermediate weapons to deal with deranged people. Mental health professionals are used to "talk down" mentally ill people in Portland, but they are not called until the situation stabilizes so they are not put in danger, which means that they can only be used when a crisis has subsided – in both cases in August 1994, officers claimed that there had been no time to call for mental health professional assistance.

Nathan Thomas shooting: On January 16, 1992, Nathan Thomas, age twelve, was taken hostage in his home.[28] Officers fired when the intruder threatened to kill Thomas, killing them both. Thomas's parents chose not to sue the city, but instead to use their son's memory to push for police reforms. The City Council hired a consultant, Pierce Brooks, to look independently at the shooting. He recommended the creation of an inspector's office outside the police bureau's internal investigations office to analyze extraordinary incidents such as shootings. No such office was created.

Civilian Review

Portland's citizen review mechanism, the Police Internal Investigations Auditing Committee (PIIAC), was created in 1982.[29] City Council members make up PIIAC, with investigations conducted by PIIAC 's citizen advisors, who are volunteers drawn largely from neighborhood associations. They do not conduct independent investigations of complaints received by PIIAC, but instead meet once a month to hear appeals from citizens dissatisfied with police internal investigations of their complaints and to perform random audits of internal investigations and review all closed use of force cases. Their review is limited to determining whether

---

[27] Erin Hoover and Nena Baker, "Police and deadly force: looking for middle ground," *Oregonian*, August 26, 1994.

[28] Editorial, "Remember Nathan Thomas," *Oregonian*, November 28, 1994.

[29] A ballot initiative was presented to voters in 1982 by opponents of citizen review. The police union opposed the City Council's creation of PIIAC and dramatically outspent PIIAC supporters. Nonetheless, the ballot initiative opposing PIIAC failed by the slimmest of margins. John Snell and Phil Manzano, "Police watchdog lacks bite?" *Oregonian*, April 28, 1992. According to its staff auditor, PIIAC is the only civilian review mechanism in the state of Oregon.

a complete and unbiased investigation took place, rather than deciding a case's merit. If they believe the investigation was sub-standard, they may request that IAD conduct a more thorough investigation. When an individual appeals IAD's findings, the PIIAC may re-examine the investigation and the city council may rule the complaint sustained. When a complaint is sustained, the police chief makes all disciplinary decisions.[30]

PIIAC's citizen advisors submit quarterly reports to the mayor and City Council, highlighting shortcomings in the investigations and abuse trends and recommending reforms. The reports also include IAD statistics regarding complaints received and their status.

After more than decade during which critics believed the PIIAC was not functioning properly and that investigations by the Internal Affairs Division (formerly Internal Investigations Division) were flawed, many in the community pushed for stronger independent review of the police. PIIAC was revised to give it a larger role in reviewing IAD investigations of complaints alleging police brutality or other misconduct. The mayor also appointed a full-time paid PIIAC staff auditor in July 1994.[31]

The PIIAC citizen advisors reviewed a total of twenty-seven appeals in 1995, affirming the police bureau's decision in fifteen; PIIAC's earlier reports did not always indicate which types of complaints were appealed.

In 1996, the advisors reviewed twenty-three appeals. They affirmed the PPB's findings in seventeen cases; two were returned to the IAD for additional investigation; two were pending at the time of the quarterly reports; and in two cases the PIIAC recommended that the PPB sustain the complaints that had not been sustained by IAD investigators originally, including one that was reported as a use of force complaint in the fourth quarter report. In that case, the IAD originally declined the case (which precludes additional investigation, formal findings, or record in the officer's complaint history) after a preliminary investigation, but the citizen advisors sided with the appellant, and PIIAC voted to accept the citizen advisors' recommendations, leading the IAD to send the case for adjudication. PIIAC cautioned the IAD against declining use of force cases, noting that one case it had randomly reviewed involved a man with serious injuries sustained during transport to jail, but because the arrestee's account differed with the officers'

---

[30] PIIAC is also overseeing the pilot mediation project, but only one case was mediated in 1996.

[31] Interview with PIIAC staff auditor Lisa Botsko, September 22, 1995.

accounts, the case was declined.[32] It was not possible to track PIIAC's review of all use of force complaints or their outcomes, because although PIIAC advisors monitored use of force investigations, their quarterly reports did not always separate appealed and monitored cases.

In 1997, PIIAC revised its reporting to incorporate breakdowns for all categories of appeals and reviews, and included brief descriptions of the allegations considered; community activists had long urged that this information be included.[33] During the first half of 1997, citizen advisors reviewed a total of ten new appeals, affirming IAD's findings in six cases, while three cases were pending and one appeal was withdrawn. And during the same period, the advisors monitored thirty-nine closed use of force investigations, showing that IAD had sustained just four – a roughly 1 percent sustained rate. In one case, a chokehold was used by an officer to subdue a suspect, and it was revealed that revised bureau policies had neglected to note that chokeholds were deadly force, meaning that IAD, rather than the district attorney and a grand jury, had made determinations on chokehold incidents until the first quarter of 1997.[34]

According to PIIAC and IAD, sometimes IAD receives a complaint, investigates the incident, and finds the officer responsible for an offense other than the one described in the complaint. For example, while an individual's complaint that an officer used excessive force may be found not sustained by the IAD, IAD will find another offense occurred, such as not reporting the use of force. PIIAC has expressed concern that while complainants receive notification that a complaint was sustained, IAD does not explain that the offense reported in the original complaint was not the offense sustained, thus misinforming the complainant.

PIIAC's mandate includes analysis of civil lawsuits against the police (risk management data), but it has expressed concern that IAD does not use these data as part of the "command review" for purposes of identifying officers with repeated complaints of abuse. In its May 1995 report, PIIAC wrote, "the Portland Police Bureau has assured the advisory committee that they [sic] are working on ways to better utilize risk management information; however, we see no evidence that the information is being used for command review purposes as mandated by the mayor's police/citizen accountability initiative....Command Review would be more

---

[32] PIIAC 1996 fourth-quarter report.

[33] Correspondence with Portland Copwatch, January 22, 1998.

[34] PIIAC 1997 first-quarter report.

effective if it could tap the information that comes through risk management."[35] A PIIAC spokesperson told Human Rights Watch that the agency receives copies of lawsuits filed against the city or bureau, alleging brutality or other misconduct by officers, and that certain names come up repeatedly in those suits.[36]

Some civilian review experts believe the PIIAC auditor system is working better than other cities' review boards with broader responsibilities. Civilian review expert Sam Walker sees "...the promise of some real progress with the auditor model that I don't quite see with other traditional civilian complaint review boards."[37] Even the police union has approved of PIIAC's approach. The former president of the local police union was quoted as stating, "It gives them [citizens] a window to look in there to be sure that this isn't a secret room...where we're in ninja suits conducting some secret cover-up. We can't cover up...."[38] Others believe that PIIAC fully utilizes its mandate but that, without the ability to receive initial complaints, conduct its own independent investigation, or recommend discipline in sustained cases, it is overly reliant on the police bureau's cooperation. These concerns are reinforced by the fact that, no matter what the PIIAC finds, the police chief is under no obligation to accept its findings, despite its neutral examination of the same facts reviewed by the IAD in making its determination.

Police Administration/Internal Affairs Division
In March 1995, the Internal Investigations Division was revamped and renamed as the Internal Affairs Division. Observers claim that its investigations have improved since that time.

During 1995, IAD received a total of 634 complaints, and in 1996 that number dropped to 506.[39] Use of force complaints made up approximately 19 percent of the total during both years (113 complaints in 1995 and ninety-nine in 1996). In the data provided by the IAD to Human Rights Watch, sustained rates and other disposition types are not broken down by complaint type, but out of the closed

---

[35] Ibid.

[36] Telephone interview with Lisa Botsko, PIIAC staff auditor, January 1997.

[37] National Public Radio's *Morning Edition*, July 31, 1997, quoting Sam Walker.

[38] Ibid., quoting PPB Sgt. Jeff Barker of the Internal Affairs Division. Another effort at transparency, led by community activists, resulted, in most cases, in the opening of appeal hearings to the public.

[39] According to data provided by IAD to Human Rights Watch, February 3, 1997.

complaints as of the end of 1995, less than 6 percent were sustained, and about 5.5 percent were sustained in 1996 (with many cases still pending). In U.S. cities, excessive force cases are commonly sustained at lower levels than other types of complaints (such as drug-related offenses, theft, procedure offenses), making it likely that the IAD is sustaining a very low percentage of excessive force cases. Indeed, according to the information provided in the PIIAC's first two quarterly reports for 1997, the IAD was sustaining about 1 percent of the use of force complaints it received. (*See* above.)

The department has initiated a "command review," an early warning system that triggers a review of officers who receive five complaints within a year, or three in six months, or two of the same type in six months. A review also occurs if two complaints are sustained in a year's time. Risk management data are not used in this review, even if a lawsuit is settled or judged in favor of a complainant alleging serious physical abuse. During 1997, fifty-five officers were reviewed.[40]

Chief Moose, in explaining why risk management data are not used, as suggested by PIIAC, stated, "I have not been able to determine a way to utilize Risk Management Information to label employees as problem officers. Tort claim notices do not contain all of the facts and I do not think it is fair to attempt to determine the involvement of an individual without examining all of the facts." The chief went on to cite attorney-client privilege as a barrier, stating, "without that information [protected by attorney-client privilege] I can only record that someone has complained about something and that it may involve some Portland Police employees in some way."[41] It is unclear to Human Rights Watch why a public document such as a tort claim, which describes alleged misconduct involving named officers, dates, and locations cannot be used to initiate a preliminary investigation by IAD staff, or why civil lawsuits settled or judged in favor of a plaintiff cannot be used as part of command review.

A grand jury reviews all shootings by Portland police officers. Precincts investigate more "minor" cases, with major cases staying with IAD. In PIIAC's April 1996 report, it states that police officials determined that IAD would handle all use of force complaints, rather than sending them to precincts for investigations. This change followed a recommendation by PIIAC based on its concerns regarding potential conflict of interest and consistency of investigative quality at the precinct-level. If a complaint is sustained, IAD sends it to the police chief for disciplinary action, if warranted. The chief can impose discipline short of dismissal, but only

---

[40] Telephone interview, Capt. Bill Bennington, IAD, January 23, 1998.

[41] December 20, 1995 memo to Mayor Vera Katz from Chief Moose.

the mayor can fire an officer.[42] No officer was dismissed as a result of an excessive force incident during 1997.[43]

An IAD representative states that files are purged after a year, except in sustained cases, and officers can request a purge of sustained complaints after five years.[44] He claimed that most supervisors do not want to deal with problem officers, and firing them is made difficult by civil service protections, so officers are transferred or ignored instead, or sometimes promoted.[45]

Civil Lawsuits

According to the city's Office of Risk Management, the city pays approximately $500,000 each year in police misconduct cases through settlements or jury awards.[46] According to press reports, twenty-five to thirty excessive force claims are filed each year.[47] The risk management office representative states that his office does not notify PIIAC when a lawsuit is filed, but does send copies of claims about the police to IAD, but he did not know what IAD does with the claims.[48]

For the city to defend the individual officers named in lawsuits, officers need to have engaged in alleged misconduct in the "course and scope of duty" and abuse cannot be "willful, wanton neglect of duty" or "outrageous." The office will defend some off-duty behavior, but only if it is connected to off-hours work.

---

[42] Interview with Lt. Ron Webber, IAD, September 21, 1995.

[43] Telephone interview, Capt. Bill Bennington, IAD, January 23, 1998.

[44] Interview with Lt. Ron Webber, IAD, September 21, 1995.

[45] Ibid.

[46] Telephone interview, Mark Stairiker, January 28, 1997. According to the police bureau's Capt. Bill Bennington, lawsuits against the police are not paid from the police budget. Telephone interview, January 23, 1998.

[47] See, for example, O'Hagan, "Good cops, bad cop," *Willamette Week.*

[48] Telephone interview, Mark Stairiker, January 28, 1997.

Criminal Prosecution

Criminal prosecution of officers for brutality-related offenses is rare in Portland, and federal criminal civil rights prosecution is rarer still.[49] Attorneys who frequently file police misconduct civil lawsuits say that local prosecution is usually for drug-related offenses or perjury, and no one had knowledge of federal prosecutions. In 1996, of the six cases decided by federal prosecutors for the federal district containing Portland (Oregon), five were prosecuted (presented to a grand jury to seek an indictment).[50] Between 1992 and 1995, sixteen cases were considered and none was prosecuted.

The Multnomah County District Attorney's office is unusual in that it reports keeping a log of criminal cases involving police officers as defendants. The office tracks police who are indicted or convicted. When, at Human Rights Watch's request, it checked for officers criminally charged during the previous two years, none were found.[51]

Unions

The Portland Police Association union is very powerful, according to attorneys, community activists and press reports. It publishes a newsletter, called "The Rap Sheet," that frequently defends officers accused of using excessive force and criticizes journalists or the PIIAC when they highlight problems in the bureau. Chief Moose was quoted in the newsletter's pages as backing Officer Fort, despite his abusive behavior. In July 1995, just after a newsweekly ran a story critical of Fort's treatment of citizens, Moose was quoted as stating that he encourages officers to tell Fort they support him, and says, "I told him [Fort] he has my support."[52]

---

[49] Capt. Bill Bennington of IAD was unaware of any federal prosecutions during 1997. Telephone interview, January 23, 1998.

[50] According to data obtained by TRAC from the Executive Office of U.S. Attorneys, Justice Department. Cases prosecuted or declined represent only a portion of the total number of complaints alleging federal criminal civil rights violations in district in a given year. Several steps prior to this decision narrow down the number of complaints actually received to those considered worthy of consideration.

[51] Multnomah County includes Portland and Gresham. Telephone inquiry with Tom Simpson, Multnomah County district attorney's office, June 3, 1997.

[52] *The Rap Sheet*, July 1995.

PROVIDENCE

Human Rights Watch chose to investigate Providence, Rhode Island and the surrounding area because the police have received an unusually large number of complaints per capita, according to a nationwide report published by the Justice Department in 1991.[1] The report cited three Rhode Island police departments as second only to New Orleans in the number of excessive force complaints. The relatively small communities – Providence, East Providence, and Pawtucket – each had complaint rates at least ten times as high as nearby Boston's.[2] Only six state police agencies were included on the Justice Department list, and Rhode Island's ranked highest for complaints, with a rate of complaints four to twenty-five times higher than any other state agency.[3]

Incidents

The case of Corey West: On January 17, 1995, white Providence Police officer Richard F. Ruggiero, Jr., a rookie, allegedly kicked Corey West, an African-American, repeatedly as he lay on the ground outside a nightclub; the encounter was captured on videotape and broadcast on local news programs.[4] Ruggiero told television reporters that he kicked West because he thought he was reaching for Ruggiero's nightstick. Ruggiero was suspended without pay after then-Chief Gannon saw the videotape. Gannon complained that Ruggiero's refusal to tell his side of the story to investigators did not help matters.[5]

---

[1] Criminal Section, Civil Rights Division, Department of Justice, "Police Brutality Study: FY 1985 - FY 1990," April 1991. Even though the report's methodology was questionable, and it lacked information necessary to reach any meaningful conclusions, it did indicate that the area may require additional scrutiny.

[2] The Pawtucket police department, with 144 officers, received more than twice as many complaints per capita as any state, county, or municipal law enforcement agency in eleven states.

[3] Ibid.

[4] Associated Press, "Officer taped kicking black man is suspended," *Boston Globe,* January 19, 1995; Associated Press, "Officer silent in R.I. kicking case," *Boston Globe*, January 20, 1995.

[5] Associated Press, "Officer silent...," *Boston Globe.*

Even with substantial publicity and with the encounter captured on videotape – and the chief's outrage over what he saw discipline of Ruggiero was not guaranteed. There was an administrative hearing, prompted by West's complaint, which was held even though police ought to have known – and were reportedly advised by West's attorney – that he was in jail in Massachusetts and could not attend.[6] Officers are automatically found "not guilty" if the complainant fails to appear at a hearing. After the hearing was canceled, Ruggiero, his lawyers, and Fraternal Order of Police (FOP, a police organization) members proceeded to the deputy chief's office (because the chief was out of town) to demand Ruggiero's reinstatement, according to press reports.[7] The deputy chief reportedly telephoned the chief, who was in Florida, and handed the phone to the FOP lawyer. The chief reportedly said Ruggiero would be reinstated, but without back-pay or lost seniority.[8] To his credit, Mayor Vincent A. Cianci, Jr. said that the hearing must be rescheduled for a time when West could be present.[9] On January 20, 1995, the FOP voted 328 to 39, expressing no confidence in Gannon and demanding his resignation because of his alleged undue haste in suspending Ruggiero.[10] Mayor Cianci responded to the dispute between the police union and the chief by stating, "Let the chips fall where they may. We will not tolerate excessive force. We will not tolerate any brutality. If the tape shows what I believe it shows, we will take action."[11] Ruggiero, who was still in his probationary period on the force when the videotaped kicking took place, was not dismissed.[12]

---

[6] John Castellucci, "Status of brutality case in dispute," *Providence Journal-Bulletin,* April 19, 1995.

[7] Ibid.

[8] Ibid.

[9] Ibid.

[10] John Castellucci, "Civil rights, religious leaders back suspension of officer," *Providence Journal-Bulletin,* January 24, 1995.

[11] "Officer silent," *Boston Globe,* January 20, 1995.

[12] John Castellucci, "Officer in kicking case sent to police academy," *Providence Journal-Bulletin,* May 9, 1995.

A federal civil rights investigation was initiated, and the case was brought before a federal grand jury in 1997. In November 1997, the grand jury deliberated for ten minutes and declined to indict Ruggiero.[13]

Frank Sherman: Frank Sherman, age sixteen, filed a brutality complaint after Foster (Providence County) police officer, Robert G. Sabetta, allegedly struck Sherman in the face with a flashlight, knocking out two teeth on January 9, 1992.[14] After an internal investigation, Sabetta was suspended with pay. He was indicted by a grand jury in March 1993, for assault with a dangerous weapon, and then suspended without pay. In April 1993, even though he was ordered to stay away from Sherman and his friends, Sabetta found them working on cars late at night at a garage in Foster, where he shot and killed Frank Sherman, his brother Charles, and friend Jeremy Bullock. The Shermans' cousin, Darryl Drake, was shot but survived.[15]

Sabetta was apprehended early the next morning and arraigned for three counts of murder, one count of assault with intent to murder and was tried in June 1994 and convicted. In October 1994, he was sentenced to three consecutive life terms plus twenty years. The trial judge called the killings a "deliberate, systematic and cold-blooded" execution.[16]

Civilian Review

There is no real civilian review mechanism in Providence. There is a Providence Human Relations Commission that is supposed to assist individuals with allegations of police misconduct to pursue their complaints, but it often merely serves as a screening office for the police department's Internal Affairs Bureau

---

[13] John Castellucci, "FBI probes kicking incident as possible civil rights violation," *Providence Journal-Bulletin,* February 1, 1995;"US jury acquits Providence officer," *Associated Press*, November 8, 1997, [Wire Service].

[14] Jerry O'Brien, "3 youths slain in Foster," *Providence Journal-Bulletin,* April 15, 1993. Although this incident took place beyond the city of Providence, but within the same county, it is included here because of the chilling effect this type of attack on brutality complainants may have on other alleged victims of abuse in the region.

[15] Ibid.

[16] Associated Press, "Ex-officer who killed 3 in R.I. is sentenced to serve 50 years," *Boston Globe*, October 5, 1994.

(IAB).[17] Many community activists believe that the commission is biased in favor of officers, and that it does not really have the mandate or will to act as an external review agency.

When the commission receives a complaint it is logged, and the complainant fills out a form that is notarized.[18] The complainant then speaks with commission staff, and if the commission deems the complaint credible it is passed to IAB. IAB investigators then interview the officer involved, and the sergeant in charge decides whether a hearing is warranted.

The hearing officer, a lieutenant or higher-ranking officer, is chosen by the police chief, and hearings are held at the courthouse. The accused officer, a Fraternal Order of Police (FOP) representative, the complainant (with an attorney, if desired), and witnesses are present, with a format similar to a trial. The officer, alleged victim and witnesses give their accounts and the hearing officer makes a guilty or not guilty finding. The chief reviews the investigation files and hearing officer's summary, and the chief decides whether he agrees with the hearing officer's finding. A letter should then be sent from the Providence police department to the complainant, advising him or her of the outcome.

A representative of the Human Relations Commission told Human Rights Watch that a legitimate complainant will pursue his or her complaint through any delays, and noted that if a complainant fails to appear at the hearing, the subject officer is found not guilty automatically. She stated that the commission receives some complaints referred by the police department, but some are sent directly to IAB and the commission is not advised. She did not have an estimate for the number of hearings held and did not know how, or if, IAB keeps track of allegations, substantiations, or repeat offenders on the force.[19]

The commission's representative repeatedly told Human Rights Watch that the Providence police force was not very abusive, and suggested investigating other nearby communities instead. She stated that the oversight "process" is worth it, even if Providence officers are not disciplined for misconduct.

In the absence of real civilian review, local advocates, particularly the American Civil Liberties Union (ACLU) of Rhode Island and DARE (Direct Action for Rights and Equality), have taken a very active role in assisting abuse victims and highlighting abuse trends. The ACLU, for example, logs each complaint it receives

---

[17] Interview with Pat Buchy, Providence Human Relations Commission, August 3, 1995.

[18] Ibid.

[19] Ibid.

and sends complainants an ACLU complaint form, and if in Providence, the completed complaint form also goes to the Human Relations Commission. They also provide an ACLU pamphlet, "Your rights and the police," explaining basic legal concerns. The pamphlet is in English, Spanish, Portuguese, Laotian, and Cambodian. When the complaint forms are returned, ACLU staff review them and decide which cases should be raised with the police chief. Despite this systematic, responsible, and informative method of reporting the most serious abuses to the police department, ACLU staff noted in 1995 that they rarely received notification from any police officials about whether specific allegations against police officers were investigated or any action taken.[20]

DARE, which closely monitors allegations of police abuse, particularly against the African-American community, told Human Rights Watch that it receives about a complaint a day about the police, and that in 90 percent of cases referred to the police department they received no response.[21] DARE contended, moreover, that complainants are intimidated or treated rudely when they attempt to file complaints at police stations.[22]

Community groups complain that the police department is excessively secretive.[23] Indeed, activists have been attempting to obtain files concerning citizen complaints, investigations, and disciplinary actions from the Providence police department for the past seventeen years.[24] In an effort to obtain information about IAB procedures and activities, DARE and the ACLU filed a lawsuit in May 1995, two years after initially requesting files about investigations. The city solicitor claimed that civilian complaints, internal investigation files and disciplinary actions

---

[20] Interview with ACLU staff, August 2, 1995.

[21] Interview with Conteh Davis, DARE, August 3, 1995.

[22] DARE also conducted a survey that appeared to confirm serious distrust of the police in many communities, with 400 people stating that they had been harassed or brutalized by police officers. Karen A. Davis, "Police officials see no problem with the process for complaints," *Providence Journal-Bulletin*, March 19, 1997.

[23] It is worth noting that Providence's police department was the only one that refused to respond in any manner to a January 1998 letter of inquiry sent by Human Rights Watch to all fourteen police departments examined in this report.

[24] Bruce Landis, "Despite challenges, police-brutality complaints remain sealed," *Providence Journal-Bulletin*, May 18, 1997.

were not public information.[25] The solicitor contended that DARE was entitled only to internal hearing officer reports if the names of the complainant and officer were deleted. The ACLU argued that the city's stance undermined the intent of open records law, and called it obstructionist. In June 1996, a Superior Court judge ruled in favor of DARE, finding that the police department had to make unedited records of complaints public, including results of hearings and reports on disciplinary actions. Superior Court Judge Stephen J. Fortunato questioned the city's lawyer, stating, "[T]ell me how it would be an unwarranted invasion of personal privacy to disclose the name of a police officer who performs his or her duties in public, who has one of the most visible and important jobs in this society, and now has been determined to have brutalized somebody. What is the privacy interest there, and why would the city want to protect the name of that individual?"[26] The State Supreme Court ordered a stay of the Superior Court order in July, after the city appealed the Superior Court decision.

Police Administration/Internal Affairs

According to Sgt. Robert Bennett, the Internal Affairs Bureau (IAB) has three investigators to handle complaints against the 435-member force.[27] Bennett estimates that the IAB receives about fifty to sixty complaints each year alleging verbal or physical abuse by police officers.[28] IAB complaint forms are only in English, with the department considering translation into Spanish. The department conducts no outreach advising residents about how to file a complaint. According to the IAB, the police department is the primary recipient of complaints, not the Human Relations Commission. When asked about reports of dissuasion efforts by officers receiving complaints about fellow officers, Bennett stated that officers might "get into dialogue" when asked for complaint forms.[29] According to IAB, the

---

[25] Mike Stanton, "Providence police sued to open brutality files," *Providence Journal-Bulletin*, May 9, 1995.

[26] Landis, "Despite challenges, police-brutality complaints remain sealed," *Providence Journal-Bulletin*, May 18, 1997.

[27] Interview with Sgt. Robert Bennett, August 3, 1995 and telephone interview with Sergeant Bennett, January 27, 1997.

[28] According to press reports, the IAB reported thirty-five complaints were filed against the police, alleging brutality or other misconduct, during 1995.

[29] Telephone interview with Sergeant Bennett, January 27, 1997.

complaint forms exist because of a 1973 court order requiring they be made available. (The complaint form provided to Human Rights Watch during our 1995 visit was precisely the same as the form required by the 1973 consent decree.) The IAB has not published any public reports, but was working on its first annual report in January 1997: it was unclear whether it would be made public.[30]

The IAB uses a photo book of black and white photos to help complainants identify accused officers. Once the officer is identified, he or she is notified of the complaint and is required to respond to the allegations. The IAB representative noted that in fifteen years at IAB, he has never heard an officer admit guilt. He was unable to provide the sustained rate for excessive force complaints, but estimated that no more than 5 percent of those accused who made it to the hearing process were actually subjected to disciplinary measures. The chief has discretion to impose suspensions up to two days, but more serious disciplinary actions must be approved during a bill of rights hearing with a police union representative, department representative, and a "neutral party" (another police officer). According to the IAB representative, officers usually prevail in bill of rights hearings, meaning that serious discipline is rarely applied.

IAB claims that complaint investigation files are only maintained until hearings are completed, and explains that the ACLU and DARE will have to settle for hearing officers' summations. Unsubstantiated complaints are reportedly kept in officer's file for two years, then discarded. IAB states that it notifies a complainant of the closure of his or her case by certified mail.

If an investigation has not already been conducted, the IAB does initiate an investigation when the City Solicitor's office notifies it an officer has been named in a lawsuit.[31] IAB sometimes works with the FBI when the FBI directly receives complaints involving the Providence police force, but IAB does not pass complaints that could be prosecutable under federal criminal civil rights statutes to the FBI.[32] However, IAB and the police department are not necessarily made aware of criminal charges filed in surrounding communities against Providence police officers. For example, Officer James J. Rodger was indicted on seven counts of assault with a dangerous weapon for pointing his loaded pistol at a group of teenagers. He was arrested by Pawtucket police for the February 1992 off-duty

---

[30] Ibid.

[31] Ibid.

[32] The IAB representative was aware of one federal civil rights prosecution involving a police officer.

incident, and filed for disability five days later.[33] According to reports, several other police officers had been granted disability pensions while facing criminal charges, even though, according to the city solicitor, officers suspended without pay should not be eligible for benefits.[34]

During a ride-along with a Providence police sergeant, he told Human Rights Watch that some complaints against officers are well founded, but most are not.[35] The sergeant stated that lawyers file false claims against officers, that most complaints are false, and officers are punished wrongly. He then described a really good officer who is now serving a five-year sentence and said he should not have been punished. The sergeant was apparently referring to an officer, Michael J. Newman, who was convicted in 1991 on federal criminal civil rights charges for beating a prisoner who was handcuffed to the bars of his cell.[36] The sergeant repeatedly mentioned that officers only fear a federal inquiry, not investigations by IAB.

Civil Lawsuits

The City Solicitor's office does not have readily available figures on police misconduct cases, but the City Solicitor, Charles Mansolillo told Human Rights Watch that he knows the amount of settlements paid in abuse cases is less than $1 million a year because the city is self-insured and has a $1 million budget for all claims against the city, including accidents.[37] He estimated that the city pays, at most, $200,000 in police misconduct suits annually, with some of that consisting of previous years' structured settlement, with payments extended since the 1980s. The IAB investigates cases involving police officers for the City Solicitor's office. Mansolillo estimated that at least 50 percent of cases that go to juries are found in favor of city.[38]

---

[33] Thomas Frank, "Patrolman facing charges gets pension," *Providence Journal-Bulletin*, October 15, 1992.

[34] Ibid.

[35] Ride-along, August 4, 1995.

[36] "Officer's sentence attacked by union," *Boston Globe*, December 8, 1991.

[37] Telephone interview, Charles Mansolillo, City Solicitor, January 28, 1997.

[38] Ibid.

Mansolillo also suggested that the reason there are not many lawsuits is because the police department makes a real effort to train and re-train. He stated that few of the sixty or so complaints filed with IAB each year end up as civil lawsuits.

Criminal Prosecution

Despite the Justice Department's own statistics showing the Providence area as problematic in terms of civilian complaints of excessive force, prosecutions of officers there are rare. In a summary of civil rights prosecutions (noting charges, indictments, pleas, convictions and acquittals) between October 1991 and July 1996, as compiled by the Justice Department's Civil Rights Division, no Rhode Island case appears.[39] In March 1998, a Providence police officer was indicted on federal criminal civil rights charges in relation to two separate beatings in 1995 and 1996; he reportedly was the first Providence officer indicted on federal civil rights charges since 1991.[40] According to a police department spokesman, the department had no record about one of the incidents.[41]

In 1996, of the thirteen cases decided by federal prosecutors for the federal district containing Providence (Rhode Island), none was prosecuted (i.e., presented to a grand jury to seek an indictment).[42] Between 1992 and 1995, 164 cases were considered, of which three were prosecuted.

---

[39] Civil Rights Division, "Official Misconduct Cases," provided to Human Rights Watch September 16, 1996.

[40] Jonathan D. Rockoff, "Providence patrolman indicted for alleged assaults," *Providence Journal-Bulletin*, March 28, 1998; Rockoff, "Patrolman denies civil rights violations in 2 alleged assaults, *Providence Journal-Bulletin*, April 2, 1998; Richard Dujardin, "Police officer charged with taking money from department funds," *Providence Journal-Bulletin*, May 5, 1998.

[41] Rockoff, "Providence patrolman indicted for alleged assaults," *Providence Journal-Bulletin*, March 28, 1998. An IAB representative refused to provide Human Rights Watch with specific information about the cases, citing the state's "bill of rights" for officers. Telephone inquiry, May 26, 1998.

[42] According to data obtained by TRAC from the Executive Office of U.S. Attorneys, Justice Department. Cases prosecuted or declined represent only a portion of the total number of complaints alleging federal criminal civil rights violations in each district in a given year. Several steps prior to this decision narrow down the number of complaints actually received to those considered worthy of consideration.

Unions

The Fraternal Order of Police in Providence is very powerful. The Ruggiero/West case, described above, was not the first time the FOP had resisted strong action by police leaders against Providence police officers caught being abusive on videotape. On January 13, 1992, three officers were suspended after a videotape aired on local television, showing a high school student, accused of assaulting an assistant principal, being restrained by two officers and struck with a baton by a third. After viewing the videotape, Mayor Cianci called for the officers' immediate suspension with pay, stating, "We're not going to have another Los Angeles here," referring to the televised beating of Rodney G. King the previous year.[43] The FOP president immediately labeled the suspensions "an overreaction" and asserted that the officers had acted properly. He warned that the suspensions would send a signal to the "criminal element [to] mess with the police."[44]

---

[43] Ken Mingis and Laura Meade Kirk, "Police's use of force at issue," *Providence Journal-Bulletin,* January 14, 1992.

[44] Ibid.

SAN FRANCISCO

The 2,000-person San Francisco police department is supervised by a civilian Police Commission. Civilian complaints of abuse are investigated by the Office of Citizen Complaints (OCC) investigators who are not part of the police force. The city's population is not passive in the face of police misconduct. Despite this outside scrutiny, however, the police force has failed, at times, to hold officers who commit abuses accountable, and high-profile violations continue. According to a 1996 investigative report by the *San Francisco Examiner*, the city was paying large amounts in civil lawsuits following officer-involved shootings, but the officers were not being disciplined by the department, or criminally prosecuted.[1] The study compared police shootings per every one hundred murders: San Francisco officers shot fatally, on average, 4.1 people for every one hundred murders in the city between 1990-95, a higher rate than Los Angeles, New York, or Oakland.[2] About 75 percent of the people shot and/or killed in shootings by the police force between 1993 and 1996 were minorities or people in low-income areas.[3]

Following a high-profile death in custody of an African-American man in June 1995, relations between the city's residents and its police force soured dramatically. San Franciscans have a well-earned reputation for community activism and protests against perceived injustices, and have organized to express outrage over incidents of brutality. Describing community criticisms, the vice president of the police officers' union recently stated that the city is "...without a doubt the most difficult city in America to be a cop. Cops are finally saying: You know what? We've had it."[4]

---

[1] Seth Rosenfeld, "S.F. pays big when cops shoot civilians," *San Francisco Examiner,* December 29, 1996.

[2] Ibid. According to the report, the average number of civilians killed each year by police, per one hundred murders, 1990-95 were: New York 1.6, Oakland 2.2, Los Angeles 2.2, San Francisco 4.1, San Diego 5.3, San Jose 5.8. Although the methodology, which is used by the highly regarded Police Executive Research Forum (PERF), was criticized by police officials as flawed, PERF states that it shows how police use deadly force relative to the level of violence of the community.

[3] Rosenfeld, "S.F. pays big when cops...,"*San Francisco Examiner.*

[4] Mary Curtius, "Despite progressive policies, S.F. police, public at odds," *Los Angeles Times*, July 21, 1997.

Incidents

A 1996 investigative report by the *San Francisco Examiner* found that the city was paying large amounts in civil lawsuits following shootings but that the involved officers were not being disciplined by the department, or criminally prosecuted.[5] In the past twenty years, the department has found only one intentional, on-duty shooting unjustified – out of a total of one hundred – according to attorneys and police officers. That is, officers have been found justified 99 percent of the time. During the same period, the district attorney's office had not prosecuted any officer for an on-duty shooting, according to current and former prosecutors.

Officer Daniel Yawczak: The killing of Michael Acosta was a case where an officer put himself in harm's way against departmental guidelines and successfully defended his use of a firearm on that basis. On November 2, 1991, Officer Daniel Yawczak shot and killed Acosta.[6] With his gun drawn, Yawczak had chased two suspected purse-snatchers to an idling car in the Pacific Heights neighborhood, where he twice shot Acosta, who was sitting in the driver's seat; the men were unarmed. Yawczak claimed that he shot Acosta while standing in front of the car, ignoring police training by placing himself in harm's way; he initially claimed he jumped on the hood of the car and then shot at Acosta, but later reportedly recanted that part of his account.[7] Yawczak also originally stated that he was bumped by the car and shot the second time while seated on the ground; when a medical examiner disputed that part of Yawczak's account, and a witness reported seeing Yawczak run alongside the car and shoot, Yawczak stated that it was possible he had not shot from a seated position.[8] If these witnesses' accounts are to be believed, the second shot would have been an unjustified use of force.

A police department firearms board cleared Yawczak, and he told a reporter he was not punished by the department for the shooting. Acosta's family reportedly received $259,358 after a civil jury found in his favor and against the city and

---

[5] Rosenfeld, "S.F. pays big...," *San Francisco Examiner;* and Seth Rosenfeld, "Cops fail to police selves in shootings," *San Francisco Examiner,* December 30, 1996.

[6] Seth Rosenfeld, "Cops fail to police...," *San Francisco Examiner.*

[7] Ibid.

[8] Ibid.

police department.[9] (Inspector Yawczak was removed from a murder-for-profit scam investigation in 1994 and was subsequently investigated for leaking information and for other misconduct in the high-profile case.[10])

Sgt. John Haggett: In another case, the Police Commission apparently violated disciplinary guidelines after finding Sgt. John Haggett guilty of four offenses that should have led to dismissal, but instead giving him a six-month suspension.[11] Prior to this case, Haggett has an extensive history of misconduct according to press reports and a local police abuse monitor.[12] According to press reports, he had received two previous ninety-day suspensions for excessive force and was involved in the fatal shooting of an unarmed man, Edwin Sheehan, in 1995 which was being investigated by the FBI.[13] He was reportedly named in six brutality-related complaints, with four settled by the city for about $75,000 as of late 1996.[14] Haggett had also been the target of dozens of citizen complaints in his fourteen years on the force.[15] In late October 1996, Sheehan's widow reportedly filed a $10

---

[9] Ibid. The case was appealed and reached the U.S. Supreme Court which let the award stand. Jim Herron Zamora, "City will pay kin of man cop shot," *San Francisco Examiner*, March 4, 1997.

[10] "Foxglove chronology," *San Francisco Examiner*, November 7, 1997.

[11] Susan Sward, Bill Wallace, "Cop's Suspension May Violate Rules," *San Francisco Chronicle*, October 18, 1996. He was found guilty of arresting three people falsely, and using excessive force at a 1995 New Year's Day police raid on an AIDS benefit.

[12] Ibid., and inquiry with John Crew, ACLU of Northern California, May 26, 1998.

[13] "S.F. cop faces $10 million suit," *San Francisco Examiner*, October 30, 1996. There was no record of an indictment on federal criminal civil rights charges, according to a Human Rights Watch inquiry with the U.S. District Court clerk, October 28, 1997.

[14] Sward and Wallace, "Cop's Suspension May...," *San Francisco Chronicle*. One of the lawsuits was dismissed and another was pending.

[15] Ibid.

million wrongful death suit against Haggett.[16] As of late 1997, Sergeant Haggett remained on the force, according to the SFPD personnel office.[17]

   Officer William Wohler: The shooting of Brian Sullivan exposed serious weaknesses in homicide investigations of police and in internal review of the use of firearms. On July 15, 1993, Brian Sullivan was shot and killed by Officer William Wohler, at Sullivan's parents' home in the Excelsior District.[18] Sullivan had an unloaded shotgun on his bike when Wohler responded to an emergency call about him.[19] He was riding on a bicycle, away from Wohler in his car, and rode into his parent's garage and closed the garage door. Wohler reportedly opened fire through the closed garage door. He then followed Sullivan to a side yard, and as Sullivan started up a ladder to the roof, unarmed, Wohler reportedly fired twice; one bullet entered Sullivan's buttocks and traveled to his heart, killing him.[20] Although Wohler later stated he had never entered the side yard, his bullet casing was found near where a neighbor said she saw him stand and shoot up at Sullivan.[21]

   The investigation by homicide detectives was seriously botched, and Wohler was allowed to remain at the crime scene as investigators collected evidence.[22] A key statement by an eyewitness disputing Wohler's account was disregarded, as were ballistics tests that undermined the officer's version of what took place. Investigators were not persuaded even when Wohler was forced to change his story after a bullet casing was later found (not by investigators) that confirmed the key eyewitness's account. Wohler claimed that Sullivan was shot while he was in the garage. When Wohler was confronted with his own conflicting testimony, he told a homicide investigator, "You know, I'm not stupid. I've been around long enough

---

[16] Ibid.

[17] Telephone inquiry, SFPD personnel office, October 28, 1997.

[18] Seth Rosenfeld, "Inside story of a killing," *San Francisco Examiner*, July 23-25, 1995, three-part series.

[19] Rosenfeld, "Cop's shooting of young man cost City $295,000, raised troubling questions about the investigation," *San Francisco Examiner,* July 23, 1995.

[20] Ibid.

[21] Ibid.

[22] Ibid.

to know the way it works. And I mean, if I'm gonna leave a casing behind, I will cover myself, you know. I'm gonna say, 'Hey the guy made a furtive move' or 'Yeah, my gun accidentally discharged.' I mean, you know...."[23]

The internal weapons discharge review board determined that the shooting was justified, even though Wohler apparently had not followed administrative rules against endangering bystanders, nor had he exhausted all other reasonable means of apprehension before firing only in necessary defense.[24] Because the weapons discharge review board's proceedings were conducted in private, the members' reasoning is not known.[25] No criminal prosecution was pursued by the district attorney's office, which reportedly did not even interview Wohler.[26] The city paid $295,000 in an out-of-court settlement, one of the largest in the city's history in a police abuse case.[27] Wohler, who reportedly had been the subject of fourteen citizen complaints of misconduct during the five-year period preceding the Sullivan shooting, was not disciplined for his actions and was back on duty by January 1995. He retired with benefits in July 1996, days before a scheduled OCC hearing about the incident.[28] Even after his departure, however, the city continue to pay for his actions while on the force; in July 1997, a $65,000 settlement was reached with a man who alleged Wohler had beaten, stomped, and pepper-sprayed him in 1995 – two weeks after the Sullivan case was settled.[29]

---

[23] Ibid.

[24] Seth Rosenfeld, "Were proper police procedures followed that summer afternoon?" *San Francisco Examiner*, July 24, 1995.

[25] Ibid.

[26] Ibid. The district attorney's office claimed there was insufficient evidence to prosecute Wohler.

[27] Ibid. In 1986, the city was ordered to pay $23,000 to a woman who alleged Wohler used excessive force during a 1981 incident.

[28] Glen Martin, "Cop retires before inquiry into fatal shooting," *San Francisco Chronicle*, July 13, 1996.

[29] "City settles lawsuit alleging police brutality," *San Francisco Chronicle*, August 1, 1997; Thaai Walker, "2 families want cop fired," *San Francisco Chronicle*, July 26, 1995; Jane Meredith Adams, "S.F. police under microscope," *Sacramento Bee,* August 3, 1995.

After the Sullivan case, and the press attention it generated, the department changed its procedures for reviewing shootings, giving the Office of Citizen Complaints (OCC) and the Police Commission a larger role in the process.

Sgt. Joseph Weatherman: The department took years to dismiss a highly decorated sergeant, Joseph Weatherman, despite his long history of citizen complaints. He was the focus of many citizen complaints and was sued for the use of excessive force six times.[30] In 1992 he was suspended for sixty days for slapping and punching a suspect; on an earlier occasion, he had to perform community service for beating a youth during an off-duty incident.[31]   All along he was promoted.[32] He was finally dismissed in August 1994 for harassing a woman officer who had ended a relationship with him.[33]

Case of Aaron Williams: Aaron Williams died in police custody on June 4, 1995 after officers subdued him and sprayed him with pepper spray in the Western Edition neighborhood. He had resisted arrest as a burglary suspect, was bound with wrist and ankle cuffs, and may have been hit and kicked after he was restrained. He was placed face down in a police van and taken to a police station; upon arrival he stopped breathing.[34] Despite many deaths in custody following the use, and misuse, of pepper spray, police departments have resisted changing their policies guiding the use of the spray. When the spray is used in conjunction with the placement of the arrestee face down on his or her chest, as in the Williams case, positional asphyxia has occurred as the individual's breathing is restricted.[35]   The county

---

[30] Bill Wallace, "S.F. police hero may be dismissed," *San Francisco Chronicle*, August 22, 1994, and Wallace, "S.F. police officer fired for misconduct," *San Francisco Chronicle*, August 25, 1994.

[31] Ibid.

[32] Ibid.

[33] Ibid., and Bill Wallace, "Disturbing complaints of police misconduct," *San Francisco Chronicle*, September 12, 1994.

[34] Eric Brazil, "Watchdog wants S.F. cop fired," *San Francisco Examiner,* January 20, 1997 and Curtius, "Despite progressive policies...," *Los Angeles Times.*

[35] Arrestees suffering from asthma, high on drugs, or in psychiatric crisis are also at particular risk, according to an American Civil Liberties Union of Southern California report, *Pepper Spray Update: More Fatalities, More Questions,* June 1995.

coroner ruled that Williams died of heart failure brought on by acute cocaine poisoning.[36] An independent pathologist listed eighteen injuries that contributed to his death.[37]

Police acknowledged that department policy was violated by using spray twice (others say many more times) on Williams, and that officers did not monitor Williams's breathing as required. Furthermore, it was reported that officers placed a surgical mask over his face at some point during the incident, but the surgical mask was not found at the scene. Experts note that examination of the mask, which never should have been applied to someone who had been sprayed, would have provided key information about the sequence of events, depending upon whether spray was found on the inside or outside of the mask.

Three of the officers involved in the Williams case had been named in previous civil suits for using excessive force, and two of the cases had been settled out of court. One of the accused officers, Marc Andaya, reportedly had been the subject of more than thirty complaints while previously with the Oakland police force, with his supervisor urging desk duty for Andaya because of his "cowboy" behavior.[38] It is not clear why the San Francisco police department hired Andaya in light of the complaints against him while he worked in Oakland.[39]

In October 1996, witnesses testified at Andaya's hearing before the Police Commission, with some stating that Andaya kicked Williams in the neck and head as others held him down. Officers claimed that Williams grabbed pepper spray from one of the officers. Andaya was accused of neglect of duty and using excessive force, but the Police Commission deadlocked on the charges (two for, two against, with one police commissioner absent), which was in effect an exoneration. The two commissioners who voted in favor of Andaya were criticized by the city's mayor and subsequently resigned. Andaya was subsequently fired by a newly

---

[36] Curtius, "Despite progressive policies...," *Los Angeles Times*..

[37] Jim Herron Zamora, "Cop kicked suspect's head, say 3 witnesses," *The San Francisco Examiner,* October 8, 1996.

[38] Rachel Gordon, "'Cowboy' cop at scene of violence," *San Francisco Examiner*, June 9, 1995; Susan Sward, "S.F. panel fires officer in Aaron Williams case," *San Francisco Chronicle*, June 28, 1997.

[39] Zamora, "Cop kicked suspect's head...," *The San Francisco Examiner*; Jim Herron Zamora, "S.F. cop cleared of using excess force," *The San Francisco Examiner,* November 21, 1996.

constituted Police Commission for lying on his 1994 application to the department.[40] Williams's family has filed two separate lawsuits against the city.

Office of Citizen Complaints

The Office of Citizen Complaints (OCC) was approved by voters in November 1982 to investigate complaints against San Francisco police officers. It is staffed by civilians who have never been police officers in San Francisco and had a budget of nearly $2 million in fiscal year 1996-97. Under new mandates, the OCC must have one full-time investigator for every 150 sworn officers, leading to an increase in staffing that is helping to deal with the OCC's case backlog.[41] Both the OCC and the police department are under the authority of the civilian Police Commission (with the police chief also reporting to the mayor). After a period of rapid turnover, the OCC has a new executive director, Mary Dunlap, who has a civil rights background and respect from local activists on police abuse issues. She is credited with improving the performance of the OCC and restoring its credibility.

Under its charter, the OCC must investigate every complaint it receives except for those that are clearly baseless. Officers are required to cooperate with the OCC, which has access to all police files, investigates complaints on its own, recommends disciplinary sanctions, makes policy recommendations and publishes quarterly reports. The public also has access to an "openness" report available from the OCC if any person requests the file on a specific investigation, but it is usually a brief one-page summary of the investigation and conclusions.[42]

On average, the OCC receives 1,000 to 1,200 complaints each year by phone, mail, and from complainants who visit its office; it accepts anonymous complaints. If the police department receives a complaint from the public, it refers it to the OCC; the Internal Affairs Division handles internally generated complaints only.[43] About 12 to 15 percent of the complaints filed each year involve allegations of

---

[40] Curtius, "Despite progressive policies...," *Los Angeles Times*.

[41] As of late 1997 there were sixteen investigators, as part of a staff of twenty-five.

[42] Telephone interview, John Crew, ACLU of Northern California, February 12, 1998.

[43] In 1988, the Police Commission adopted resolution 1159-88 which prohibits police from threatening, intimidating, misleading or harassing potential or actual OCC complainants, witnesses or staff members.

unnecessary force.[44] In 1996, African-Americans made up 26 percent of the OCC's complainants – the OCC notes that this percentage "is higher than the percentage of African-Americans in the city's population," which in the 1990 census was just under 11 percent.[45] The OCC generally sustained approximately 6 to 7 percent of the cases closed each year.[46]

OCC conducts its own investigations.[47] Investigative hearings are held after an OCC investigation if either the complainant or officer is dissatisfied and if the hearing is approved by the OCC to facilitate fact-finding. Hearings are as nonadversarial as possible, and hearing officers are not drawn from the OCC. Cases sustained by the OCC are sent to the police chief with recommendations for disciplinary or other action if the OCC recommends less than a ten-day suspension. For any longer period of suspension or termination, cases are sent to the Police Commission for a hearing.

Until recently, the chief had the option of ignoring the OCC's recommendation, and did so in the past. In 1994, the American Civil Liberties Union of Northern California reviewed cases and found that, in more than 80 percent of sustained complaint findings, no discipline was imposed at all, even for very serious violations. The OCC has been criticized for failing to challenge the police chiefs when they have lessened, or lifted, OCC's recommended penalties. The procedures were changed, and now the OCC may take any case to the Police Commission for an ultimate decision if the chief declines to take disciplinary action.

The OCC maintains its own database to track complaints and other information about investigations. The department's Management Control Division (MCD) has its own database dealing with deaths in custody. According to OCC, the two offices have access to each other's tracking data. Every six months, supervisors have to update a "multiple card" for officers, tracking complaints and other information to

---

[44] In 1995 and 1996, other complaint categories were "unwarranted action" which made up 38 to 39 percent of complaints, neglect of duty complaints made up approximately 23 percent, "conduct reflecting discredit" on the department made up 15 to 18 percent, with the remaining complaints concerning discourtesy and sexual or racial slurs.

[45] Office of Citizen Complaints, *1996 Annual Report*, p. 13.

[46] Ibid., p. 3.

[47] During 1996 when the OCC hired eight new investigators, four were women and four men, and included an African-American, one Latina- American, one Latino-American, one Chinese-American, and one Siberian-American, thus adding to language expertise and cultural breadth at the OCC.

identify officers who may need discipline, training, or counseling. There is an early warning system, adopted in April 1995 and administered by OCC. The OCC reports on a quarterly basis a list of officers who have received three or more complaints within a six-month period or four or more complaints within a year. The complaint histories are also used for general performance evaluations. Mediation is now part of the process, so if an officer agrees to mediation and the complaint is mediated successfully, nothing appears on his or her personnel record. OCC retains its findings for a minimum of five years.[48]

The OCC has a unique procedure for responding to civil lawsuits alleging police abuse that falls within its mandate.[49] Whenever the office receives a copy of a civil claim form from the City Attorney's office, it sends the complainant information about the OCC and a complaint form, to allow the plaintiff to file an OCC complaint if he or she is so inclined. Civil attorneys frequently advise clients not to file a complaint with the OCC, because the client's statement could be used against him or her in the civil lawsuit. But OCC explains that a timely investigation is crucial, and if they do not investigate until a civil suit is settled, the investigation suffers. The OCC contends that its investigation will be of high quality and that civil attorneys could benefit from using the information uncovered (or they could save time by dropping an unwinnable case).

There is no procedure for the OCC to notify the district attorney's office if a case may be prosecutable; the victim or another involved party must report directly to the district attorney's office. There is no link between the OCC and federal prosecutors, with the OCC relying on civil lawyers to provide information to federal authorities.

Police Administration

An investigative report by the *San Francisco Examiner* in 1996 found that the city was paying large amounts in civil lawsuits following officer-involved shootings, but the officers were not being disciplined by the department, or criminally prosecuted. Between 1988 and September 1996, according to this report, San Francisco police officers shot eighty-six people, killing thirty-one and injuring fifty-five.[50]

---

[48] According to press reports, twenty-five files of fully investigated or closed cases were lost in 1994; eighteen files were similarly lost in 1990. Thaai Walker, "Files missing at police watchdog agency in S.F.," *San Francisco Chronicle*, August 18, 1994.

[49] This change was implemented after the Wohler case, see above.

[50] Rosenfeld, "S.F. pays big...," *San Francisco Examiner.*

According to the investigative series, homicide investigations of police shootings quickly affirm officers' accounts, and the district attorney's office does not serve as a check on the homicide investigation but merely confirms the findings. The explanation for this record is similar to that in other cities – top police administrators have shown little observable commitment to holding officers accountable, instead shielding officers who commit human rights violations from exposure and punishment. The district attorney's office often does not want to prosecute officers on whom it relies in criminal cases, and the city wants to avoid lawsuits for large amounts that would be easier if the facts were proven against the officer by the internal investigators or in a criminal proceeding.

After several shooting investigations were criticized (*See* above), the department established new procedures in 1995 that allow more review by the OCC and the Police Commission, but many police abuse experts believe the process is still too secretive. Prior to 1995, the Discharge Review Board was a panel of three deputy chiefs, including current Chief Fred Lau, who met privately, kept no minutes and made no public reports. Now, the chief makes public a summary of the internal Management Control Division (MCD) review and sends a copy of its findings to the OCC. Critics of the revised procedure have noted that no information identifying the officer may be disclosed.

The new policy also requires that homicide investigators explore whether the shooting broke the law, while MCD investigates whether it broke department policy, with the homicide unit retaining initial control of witnesses and the scene. This dual investigative authority has led to disagreements between homicide investigators and the MCD, with each unit criticizing the other's investigative efforts, while coming to different conclusions about what occurred.

Also in 1995, the police department revised its policy guiding when an officer may shoot.[51] The old policy allowed officers to shoot when necessary to arrest a suspect in a felony involving deadly force. Prior to the change in policy, the department had not been in compliance with international human rights standards, or with the 1985 U.S. Supreme Court ruling, *Tennessee v. Garner*, which requires that police officers only shoot at fleeing felony suspects when necessary to prevent escape and when there was probable cause to believe that they posed a significant danger.[52] The new policy permits them to shoot only if the suspect also poses a risk

---

[51] Seth Rosenfeld, "SFPD quietly changed policy on officer-involved shootings," *San Francisco Examiner*, December 30, 1996.

[52] *Tennessee v. Garner*, 471 U.S. 1 (1985). The old policy was in clear violation of international human rights standards. For example, the U.N. Basic Principles on the Use of Force and Firearms by Law Enforcement Officials, requiring that "law enforcement officials

of serious injury if not arrested quickly. It also urges officers to give a warning before firing.

Civil Lawsuits

In response to a request from Rep. John Conyers of the House Judiciary Committee of the U.S. Congress, the Office of the City Attorney provided the following information regarding police misconduct cases handled by the City Attorney's office from 1993 to 1995.[53] All cases resulting in payment were settlements, except for one judgment in 1994. During the three-year period, there were twenty-seven claims resulting in total payments of $1,929,057. In 1993, the city paid $446,324; in 1994, the city paid $755,500; and in 1995, the city paid $727,233. The cases included charges of unnecessary force, unwarranted or unlawful action, sexual harassment, conduct reflecting discredit, neglect of duty, racial slurs, and discourtesy. The Police Commission and the Board of Supervisors must authorize settlements.

In November 1995, voters approved Proposition G, which among other things requires that settlement of civil cases alleging police misconduct must come out of the police department's budget, beginning in fiscal year 1996. At the same time, the city is not allowed to diminish the police force beyond a set level, so if civil suits are paid out of the budget and the department needs more funding, it must go back to the Board of Supervisors and request it. Advocates believe that by making the department track the amounts and request additional funding, this process may focus more attention on officers who are repeatedly sued but not retrained or disciplined appropriately. Advocates also state that the new procedure provides more accountability, because these settlements and judgments can no longer be hidden in a general liability account. A new position has been created within the police department to serve as a risk manager, to monitor and respond to civil suits against the police.

---

shall not use firearms against persons except in self-defence or defence of others against imminent threat of death or serious injury, to prevent the perpetration of a particularly serious crime involving grave threat to life, to arrest a person presenting such a danger and resisting their authority, or to prevent his or her escape, and only when less extreme means are insufficient to achieve these objectives. In any event, intentional lethal use of firearms may only be made when strictly unavoidable to protect life." (*See* overview for additional international human rights standards.)

[53] Letter from Delia Schletter, Executive Officer in the City Attorney's office, to Rep. Conyers dated May 21, 1996.

Criminal Prosecution

The district attorney's office rarely prosecutes officers for crimes relating to excessive force. Nor does the district attorney's office acknowledge compiling information that would allow its staff to identify and monitor prosecutions of police officers. In September 1996, Officer Francis Hogue was convicted and sentenced to six years in state prison for kidnaping a woman and forcing her to perform sexual acts in his squad car.[54] But according to the December 1996 *San Francisco Examiner* series, no officer had been prosecuted for an on-duty shooting for twenty years. As to federal action, no one we interviewed from the OCC or City Attorney's office, and no local police abuse experts, knew of any federal criminal civil rights investigation in San Francisco in recent years.

In 1996, of the sixty-four cases decided by federal prosecutors for the federal district containing San Francisco (Northern District of California), none was prosecuted (presented to a grand jury to seek an indictment). Between 1992 and 1995, 342 cases were considered, of which two were prosecuted.[55]

---

[54] Dennis J. Opatrny, "SF hookers accuse vice officer of forcing them into fellatio," *San Francisco Examiner*, April 10, 1997.

[55] According to data obtained by the Transactional Records Access Clearinghouse (TRAC) from the Executive Office of U.S. Attorneys, Justice Department. Cases prosecuted or declined represent only a portion of the total number of complaints alleging federal criminal civil rights violations because several steps prior to this decision narrow down the number of complaints actually received to those considered worthy of consideration.

WASHINGTON, D.C.

Scandals involving the District of Columbia's Metropolitan Police Department (MPD) have had less to do with allegations of excessive force by its 3,600 officers than with political infighting and gross mismanagement.[1] Although in crisis, the department is embarking on a "zero tolerance" campaign, meaning that police-resident encounters, and presumably the opportunity to commit abuses, will increase.[2] With the internal affairs unit exercising excessive secrecy and the recent abolition of the city's civilian review board, the department is left with very little external scrutiny regarding its handling of brutality complaints.[3]

In November 1997, Chief Larry Soulsby resigned amid allegations of impropriety.[4] Soulsby had been sharing an apartment where the rent had reportedly been reduced dramatically after Soulsby's friend and roommate, Lt. Jeffrey Stowe, reportedly told the landlords that it would be used for undercover work. Also in November, Stowe – who headed the investigations unit on extortion and fraud – was himself charged with embezzlement and extortion.[5] Stowe was accused of stealing money from department funds, attempting to blackmail married men who

---

[1] A detailed study by the consulting firm Booz-Allen and Hamilton concluded in 1997 that "chronic" problems plagued the force and that the department had poor leadership. Cheryl Thompson, "Detailing Failings of D.C. Police Department," *Washington Post,* April 9, 1997.

[2] Meanwhile, tragedy has also affected the police force. During the first six months of 1997, three MPD officers were shot and killed. One, Brian T. Gibson, was shot in his squad car while on duty, another had just gotten off work and was shot as he stood outside his precinct, and a third was shot in a suburb while off-duty by an assailant believed to have known that he was an officer.

[3] It is also very unresponsive to requests for information, even when they are submitted in the form of a Freedom of Information Act request. The police department did not respond to a FOIA request originally sent by Human Rights Watch in September 1996 and did not respond to a letter requesting an interview with the acting chief, or a response in writing to several questions, sent in January 1998 – twice by facsimile and once by mail.

[4] Cheryl W. Thompson, Sari Horwitz, "Embattled D.C. police chief resigns," *Washington Post*, November 26, 1997; Sari Horwitz, Cheryl W. Thompson, "D.C. police chief weighs resigning," *Washington Post*, November 25, 1997.

[5] Stowe pleaded guilty to charges of wire fraud, theft, and extortion. Toni Locy, "Luxury unit allegedly for Soulsby," *Washington Post*, January 27, 1998.

frequented a gay nightclub, and using his subordinates to get information about the FBI's investigation of Stowe.[6] A former deputy superintendent from Chicago's police force, Charles Ramsey, was chosen as the new chief in early 1998, and there were hopes that an "outsider" might help improve the management of the force.

In addition to serious scandals involving the department's leaders, the rank-and-file of the force have also gotten into trouble. According to press reports, some one hundred officers who joined the force during a 1989-90 hiring drive, when standards and background screening were all but absent, were later charged with criminal offenses.[7] Nearly one quarter of those were charged with crimes involving domestic violence.[8] More recently it was reported that during late 1996 and early 1997, background checks of new recruits were incomplete.[9]

Prior to his own problems, in early 1997 Chief Soulsby gained enhanced powers as chief, and he used them to dismiss top-level police officials. (As described below, two of the deputy chiefs who were dismissed were allegedly involved in domestic violence and sexual harassment incidents.) The changes came about due to the D.C. financial control board's increased oversight of the police department and Mayor Marion Barry's decreased powers. Observers credited Chief Soulsby, who became chief in July 1995, with emphasizing that he would not tolerate abuse by officers. He also called for retraining for about three-quarters of the force. The need for training became apparent when one officer at the initial training session asked, "When are they going to change the laws about suing the department? So when a guy does something and gets smacked, he can't go and sue." None of the officers in the training class could articulate what constituted a legal search, and when the group did a word association exercise, responses to the word "gays" were "wrong, weird, faggots, AIDS, ungodly, don't like em, immoral."[10]

---

[6] Avis Thomas-Lester and Toni Locy, "Soulsby's friend accused of extortion," *Washington Post*, November 26, 1997.

[7] Carl T. Rowan, Jr., "Who's Policing D.C. Cops?" *Washington Post*, October 8, 1995; and Michael Powell, Sari Horwitz, Cheryl W. Thompson, "Problems in D.C. police dept. festered for decades," *Washington Post*, October 12, 1997.

[8] Stephanie Mencimer, "Battered Blue," *Washington City Paper,* August 23-29, 1996.

[9] Cheryl W. Thompson, "Half of officers lack firearm certification," *Washington Post*, March 28, 1998.

[10] Sari Horwitz, "Getting back to basics," *Washington Post*, April 1, 1996.

Latino activists have reported that community relations with the police improved after the riots in Washington's Mt. Pleasant neighborhood in May 1991, but there are still language and cultural barriers for the approximately 10 to 12 percent of the D.C. population that is of Hispanic origin.[11] The benchmark for this assessment is a January 1993 U.S. Commission on Civil Rights report issued about the rioting that followed the May 5, 1991 shooting by a rookie officer of a Salvadoran man. After the shooting, there was looting and arson described as a "manifestation of frustration...years of harassment, resentment and rejection."[12] The city's Latino task force complained of "a real or perceived pattern of widespread, endemic racism and physical and verbal abuse by the MPD against the Latino community, particularly in the 3rd District, which has the highest concentration of Latino residents...."[13] Racial epithets like "wetback" and "spic" were allegedly used by officers. As noted, there have been improvements in recent years, but some unease persists.[14]

Some observers have speculated that the reason there have not been more recent incidents of excessive force is because – in addition to the lack of information about how to file a complaint or any evidence that it makes any difference – officers have been so demoralized by the budgetary and leadership crises that they were avoiding contact with citizens, thus possibly reducing the potential for complaints. The Booz-Allen reports found that two-thirds of the department's officers made ten or fewer arrests a year, with half of those officers making no arrests at all.[15] Yet by March 1997, efforts were underway to copy the New York City Police Department's "zero tolerance" efforts by policing minor offenses more aggressively and becoming a more visible presence throughout the city. Residents' responses to the new efforts were mixed and echoed those in New York: some welcomed the new activism while others complained that the police were overzealous. Said one officer, "[Police officials] want to see numbers, so

---

[11] Telephone interview with Elena Rocha, member of the Police-Latino Relations Task Force, October 24, 1996.

[12] Preface, "Racial and Ethnic Tensions in American Communities: The Mount Pleasant Report," U.S. Commission on Civil Rights, January 1993.

[13] Ibid., p 20.

[14] More than 67 percent of the police force is African-American, 27 percent is white, and less than 5 percent Hispanic.

[15] Cheryl Thompson, "Detailing Failings," *Washington Post*, April 9, 1997.

we're arresting people and locking them up for almost anything."[16] The initiative began with little or no training for officers, including 400 who were moved to the streets from specialty units and desk jobs and who had not patrolled the streets for years.

In an alarming indication that training remains grossly inadequate, it was reported in March 1998 that roughly half of the city's police officers had not been certified on their firearms, as required by department regulations.[17] As in most police departments, MPD officers are required to demonstrate their proficiency at a shooting range at regular intervals. When questioned about this development, interim police chief Sonya T. Proctor – who was responsible for recruitment and training before being named acting chief – had no explanation for the lapse but noted that the department "needed to be more diligent about scheduling these people [for shooting certification tests]."[18] Almost a year before the latest disclosures, a consulting firm reportedly had brought the poor certification record to the department's attention, apparently with little impact.[19]

Civilian Review
Washington's Civilian Complaint Review Board (CCRB), created in 1980, was abolished in mid-1995. Opinions differ about why the board was not successful, with most agreeing that budgetary cuts and its requirement that it must investigate and hold an adjudicatory hearing for each complaint dooming the board to an insurmountable backlog and dissatisfaction for all. Even when the board was able to sustain cases, police administrative trial boards often overturned CCRB's findings.

The failure of the oversight system, including the CCRB and IAD, was apparent when the city was held liable for damages for police abuse in a case filed in 1991. In 1993, the U.S. District Court found that the MPD maintained a "patently inadequate system of investigation of excessive force complaints."[20]

---

[16] Cheryl Thompson, "D.C. Police Zero in on petty crime," *Washington Post*, May 5, 1997. During the first month of the new initiative, eight in ten arrests were for offenses such as disorderly conduct, panhandling, and traffic violations.

[17] Thompson, "Half of officers lack...," *Washington Post*.

[18] Ibid.

[19] Ibid.

[20] *Cox v. District of Columbia*, 821 F. Supp. 1 (1993), aff'd 40 F.3d 475 (1994).

Furthermore, the department showed a "deliberate indifference to the rights of persons who come in contact with District police officers."[21] The court held the department and city responsible for allowing the CCRB to conduct poor, or no, investigations and not disciplining officers regardless of the CCRB's actions.

The CCRB would receive approximately 500 complaints a year, but it was only able to dispose of about one hundred. As the board's funding was cut, the head of the MPD police union Det. J.C. Stamps, said, "That's what they have the court system for; that's what they have internal affairs for," when asked whether independent review necessary.[22]

In October 1995, the City Council's judiciary committee held hearings on the need for civilian review and proposals for creating a new, less burdensome and less expensive mechanism similar to the one used in Minneapolis, Minnesota.[23] Faced with the prospect of the police department's zero tolerance initiative without any mechanism for external review, an independent task force was created by city activists in early 1997, made up of twenty-five members, including representatives from nongovernmental groups, four retired MPD officers, and the former chairperson of the CCRB.[24] The task force, called the Metropolitan Police and Criminal Justice Review Task Force, planned to review and evaluate the MPD and assist individuals who have complaints about police misconduct. Its creation highlighted the absence of any formal external review of the police force. In September 1997, the City Council discussed the possibility of creating some new external review mechanism, with police officials favoring the use of police officers as investigators and retired judges as the review panel. Civil rights groups opposed this proposal, advocating an independent review agency instead.[25]

---

[21] Ibid.

[22] Michael A. Fletcher, "City's Police Review Panel Loses Funding in Budget," *Washington Post*, April 20, 1995.

[23] *See* Minneapolis chapter.

[24] Cheryl W. Thompson, "Panel to Review D.C. Police, NAACP Says," *Washington Post*, April 18, 1997.

[25] In March 1997, an inspector general post to investigate allegations of corruption was created, but there were long delays in appointing anyone to fill the position.

Police Administration/Internal Affairs

High-level city and police officials have often failed to provide the police force with adequate leadership and instead have been involved in inappropriate behavior themselves.[26] As part of a general review of the police department in 1997, consultants found that performance reviews of officers and supervisors were terminated in 1985.[27] It appeared that promotion through the ranks was based on positive relations with the chief or mayor, rather than on job performance. The cronyism in the department is one of the factors widely blamed for the force's poor performance.[28] The others are a flood of recruits during a short period in the late 1980s and early 1990s, and subsequent budget cuts.[29] The congressionally mandated hiring of 1,500 recruits in a two-year period meant that new officers were put on the streets without adequate, or in some cases any, background checks; many were later found to have criminal backgrounds. The 1989-90 classes accounted for half of the 200 officers arrested during the subsequent three years on charges from shoplifting to rape and murder.[30]

Until the February 1997 purging of the city's highest police officials, two of the city's deputy chiefs were the subjects of serious allegations. One former deputy chief was charged with assault with intent to commit murder after he reportedly shot at a girlfriend; the woman refused to testify and the charges were dropped.[31] An internal affairs investigation found the deputy chief guilty of misconduct and recommended he be demoted, but he successfully appealed, and was instead promoted. In 1993, another former girlfriend claimed that the deputy chief intentionally rammed his car into hers, but prosecutors did not bring charges against

---

[26] Mayor Barry was caught on videotape smoking crack cocaine and was convicted on misdemeanor charges in 1990. And former police Chief Soulsby was caught on audiotape reportedly promising the head of the homicide squad a choice assignment if he would agree not to oppose Soulsby at the chief's confirmation hearings.

[27] Powell, Horwitz, and Thompson, "Problems in D.C. police dept. festered for decades," *Washington Post*, October 12, 1997.

[28] Ibid.

[29] Ibid.

[30] Carl T. Rowan, Jr., "Who's Policing D.C. Cops?" *Washington Post*, October 8, 1995.

[31] Ibid.

him.[32] For years, officers under investigation for serious abuses argued that, since the deputy chief was not fired for his actions, why should they be let go? Another former deputy chief was accused of sexually harassing a female sergeant while he was a commander. An internal investigation found that he had harassed the woman, but the finding was later overturned by an administrative judge who found the complainant's account inconsistent.[33] Neither of the deputy chiefs' records were mentioned as reasons for their dismissals in 1997.

Since the abolition of the CCRB, the Internal Affairs Division (IAD) of the police department has been responsible for handling all citizen complaints of police misconduct.[34] Unfortunately, IAD's budget reportedly has not increased accordingly and perhaps potentially for this reason, IAD did not in fact become more active.[35] Rather, it established a system that allows district supervisors, rather than IAD, to investigate most complaints. Therefore, supervisors who work closely with an accused officer must decide whether he or she committed an abuse, and if the supervisor acknowledges abusive behavior, this may reflect poorly on his or her own leadership and training skills. It would appear that such a system inherently favors officers and removes impartiality from investigations. During a 1996 interview with Inspector Lloyd L. Coward, Jr. of IAD, he disagreed with this negative assessment and told Human Rights Watch that local investigating is desirable because supervisors and officers know each other best.[36] Coward stated that, if there is a lot of publicity, IAD handles excessive force cases, rather than referring them to districts for investigations. Noting that CCRB no longer exists, the city's corporation counsel provided his assessment of the way the MPD handles

---

[32] Ibid.

[33] Avis Thomas-Lester, "D.C. reverses suspension of police commander," *Washington Post*, July 24, 1995. Avis Thomas-Lester, "Police official calls demotion political," *Washington Post*, December 2, 1996. The city's Office of Human Rights told Human Rights Watch that, as of April 1998, the woman's complaint against the police department was still pending.

[34] The now-abolished CCRB mandate did not permit IAD to investigate complaints under the board's purview, although excessive force cases that were possibly criminal should have been handled by IAD.

[35] IAD had a staff of fifty in 1996.

[36] Human Rights Watch interview, Inspector Lloyd L. Coward, Jr., IAD, September 27, 1996.

citizen complaints, "Currently, there is an informal process within the Department for handling these [citizen] kinds of complaints."[37]

The changeover from CCRB to IAD left a number of pending complaint cases – possibly several hundred – shrouded in secrecy. IAD's Inspector Coward was unable or unwilling to provide information to us about the status of the CCRB complaints, or where the board's files as a whole ended up. He suggested Human Rights Watch file a Freedom of Information Act (FOIA) request for this information and other basic guidelines about how the department handles complaints. A FOIA request was sent in September 1996 and acknowledged on October 2, 1996 but remained unanswered as of May 1998. In an undated letter to a community activist, received in September 1996, IAD provided some information about the CCRB complaints, reporting that of the 824 transferred complaints, 246 were categorized as priority 1 (excessive force requiring medical attention). The lesser priorities included 334 complaints of excessive force not requiring medical treatment, 229 complaints of harassment and/or demeaning language, and fourteen that were not within CCRB jurisdiction (one complaint was not accounted for). In earlier correspondence in response to an advocacy group, IAD reported that of the 824 complaints, 232 had been investigated and resolved, with just seven sustained – a very low 3 percent sustained rate for investigated cases.[38] A letter of prejudice was issued in three sustained cases, an official reprimand issued in two cases, and suspensions (length not defined) were ordered in two cases.[39] IAD reported 184 new citizen complaints between January and September 1996, including fifty-five of excessive force, with the 4th and 7th district officers the subjects of thirty of the excessive force cases.

IAD's system for the intake of complaints is imperfect. Complaint forms are only in English, but the U.S. State Department reportedly assists the department when it needs interpreting. Attorneys in police abuse cases claim that officers attempt to dissuade individuals attempting to file complaints.

IAD Inspector Coward stated that complaints have little impact on promotions, but they do affect assignments so that if someone has a history of complaints, he or she will not be assigned to "sensitive" units. The department does have an "early

---

[37] Letter to Human Rights Watch from Charles F.C. Ruff, D.C. Corporation Counsel, November 1, 1996.

[38] Letter to the National Capital Area ACLU from Chief Soulsby, July 16, 1996.

[39] Ibid. A letter of prejudice is described as "a written notice to a member outlining specific unsatisfactory job performance or conduct." An official reprimand is a "formal written censor for specific unsatisfactory performance or conduct."

warning system" to identify officers who are the subject of several complaints. The tracking is done by a separate office, the Office of Audit and Compliance. If, during a two-year period, three or more sustained or not sustained complaints have been lodged against an officer, a report is sent to the district commander or supervisor, who is asked to provide an evaluation before any action is proposed for dealing with the officer.[40] Supervisors may consider civil lawsuits against the officer, but IAD does not initiate an investigation when it learns of a civil suit against an officer alleging excessive force or other serious misconduct. Moreover, IAD will not investigate a complaint made with its office if a civil lawsuit is pending.[41]

Domestic violence is an area where IAD has been reluctant to tread, although it is clearly a problem for the MPD. One IAD representative interviewed by Human Rights Watch stated that IAD was not involved in investigating domestic violence complaints against police officers, and that those allegations are handled by district command. This is because, as Inspector Coward explained, "It's usually a one-time incident."[42] IAD only handles long-term, "serious" violations, said Coward, apparently considering alleged domestic battery a minor issue.[43]

A 1996 investigative report in the *Washington City Paper,* however, underscored the fact that domestic violence was a problem on the force, and raised serious doubts about the department's interest in dealing with officers who are abusive at home.[44] According to that report, victims of domestic abuse at the hands of police officers were left with nowhere to turn to report the incident and were often intimidated out of pursuing cases against their boyfriends or husbands.

Some examples were provided in the same report. One officer who allegedly beat his girlfriend in July 1994 was not arrested or reported because a lieutenant on the scene ordered no charges be filed, according to an officer present. The officer

---

[40] It should be noted that, as of August 1997, officers in the MPD did not receive written performance evaluations, meaning that recording abuse complaints or civil lawsuits may have little effect on the subject officer's personnel records. Cheryl W. Thompson, "Progress, problems mark D.C. police overhaul," *Washington Post*, August 25, 1997.

[41] Interview with Inspector Coward, September 27, 1996.

[42] Interview with Inspector Coward and then-Capt. Stanly E. Wiggington, September 27, 1996.

[43] Ibid.

[44] Mencimer, "Battered Blue," *Washington City Paper.*

reportedly remained on the force, working in the 1st District. He reportedly told his girlfriend, "I'm blue, baby....All cops stick together."[45]

In another case, MPD Officer George Batista allegedly beat his girlfriend severely in May 1994.[46] The Maryland state's attorney charged him with felony counts of assault, but his girlfriend backed down and tried to drop the charges. Because the police in Prince George's County, where the incident had occurred, did a good investigation with photographs and other evidence, the prosecutor went ahead with the case without the victim, who ended up marrying Batista. Batista was convicted, but his attorneys argued for a new trial; the judge then dismissed the convictions, and the state declined to retry the case. After Batista was dismissed, fellow officers campaigned to get him reinstated. Citing the deputy chief who was not fired for allegedly abusive behavior, lawyers argued that Batista should get his job back.[47]

Incidents of violence against women have also been alleged in off-duty sexual assaults. In 1997, for example, an MPD sergeant was arrested for allegedly beating a woman in nearby Anne Arundel County, then binding her arms and legs with duct tape before raping her.[48] MPD officers arrested the sergeant on charges of being a fugitive from justice in Maryland. He later reportedly pleaded not guilty to charges in Anne Arundel County of first- and second-degree rape, first- and second-degree sexual offense and second-degree assault.[49]

At the time of this writing, an MPD officer faces second-degree rape charges for allegedly having sexual relations with a thirteen-year-old girl.[50] The officer was placed on administrative leave when the MPD first learned of the allegations a month prior to his indictment in a nearby county where a majority of the incidents took place. According to initial reports, the MPD did not report the allegations to

---

[45] Ibid.

[46] Ibid., and Avis Thomas-Lester, "D.C. police to rid ranks of spouse abusers," *Washington Post*, September 10, 1997.

[47] As of August 1997, Batista's name did not appear on an employee printout.

[48] Jennifer Ordonez and Fern Shen, "D.C. police sergeant accused of raping Arundel resident," *Washington Post*, September 6, 1997.

[49] Ibid.

[50] Philip P. Pan, "D.C. officer is charged with rape," *Washington Post*, February 18, 1998.

the police department in the nearby county; investigators there learned of the allegations through a social service agency instead.[51]

In September 1997, Chief Soulsby announced a comprehensive review of domestic violence complaints against members of the force.[52] Soulsby stated that he would fire any officer who had pleaded guilty or been convicted in a domestic violence case – he also threatened to fire officers who were accused but not criminally charged, acquitted, or whose cases were dismissed. At the time of his announcement, approximately eighteen officers were suspended pending disciplinary hearings related to domestic violence, and MPD sources told a reporter that at least one hundred officers had been accused of domestic violence in the past. In a welcome, if belated, acknowledgment of this issue, Soulsby stated, "[D]omestic violence is one of [the department's] worst behavioral problems."[53] There were still those who resisted addressing the issue, however. Fraternal Order of Police labor committee chairman for the MPD, Ron Robertson stated, "[I]f you went around firing all the people who did it, nobody would have a job...What other profession do you know that [people] get fired for beating their wives?"[54]

As in many other cities' police forces, lack of cooperation from police officers involved in incidents under investigation is part of the MPD culture. In a fatal 1994 shooting, Detective Roosevelt Askew shot motorist Sutoria Moore and alleged that he fired because he feared another officer, Sgt. William Middleton, would be run over by Moore's car. Middleton backed him up and the officers were not disciplined. An assistant U.S. attorney allegedly uncovered evidence discrediting their story, however, and Askew agreed to plead guilty to making a false statement and to cooperate with a Justice Department investigation into the alleged coverup involving other officers from the 7th District, as well as the conduct of homicide detectives who determined that the shooting was justified.[55]

In court documents filed in July 1997, Askew (who retired shortly after the July 1994 shooting) admitted he lied about what had taken place and said that the

---

[51] Ibid.

[52] A new federal law bars convicted domestic abuser, including police officers, from possessing firearms. Avis Thomas-Lester, "D.C. police to rid ranks of spouse abusers," *Washington Post*, September 10, 1997.

[53] Ibid.

[54] Mencimer, "Battered Blue," *Washington City Paper*, August 23-19, 1996.

[55] Bill Miller, "Ex-officer pleads guilty to coverup," *Washington Post*, July 16, 1997.

motorist posed no immediate threat of harm, but that his gun accidentally discharged.[56] In September 1997, Middleton pleaded guilty to making a false statement in the case, and agreed to resign.[57] In January 1998, a federal judge placed Askew on probation for two years and fined him $5,000.

Civil Lawsuits

According to the city's corporation counsel, "[T]here is no formalized notification procedure implemented by this office" to advise the police department about the filing of civil lawsuits against officers.[58] Washington is self-insured by putting aside a set amount each year for anticipated claims against city employees. During a three-year period it spent $4 million in settlement or post-verdict payments in police misconduct suits by individuals claiming false arrest/assault ($1.29 million in fiscal year 1995, $1.5 million in FY94, and about $1.3 million in FY93).[59] The data chart used by the corporation counsel provides a space for "descriptions" of cases, but few are provided, making the combined false arrest/assault section less than informative. The vast majority of suits do not go to trial but are settled out of court.

Criminal Prosecution

The U.S. Attorney's office is responsible for all criminal prosecutions in the District of Columbia. According to press reports, twenty-nine officers have been prosecuted "for assaultive behavior" since 1990, according to a U.S. Attorney's office spokesman, with the figure including off-duty incidents; the relatively high number of prosecutions may reflect poor background screening during the 1989-1990 hiring period.[60] A U.S. Attorney's office spokesman told the press that convictions are difficult because victims "don't have clean hands themselves."[61]

---

[56] Toni Lacy, "D.C. Police Accused of Coverup," *Washington Post,* July 3, 1997.

[57] "D.C. officer admits false statement," *Washington Post,* September 27, 1997.

[58] Letter to Human Rights Watch from Charles F.C. Ruff, Corporation Counsel, November 1, 1996.

[59] Ibid.

[60] Avis Thomas-Lester, "DC officer indicted in brutality case," *Washington Post,* May 19, 1996.

[61] Ibid.

In November 1996, Officer Richard Fitzgerald, white, was convicted in D.C. Superior Court of assault charges for beating a drug suspect, who was black, after a chase on August 25, 1993.[62] The 4th District officer, a member of the troubled 1990 class, allegedly hit the man in the head repeatedly with his nightstick. The department considered Fitzgerald's actions justified, and Fitzgerald claims that his supervisors told him that he deserved praise for making a difficult arrest. Yet fellow officers reported that he did not have to keep hitting the suspect, and since fellow officers' testimony is usually taken more seriously than citizens', the officer was convicted. Fitzgerald had been the subject of six complaints and was formally reprimanded when he was questioning a Latino in 1995 and told an ethnic joke about hitting Latinos harder to make them speak English. An MPD detective and former union steward said that Fitzgerald's behavior "showed no pattern," and that, to his credit, Fitzgerald was "one of the most aggressive officers in 4D."[63]

In 1996, of the two federal criminal civil rights cases decided by prosecutors for the federal district (containing the District of Columbia), neither was prosecuted (presented to a grand jury to seek an indictment).[64] Between 1992 and 1995, seven cases were considered, of which none were prosecuted.

---

[62] Bill Miller, "DC Officer Convicted of assault on suspect," *Washington Post*, November 2, 1996. He was scheduled to be sentenced in September 1997, according the U.S. Attorney's office by telephone August 20, 1997.

[63] Thomas-Lester, "DC Officer indicted...," *Washington Post.*

[64] According to data obtained by TRAC from the Executive Office of U.S. Attorneys, Justice Department. Cases prosecuted or declined represent only a portion of the total number of complaints alleging federal criminal civil rights violations in each district in a given year. Several steps prior to this decision narrow down the number of complaints actually received to those considered worthy of consideration.

Federal Criminal Civil Rights Prosecutorial Decisions[1]

U.S. FEDERAL JUDICIAL DISTRICTS FY 1996 PROSECUTORIAL DECISIONS (18 U.S.C. §§241 AND 242)		
Federal Judicial District[1]	Total Referrals	Prosecutions (Sent to grand jury)
Alabama, M [2]	9	0
Alabama, N	28	1
Alabama, S	22	9
Alaska	3	0
Arizona	15	0
Arkansas, E	32	2
Arkansas, W	2	0
California, C	12	1
California, E	27	4
California, N	64	0
California, S	455	1
Colorado	27	0
Connecticut	3	0

[1] According to data obtained by TRAC from the Executive Office of U.S. Attorneys, Justice Department. Cases prosecuted or declined represent only a portion of the total number of complaints alleging federal criminal civil rights violations in each district in a given year.

[2] *M* refers to Middle, *N* to Northern, *S* to Southern, *E* to Eastern, *W* to Western, and *C* to Central

U.S. FEDERAL JUDICIAL DISTRICTS FY 1996 PROSECUTORIAL DECISIONS (18 U.S.C. §§241 AND 242)		
Federal Judicial District[1]	Total Referrals	Prosecutions (Sent to grand jury)
District of Columbia	2	0
Delaware	3	0
Florida, M	41	0
Florida, N	38	0
Florida, S	1	1
Georgia, M	22	0
Georgia, N	20	4
Georgia, S	29	1
Hawaii	85	0
Idaho	2	0
Illinois, C	1	0
Illinois, N	18	0
Illinois, S	15	3
Indiana, N	13	0
Indiana, S	12	0
Iowa, N	44	0
Iowa, S	17	0
Kansas	44	1
Kentucky, E	18	0
Kentucky, W	10	0

U.S. FEDERAL JUDICIAL DISTRICTS FY 1996 PROSECUTORIAL DECISIONS (18 U.S.C. §§241 AND 242)		
Federal Judicial District[1]	Total Referrals	Prosecutions (Sent to grand jury)
Louisiana, E	80	0
Louisiana, M	23	1
Louisiana, W	42	8
Maryland	26	0
Massachusetts	18	2
Michigan, E	37	1
Michigan, W	8	0
Minnesota	6	0
Mississippi, N	29	3
Mississippi, S	86	7
Missouri, E	20	0
Missouri, W	5	0
Montana	109	0
North Carolina, M	4	0
North Carolina, W	6	5
North Dakota	5	0
N. Mariana Islands	1	0
New Mexico	107	0
New Jersey	94	6
New York, E	4	2

U.S. FEDERAL JUDICIAL DISTRICTS FY 1996 PROSECUTORIAL DECISIONS (18 U.S.C. §§241 AND 242)		
Federal Judicial District[1]	Total Referrals	Prosecutions (Sent to grand jury)
New York, N	54	5
New York, S	18	3
New York, W	25	1
Nebraska	9	0
Nevada	13	0
New Hampshire	7	1
Ohio, N	64	4
Ohio, S	16	0
Oklahoma, E	34	4
Oklahoma, N	6	0
Oklahoma, W	19	0
Oregon	6	5
Pennsylvania, E	2	0
Pennsylvania, M	19	0
Pennsylvania, W	30	0
Puerto Rico	2	0
Rhode Island	13	0
South Carolina	11	2
Tennessee, E	53	0
Tennessee, M	5	0

U.S. FEDERAL JUDICIAL DISTRICTS FY 1996 PROSECUTORIAL DECISIONS (18 U.S.C. §§241 AND 242)		
Federal Judicial District[1]	Total Referrals	Prosecutions (Sent to grand jury)
Tennessee, W	87	0
Texas, E	73	0
Texas, N	63	4
Texas, S	241	1
Texas, W	111	0
Utah	30	0
Virginia, E	7	2
Virginia, W	9	0
West Virginia, N	15	0
West Virginia, S	69	0
Washington, E	30	0
Washington, W	33	1
Wisconsin, E	5	0
Wisconsin, W	4	0
Wyoming	1	0

APPENDIX B
Reasons Provided by Justice Department for Declining Prosecution under 18 U.S.C. §§241 and 242[1]

FY 1994 - AND FY 1995 CIVIL RIGHTS DIVISION REASONS FOR NOT PROSECUTING, BY FREQUENCY		
Declination Reasons	**# of Cases in 1994**	**# of Cases in 1995**
Weak or insufficient admissible evidence	904	778
Lack of evidence of criminal intent	480	497
No federal offense evident	426	482
Declined per instructions from DOJ	737	477
Suspect to be prosecuted by other authorities	98	121
Lack of investigative or prosecutive resources	59	80
Witness Problems	98	70
Agency Request	66	68
Civil, administrative, or other disciplinary alternatives	36	62
Minimal federal interest or no deterrent value	48	23
Statute of Limitations	105	22

---

[1] According to data obtained by TRAC from the Executive Office of U.S. Attorneys, Justice Department. Cases prosecuted or declined represent only a portion of the total number of complaints alleging federal criminal civil rights violations in each district in a given year.

FY 1994 - AND FY 1995 CIVIL RIGHTS DIVISION REASONS FOR NOT PROSECUTING, BY FREQUENCY		
Declination Reasons	**# of Cases in 1994**	**# of Cases in 1995**
Suspect being prosecuted on other charges (e.g., UFAPs)	7	22
Office policy	55	20
No known suspect	49	19
Staleness	121	19
Lack of prosecutive resources	0	15
Jurisdiction or venue problems	25	14
Department Policy	23	13
Petite policy	3	6
By government from Magistrate Court with DOJ authorization	0	6
Juvenile Suspect	1	4
Lack of investigative resources	0	2
Suspect deceased	2	2
Transfer within District	0	2
Suspect's cooperation	1	1
By government from District Court without DOJ authorization	3	1
By government from Magistrate Court without DOJ authorization	3	1
Rule 40	2	1

FY 1994 - AND FY 1995 CIVIL RIGHTS DIVISION REASONS FOR NOT PROSECUTING, BY FREQUENCY		
Declination Reasons	**# of Cases in 1994**	**# of Cases in 1995**
Plea to other charge(s) (Magistrate Court)	0	1
Suspect a fugitive	0	1
Pretrial Diversion Completed	1	0
Suspect serving sentence	2	0
Action of the Grand Jury	1	0
Proceedings suspended indefinitely by court	5	0
TOTAL	3,361	2,830

APPENDIX C
Sentencing for Civil Rights Convictions under 18 U.S.C. §§241 and 242[1]

Sentences for Civil Rights Convictions (0 - 27 months)

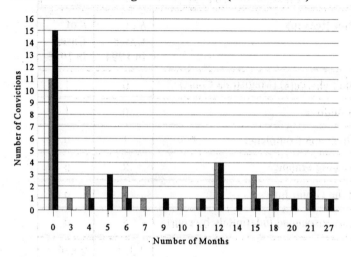

1994

1995

---

[1] According to data obtained by TRAC from the Executive Office of U.S. Attorneys, Justice Department. Cases prosecuted or declined represent only a portion of the total number of complaints alleging federal criminal civil rights violations in each district in a given year.

Sentences for Civil Rights Convictions (30 - 180 months)

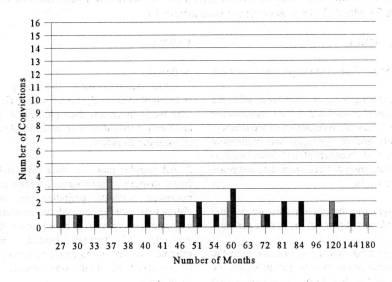

 1994

1995

APPENDIX D
International Covenant on Civil and Political Rights

Adopted and opened for signature, ratification, and accession by United Nations General Assembly resolution 2200A (XXI) on 16 December 1966. Entered into force 23 March 1976 in accordance with article 49.

PREAMBLE

The States Parties to the present Covenant,

Considering that, in accordance with the principles proclaimed in the Charter of the United Nations, recognition of the inherent dignity and of the equal and inalienable rights of all members of the human family is the foundation of freedom, justice and peace in the world,

Recognizing that these rights derive from the inherent dignity of the human person,

Recognizing that, in accordance with the Universal Declaration of Human Rights, the ideal of free human beings enjoying civil and political freedom and freedom from fear and want can only be achieved if conditions are created whereby everyone may enjoy his civil and political rights, as well as his economic, social and cultural rights,

Considering the obligation of States under the Charter of the United Nations to promote universal respect for and observance of, human rights and freedoms,

Realizing that the individual, having duties to other individuals and to the community to which he belongs, is under a responsibility to strive for the promotion and observance of the rights recognized in the present Covenant,

Agree upon the following articles:

PART I

Article 1
1. All peoples have the right of self-determination. By virtue of that right they freely determine their political status and freely pursue their economic, social and cultural development.

2. All peoples may, for their own ends, freely dispose of their natural wealth and resources without prejudice to any obligations arising out of international economic co-operation, based upon the principle of mutual benefit, and international law. In no case may a people be deprived of it its own means of subsistence.

3. The States Parties to the present Covenant, including those having responsibility for the administration of Non-Self-Governing and Trust Territories, shall promote the realization of the right of self-determination, and shall respect that right, in conformity with the provisions of the Charter of the United Nations.

PART II

Article 2
1. Each State Party to the present Covenant undertakes to respect and to ensure to all individuals within its territory and subject to its jurisdiction the rights recognized in the present Covenant, without distinction of any kind, such as race, colour, sex, language, religion, political or other opinion, national

or social origin, property, birth or other status.

2. Where not already provided for by existing legislative or other measures, each State Party to the present Covenant undertakes to take the necessary steps, in accordance with its constitutional processes and with the provisions of the present Covenant, to adopt such legislative or other measures as may be necessary to give effect to the rights recognized in the present Covenant.

3. Each State Party to the present Covenant undertakes:

(a) To ensure that any person whose rights or freedoms as herein recognized are violated shall have an effective remedy, notwithstanding that the violation has been committed by persons acting in an official capacity;

(b) To ensure that any person claiming such a remedy shall have his right thereto determined by competent judicial, administrative or legislative authorities, or by any other competent authority provided for by the legal system of the State, and to develop the possibilities of judicial remedy;

(c) To ensure that the competent authorities shall enforce such remedies when granted.

Article 3
The States Parties to the present Covenant undertake to ensure the equal right of men and women to the enjoyment of all civil and political rights set forth in the present Covenant.

Article 4
1. In time of public emergency which threatens the life of the nation and the existence of which is officially proclaimed, the States Parties to the present Covenant may take measures derogating from their obligations under the present Covenant to the extent strictly required by the exigencies of the situation, provided that such measures are not inconsistent with their other obligations under international law and do not involve discrimination solely on the ground of race, colour, sex, language, religion or social origin.

2. No derogation from articles 6, 7, 8 (paragraphs 1 and 2), 11 ,15, 16 and 18 may be made under this provision.

3. Any State Party to the present Covenant availing itself of the right of derogation shall immediately inform the other States Parties to the present Covenant, through the intermediary of the Secretary-General of the United Nations, of the provisions from which it has derogated and of the reasons by which it was actuated. A further communication shall be made, through the same intermediary, on the date on which it terminates such derogation.

Article 5
1. Nothing in the present Covenant may be interpreted as implying for any State, group or person any right to engage in any activity or perform any act aimed at the destruction of any of the rights and freedoms recognized herein or at their limitation to a greater extent than is provided for in the present Covenant. 2. There shall be no restriction upon or derogation from any of the fundamental human rights recognized or existing in any State Party to the present Covenant pursuant to law, conventions, regulations or custom on the pretext that the

present Covenant does not recognize such rights or that it recognizes them to a lesser extent.

PART III

Article 6

1. Every human being has the inherent right to life. This right shall be protected by law. No one shall be arbitrarily deprived of his life.

2. In countries which have not abolished the death penalty, sentence of death may be imposed only for the most serious crimes in accordance with the law in force at the time of the commission of the crime and not contrary to the provisions of the present Covenant and to the Convention on the Prevention and Punishment of the Crime of Genocide. This penalty can only be carried out pursuant to a final judgement rendered by a competent court.

3. When deprivation of life constitutes the crime of genocide, it is understood that nothing in this article shall authorize any State Party to the present Covenant to derogate in any way from any obligation assumed under the provisions of the Convention on the Prevention and Punishment of the Crime of Genocide.

4. Anyone sentenced to death shall have the right to seek pardon or commutation of the sentence. Amnesty, pardon or commutation of the sentence of death may be granted in all cases.

5. Sentence of death shall not be imposed for crimes committed by persons below eighteen years of age and shall not be carried out on pregnant women.

6. Nothing in this article shall be invoked to delay or to prevent the abolition of capital punishment by any State Party to the present Covenant.

Article 7

No one shall be subjected to torture or to cruel, inhuman or degrading treatment or punishment. In particular, no one shall be subjected without his free consent to medical or scientific experimentation.

Article 8

1. No one shall be held in slavery; slavery and the slave-trade in all their forms shall be prohibited.

2. No one shall be held in servitude.

3. (a) No one shall be required to perform forced or compulsory labour

  (b) Paragraph 3 (a) shall not be held to preclude, in countries where imprisonment with hard labour may be imposed as a punishment for a crime, the performance of hard labour in pursuance of a sentence to such punishment by a competent court.

  (c) For the purpose of this paragraph the term "forced or compulsory labour" shall not include:

    (i) Any work or service, not referred to in sub-paragraph (b), normally required of a person who is under detention in consequence of a lawful order of a court, or of a person during conditional release from such detention;

    (ii) Any service of a military character and, in countries where conscientious objection is recognized, any national service required by law of conscientious objectors;

(iii) Any service exacted in cases of emergency or calamity threatening the life or well-being of the community;

(iv) Any work or service which forms part of normal civil obligations.

Article 9

1. Everyone has the right to liberty and security of person. No one shall be subjected to arbitrary arrest or detention. No one shall be deprived of his liberty except on such grounds and in accordance with such procedure as are established by law.

2. Anyone who is arrested shall be informed, at the time of arrest, of the reasons for his arrest and shall be promptly informed of any charges against him.

3. Anyone arrested or detained on a criminal charge shall be brought promptly before a judge or other officer authorized by law to exercise judicial power and shall be entitled to trial within a reasonable time or to release. It shall not be the general rule that persons awaiting trial shall be detained in custody, but release may be subject to guarantees to appear for trial, at any other stage of the judicial proceedings, and, should occasion arise, for execution of the judgement.

4. Anyone who is deprived of his liberty by arrest or detention shall be entitled to take proceedings before a court, in order that that court may decide without delay on the lawfulness of his detention and order his release if the detention is not lawful.

5. Anyone who has been the victim of unlawful arrest or detention shall have an enforceable right to compensation.

Article 10

1. All persons deprived of their liberty shall be treated with humanity and with respect for the inherent dignity of the human person.

2. (a) Accused persons shall, save in exceptional circumstances, be segregated from convicted persons and shall be subject to separate treatment appropriate to their status as unconvicted persons;

(b) Accused juvenile persons shall be separated from adults and brought as speedily as possible for adjudication.

3. The penitentiary system shall comprise treatment of prisoners the essential aim of which shall be their reformation and social rehabilitation. Juvenile offenders shall be segregated from adults and be accorded treatment appropriate to their age and legal status. Article 11 No one shall be imprisoned merely on the ground of inability to fulfil a contractual obligation.

Article 12

1. Everyone lawfully within the territory of a State shall, within that territory, have the right to liberty of movement and freedom to choose his residence.

2. Everyone shall be free to leave any country, including his own.

3. The above-mentioned rights shall not be subject to any restrictions except those which are provided by law, are necessary to

protect national security, public order (ordre public), public health or morals or the rights and freedoms of others, and are consistent with the other rights recognized in the present Covenant.

4. No one shall be arbitrarily deprived of the right to enter his own country.

Article 13
An alien lawfully in the territory of a State Party to the present Covenant may be expelled therefrom only in pursuance of a decision reached in accordance with law and shall, except where compelling reasons of national security otherwise require, be allowed to submit the reasons against his expulsion and to have his case reviewed by, and be represented for the purpose before, the competent authority or a person or persons especially designated by the competent authority.

Article 14
1. All persons shall be equal before the courts and tribunals. In the determination of any criminal charge against him, or of his rights and obligations in a suit at law, everyone shall be entitled to a fair and public hearing by a competent, independent and impartial tribunal established by law. The Press and the public may be excluded from all or part of a trial for reasons of morals, public order (ordre public) or national security in a democratic society, or when the interest of the private lives of the parties so requires, or to the extent strictly necessary in the opinion of the court in special circumstances where publicity would prejudice the interests of justice; but any judgement rendered in a criminal case or in a suit at law shall be made public except where the interest of juvenile persons otherwise requires or the proceedings concern matrimonial disputes or the guardianship of children.

2. Everyone charged with a criminal offence shall have the right to be presumed innocent until proved guilty according to law.

3. In the determination of any criminal charge against him, everyone shall be entitled to the following minimum guarantees, in full equality:

(a) To be informed promptly and in detail in a language which he understands of the nature and cause of the charge against him;

(b) To have adequate time and facilities for the preparation of his defence and to communicate with counsel of his own choosing;

(c) To be tried without undue delay;

(d) To be tried in his presence, and to defend himself in person or through legal assistance of his own choosing; to be informed, if he does not have legal assistance, of this right; and to have legal assistance assigned to him, in any case where the interests of justice so require, and without payment by him in any such case if he does not have sufficient means to pay for it;

(e) To examine, or have examined the witnesses against him and to obtain the attendance and examination of witnesses on his behalf under the same conditions as witnesses against him;

(f) To have the free assistance of an interpreter if he cannot understand or speak the language used in court;

(g) Not to be compelled to testify against himself or to confess guilt.

4. In the case of juvenile persons, the procedure shall be such as will take account of their age and the desirability of promoting their rehabilitation.

5. Everyone convicted of a crime shall have the right to his conviction and sentence being reviewed by a higher tribunal according to law.

6. When a person has by a final decision been convicted of a criminal offence and when subsequently his conviction has been reversed or he has been pardoned on the ground that a new or newly discovered fact shows conclusively that there has been a miscarriage of justice, the person who has suffered punishment as a result of such conviction shall be compensated according to law, unless it is proved that the non-disclosure of the unknown fact in time is wholly or partly attributable to him.

7. No one shall be liable to be tried or punished again for an offence for which he has already been finally convicted or acquitted in accordance with the law and penal procedure of each country.

Article 15
1. No one shall be held guilty of any criminal offence on account of any act or omission which did not constitute a criminal offence, under national or international law, at the time when it was committed. Nor shall a heavier penalty be imposed than the one that was applicable at the time when the criminal offence was committed. If, subsequent to the commission of the offence, provision is made by law for the imposition of a lighter penalty, the offender shall benefit thereby.

2. Nothing in this article shall prejudice the trial and punishment of any person for any act or omission which, at the time when it was committed. was criminal according to the general principles of law recognized by the community of nations.

Article 16
Everyone shall have the right to recognition everywhere as a person before the law.

Article 17
1. No one shall be subjected to arbitrary or unlawful interference with his privacy, family, home or correspondence, nor to unlawful attacks on his honour and reputation.

2. Everyone has the right to the protection of the law against such interference or attacks.

Article 18
1. Everyone shall have the right to freedom of thought, conscience and religion. This right shall include freedom to have or to adopt a religion or belief of his choice, and freedom, either individually or in community with others and in public or private, to manifest his religion or belief in worship, observance, practice and teaching.

2. No one shall be subject to coercion which would impair his freedom to have or to adopt a religion or belief of his choice.

3. Freedom to manifest one's religion or beliefs may be subject only to such limitations as are prescribed by law and are necessary to protect public safety, order, health, or morals or the fundamental rights and freedoms of others.

4. The States Parties to the present Covenant undertake to have respect for the

liberty of parents and, when applicable, legal guardians to ensure the religious and moral education of their children in conformity with their own convictions.

Article 19

1. Everyone shall have the right to hold opinions without interference.

2. Everyone shall have the right to freedom of expression; this right shall include freedom to seek, receive and impart information and ideas of all kinds, regardless of frontiers, either orally, in writing or in print, in the form of art, or through any other media of his choice.

3. The exercise of the rights provided for in paragraph 2 of this article carries with it special duties and responsibilities. It may therefore be subject to certain restrictions, but these shall only be such as are provided by law and are necessary:

(a) For respect of the rights or reputations of others;

(b) For the protection of national security or of public order (ordre public), or of public health or morals.

Article 20

1. Any propaganda for war shall be prohibited by law.

2. Any advocacy of national, racial or religious hatred that constitutes incitement to discrimination, hostility or violence shall be prohibited by law.

Article 21

The right of peaceful assembly shall be recognized. No restrictions may be placed on the exercise of this right other than those imposed in conformity with the law and which are necessary in a democratic society in the interests of national security or public safety, public order (ordre public), the protection of public health or morals or the protection of the rights and freedoms of others.

Article 22

1. Everyone shall have the right to freedom of association with others, including the right to form and join trade unions for the protection of his interests.

2. No restrictions may be placed on the exercise of this right other than those which are prescribed by law and which are necessary in a democratic society in the interests of national security or public safety, public order (ordre public), the protection of public health or morals or the protection of the rights and freedoms of others. This article shall not prevent the imposition of lawful restrictions on members of the armed forces and of the police in their exercise of this right.

3. Nothing in this article shall authorize States Parties to the International Labour Organisation Convention of 1948 concerning Freedom of Association and Protection of the Right to Organize to take legislative measures which would prejudice, or to apply the law in such a manner as to prejudice, the guarantees provided for in that Convention.

Article 23

1. The family is the natural and fundamental group unit of society and is entitled to protection by society and the State.

2. The right of men and women of marriageable age to marry and to found a family shall be recognized.

3. No marriage shall be entered into without the free and full consent of the intending spouses.

4. States Parties to the present Covenant shall take appropriate steps to ensure equality of rights and responsibilities of spouses as to marriage, during marriage and at its dissolution. In the case of dissolution, provision shall be made for the necessary protection of any children.

Article 24

1. Every child shall have, without any discrimination as to race, colour sex, language, religion, national or social origin, property or birth, the right to such measures of protection as are required by his status as a minor, on the part of his family, society and the State.

2. Every child shall be registered immediately after birth and shall have a name.

3. Every child has the right to acquire a nationality.

Article 25

Every citizen shall have the right and the opportunity, without any of the distinctions mentioned in article 2 and without unreasonable restrictions:

(a) To take part in the conduct of public affairs, directly or through freely chosen representatives;

(b) To vote and to be elected at genuine periodic elections which shall be by universal and equal suffrage and shall be held by secret ballot, guaranteeing the free expression of the will of the electors;

(c) To have access, on general terms of equality, to public service in his country.

Article 26

All persons are equal before the law and are entitled without any discrimination to the equal protection of the law. In this respect, the law shall prohibit any discrimination and guarantee to all persons equal and effective protection against discrimination on any ground such as race, colour, sex, language, religion, political or other opinion, national or social origin, property, birth or other status.

Article 27

In those States in which ethnic, religious or linguistic minorities exist persons belonging to such minorities shall not be denied the right, in community with the other members of their group, to enjoy their own culture, to profess and practise their own religion, or to use their own language.

PART IV

Article 28

1. There shall be established a Human Rights Committee (hereafter referred to in the present Covenant as the Committee). It shall consist of eighteen members and shall carry out the functions hereinafter provided.

2. The Committee shall be composed of nationals of the States Parties to the present Covenant who shall be persons of high moral character and recognized competence in the field of human rights, consideration being given to the usefulness of the participation of some persons having legal experience.

3. The members of the Committee shall be elected and shall serve in their personal capacity.

Article 29
1. The members of the Committee shall be elected by secret ballot from a list of persons possessing the qualifications prescribed in article 28 and nominated for the purpose by the States Parties to the present Covenant.

2. Each State Party to the present Covenant may nominate not more than two persons. These persons shall be nationals of the nominating State.

3. A person shall be eligible for renomination.

Article 30
1. The initial election shall be held no later than six months after the date of the entry into force of the present Covenant.

2. At least four months before the date of each election to the Committee other than an election to fill a vacancy declared in accordance with article 34, the Secretary-General of the United Nations shall address a written invitation to the States Parties to the present Covenant to submit their nominations for membership of the Committee within three months.

3. The Secretary-General of the United Nations shall prepare a list in alphabetical order of all the persons thus nominated, with an indication of the States Parties which have nominated them, and shall submit it to the States Parties to the present Covenant no later than one month before the date of each election.

4. Elections of the members of the Committee shall be held at a meeting of the States Parties to the present Covenant convened by the Secretary-General of the United Nations at the Headquarters of the United Nations. At that meeting, for which two thirds of the States Parties to the present Covenant shall constitute a quorum, the persons elected to the Committee shall be those nominees who obtain the largest number of votes and an absolute majority of the votes of the representatives of States Parties present and voting.

Article 31
1. The Committee may not include more than one national of the same State.

2. In the election of the Committee, consideration shall be given to equitable geographical distribution of membership and to the representation of the different forms of civilization and of the principal legal systems.

Article 32
1. The members of the Committee shall be elected for a term of four years. They shall be eligible for re-election if renominated. However, the terms of nine of the members elected at the first election shall expire at the end of two years; immediately after the first election, the names of these nine members elected at the first election shall expire at the end of two years; immediately after the first election, the names of these nine members shall be chosen by lot by the Chairman of the meeting referred to in article 30, paragraph 4.

2. Elections at the expiry of office shall be held in accordance with the preceding articles of this part of the present Covenant.

Article 33

1. If, in the unanimous opinion of the other members, a member of the Committee has ceased to carry out his functions for any cause other than absence of a temporary character, the Chairman of the Committee shall notify the Secretary-General of the United Nations, who shall then declare the seat of that member to be vacant.

2. In the event of the death or the resignation of a member of the Committee, the Chairman shall immediately notify the Secretary-General of the United Nations, who shall declare the seat vacant from the date of death or the date on which the resignation takes effect.

Article 34

1. When a vacancy is declared in accordance with article 33 and if the term of office of the member to be replaced does not expire within six months of the declaration of the vacancy, the Secretary-General of the United Nations shall notify each of the States Parties to the present Covenant, which may within two months submit nominations in accordance with article 29 for the purpose of filling the vacancy.

2. The Secretary-General of the United Nations shall prepare a list in alphabetical order of the persons thus nominated and shall submit it to the States Parties to the present Covenant. The election to fill the vacancy shall then take place in accordance with the relevant provisions of this part of the present Covenant.

3. A member of the Committee elected to fill a vacancy declared in accordance with Article 33 shall hold office for the remainder of the term of the member who vacated the seat on the Committee under the provisions of that article.

Article 35

The members of the Committee shall, with the approval of the General Assembly of the United Nations, receive emoluments from United Nations resources on such terms and conditions as the General Assembly may decide, having regard to the importance of the Committee's responsibilities.

Article 36

The Secretary-General of the United Nations shall provide the necessary staff and facilities for the effective performance of the functions of the Committee under the present Covenant.

Article 37

1. The Secretary-General of the United Nations shall convene the initial meeting of the Committee at the Headquarters of the United Nations.

2. After its initial meeting, the Committee shall meet at such times as shall be provided in its rules of procedure.

3. The Committee shall normally meet at the Headquarters of the United Nations or at the United Nations Office at Geneva.

Article 38

Every member of the Committee shall, before taking up his duties, make a solemn declaration in open committee that he will perform his functions impartially and conscientiously.

Article 39

1. The Committee shall elect its officers for a term of two years. They may be re-elected.

2. The Committee shall establish its own rules of procedure, but these rules shall provide, inter alia, that:

(a) Twelve members shall constitute a quorum;

(b) Decisions of the Committee shall be made by a majority vote of the members present.

Article 40

1. The States Parties to the present Covenant undertake to submit reports on the measures they have adopted which give effect to the rights recognized herein and on the progress made in the enjoyment of those rights:

(a) Within one year of the entry into force of the present Covenant for the States Parties concerned;

(b) Thereafter whenever the Committee so requests.

2. All reports shall be submitted to the Secretary-General of the United Nations, who shall transmit them to the Committee for consideration. Reports shall indicate the factors and difficulties, if any, affecting the implementation of the present Covenant.

3. The Secretary-General of the United Nations may, after consultation with the Committee, transmit to the specialized agencies concerned copies of such parts of the reports as may fall within their field of competence.

4. The Committee shall study the reports submitted by the States Parties to the present Covenant. It shall transmit its reports, and such general comments as it may consider appropriate, to the States

Parties. The Committee may also transmit to the Economic and Social Council these comments along with the copies of the reports it has received from States Parties to the present Covenant.

5. The States Parties to the present Covenant may submit to the Committee observations on any comments that may be made in accordance with paragraph 4 of this article.

Article 41

1. A State Party to the present Covenant may at any time declare under this article that it recognizes the competence of the Committee to receive and consider communications to the effect that a State Party claims that another State Party is not fulfilling its obligations under the present Covenant. Communications under this article may be received and considered only if submitted by a State Party which has made a declaration recognizing in regard to itself the competence of the Committee. No communication shall be received by the Committee if it concerns a State Party which has not made such a declaration. Communications received under this article shall be dealt with in accordance with the following procedure:

(a) If a State Party to the present Covenant considers that another State Party is not giving effect to the provisions of the present Covenant, it may, by written communication, bring the matter to the attention of that State Party. Within three months after the receipt of the communication, the receiving State shall afford the State which sent the communication an explanation or any other statement in writing clarifying the matter, which should include, to the extent possible and pertinent, reference to domestic procedures and remedies taken, pending, or available in the matter.

(b) If the matter is not adjusted to the satisfaction of both States Parties concerned within six months after the receipt by the receiving State of the initial communication, either State shall have the right to refer the matter to the Committee, by notice given to the Committee and to the other State.

(c) The Committee shall deal with a matter referred to it only after it has ascertained that all available domestic remedies have been invoked and exhausted in the matter, in conformity with the generally recognized principles of international law. This shall not be the rule where the application of the remedies is unreasonably prolonged.

(d) The Committee shall hold closed meetings when examining communications under this article.

(e) Subject to the provisions of sub-paragraph (c), the Committee shall make available its good offices to the States Parties concerned with a view to a friendly solution of the matter on the basis of respect for human rights and fundamental freedoms as recognized in the present Covenant.

(f) In any matter referred to it, the Committee may call upon the States Parties concerned, referred to in sub-paragraph (b), to supply any relevant information.

(g) The States Parties concerned, referred to in sub-paragraph (b), shall have the right to be represented when the matter is being considered in the Committee and to make submissions orally and/or in writing.

(h) The Committee shall, within twelve months after the date of receipt of notice under sub-paragraph (b), submit a report:

(i) If a solution within the terms of sub-paragraph (e) is reached, the Committee shall confine its report to a brief statement of the facts and of the solution reached;

(ii) If a solution within the terms of sub-paragraph (e) is not reached, the Committee shall confine its report to a brief statement of the facts; the written submissions and record of the oral submissions made by the States Parties concerned shall be attached to the report.

In every matter, the report shall be communicated to the States Parties concerned.

2. The provisions of this article shall come into force when ten States Parties to the present Covenant have made declarations under paragraph 1 of this article. Such declarations shall be deposited by the States Parties with the Secretary-General of the United Nations, who shall transmit copies thereof to the other States Parties. A declaration may be withdrawn at any time by notification to the Secretary-General. Such a withdrawal shall not prejudice the consideration of any matter which is the subject of a communication already transmitted under this article; no further communication by any State Party shall be

received after the notification of withdrawal of the declaration has been received by the Secretary-General, unless the State Party concerned had made a new declaration.

Article 42

1. (a) If a matter referred to the Committee in accordance with article 41 is not resolved to the satisfaction of the States Parties concerned, the Committee may, with the prior consent of the States Parties concerned, appoint an ad hoc Conciliation Commission (hereinafter referred to as the Commission). The good offices of the Commission shall be made available to the States Parties concerned with a view to an amicable solution of the matter on the basis of respect for the present Covenant;

    (b) The Commission shall consist of five persons acceptable to the States Parties concerned. If the States Parties concerned fail to reach agreement within three months on all or part of the composition of the Commission the members of the Commission concerning whom no agreement has been reached shall be elected by secret ballot by a two-thirds majority vote of the Committee from among its members.

2. The members of the Commission shall serve in their personal capacity. They shall not be nationals of the States Parties concerned, or of a State not party to the present Covenant, or of a State Party which has not made a declaration under article 41.

3. The Commission shall elect its own Chairman and adopt its own rules of procedure.

4. The meetings of the Commission shall normally be held at the Headquarters of the United Nations or at the United Nations Office at Geneva. However, they may be held at such other convenient places as the Commission may determine in consultation with the Secretary-General of the United Nations and the States Parties concerned.

5. The secretariat provided in accordance with article 36 shall also service the commissions appointed under this article.

6. The information received and collated by the Committee shall be made available to the Commission and the Commission may call upon the States Parties concerned to supply any other relevant information.

7. When the Commission has fully considered the matter, but in any event not later than twelve months after having been seized of the matter, it shall submit to the Chairman of the Committee a report for communication to the States Parties concerned:

    (a) If the Commission is unable to complete its consideration of the matter within twelve months, it shall confine its report to a brief statement of the status of its consideration of the matter;

    (b) If an amicable solution to the matter on the basis of respect for human rights as recognized in the present Covenant is reached, the Commission shall confine its report to a brief statement of the facts and of the solution reached;

    (c) If a solution within the terms of sub-paragraph (b) is not reached, the Commission's report shall embody its findings on all questions of fact relevant to the issues between the

States Parties concerned, and its views on the possibilities of an amicable solution of the matter. This report shall also contain the written submissions and a record of the oral submissions made by the States Parties concerned;

(d) If the Commission's report is submitted under sub-paragraph (c), the States Parties concerned shall, within three months of the receipt of the report, notify the Chairman of the Committee whether or not they accept the contents of the report of the Commission.

8. The provisions of this article are without prejudice to the responsibilities of the Committee under article 41.

9. The States Parties concerned shall share equally all the expenses of the members of the Commission in accordance with estimates to be provided by the Secretary-General of the United Nations .

10. The Secretary-General of the United Nations shall be empowered to pay the expenses of the members of the Commission, if necessary, before reimbursement by the States Parties concerned, in accordance with paragraph 9 of this article.

Article 43
The members of the Committee, and of the ad hoc conciliation commissions which may be appointed under article 42, shall be entitled to the facilities, privileges and immunities of experts on mission for the United Nations as laid down in the relevant sections of the Convention on the Privileges and Immunities of the United Nations.

Article 44
The provisions for the implementation of the present Covenant shall apply without prejudice to the procedures prescribed in the field of human rights by or under the constituent instruments and the conventions of the United Nations and of the specialized agencies and shall not prevent the States Parties to the present Covenant from having recourse to other procedures for settling a dispute in accordance with general or special international agreements in force between them.

Article 45
The Committee shall submit to the General Assembly of the United Nations, through the Economic and Social Council, an annual report on its activities.

PART V

Article 46
Nothing in the present Covenant shall be interpreted as impairing the provisions of the Charter of the United Nations and of the constitutions of the specialized agencies which define the respective responsibilities of the various organs of the United Nations and of the specialized agencies in regard to the matters dealt with in the present Covenant.

Article 47
Nothing in the present Covenant shall be interpreted as impairing the inherent right of all peoples to enjoy and utilize fully and freely their natural wealth and resources.

PART VI

Article 48
1. The present Covenant is open for signature by any State Member of the United Nations or member of any of its

specialized agencies, by any State Party to the Statute of the International Court of Justice, and by any other State which has been invited by the General Assembly of the United Nations to become a party to the present Covenant.

2. The present Covenant is subject to ratification. Instruments of ratification shall be deposited with the Secretary-General of the United Nations.

3. The present Covenant shall be open to accession by any State referred to in paragraph 1 of this article.

4. Accession shall be effected by the deposit of an instrument of accession with the Secretary-General of the United Nations.

5. The Secretary-General of the United Nations shall inform all States which have signed this Covenant or acceded to it of the deposit of each instrument of ratification or accession.

Article 49

1. The present Covenant shall enter into force three months after the date of the deposit with the Secretary-General of the United Nations of the thirty-fifth instrument of ratification or instrument of accession.

2. For each State ratifying the present Covenant or acceding to it after the deposit of the thirty-fifth instrument of ratification or instrument of accession, the present Covenant shall enter into force three months after the date of the deposit of its own instrument of ratification or instrument of accession.

Article 50

The provisions of the present Covenant shall extend to all parts of federal States without any limitations or exceptions.

Article 51

1. Any State Party to the present Covenant may propose an amendment and file it with the Secretary-General of the United Nations. The Secretary-General of the United Nations shall thereupon communicate any proposed amendments to the States Parties to the present Covenant with a request that they notify him whether they favour a conference of States Parties for the purpose of considering and voting upon the proposals. In the event that at least one third of the States Parties favours such a conference, the Secretary-General shall convene the conference under the auspices of the United Nations. Any amendment adopted by a majority of the States Parties present and voting at the conference shall be submitted to the General Assembly of the United Nations for approval.

2. Amendments shall come into force when they have been approved by the General Assembly of the United Nations and accepted by a two-thirds majority of the States Parties to the present Covenant in accordance with their respective constitutional processes.

3. When amendments come into force, they shall be binding on those States Parties which have accepted them, other States Parties still being bound by the provisions of the present Covenant and any earlier amendment which they have accepted.

Article 52

Irrespective of the notifications made under article 48, paragraph 5, the Secretary-General of the United Nations shall inform all States referred to in paragraph 1 of the same article of the following particulars:

(a) Signatures, ratifications and accessions under article 48;

(b) The date of the entry into force of the present Covenant under article 49 and the date of the entry into force of any amendments under article 51.

Article 53
1. The present Covenant, of which the Chinese, English, French, Russian and Spanish texts are equally authentic, shall be deposited in the archives of the United Nations.

2. The Secretary-General of the United Nations shall transmit certified copies of the present Covenant to all States referred to in article 48.

IN FAITH WHEREOF the undersigned, being duly authorized thereto by their respective Governments, have signed the present Covenant, opened for signature at New York, on the nineteenth day of December, one thousand nine hundred and sixty-six.

APPENDIX E
Convention Against Torture and Other Cruel, Inhuman or Degrading Treatment or Punishment

Adopted and opened for signature, ratification and accession by General Assembly resolution 39/46 of 10 December 1984. Entered into force 26 June 1987, in accordance with article 27 (1).

The States Parties to this Convention,

Considering that, in accordance with the principles proclaimed in the Charter of the United Nations, recognition of the equal and inalienable rights of all members of the human family is the foundation of freedom, justice and peace in the world,

Recognizing that those rights derive from the inherent dignity of the human person,

Considering the obligation of States under the Charter, in particular Article 55, to promote universal respect for, and observance of, human rights and fundamental freedoms,

Having regard to article 5 of the Universal Declaration of Human Rights and article 7 of the International Covenant on Civil and Political Rights, both of which provide that no one may be subjected to torture or to cruel, inhuman or degrading treatment or punishment,

Having regard also to the Declaration on the Protection of All Persons from Being Subjected to Torture and Other Cruel, Inhuman or Degrading Treatment or Punishment, adopted by the General Assembly on 9 December 1975 (resolution 3452 (XXX)),

Desiring to make more effective the struggle against torture and other cruel, inhuman or degrading treatment or punishment throughout the world,

Have agreed as follows:

PART I

Article 1
1. For the purposes of this Convention, torture means any act by which severe pain or suffering, whether physical or mental, is intentionally inflicted on a person for such purposes as obtaining from him or a third person information or a confession, punishing him for an act he or a third person has committed or is suspected of having committed, or intimidating or coercing him or a third person, or for any reason based on discrimination of any kind, when such pain or suffering is inflicted by or at the instigation of or with the consent or acquiescence of a public official or other person acting in an official capacity. It does not include pain or suffering arising only from, inherent in or incidental to lawful sanctions.

2. This article is without prejudice to any international instrument or national legislation which does or may contain provisions of wider application.

Article 2
1. Each State Party shall take effective legislative, administrative, judicial or other

measures to prevent acts of torture in any territory under its jurisdiction.

2. No exceptional circumstances whatsoever, whether a state of war or a threat or war, internal political instability or any other public emergency, may be invoked as a justification of torture.

3. An order from a superior officer or a public authority may not be invoked as a justification of torture.

Article 3
1. No State Party shall expel, return ("refouler") or extradite a person to another State where there are substantial grounds for believing that he would be in danger of being subjected to torture.

2. For the purpose of determining whether there are such grounds, the competent authorities shall take into account all relevant considerations including, where applicable, the existence in the State concerned of a consistent pattern of gross, flagrant or mass violations of human rights.

Article 4
1. Each State Party shall ensure that all acts of torture are offences under its criminal law. The same shall apply to an attempt to commit torture and to an act by any person which constitutes complicity or participation in torture.

2. Each State Party shall make these offences punishable by appropriate penalties which take into account their grave nature.

Article 5
1. Each State Party shall take such measures as may be necessary to establish its jurisdiction over the offences referred to in article 4 in the following cases:

(a) When the offences are committed in any territory under its jurisdiction or on board a ship or aircraft registered in that State;

(b) When the alleged offender is a national of that State;

(c) When the victim os a national of that State if that State considers it appropriate.

2. Each State Party shall likewise take such measures as may be necessary to establish its jurisdiction over such offences in cases where the alleged offender is present in any territory under its jurisdiction and it does not extradite him pursuant to article 8 to any of the States mentioned in Paragraph 1 of this article.

3. This Convention does not exclude any criminal jurisdiction exercised in accordance with internal law.

Article 6
1. Upon being satisfied, after an examination of information available to it, that the circumstances so warrant, any State Party in whose territory a person alleged to have committed any offence referred to in article 4 is present, shall take him into custody or take other legal measures to ensure his presence. The custody and other legal measures shall be as provided in the law of that State but may be continued only for such time as is necessary to enable any criminal or extradition proceedings to be instituted.

2. Such State shall immediately make a preliminary inquiry into the facts.

3. Any person in custody pursuant to paragraph 1 of this article shall be assisted

in communicating immediately with the nearest appropriate representative of the State of which he is a national, or, if he is a stateless person, to the representative of the State where he usually resides.

4. When a State, pursuant to this article, has taken a person into custody, it shall immediately notify the States referred to in article 5, paragraph 1, of the fact that such person is in custody and of the circumstances which warrant his detention. The State which makes the preliminary inquiry contemplated in paragraph 2 of this article shall promptly report its findings to the said State and shall indicate whether it intends to exercise jurisdiction.

Article 7
1. The State Party in territory under whose jurisdiction a person alleged to have committed any offence referred to in article 4 is found, shall in the cases contemplated in article 5, if it does not extradite him, submit the case to its competent authorities for the purpose of prosecution.

2. These authorities shall take their decision in the same manner as in the case of any ordinary offence of a serious nature under the law of that State. In the cases referred to in article 5, paragraph 2, the standards of evidence required for prosecution and conviction shall in no way be less stringent than those which apply in the cases referred to in article 5, paragraph 1.

3. Any person regarding whom proceedings are brought in connection with any of the offences referred to in article 4 shall be guaranteed fair treatment at all stages of the proceedings.

Article 8
1. The offences referred to in article 4 shall be deemed to be included as extraditable offences in any extradition treaty existing between States Parties. States Parties undertake to include such offences as extraditable offences in every extradition treaty to be concluded between them.

2. If a State Party which makes extradition conditional on the existence of a treaty receives a request for extradition from another State Party with which it has no extradition treaty, it may consider this Convention as the legal basis for extradition in respect of such offenses. Extradition shall be subject to the other conditions provided by the law of the requested State.

3. States Parties which do not make extradition conditional on the existence of a treaty shall recognize such offences as extraditable offences between themselves subject to the conditions provided by the law of the requested state.

4. Such offences shall be treated, for the purpose of extradition between States Parties, as if they had been committed not only in the place in which they occurred but also in the territories of the States required to establish their jurisdiction in accordance with article 5, paragraph 1.

Article 9
1. States Parties shall afford one another the greatest measure of assistance in connection with civil proceedings brought in respect of any of the offences referred to in article 4, including the supply of all evidence at their disposal necessary for the proceedings.

2. States Parties shall carry out their obligations under paragraph 1 of this article in conformity with any treaties on mutual

judicial assistance that may exist between them.

Article 10

1. Each State Party shall ensure that education and information regarding the prohibition against torture are fully included in the training of law enforcement personnel, civil or military, medical personnel, public officials and other persons who may be involved in the custody, interrogation or treatment of any individual subjected to any form of arrest, detention or imprisonment.

2. Each State Party shall include this prohibition in the rules or instructions issued in regard to the duties and functions of any such persons.

Article 11

Each State Party shall keep under systematic review interrogation rules, instructions, methods and practices as well as arrangements for the custody and treatment of persons subjected to any form of arrest, detention or imprisonment in any territory under its jurisdiction, with a view to preventing any cases of torture.

Article 12

Each State Party shall ensure that its competent authorities proceed to a prompt and impartial investigation, wherever there is reasonable ground to believe that an act of torture has been committee in any territory under its jurisdiction.

Article 13

Each State Party shall ensure that any individual who alleges he has been subjected to torture in any territory under its jurisdiction has the right to complain to and to have his case promptly and impartially examined its competent authorities. Steps shall be taken to ensure that the complainant and witnesses are protected against all ill-treatment or intimidation as a consequence of his complaint or any evidence given.

Article 14

1. Each State Party shall ensure in its legal system that the victim of an act of torture obtains redress and has an enforceable right to fair and adequate compensation including the means for as full rehabilitation as possible. In the event of the death of the victim as a result of an act of torture, his dependents shall be entitled to compensation.

2. Nothing in this article shall affect any right of the victim or other person to compensation which may exist under national law.

Article 15

Each State Party shall ensure that any statement which is established to have been made as a result of torture shall not be invoked as evidence in any proceedings, except against a person accused of torture as evidence that the statement was made.

Article 16

1. Each State Party shall undertake to prevent in any territory under its jurisdiction other acts of cruel, inhuman or degrading treatment or punishment which do not amount to torture as defined in article 1, when such acts are committed by or at the instigation of or with the consent or acquiescence of a public official or other person acting in an official capacity. In particular, the obligations contained in articles 10, 11, 12 and 13 shall apply with the substitution for references to torture or references to other forms of cruel, inhuman or degrading treatment or punishment.

2. The provisions of this Convention are without prejudice to the provisions of any other international instrument or national law which prohibit cruel, inhuman or degrading treatment or punishment or which relate to extradition or expulsion.

Part II

Article 17

1. There shall be established a Committee against Torture (hereinafter referred to as the Committee) which shall carry out the functions hereinafter provided. The Committee shall consist of 10 experts of high moral standing and recognized competence in the field of human rights, who shall serve in their personal capacity. The experts shall be elected by the States Parties, consideration being given to equitable geographical distribution and to the usefulness of the participation of some persons having legal experience.

2. The members of the Committee shall be elected by secret ballot from a list of persons nominated by States Parties. Each State Party may nominate one person from among its own nationals. States Parties shall bear in mind the usefulness of nominating persons who are also members of the Human Rights Committee established under the International Covenant on Civil and Political Rights and are willing to serve on the Committee against Torture.

3. Elections of the members of the Committee shall be held at biennial meetings of States Parties convened by the Secretary-General of the United Nations. At those meetings, for which two thirds of the States Parties shall constitute a quorum, the persons elected to the Committee shall be those who obtain the largest number of votes and an absolute majority of the votes of the representatives of States Parties present and voting.

4. The initial election shall be held no later than six months after the date of the entry into force of this Convention. At least four months before the date of each election, the Secretary-General of the United Nations shall address a letter to the States Parties inviting them to submit their nominations within three months. The Secretary-General shall prepare a list in alphabetical order of all persons thus nominated, indicating the States Parties which have nominated them, and shall submit it to the States Parties.

5. The members of the Committee shall be elected for a term of four years. They shall be eligible for re-election if renominated. However, the term of five of the members elected at the first election shall expire at the end of two years; immediately after the first election the names of these five members shall be chosen by lot by the chairman of the meeting referred to in paragraph 3.

6. If a member of the Committee dies or resigns or for any other cause can no longer perform his Committee duties, the State Party which nominated him shall appoint another expert from among its nationals to serve for the remainder of his term, subject to the approval of the majority of the States Parties. The approval shall be considered given unless half or more of the States Parties respond negatively within six weeks after having been informed by the Secretary-General of the United Nations of the proposed appointment.

7. States Parties shall be responsible for the expenses of the members of the Committee while they are in performance of Committee duties.

Article 18

1. The Committee shall elect its officers for a term of two years. They may be re-elected.

2. The Committee shall establish its own rules of procedure, but these rules shall provide, inter alia, that

(a) Six members shall constitute a quorum;

(b) Decisions of the Committee shall be made by a majority vote of the members present.

3 . The Secretary-General of the United Nations shall provide the necessary staff and facilities for the effective performance of the functions of the Committee under this Convention.

4. The Secretary-General of the United Nations shall convene the initial meeting of the Committee. After its initial meeting, the Committee shall meet at such times as shall be provided in its rules of procedure.

5. The State Parties shall be responsible for expenses incurred in connection with the holding of meetings of the States Parties and of the Committee, including reimbursement of the United Nations for any expenses, such as the cost of staff and facilities, incurred by the United Nations pursuant to paragraph 3 above.

Article 19

1. The States Parties shall submit to the Committee, through the Secretary- General of the United Nations, reports on the measures they have taken to give effect to their undertakings under this Convention, within one year after the entry into force of this Convention for the State Party concerned. Thereafter the States Parties shall submit supplementary reports every four years on any new measures taken, and such other reports as the Committee may request.

2. The Secretary-General shall transmit the reports to all States Parties.

3. Each report shall be considered by the Committee which may make such comments or suggestions on the report as it considers appropriate, and shall forward these to the State Party concerned. That State Party may respond with any observations it chooses to the Committee.

4. The Committee may, at its discretion, decide to include any comments or suggestions made by it in accordance with paragraph 3, together with the observations thereon received from the State Party concerned, in its annual report made in accordance with article 24. If so requested by the State Party concerned, the Committee may also include a copy of the report submitted under paragraph 1.]

Article 20

1. If the Committee receives reliable information which appears to it to contain well-founded indications that torture is being systematically practised in the territory of a State Party, the Committee shall invite that State Party to co-operate in the examination of the information and to this end to submit observations with regard to the information concerned.

2. Taking into account any observations which may have been submitted by the State Party concerned as well as any other relevant information available to it, the Committee may, if it decides that this is warranted, designate one or more of its

members to make a confidential inquiry and to report to the Committee urgently.

3. If an inquiry is made in accordance with paragraph 2, the Committee shall seek the co-operation of the State Party concerned. In agreement with that State Party, such an inquiry may include a visit to its territory.

4. After examining the findings of its member or members submitted in accordance with paragraph 2, the Committee shall transmit these findings to the State Party concerned together with any comments or suggestions which seem appropriate in view of the situation.

5. All the proceedings of the Committee referred to in paragraphs 1 to 4 of this article shall be confidential, and at all stages of the proceedings the co-operation of the State Party shall be sought. After such proceedings have been completed with regard to an inquiry made in accordance with paragraph 2, the Committee may, after consultations with the State Party concerned, decide to include a summary account of the results of the proceedings in its annual report made in accordance with article 24.

Article 21
1. A State Party to this Convention may at any time declare under this article 3 that it recognizes the competence of the Committee to receive and consider communications to the effect that a State Party claims that another State Party is not fulfilling its obligations under this Convention. Such communications may be received and considered according to the procedures laid down in this article only if submitted by a State Party which has made a declaration recognizing in regard to itself the competence of the Committee. No

communication shall be dealt with by the Committee under this article if it concerns a State Party which has not made such a declaration. Communications received under this article shall be dealt with in accordance with the following procedure:

(a) If a State Party considers that another State Party is not giving effect to the provisions of this Convention, it may, by written communication, bring the matter to the attention of that State Party. Within three months after the receipt of the communication the receiving State shall afford the State which sent the communication an explanation or any other statement in writing clarifying the matter which should include, to the extent possible and pertinent, references to domestic procedures and remedies taken, pending, or available in the matter.

(b) If the matter is not adjusted to the satisfaction of both States Parties concerned within six months after the receipt by the receiving State of the initial communication, either State shall have the right to refer the matter to the Committee by notice given to the Committee and to the other State.

(c) The Committee shall deal with a matter referred to it under this article only after it has ascertained that all domestic remedies have been invoked and exhausted in the matter, in conformity with the generally recognized principles of international law. This shall not be the rule where the application of the remedies is unreasonably prolonged or is unlikely to bring effective relief to the person who is the victim of the violation of this Convention.

(d) The Committee shall hold closed meetings when examining communications under this article.

(e) Subject to the provisions of subparagraph (c), the Committee shall make available its good offices to the States Parties concerned with a view to a friendly solution of the matter on the basis of respect for the obligations provided for in the present Convention. For this purpose, the Committee may, when appropriate, set up an ad hoc conciliation commission.

(f) In any matter referred to it under this article, the Committee may call upon the States Parties concerned, referred to in subparagraph (b), to supply any relevant information.

(g) The States Parties concerned, referred to in subparagraph (b), shall have the right to be represented when the matter is being considered by the Committee and to make submissions orally and/or in writing.

(h) The Committee shall, within 12 months after the date of receipt of notice under subparagraph (b), submit a report.

(i) If a solution within the terms of subparagraph (e) is reached, the Committee shall confine its report to a brief statement of the facts and of the solution reached.

(ii) If a solution within the terms of subparagraph (e) is not reached, the Committee shall confine its report to a brief statement of the facts; the written submissions and record of the oral submissions made by the States Parties concerned shall be attached to the report.

In every matter, the report shall be communicated to the States Parties concerned.

2. The provisions of this article shall come into force when five States Parties to this Convention have made declarations under paragraph 1 of this article. Such declarations shall be deposited by the States Parties with the Secretary-General of the United Nations, who shall transmit copies thereof to the other States Parties. A declaration may be withdrawn at any time by notification to the Secretary-General. Such a withdrawal shall not prejudice the consideration of any matter which is the subject of a communication already transmitted under this article; no further communication by any State Party shall be received under this article after the notification of withdrawal of the declaration has been received by the Secretary-General, unless the State Party concerned has made a new declaration.

Article 22
1. A State Party to this Convention may at any time declare under this article that it recognizes the competence of the Committee to receive and consider communications from or on behalf of individuals subject to its jurisdiction who claim to be victims of a violation by a State Party of the provisions of the Convention. No communication shall be received by the Committee if it concerns a State Party to the Convention which has not made such a declaration.

2. The Committee shall consider inadmissible any communication under this

article which is anonymous, or which it considers to be an abuse of the right of submission of such communications or to be incompatible with the provisions of this Convention.

3. Subject to the provisions of paragraph 2, the Committee shall bring any communication submitted to it under this article to the attention of the State Party to this Convention which has made a declaration under paragraph 1 and is alleged to be violating any provisions of the Convention. Within six months, the receiving State shall submit to the Committee written explanations or statements clarifying the matter and the remedy, if any, that may have been taken by that State.

4. The Committee shall consider communications received under this article in the light of all information made available to it by or on behalf of the individual and by the State Party concerned.

5. The Committee shall not consider any communication from an individual under this article unless it has ascertained that:

> (a) The same matter has not been, and is not being examined under another procedure of international investigation or settlement;

> (b) The individual has exhausted all available domestic remedies; this shall not be the rule where the application of the remedies is unreasonably prolonged or is unlikely to bring effective relief to the person who is the victim of the violation of this Convention.

6. The Committee shall hold closed meetings when examining communications under this article.

7. The Committee shall forward its views to the State Party concerned and to the individual.

8. The provisions of this article shall come into force when five States Parties to this Convention have made declarations under paragraph 1 of this article. Such declarations shall be deposited by the States Parties with the Secretary-General of the United Nations, who shall transmit parties thereof to the other States Parties. A declaration may be withdrawn at any time by notification to the Secretary-General. Such a withdrawal shall not prejudice the consideration of any matter which is the subject of a communication already transmitted under this article; no further communication by or on behalf of an individual shall be received under this article after the notification of withdrawal of the declaration has been received by the Secretary-General, unless the State Party concerned has made a new declaration.

Article 23
The members of the Committee, and of the ad hoc conciliation commissions which may be appointed under article 21, paragraph 1 (e), shall be entitled to the facilities, privileges and immunities of experts on missions for the United Nations as laid down in the relevant sections of the Convention on the Privileges and Immunities of the United Nations.

Article 24
The Committee shall submit an annual report on its activities under this Convention to the States Parties and to the General Assembly of the United Nations.

Part III

Article 25
1. This Convention is open for signature by all States.

2. This Convention is subject to ratification. Instruments of ratification shall be deposited with the Secretary-General of the United Nations.

Article 26
This Convention is open to accession by all States. Accession shall be effected by the deposit of an instrument of accession with the Secretary-General of the United Nations.

Article 27
1. This Convention shall enter into force on the thirtieth day after the date of the deposit with the Secretary-General of the United Nations of the twentieth instrument of ratification or accession.

2. For each State ratifying this Convention or acceding to it after the deposit of the twentieth instrument of ratification or accession, the Convention shall enter into force on the thirtieth day after the date of the deposit of its own instrument of ratification or accession.

Article 28
1. Each State may, at the time of signature or ratification of this Convention or accession thereto, declare that it does not recognize the competence of the Committee provided for in article 20.

2. Any State Party having made a reservation in accordance with paragraph 1 of this article may, at any time, withdraw this reservation by notification to the Secretary-General of the United Nations.

Article 29
1. Any State Party to this Convention may propose an amendment and file it with the Secretary-General of the United Nations. The Secretary-General shall thereupon communicate the proposed amendment to the States Parties to this Convention with a request that they notify him whether they favour a conference of States Parties for the purpose of considering and voting upon the proposal. In the event that within four months from the date of such communication at least one third of the State Parties favours such a conference, the Secretary-General shall convene the conference under the auspices of the United Nations. Any amendment adopted by a majority of the States Parties present and voting at the conference shall be submitted by the Secretary-General to all the States Parties for acceptance.

2. An amendment adopted in accordance with paragraph 1 shall enter into force when two thirds of the States Parties to this Convention have notified the Secretary-General of the United Nations that they have accepted it in accordance with their respective constitutional processes.

3. When amendments enter into force, they shall be binding on those States Parties which have accepted them, other States Parties still being bound by the provisions of this Convention and any earlier amendments which they have accepted.

Article 30
1. Any dispute between two or more States Parties concerning the interpretation or application of this Convention which cannot be settled through negotiation, shall, at the request of one of them, be submitted to arbitration. If within six months from the

date of the request for arbitration the Parties are unable to agree on the organization of the arbitration, any one of those Parties may refer the dispute to the International Court of Justice by request in conformity with the Statute of the Court.

2. Each State may at the time of signature or ratification of this Convention or accession thereto, declare that it does not consider itself bound by the preceding paragraph. The other States Parties shall not be bound by the preceding paragraph with respect to any State Party having made such a reservation.

3. Any State Party having made a reservation in accordance with the preceding paragraph may at any time withdraw this reservation by notification to the Secretary-General of the United Nations.

Article 31

1 A State Party may denounce this Convention by written notification to the Secretary-General of the United Nations. Denunciation becomes effective one year after the date of receipt of the notification by the Secretary- General.

2. Such a denunciation shall not have the effect of releasing the State Party from its obligations under this Convention in regard to any act or omission which occurs prior to the date at which the denunciation becomes effective. Nor shall denunciation prejudice in any way the continued consideration of any matter which is already under consideration by the Committee prior to the date at which the denunciation becomes effective.

3. Following the date at which the denunciation of a State Party becomes

effective, the Committee shall not commence consideration of any new matter regarding that State.

Article 32

The Secretary-General of the United Nations shall inform all members of the United Nations and all States which have signed this Convention or acceded to it, or the following particulars:

(a) Signatures, ratifications and accessions under articles 25 and 26;

(b) The date of entry into force of this Convention under article 27, and the date of the entry into force of any amendments under article 29;

(c) Denunciations under article 31.

Article 33

1. This Convention, of which the Arabic, Chinese, English, French, Russian and Spanish texts are equally authentic, shall be deposited in the archives of the United Nations.

2. The Secretary-General of the United Nations shall transmit certified copies of this Convention to all States.

APPENDIX F
International Convention on the Elimination of All Forms of Racial Discrimination

Adopted and opened for signature and ratification by General Assembly resolution 2106A (XX) of 21 December 1965. Entered into force on 4 January 1965, in accordance with article 19.

The States Parties to this Convention,

Considering that the Charter of the United Nations is based on the principles of the dignity and equality inherent in all human beings, and that all Member States have pledged themselves to take joint and separate action, in co-operation with the Organization, for the achievement of one of the purposes of the United Nations which is to promote and encourage universal respect for and observance of human rights and fundamental freedoms for all, without distinction as to race, sex, language or religion,

Considering that the Universal Declaration of Human Rights proclaims that all human beings are born free and equal in dignity and rights and that everyone is entitled to all the rights and freedoms set out therein, without distinction of any kind, in particular as to race, colour or national origin,

Considering that all human beings are equal before the law and are entitled to equal protection of the law against any discrimination and against any incitement to discrimination,

Considering that the United Nations has condemned colonialism and all practices of segregation and discrimination associated therewith, in whatever form and wherever they exist, and that the Declaration on the Granting of Independence to Colonial Countries and Peoples of 14 December 1960 (General Assembly resolution 1514 (XV)) has affirmed and solemnly proclaimed the necessity of bringing them to a speedy and unconditional end,

Considering that the United Nations Declaration on the Elimination of All Forms of Racial Discrimination of 20 November 1963 (General Assembly resolution 1904 (XVIII)) solemnly affirms the necessity of speedily eliminating racial discrimination throughout the world in all its forms and manifestations and of securing understanding of and respect for the dignity of the human person,

Convinced that any doctrine of superiority based on racial differentiation is scientifically false, morally condemnable, socially unjust and dangerous, and that there is no justification for racial discrimination, in theory or in practice, anywhere,

Reaffirming that discrimination between human beings on the grounds of race, colour or ethnic origin in an obstacle to friendly and peaceful relations among nations and is capable of disturbing peace and security among peoples and the harmony of persons living side by side even within one and the same State,

Convinced that the existence of racial barriers is repugnant to the ideals of any human society,

Alarmed by manifestations of racial discrimination still in evidence in some areas of the world and by governmental policies based on racial superiority or hatred, such as policies of apartheid, segregation or separation, Resolved to adopt all necessary measures for speedily eliminating racial discrimination in all its forms and manifestations, and to prevent and combat racist doctrines and practices in order to promote understanding between races and to build an international community free from all forms of racial segregation and racial discrimination,

Bearing in mind the Convention concerning Discrimination in respect of Employment and Occupation adopted by the International Labour Organisation in 1958, and the Convention against Discrimination in Education adopted by the United Nations Educational, Scientific and Cultural Organization in 1960,

Desiring to implement the principles embodied in the United Nations Declaration on the Elimination of All Forms of Racial Discrimination and to secure the earliest adoption of practical measures to that end,

Have agreed as follows:

PART I

Article 1
1. In this Convention, the term "racial discrimination" shall mean any distinction, exclusion, restriction or preference based on race, colour, descent, or national or ethnic origin which has the purpose or effect of nullifying or impairing the recognition, enjoyment or exercise, on an equal footing, of human rights and fundamental freedoms in the political, economic, social, cultural or any other field of public life.

2. This Convention shall not apply to distinctions, exclusions, restrictions or preferences made by a State Party to this Convention between citizens and non-citizens.

3. Nothing in this Convention may be interpreted as affecting in any way the legal provisions of States Parties concerning nationality, citizenship or naturalization, provided that such provisions do not discriminate against any particular nationality.

4. Special measures taken for the sole purpose of securing adequate advancement of certain racial or ethnic groups or individuals requiring such protection as may be necessary in order to ensure such groups or individuals equal enjoyment or exercise of human rights and fundamental freedoms shall not be deemed racial discrimination, provided, however, that such measures do not, as a consequence, lead to the maintenance of separate rights for different racial groups and that they shall not be continued after the objectives for which they were taken have been achieved.

Article 2
1. States Parties condemn racial discrimination and undertake to pursue by all appropriate means and without delay a policy of eliminating racial discrimination in all its forms and promoting understanding among all races, and, to this end:

(a) Each State Party undertakes to engage in no act or practice of racial discrimination against persons, groups of persons or institutions and to ensure that all public authorities and public institutions, national and local, shall act in conformity with this obligation;

(b) Each State Party undertakes not to sponsor, defend or support racial discrimination by any persons or organizations;

(c) Each State Party shall take effective measures to review governmental, national and local policies, and to amend, rescind or nullify any laws and regulations which have the effect of creating or perpetuating racial discrimination wherever it exists;

(d) Each State Party shall prohibit and bring to an end, by all appropriate means, including legislation as required by circumstances, racial discrimination by any persons, group or organization;

(e) Each State Party undertakes to encourage, where appropriate, integrationist multi-racial organizations and movements and other means of eliminating barriers between races, and to discourage anything which tends to strengthen racial division.

2. States Parties shall, when the circumstances so warrant, take, in the social, economic, cultural and other fields, special and concrete measures to ensure the adequate development and protection of certain racial groups or individuals belonging to them, for the purpose of guaranteeing them the full and equal enjoyment of human rights and fundamental freedoms. These measures shall in no case entail as a consequence the maintenance of unequal or separate rights for different racial groups after the objectives for which they were taken have been achieved.

Article 3

States Parties particularly condemn racial segregation and apartheid and undertake to prevent, prohibit and eradicate all practices of this nature in territories under their jurisdiction.

Article 4

States Parties condemn all propaganda and all organizations which are based on ideas or theories of superiority of one race or group of persons of one colour or ethnic origin, or which attempt to justify or promote racial hatred and discrimination in any form, and undertake to adopt immediate and positive measures designed to eradicate all incitement to, or acts of, such discrimination and, to this end, with due regard to the principles embodied in the Universal Declaration of Human Rights and the rights expressly set forth in article 5 of this Convention, inter alia:

(a) Shall declare an offence punishable by law all dissemination of ideas based on racial superiority or hatred, incitement to racial discrimination, as well as all acts of violence or incitement to such acts against any race or group of persons of another colour or ethnic origin, and also the provision of any assistance to racist activities, including the financing thereof;

(b) Shall declare illegal and prohibit organizations, and also organized and all other propaganda activities, which promote and incite racial discrimination, and shall recognize participation in such organizations or activities as an offence punishable by law;

(c) Shall not permit public authorities or public institutions, national or local, to promote or incite racial discrimination.

Article 5

In compliance with the fundamental obligations laid down in article 2 of this Convention, States Parties undertake to prohibit and to eliminate racial discrimination in all its forms and to guarantee the right of everyone, without distinction as to race, colour, or national or ethnic origin, to equality before the law, notably in the enjoyment of the following rights:

(a) The right to equal treatment before the tribunals and all other organs administering justice;

(b) The right to security of person and protection by the State against violence or bodily harm, whether inflicted by government officials or by any individual, group or institution;

(c) Political rights, in particular the rights to participate in elections--to vote and to stand for election--on the basis of universal and equal suffrage, to take part in the Government as well as in the conduct of public affairs at any level and to have equal access to public service;

(d) Other civil rights, in particular:

(i) The right to freedom of movement and residence within the border of the State;

(ii) The right to leave any country, including one's own, and to return to one's country;

(iii) The right to nationality;

(iv) The right to marriage and choice of spouse;

(v) The right to own property alone as well as in association with others;

(vi) The right to inherit;

(vii) The right to freedom of thought, conscience and religion;

(viii) The right to freedom of opinion and expression;

(ix) The right to freedom of peaceful assembly and association;

(e) Economic, social and cultural rights, in particular:

(i) The rights to work, to free choice of employment, to just and favourable conditions of work, to protection against unemployment, to equal pay for equal work, to just and favourable remuneration;

(ii) The right to form and join trade unions;

(iii) The right to housing;

(iv) The right to public health, medical care, social security and social services;

(v) The right to education and training;

(vi) The right to equal participation in cultural activities;

(f) The right of access to any place or service intended for use by the general public, such as transport, hotels, restaurants, cafes, theatres and parks.

Article 6

States Parties shall assure to everyone within their jurisdiction effective protection and remedies, through the competent national tribunals and other State institutions, against any acts of racial discrimination which violate his human rights and fundamental freedoms contrary to this Convention, as well as the right to seek from such tribunals just and adequate reparation or satisfaction for any damage suffered as a result of such discrimination.

Article 7

States Parties undertake to adopt immediate and effective measures, particularly in the fields of teaching, education, culture and information, with a view to combating prejudices which lead to racial discrimination and to promoting understanding, tolerance and friendship among nations and racial or ethnical groups, as well as to propagating the purposes and principles of the Charter of the United Nations, the Universal Declaration of Human Rights, the United Nations Declaration on the Elimination of All Forms of Racial Discrimination, and this Convention.

PART II

Article 8

1. There shall be established a Committee on the Elimination of Racial Discrimination (hereinafter referred to as the Committee) consisting of eighteen experts of high moral standing and acknowledged impartiality elected by States Parties from among their nationals, who shall serve in their personal capacity, consideration being given to equitable geographical distribution and to the representation of the different forms of civilization as well as of the principal legal systems.

2. The members of the Committee shall be elected by secret ballot from a list of persons nominated by the States Parties. Each State Party may nominate one person from among its own nationals.

3. The initial election shall be held six months after the date of the entry into force of this Convention. At least three months before the date of each election the Secretary-General of the United Nations shall address a letter to the States Parties inviting them to submit their nominations within two months. The Secretary-General shall prepare a list in alphabetical order of all persons thus nominated, indicating the States Parties which have nominated them, and shall submit it to the States Parties.

4. Elections of the members of the Committee shall be held at a meeting of States Parties convened by the Secretary-General at United Nations Headquarters. At that meeting, for which two-thirds of the States Parties shall constitute a quorum, the persons elected to the Committee shall be those nominees who obtain the largest number of votes and an absolute majority of the votes of the

representatives of States Parties present and voting.

5. (a) The members of the Committee shall be elected for a term of four years. However, the terms of nine of the members elected at the first election shall expire at the end of two years; immediately after the first election the names of these nine members shall be chosen by lot by the Chairman of the Committee.

(b) For the filling of casual vacancies, the State Party whose expert has ceased to function as a member of the Committee shall appoint another expert from among its nationals, subject to the approval of the Committee. 6. States Parties shall be responsible for the expenses of the members of the Committee while they are in performance of Committee duties.

Article 9
1. States Parties undertake to submit to the Secretary-General of the United Nations, for consideration by the Committee, a report on the legislative, judicial, administrative or other measures which they have adopted and which give effect to the provisions of this Convention:

(a) within one year after the entry into force of the Convention for the State concerned; and

(b) thereafter every two years and whenever the Committee so requests. The Committee may request further information from the States Parties.

2. The Committee shall report annually, through the Secretary-General, to the General Assembly of the United Nations on

its activities and may make suggestions and general recommendations based on the examination of the reports and information received from the States Parties. Such suggestions and general recommendations shall be reported to the General Assembly together with comments, if any, from States Parties.

Article 10
1. The Committee shall adopt its own rules of procedure.

2. The Committee shall elect its officers for a term of two years.

3. The secretariat of the Committee shall be provided by the Secretary-General of the United Nations.

4. The meetings of the Committee shall normally be held at United Nations Headquarters.

Article 11
1. If a State Party considers that another State Party is not giving effect to the provisions of this Convention, it may bring the matter to the attention of the Committee. The Committee shall then transmit the communication to the State Party concerned. Within three months, the receiving State shall submit to the Committee written explanations or statements clarifying the matter and the remedy, if any, that may have been taken by that State.

2. If the matter is not adjusted to the satisfaction of both parties, either by bilateral negotiations or by any other procedure open to them, within six months after the receipt by the receiving State of the initial communication, either State shall have the right to refer the matter again to the

Committee by notifying the Committee and also the other State.

3. The Committee shall deal with a matter referred to it in accordance with paragraph 2 of this article after it has ascertained that all available domestic remedies have been invoked and exhausted in the case, in conformity with the generally recognized principles of international law. This shall not be the rule where the application of the remedies is unreasonably prolonged. 4. In any matter referred to it, the Committee may call upon the States Parties concerned to supply any other relevant information.

5. When any matter arising out of this article is being considered by the Committee, the States Parties concerned shall be entitled to send a representative to take part in the proceedings of the Committee, without voting rights, while the matter is under consideration.

Article 12
1. (a) After the Committee has obtained and collated all the information it deems necessary, the Chairman shall appoint an ad hoc Conciliation Commission (hereinafter referred to as the Commission) comprising five persons who may or may not be members of the Committee. The members of the Commission shall be appointed with the unanimous consent of the parties to the dispute, and its good offices shall be made available to the States concerned with a view to an amicable solution of the matter on the basis of respect for this Convention.

(b) If the States parties to the dispute fail to reach agreement within three months on all or part of the composition of the Commission, the members of the Commission not agreed upon by the States parties to the

dispute shall be elected by secret ballot by a two-thirds majority vote of the Committee from among its own members.

2. The members of the Commission shall serve in their personal capacity. They shall not be nationals of the States parties to the dispute or of a State not Party to this Convention.

3. The Commission shall elect its own Chairman and adopt its own rules of procedure.

4. The meetings of the Commission shall normally be held at United Nations Headquarters or at any other convenient place as determined by the Commission.

5. The secretariat provided in accordance with article 10, paragraph 3, of this Convention shall also service the Commission whenever a dispute among States Parties brings the Commission into being.

6. The States parties to the dispute shall share equally all the expenses of the members of the Commission in accordance with estimates to be provided by the Secretary-General of the United Nations.

7. The Secretary-General shall be empowered to pay the expenses of the members of the Commission, if necessary, before reimbursement by the States parties to the dispute in accordance with paragraph 6 of this article.

8. The information obtained and collated by the Committee shall be made available to the Commission, and the Commission may call upon the States concerned to supply any other relevant information.

Article 13

1. When the Commission has fully considered the matter, it shall prepare and submit to the Chairman of the Committee a report embodying its findings on all questions of fact relevant to the issue between the parties and containing such recommendations as it may think proper for the amicable solution of the dispute.

2. The Chairman of the Committee shall communicate the report of the Commission to each of the States parties to the dispute. These States shall, within three months, inform the Chairman of the Committee whether or not they accept the recommendations contained in the report of the Commission.

3. After the period provided for in paragraph 2 of this article, the Chairman of the Committee shall communicate the report of the Commission and the declarations of the States Parties concerned to the other States Parties to this Convention.

Article 14

1. A State Party may at any time declare that it recognizes the competence of the Committee to receive and consider communications from individuals or groups of individuals within its jurisdiction claiming to be victims of a violation by that State Party of any of the rights set forth in this Convention. No communication shall be received by the Committee if it concerns a State Party which has not made such a declaration.

2. Any State Party which makes a declaration as provided for in paragraph 1 of this article may establish or indicate a body within its national legal order which shall be competent to receive and consider petitions from individuals and groups of individuals within its jurisdiction who claim to be victims of a violation of any of the rights set forth in this Convention and who have exhausted other available local remedies.

3. A declaration made in accordance with paragraph 1 of this article and the name of any body established or indicated in accordance with paragraph 2 of this article shall be deposited by the State Party concerned with the Secretary-General of the United Nations, who shall transmit copies thereof to the other States Parties. A declaration may be withdrawn at any time by notification to the Secretary-General, but such a withdrawal shall not affect communications pending before the Committee.

4. A register of petitions shall be kept by the body established or indicated in accordance with paragraph 2 of this article, and certified copies of the register shall be filed annually through appropriate channels with the Secretary-General on the understanding that the contents shall not be publicly disclosed.

5. In the event of failure to obtain satisfaction from the body established or indicated in accordance with paragraph 2 of this article, the petitioner shall have the right to communicate the matter to the Committee within six months.

6. (a) The Committee shall confidentially bring any communication referred to it to the attention of the State Party alleged to be violating any provision of this Convention, but the identity of the individual or groups of individuals concerned shall not be revealed without his or their express consent. The Committee shall not receive anonymous communications.

(b) Within three months, the receiving State shall submit to the Committee written explanations or statements clarifying the matter and the remedy, if any, that may have been taken by that State.

7. (a) The Committee shall consider communications in the light of all information made available to it by the State Party concerned and by the petitioner. The Committee shall not consider any communication from a petitioner unless it has ascertained that the petitioner has exhausted all available domestic remedies. However, this shall not be the rule where the application of the remedies is unreasonably prolonged.

(b) The Committee shall forward its suggestions and recommendations, if any, to the State Party concerned and to the petitioner.

8. The Committee shall include in its annual report a summary of such communications and, where appropriate, a summary of the explanations and statements of the States Parties concerned and of its own suggestions and recommendations.

9. The Committee shall be competent to exercise the functions provided for in this article only when at least ten States Parties to this Convention are bound by declarations in accordance with paragraph I of this article.

Article 15
1. Pending the achievement of the objectives of the Declaration on the Granting of Independence to Colonial Countries and Peoples, contained in General Assembly resolution 1514 (XV) of 14 December 1960, the provisions of this

Convention shall in no way limit the right of petition granted to these peoples by other international instruments or by the United Nations and its specialized agencies.

2. (a) The Committee established under article 8, paragraph 1, of this Convention shall receive copies of the petitions from, and submit expressions of opinion and recommendations on these petitions to, the bodies of the United Nations which deal with matters directly related to the principles and objectives of this Convention in their consideration of petitions from the inhabitants of Trust and Non-Self-Governing Territories and all other territories to which General Assembly resolution 1514 (XV) applies, relating to matters covered by this Convention which are before these bodies.

(b) The Committee shall receive from the competent bodies of the United Nations copies of the reports concerning the legislative, judicial, administrative or other measures directly related to the principles and objectives of this Convention applied by the administering Powers within the Territories mentioned in sub-paragraph (a) of this paragraph, and shall express opinions and make recommendations to these bodies.

3. The Committee shall include in its report to the General Assembly a summary of the petitions and reports it has received from United Nations bodies, and the expressions of opinion and recommendations of the Committee relating to the said petitions and reports.

4. The Committee shall request from the Secretary-General of the United Nations all information relevant to the objectives of this

Convention and available to him regarding the Territories mentioned in paragraph 2 (a) of this article.

Article 16

The provisions of this Convention concerning the settlement of disputes or complaints shall be applied without prejudice to other procedures for settling disputes or complaints in the field of discrimination laid down in the constituent instruments of, or in conventions adopted by, the United Nations and its specialized agencies, and shall not prevent the States Parties from having recourse to other procedures for settling a dispute in accordance with general or special international agreements in force between them.

PART III

Article 17

1. This Convention is open for signature by any State Member of the United Nations or member of any of its specialized agencies, by any State Party to the Statute of the International Court of Justice, and by any other State which has been invited by the General Assembly of the United Nations to become a Party to this Convention.

2. This Convention is subject to ratification. Instruments of ratification shall be deposited with the Secretary-General of the United Nations.

Article 18

1. This Convention shall be open to accession by any State referred to in article 17, paragraph 1, of the Convention.

2. Accession shall be effected by the deposit of an instrument of accession with the Secretary-General of the United Nations.

Article 19

1. This Convention shall enter into force on the thirtieth day after the date of the deposit with the Secretary-General of the United Nations of the twenty-seventh instrument of ratification or instrument of accession.

2. For each State ratifying this Convention or acceding to it after the deposit of the twenty-seventh instrument of ratification or instrument of accession, the Convention shall enter into force on the thirtieth day after the date of the deposit of its own instrument of ratification or instrument of accession.

Article 20

1. The Secretary-General of the United Nations shall receive and circulate to all States which are or may become Parties to this Convention reservations made by States at the time of ratification or accession. Any State which objects to the reservation shall, within a period of ninety days from the date of the said communication, notify the Secretary-General that it does not accept it.

2. A reservation incompatible with the object and purpose of this Convention shall not be permitted, nor shall a reservation the effect of which would inhibit the operation of any of the bodies established by this Convention be allowed. A reservation shall be considered incompatible or inhibitive if at least two-thirds of the States Parties to this Convention object to it.

3. Reservations may be withdrawn at any time by notification to this effect addressed to the Secretary-General. Such notification shall take effect on the date on which it is received.

Article 21

A State Party may denounce this Convention by written notification to the Secretary-General of the United Nations. Denunciation shall take effect one year after the date of receipt of the notification by the Secretary-General.

Article 22

Any dispute between two or more States Parties with respect to the interpretation or application of this Convention, which is not settled by negociation or by the procedures expressly provided for in this Convention, shall, at the request of any of the parties to the dispute, be referred to the International Court of Justice for decision, unless the disputants agree to another mode of settlement.

Article 23

1. A request for the revision of this Convention may be made at any time by any State Party by means of a notification in writing addressed to the Secretary-General of the United Nations.

2. The General Assembly of the United Nations shall decide upon the steps, if any, to be taken in respect of such a request.

Article 24

The Secretary-General of the United Nations shall inform all States referred to in article 17, paragraph 1, of this Convention of the following particulars

(a) Signatures, ratifications and accessions under articles 17 and 18;

(b) The date of entry into force of this Convention under article 19;

(c) Communications and declarations received under articles 14, 20 and 23;

(d) Denunciations under article 21.

Article 25

1. This Convention, of which the Chinese, English, French, Russian and Spanish texts are equally authentic, shall be deposited in the archives of the United Nations.

2. The Secretary-General of the United Nations shall transmit certified copies of this Convention to all States belonging to any of the categories mentioned in article 17, paragraph 1, of the Convention.

IN FAITH WHEREOF the undersigned, being duly authorized thereto by their respective Governments, have signed the present Convention, opened for signature at New York, on the seventh day of March, one thousand nine hundred and sixty-six.

APPENDIX G
Basic Principles on the Use of Force and Firearms by Law Enforcement Officials

Adopted by the Eighth United Nations Congress on the Prevention of Crime and the Treatment of Offenders, Havana, 27 August to 7 September 1990.

Whereas the work of law enforcement officials[1] is a social service of great importance and there is, therefore, a need to maintain and, whenever necessary, to improve the working conditions and status of these officials,

Whereas a threat to the life and safety of law enforcement officials must be seen as a threat to the stability of society as a whole,

Whereas law enforcement officials have a vital role in the protection of the right to life, liberty and security of the person, as guaranteed in the Universal Declaration of Human Rights and reaffirmed in the International Covenant on Civil and Political Rights,

Whereas the Standard Minimum Rules for the Treatment of Prisoners provide for the circumstances in which prison officials may use force in the course of their duties,

Whereas article 3 of the Code of Conduct for Law Enforcement Officials provides that law enforcement officials may use force only when strictly necessary and to the extent required for the performance of their duty,

Whereas the preparatory meeting for the Seventh United Nations Congress on the Prevention of Crime and the Treatment of Offenders, held at Varenna, Italy, agreed on elements to be considered in the course of further work on restraints on the use of force and firearms by law enforcement officials,

Whereas the Seventh Congress, in its resolution 14, inter alia, emphasizes that the use of force and firearms by law enforcement officials should be commensurate with due respect for human rights,

Whereas the Economic and Social Council, in its resolution 1986/10, section IX, of 21 May 1986, invited Member States to pay particular attention in the implementation of the Code to the use of force and firearms by law enforcement officials, and the General Assembly, in its resolution 41/149 of 4 December 1986, inter alia, welcomed this recommendation made by the Council,

Whereas it is appropriate that, with due regard to their personal safety, consideration be given to the role of law enforcement officials in relation to the administration of

---

[1] In accordance with the commentary to article 1 of the Code of Conduct for Law Enforcement Officials, the term "law enforcement officials" includes all officers of the law, whether appointed or elected, who exercise police powers, especially the powers of arrest or detention. In countries where police powers are exercised by military authorities. whether uniformed or not, or by State security forces, the definition of law enforcement officials shall be regarded as including officers of such services.

432

justice, to the protection of the right to life, liberty and security of the person, to their responsibility to maintain public safety and social peace and to the importance of their qualifications, training and conduct,

The basic principles set forth below, which have been formulated to assist Member States in their task of ensuring and promoting the proper role of law enforcement officials, should be taken into account and respected by Governments within the framework of their national legislation and practice, and be brought to the attention of law enforcement officials as well as other persons, such as judges, prosecutors, lawyers, members of the executive branch and the legislature, and the public.

General Provisions

1. Governments and law enforcement agencies shall adopt and implement rules and regulations on the use of force and firearms against persons by law enforcement officials. In developing such rules and regulations, Governments and law enforcement agencies shall keep the ethical issues associated with the use of force and firearms constantly under review.

2. Governments and law enforcement agencies should develop a range of means as broad as possible and equip law enforcement officials with various types of weapons and ammunition that would allow for a differentiated use of force and firearms. These should include the development of non-lethal incapacitating weapons for use in appropriate situations, with a view to increasingly restraining the application of means capable of causing death or injury to persons. For the same purpose, it should also be possible for law enforcement officials to be equipped with

self-defensive equipment such as shields, helmets, bullet-proof vests and bullet-proof means of transportation, in order to decrease the need to use weapons of any kind.

3. The development and deployment of non-lethal incapacitating weapons should be carefully evaluated in order to minimize the risk of endangering uninvolved persons, and the use of such weapons should be carefully controlled.

4. Law enforcement officials, in carrying out their duty, shall, as far as possible, apply non-violent means before resorting to the use of force and firearms. They may use force and firearms only if other means remain ineffective or without any promise of achieving the intended result.

5. Whenever the lawful use of force and firearms is unavoidable, law enforcement officials shall:

(a) Exercise restraint in such use and act in proportion to the seriousness of the offence and the legitimate objective to be achieved;

(b) Minimize damage and injury, and respect and preserve human life;

(c) Ensure that assistance and medical aid are rendered to any injured or affected persons at the earliest possible moment;

(d) Ensure that relatives or close friends of the injured or affected person are notified at the earliest possible moment.

6. Where injury or death is caused by the use of force and firearms by law enforcement officials, they shall report the

incident promptly to their superiors, in accordance with principle 22.

7. Governments shall ensure that arbitrary or abusive use of force and firearms by law enforcement officials is punished as a criminal offence under their law.

8. Exceptional circumstances such as internal political instability or any other public emergency may not be invoked to justify any departure from these basic principles.

Special Provisions
9. Law enforcement officials shall not use firearms against persons except in self-defence or defence of others against the imminent threat of death or serious injury, to prevent the perpetration of a particularly serious crime involving grave threat to life, to arrest a person presenting such a danger and resisting their authority, or to prevent his or her escape, and only when less extreme means are insufficient to achieve these objectives. In any event, intentional lethal use of firearms may only be made when strictly unavoidable in order to protect life.

10. In the circumstances provided for under principle 9, law enforcement officials shall identify themselves as such and give a clear warning of their intent to use firearms, with sufficient time for the warning to be observed, unless to do so would unduly place the law enforcement officials at risk or would create a risk of death or serious harm to other persons, or would be clearly inappropriate or pointless in the circumstances of the incident.

11. Rules and regulations on the use of firearms by law enforcement officials should include guidelines that:

(a) Specify the circumstances under which law enforcement officials are authorized to carry firearms and prescribe the types of firearms and ammunition permitted;

(b) Ensure that firearms are used only in appropriate circumstances and in a manner likely to decrease the risk of unnecessary harm;

(c) Prohibit the use of those firearms and ammunition that cause unwarranted injury or present an unwarranted risk;

(d) Regulate the control, storage and issuing of firearms, including procedures for ensuring that law enforcement officials are accountable for the firearms and ammunition issued to them;

(e) Provide for warnings to be given, if appropriate, when firearms are to be discharged;

(f) Provide for a system of reporting whenever law enforcement officials use firearms in the performance of their duty.

Policing Unlawful Assemblies
12. As everyone is allowed to participate in lawful and peaceful assemblies, in accordance with the principles embodied in the Universal Declaration of Human Rights and the International Covenant on Civil and Political Rights, Governments and law enforcement agencies and officials shall recognize that force and firearms may be used only in accordance with principles 13 and 14.

13. In the dispersal of assemblies that are unlawful but non-violent, law enforcement officials shall avoid the use of force or, where that is not practicable, shall restrict such force to the minimum extent necessary.

14. In the dispersal of violent assemblies, law enforcement officials may use firearms only when less dangerous means are not practicable and only to the minimum extent necessary. Law enforcement officials shall not use firearms in such cases, except under the conditions stipulated in principle 9.

Policing Persons in Custody or Detention
15. Law enforcement officials, in their relations with persons in custody or detention, shall not use force, except when strictly necessary for the maintenance of security and order within the institution, or when personal safety is threatened.

16. Law enforcement officials, in their relations with persons in custody or detention, shall not use firearms, except in self-defence or in the defence of others against the immediate threat of death or serious injury, or when strictly necessary to prevent the escape of a person in custody or detention presenting the danger referred to in principle 9.

17. The preceding principles are without prejudice to the rights, duties and responsibilities of prison officials, as set out in the Standard Minimum Rules for the Treatment of Prisoners, particularly rules 33, 34 and 54.

Qualifications, Training and Counselling
18. Governments and law enforcement agencies shall ensure that all law enforcement officials are selected by proper screening procedures, have appropriate moral, psychological and physical qualities

for the effective exercise of their functions and receive continuous and thorough professional training. Their continued fitness to perform these functions should be subject to periodic review.

19. Governments and law enforcement agencies shall ensure that all law enforcement officials are provided with training and are tested in accordance with appropriate proficiency standards in the use of force. Those law enforcement officials who are required to carry firearms should be authorized to do so only upon completion of special training in their use.

20. In the training of law enforcement officials, Governments and law enforcement agencies shall give special attention to issues of police ethics and human rights, especially in the investigative process, to alternatives to the use of force and firearms, including the peaceful settlement of conflicts, the understanding of crowd behaviour, and the methods of persuasion, negotiation and mediation, as well as to technical means, with a view to limiting the use of force and firearms. Law enforcement agencies should review their training programmes and operational procedures in the light of particular incidents.

21. Governments and law enforcement agencies shall make stress counselling available to law enforcement officials who are involved in situations where force and firearms are used.

Reporting and Review Procedures
22. Governments and law enforcement agencies shall establish effective reporting and review procedures for all incidents referred to in principles 6 and 11 (f). For incidents reported pursuant to these principles, Governments and law

enforcement agencies shall ensure that an
effective review process is available and
that independent administrative or
prosecutorial authorities are in a position to
exercise jurisdiction in appropriate
circumstances. In cases of death and serious
injury or other grave consequences, a
detailed report shall be sent promptly to the
competent authorities responsible for
administrative review and judicial control.

23. Persons affected by the use of force and
firearms or their legal representatives shall
have access to an independent process,
including a judicial process. In the event of
the death of such persons, this provision
shall apply to their dependants accordingly.

24. Governments and law enforcement
agencies shall ensure that superior officers
are held responsible if they know, or should
have known, that law enforcement officials
under their command are resorting, or have
resorted, to the unlawful use of force and
firearms, and they did not take all measures
in their power to prevent, suppress or report
such use.

25. Governments and law enforcement
agencies shall ensure that no criminal or
disciplinary sanction is imposed on law
enforcement officials who, in compliance
with the Code of Conduct for Law
Enforcement Officials and these basic
principles, refuse to carry out an order to
use force and firearms, or who report such
use by other officials.

26. Obedience to superior orders shall be no
defence if law enforcement officials knew
that an order to use force and firearms
resulting in the death or serious injury of a
person was manifestly unlawful and had a
reasonable opportunity to refuse to follow

it. In any case, responsibility also rests on
the superiors who gave the unlawful orders.

APPENDIX H
Code of Conduct for Law Enforcement Officials

Adopted by General Assembly 34/169 of 17 December 1979.

Article 1

Law enforcement officials shall at all times fulfil the duty imposed upon them by law, by serving the community and by protecting all persons against illegal acts, consistent with the high degree of responsibility required by their profession.

Commentary:

(a) The term 'law enforcement officials', includes all officers of the law, whether appointed or elected, who exercise police powers, especially the powers of arrest or detention.

(b) In countries where police powers are exercised by military authorities, whether uniformed or not, or by State security forces, the definition of law enforcement officials shall be regarded as including officers of such services.

(c) Service to the community is intended to include particularly the rendition of services of assistance to those members of the community who by reason of personal, economic, social or other emergencies are in need of immediate aid.

(d) This provision is intended to cover not only all violent, predatory and harmful acts, but extends to the full range of prohibitions under penal statutes. It extends to conduct by persons not capable of incurring criminal liability.

Article 2

In the performance of their duty, law enforcement officials shall respect and protect human dignity and maintain and uphold the human rights of all persons.

Commentary:

(a) The human rights in question are identified and protected by national and international law. Among the relevant international instruments are the Universal Declaration of Human Rights, the International Covenant on Civil and Political Rights, the Declaration on the Protection of All Persons from Being Subjected to Torture and Other Cruel, Inhuman or Degrading Treatment or Punishment, the United Nations Declaration on the Elimination of All Forms of Racial Discrimination, the International Convention on the Elimination of All Forms of Racial Discrimination, the International Convention on the Suppression and Punishment of the Crime of Apartheid, the Convention on the Prevention and Punishment of the Crime of Genocide, the Standard Minimum Rules for the Treatment of Prisoners and the Vienna Convention on Consular Relations.

(b) National commentaries to this provision should indicate regional or national provisions identifying and protecting these rights.

Article 3

Law enforcement officials may use force only when strictly necessary and to the extent required for the performance of their duty.

Commentary:

(a) This provision emphasizes that the use of force by law enforcement officials should be exceptional; while it implies that law enforcement officials may be authorized to use force as is reasonably necessary under the circumstances for the prevention of crime or in effecting or assisting in the lawful arrest of offenders or suspected offenders, no force going beyond that may be used.

(b) National law ordinarily restricts the use of force by law enforcement officials in accordance with a principle of proportionality. It is to be understood that such national principles of proportionality are to be respected in the interpretation of this provision. In no case should this provision be interpreted to authorize the use of force which is disproportionate to the legitimate objective to be achieved.

(c) The use of firearms is considered an extreme measure. Every effort should be made to exclude the use of firearms, especially against children. In general, firearms should not be used except when a suspected offender offers armed resistance or otherwise jeopardizes the lives of others and less extreme measures are not sufficient to restrain or apprehend the suspected offender. In every instance in which a firearm is discharged, a report should be made promptly to the competent authorities.

Article 4

Matters of a confidential nature in the possession of law enforcement officials shall be kept confidential , unless the

performance of duty or the needs of justice strictly require otherwise.

Commentary:

By the nature of their duties, law enforcement officials obtain information which may relate to private lives or be potentially harmful to the interests, and especially the reputation, of others. Great care should be exercised in safeguarding and using such information, which should be disclosed only in the performance of duty or to serve the needs of justice. Any disclosure of such information for other purposes is wholly improper.

Article 5

No law enforcement official may inflict, instigate or tolerate any act of torture or other cruel, inhuman or degrading treatment or punishment, nor may any law enforcement official invoke superior orders or exceptional circumstances such as a state of war or a threat of war, a threat to national security, internal political instability or any other public emergency as a justification of torture or other cruel, inhuman or degrading treatment or punishment .

Commentary:

(a) This prohibition derives from the Declaration on the Protection of All Persons from Being Subjected to Torture and Other Cruel, Inhuman or Degrading Treatment or Punishment, adopted by the General Assembly, according to which: "[Such an act is] an offence to human dignity and shall be condemned as a denial of the purposes of the Charter of the United Nations and as a violation of the human rights and fundamental freedoms proclaimed in the Universal

Declaration of Human Rights [and other international human rights instruments]."

(b) The Declaration defines torture as follows:

". . . torture means any act by which severe pain or suffering, whether physical or mental, is intentionally inflicted by or at the instigation of a public official on a person for such purposes as obtaining from him or a third person information or confession, punishing him for an act he has committed or is suspected of having committed, or intimidating him or other persons. It does not include pain or suffering arising only from, inherent in or incidental to, lawful sanctions to the extent consistent with the Standard Minimum Rules for the Treatment of Prisoners."

(c) The term "cruel, inhuman or degrading treatment or punishment" has not been defined by the General Assembly but should be interpreted so as to extend the widest possible protection against abuses, whether physical or mental.

Article 6
Law enforcement officials shall ensure the full protection of the health of persons in their custody and, in particular, shall take immediate action to secure medical attention whenever required.

Commentary:
(a) "Medical attention", which refers to services rendered by any medical

personnel, including certified medical practitioners and paramedics, shall be secured when needed or requested.

(b) While the medical personnel are likely to be attached to the law enforcement operation, law enforcement officials must take into account the judgement of such personnel when they recommend providing the person in custody with appropriate treatment through, or in consultation with, medical personnel from outside the law enforcement operation.

(c) It is understood that law enforcement officials shall also secure medical attention for victims of violations of law or of accidents occurring in the course of violations of law.

Article 7
Law enforcement officials shall not commit any act of corruption. They shall also rigorously oppose and combat all such acts.

Commentary:
(a) Any act of corruption, in the same way as any other abuse of authority, is incompatible with the profession of law enforcement officials. The law must be enforced fully with respect to any law enforcement official who commits an act of corruption, as Governments cannot expect to enforce the law among their citizens if they cannot, or will not, enforce the law against their own agents and within their agencies.

(b) While the definition of corruption must be subject to national law, it should be understood to encompass the commission or omission of an act in the performance of or in connection with one's duties, in response to gifts, promises or incentives demanded or accepted, or the wrongful receipt of these once the act has been committed or omitted.

(c) The expression "act of corruption" referred to above should be understood to encompass attempted corruption.

Article 8

Law enforcement officials shall respect the law and the present Code. They shall also, to the best of their capability, prevent and rigorously oppose any violations of them.

Law enforcement officials who have reason to believe that a violation of the present Code has occurred or is about to occur shall report the matter to their superior authorities and, where necessary, to other appropriate authorities or organs vested with reviewing or remedial power.

Commentary:

(a) This Code shall be observed whenever it has been incorporated into national legislation or practice. If legislation or practice contains stricter provisions than those of the present Code, those stricter provisions shall be observed.

(b) The article seeks to preserve the balance between the need for internal discipline of the agency on which public safety is largely dependent, on the one hand, and the need for dealing with violations of basic human rights, on the other. Law enforcement officials shall report violations within the chain of command and take other lawful action outside the chain of command only when

no other remedies are available or effective. It is understood that law enforcement officials shall not suffer administrative or other penalties because they have reported that a violation of this Code has occurred or is about to occur.

(c) The term "appropriate authorities or organs vested with reviewing or remedial power" refers to any authority or organ existing under national law, whether internal to the law enforcement agency or independent thereof, with statutory, customary or other power to review grievances and complaints arising out of violations within the purview of this Code.

(d) In some countries, the mass media may be regarded as performing complaint review functions similar to those described in subparagraph (c) above. Law enforcement officials may, therefore, be justified if, as a last resort and in accordance with the laws and customs of their own countries and with the provisions of article 4 of the present Code, they bring violations to the attention of public opinion through the mass media.

(e) Law enforcement officials who comply with the provisions of this Code deserve the respect, the full support and the co-operation of the community and of the law enforcement agency in which they serve, as well as the law enforcement profession.